ECONOMICS
TODAY AND TOMORROW

ECONOMICS
TODAY AND TOMORROW

Roger LeRoy Miller

Law & Economics Center

University of Miami

 HARPER & ROW, Publishers
New York   Hagerstown   San Francisco   London

Sponsoring Editor: George Provol
Interior and cover design: James Stockton
Cover and Unit Opener photographs: Nikolay Žurek
Technical art: Barbara Hack
Photographic research: Kay Y. James
Marketing: Ronald Blauer
Production Manager: Laura Argento
Production coordinator: Thomas Dorsaneo

ECONOMICS Today and Tomorrow

Library of Congress Cataloging in Publication Data

Miller, Roger LeRoy.
  Economics, today and tomorrow.

  SUMMARY: Applies traditional economic theory to contemporary problems such as unemployment, inflation, and conflicting economic systems.
  1. Economics—Juvenile literature. 2. United States—Economic conditions—1971-   —Juvenile literature. 3. Consumer protection—Juvenile literature. [1. Economics. 2. Consumer protection] I. Title.
HB171.7.M66   330   77-12974
ISBN 06-552500-0

79 80 10 9 8 7 6 5 4 3

Credits begin on page 415

CONTENTS

PREFACE

No matter who you are, where you live, or how much money you have to spend, the subject of economics is important to *you*.

The understanding of economics has become progressively essential as our society becomes increasingly complex. *Economics Today & Tomorrow (ETT)* has been conceived and designed to provide young adults with a clear and *meaningful* understanding of our amazing complex economic society. Central to this purpose is the belief that students learn more when given the opportunity to relate what they have learned to their daily life experiences.

Wherever possible, *ETT* involves students with each new concept in a manner that relates their learning to activities they are involved in on a day-to-day basis. *ETT* encourages students to make *immediate* use of what they learn. It is this feature which clearly distinguishes *ETT* from other basic economic texts.

ETT is one of a series of texts designed for the young adult. Each book has been carefully developed to provide for the *student's* interests and needs. Prior to the development of this text many educational consortiums were held and hundreds of educators were consulted; you, the educator, told us what kind of book would best serve the needs of your students. This information was combined with extensive national surveys, resulting in an economics text which presents a usually difficult subject in an imaginative and innovative manner.

Roger LeRoy Miller, author of many best-selling college texts and popular economics books, offers students a unique synthesis of traditional economic topics interwoven with practical information and a series of student related issues. He addresses students as intelligent young adults who face difficult economic decisions.

ETT has been organized into eight major units, including principles of economics, consumer economics, and private enterprise. The existing organization provides maximum flexibility to allow you to emphasize those areas and approaches which most closely fit the needs of your students.

Such stimulating issues as living within your means, business and advertising, labor and wages, the cost of education, and inflation are designed to create interest and understanding; they follow many of the chapters on subjects which traditionally are difficult for students to grasp. Biographies of major economists further enhance economic awareness and understanding.

This text has been designed for study. Definitions of new terms appear at chapter openings to alert the student to key words and further reinforce learning. Each chapter contains opening previews and important terms, review and discussion questions at chapter end. Projects are also included for either classroom use or additional projects.

The illustrative material in this text is specifically selected to reinforce the concept that economics is a human activity that involves *everyone*. An inquiry approach has been used to caption the photographs, further engaging the students in the learning process.

The accompanying instructor's resource manual provides additional support and includes answers to end of chapter material, chapter outlines, learning objectives, additional test questions with answers, activities, and a free materials list.

A student study guide which further expands and reinforces the learning of key concepts is available from the publisher. Included are learning objectives, definitions of concepts and terms, chapter summaries, and additional true-false, multiple choice, and fill-in questions, with answers provided for immediate reinforcement.

ABOUT THE AUTHOR

Roger LeRoy Miller is much more than just an economist—he is a brilliant thinker, a prolific writer, and an academician who has brought the study of economics into a new and relevant perspective by teaching the economic realities of modern life rather than merely espousing economic theories.

Professor Miller grew up on the West Coast and graduated *summa cum laude* and Phi Beta Kappa in 1965 from the University of California at Berkeley, where he was a California Senior Regent's Scholar. Upon graduation he was awarded the National Science Foundation Fellowship and the Woodrow Wilson Fellowship. He then went on to Bordeaux, France to study French literature for a year before returning to the States, where he continued his graduate studies and received a Ph.D. in 1968.

Dr. Miller has taught methodology and technique to teachers of high school economics through the Joint Council on Economics Education. He has also taught economics at the University of Washington in Seattle, and is currently Professor of Economics at the Law and Economics Center of the University of Miami. He continues to apply economic theory to real world problems, particularly in the areas of ecology and environmental concerns, by working with lawyers, the government and private firms.

Dr. Miller has recently completed a television series on teaching economics through different medias. He has written over 30 books on economics and statistics, including the best-selling textbook *ECONOMICS TODAY*. When he is not teaching or writing or consulting, Professor Miller enjoys a variety of outdoor sports including swimming, fishing and surfing near his home in Coral Gables.

"I can't tell you the secret of life . . . Ask me about economics"

UNIT ONE

An Introduction

Can We Save Our Environment?

Definitions of New Terms

Private or personal cost: Private or personal cost is what the individual pays for something he or she buys or does. Private costs are what people consider in their personal decision making.

Social costs: Social costs are what society pays for any action by individuals in the society. These costs include not only all private or personal costs but also all costs that individuals do not consider. For example, individuals pay the private costs of driving an automobile, such as gas, oil, and repairs. Society pays not only those costs but also such costs as air pollution, noise pollution, and congestion.

Pollution and the Quality of Life

If you live in a large city such as New York, Chicago, or Los Angeles, you know what air pollution is. If you live in an industrial city, such as Gary, Indiana, or Tacoma, Washington, with their many mills, you know what air pollution is. If you live near a busy airport, you know what noise pollution is. If you have tried to swim in such bodies of water as Lake Erie, the Hudson River, or the Houston Ship Channel, you know what water pollution is.

Can People Escape a Changed Environment?

The fact is that neither you nor anyone else can escape the pollution that has become part of everyday life in the United States. Some people believe that pollution and the quality of life in general are problems that can only be solved by scientists using improved technology. After all, a polluted river is first and foremost a *physical* fact of life. But, while all pollution is physical, because it involves physical destruction of the environment, there cannot be any real analysis of pollution problems without economic considerations.

You may be wondering what this means. Without going into detail, consider the fact that when automobile manufacturers were required to put pollution control equipment on engines, the price of automobiles increased. Similarly, when electric companies were forced to put pollution control equipment on generators, the price of electricity increased.

The point is that any discussion about improving the quality of life requires a discussion of the *price* people must pay for that improvement. Among other matters, economics concerns itself

Pollution has many economic and social consequences. How many different ways does pollution both improve and worsen the quality of your life?

with the price people must pay for their actions. Thus, economics plays an important part in any analysis of the environment.

Is Pollution a Problem of the 1970s and 1980s?

Many people think that pollution is a modern problem—that people who lived in the past did not experience pollution. This is not the case. Pollution began when civilization began. Since pollution can be defined as the production of unwanted by-products of human activity, then pollution has occurred whenever people have done something—even when they have merely existed.

For example, we know smog has been a problem in Los Angeles for 40 years or more. More than a century ago, London's air was polluted by the unrestricted burning of soft Newcastle coal. Today we are all aware of the problem of noise pollution caused by supersonic jets. Yet noise pollution was a problem as far back as Roman times. Julius Caesar banned chariots from the cobblestone streets during evening hours because of the noise they made.

Various forms of pollution have long troubled civilization. Recently, more people have become aware of a general decline in the environment.

Can the Earth Clean Itself?

Throughout most of history, the earth's air, water, and land were able to clean themselves sufficiently to take care of the by-products of human pollution. However, within the last hundred years the situation has changed, for two important reasons. First, the tremendous increase in population during the last century or so has led to ever-increasing pollution. Second, and

Although pollution is not a new problem to man, rapid population and technological growth have dramatically increased the amount of pollution and its impact on the environment. Can there be economic growth without increased pollution? How?

perhaps even more important, as the material well-being of people has increased, so have their purchases of products that use resources and, at the same time, cause pollution. In fact, a major determinant of the levels of pollution has been how much income people have had to spend for manufactured products. The manufacture of these products first caused the by-products that are pollution and increased them many times over the years.

Why Have People Been Allowed to Pollute?

You may have asked yourself a very important question: Why have people been allowed to pollute? Or, as one example, why have factories until recently been allowed to emit polluted smoke into the atmosphere so that people had difficulty breathing?

The answer lies in the way people have treated air. Nearly everyone has treated air as if no one owned it. Since no one person really does own the air, it has been to no one's *personal* advantage to make sure that it was not polluted and that a general high quality of life was maintained. Herein lies the heart of the pollution problem. It will become more evident as we examine more closely one of the main types of environmental destruction.

Water Pollution

Water can clean itself of a certain amount of pollution. But if the pollution becomes too great, it cannot purify itself. Water pollution comes from three major sources: sewage, industrial waste, and agricultural waste.

Sewage

Two basic types of sewage, or waste water, treatment processes are used today. The first is a primary treatment. This is merely the removal of solids, grease, and scum. The second is a secondary treatment, in which controlled bacteria are used to destroy raw sewage. Neither treatment, however, removes all of the minerals in polluted water that are harmful to human beings.

Thus, municipal waste water that has passed through both primary and secondary treatment cannot be directly reused for human beings. It must be exposed to still a third treatment. And this treatment is twice as expensive as the secondary treatment.

The Federal Water Quality Administration reported at the beginning of the 1970s that only about 40 percent of the nation's municipal sewage treatment systems were adequate. About 5 percent of the American population still lives in areas where sewers are available but where communities have no sewage treatment.

Industrial Waste

Today industry probably contributes more to water pollution than do household users. The major industrial polluters are the chemical, primary metals, paper, and food industries. The chemical industry alone pours more waste into the nation's waterways than the entire population served by municipal sewer systems.

Water pollution caused by industrial waste is a more complicated problem than that caused by sewage. For one thing, industrial waste generally contains many more exotic chemicals that resist biological destruction than does household sewage. Moreover, the chemicals with which industry pollutes water tend to stay for a longer period of time. Last, industrial waste is increasing at a greater rate than sewage because industry is producing more and more goods, whereas the population is growing only slowly.

Recently a new type of water pollution has developed that is particularly evident around industrial power plants. This type is known as *thermal* water pollution. It comes from water that has been heated, used in some production process as a coolant, and then returned to its source.

There is much dispute over the effects of thermal pollution. In some cases thermal pollution has actually led to more fish growing in a particular lake or stream. In other cases it has led to

"Another pact to clean up the environment . . . frankly I WAS getting worried"

a dramatic change in the types of water life that can exist in the warmer waters.

Agricultural Waste

The third major source of water pollution is agricultural waste. Much water pollution is caused by sediment from the erosion of crop lands, by animal wastes, by pesticides, and by the runoff of commercial fertilizers.

The disposal of domestic animal wastes, which contain organisms and nutrients that can cause diseases, is a growing problem. The polluting matter from this source in the United States is estimated to be equivalent to that of a human population of about 2 billion.

The latest estimates of waste water and undissolved solids are shown in Figure I–1–1.

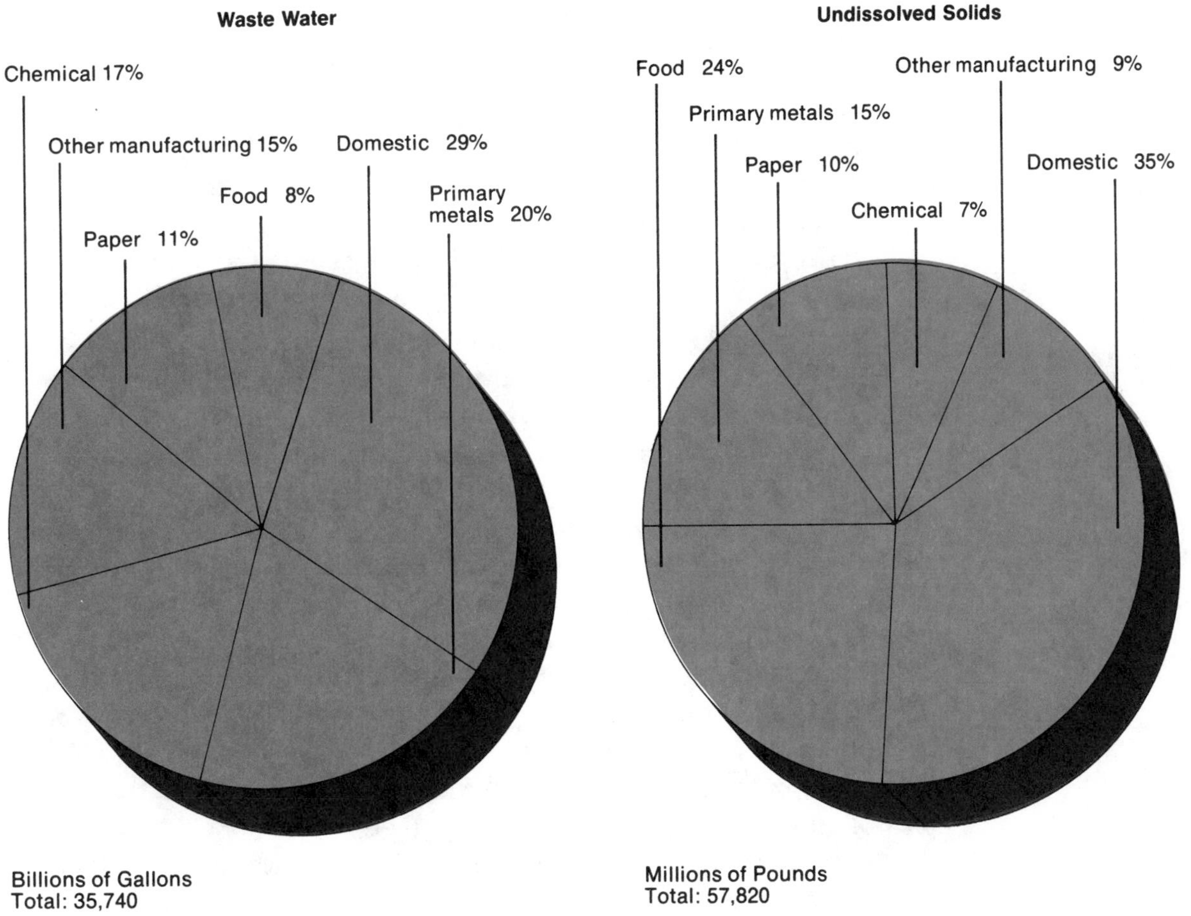

Waste Water

Chemical 17%

Other manufacturing 15%   Domestic 29%

Food 8%

Paper 11%   Primary metals 20%

Billions of Gallons
Total: 35,740

Undissolved Solids

Food 24%   Other manufacturing 9%

Primary metals 15%

Paper 10%   Domestic 35%

Chemical 7%

Millions of Pounds
Total: 57,820

Figure I-1-1. Water Pollution. Estimated industrial and domestic wastes before treatment (1977 estimates).

The Cost of Water Pollution

Why have Americans allowed the nation's waterways to become polluted? Why, for example, have factories poured harmful wastes into nearby rivers so that people downstream cannot use those rivers for swimming, fishing, or drinking? Until recently, most rivers have been treated as if no one owned them. Thus, factories located near rivers had no reason not to pollute. After all, if the rivers would carry off waste, the factory owners would not have to pay for waste disposal. The owners would, therefore, have lower costs in producing their products. Lower costs, in turn, would allow the owners to sell their products at a lower price, to get more business.

Only recently have municipalities, states, and the federal government begun to make individual firms treat waterways with some respect. For example, the 140 or so plants along the Houston Ship Channel spent more than $140 million in the first five years of a clean-up campaign to purge 85 percent of the carbon wastes in that waterway. This was not a voluntary effort. The U.S. Environmental Protection Agency (EPA) prodded the plants, perhaps not so gently, into doing it.

The question remains as to why municipalities, states, and the federal government have had to force industry to stop polluting waterways. In order to understand why, let us look at the case of an individual living along the edge of a lake. What are the **private** or **personal costs**[1] that the person must incur? They would be the costs of running a house, buying food, and the like.

Now consider that the person is allowed to dispose of household sewage or the runoff of dirty water from a washing machine in the lake. Is there additional cost? Yes—that of polluting the lake. If we add this cost to the private or personal costs of the individual's actions, we get what is known as **social costs,** or the costs to society. Social costs can be defined as *all costs of an action borne by society.* Private or personal costs are merely *those costs of an action that are borne by an individual.*

Whenever a resource such as water or air is treated as if no one owned it, we find that the individual's private or personal costs are not the same as the social costs of his or her actions. That is why we talk in terms of a government agency forcing people, business firms, and industries to take account of their pollution-creating activities. Then people must take account of the (higher) social costs of their actions, rather than just their private costs.

[1]In this book new words important to the study of economics are printed in **boldface** or **darker type.** These words are defined at the beginning of the issue or chapter in which they first appear.

The Houston Ship Canal was until recently considered to be one of the most polluted bodies of water in the United States. In what ways does industrial waste dumped into waterways become a social cost?

When they do, they find that pollution is reduced. The Houston Ship Channel, for example, is now cleaner than it was 10 years ago. But this improvement did not come free of charge. All the plants along the channel had to install antipollution equipment to reduce the amounts of pollutants going into the water. Because that equipment cost money, the plants had higher expenses. Ultimately, the people who have bought products made in those plants have paid higher prices for them.

This, of course, gives rise to political issues. For example, the owners of the plants along the Houston Ship Channel are in competition with the owners of plants located elsewhere in the United States. Thus, when the federal government required the Houston Ship Channel plants to install costly pollution-reducing equipment, the owners of the plants were faced with an increase in the costs of production. If we disregard other factors, we might expect that the costs of production for the Houston Ship Channel plants would become greater than the costs of production elsewhere in the country. The owners would then find themselves at a competitive disadvantage. They might even have to close down. Therefore, it is not surprising that the owners politically opposed reducing the pollution from their plants.

Political issues of this sort must always be faced when the government decides to impose restrictions on specific parts of the economy. Ultimately, such restrictions mean extra costs in those sections of the economy. And the extra costs sooner or later have to be translated into higher-priced products.

Usually, we see only the results of the political give-and-take that goes on behind the scene when government imposes rules, restrictions, or standards on industry. Nevertheless, we can be sure that both industry and government had to make some compromises along the way, because a choice had to be made. What is the choice? In the case of the Houston Ship Channel, the choice was between the continued polluting of the channel and a combination of higher-priced products made in the channel's factories and rising unemployment resulting from the closing of those plants that "couldn't make it" under more stringent pollution controls.

Economics and the Environment

The choice between a polluted waterway and paying the price to clean it up raises other questions. A basic question is how far people should go in cleaning up the environment. A dedicated ecologist might say, "All the way." But what does this mean? Does it mean to have no pollution at all? To eliminate all pollution would be literally impossible. Remember that humans pollute merely by living.

If we look at it from society's viewpoint, people should eliminate pollution up to the point where it is no longer worth it. When does that point occur? In theory, it occurs when the *cost* of eliminating any additional pollution outweighs the benefit to society created by eliminating more pollution.

In practice, it may be difficult to measure the benefit to society of additional pollution reduction. We know most people would like a cleaner environment. But how much do they value increased purity compared to what it costs them to obtain it? When we begin talking about costs, we are talking about economics.

Summary

This Issue introduces some important concepts. Several are fundamental to the study of economics. For example:

1. Almost everything that happens on earth involves a cost. If people want to clean up the environment, they must pay for it. A cleaner environment does not happen free of charge. Thus, the question arises: Are the benefits worth the cost? People need to make that comparison when they talk about cleaning up their surroundings. Otherwise, they might spend too much money to control pollution and not enough for some other socially worth-while task, such as crime prevention or cancer research.

2. There are various types of costs. When most individuals make decisions, they consider primarily the private cost of their actions. They do not look at the additional costs that might fall to society as a whole. Specifically, private costs are important in

personal decision making, but social costs are important in decision making for an entire economy.

3.   Implied in some of the previous discussion is the concept that life involves choosing among alternatives. In fact, *economics basically involves making choices among alternatives.* Let's face it: people make choices all the time. They cannot escape decision making, even when it gets down to such basic problems as what to wear to school or which movie to see on Saturday night.

Important Terms   private or personal cost   social cost

Questions for Thought and Discussion

1.   Have you ever been anywhere that you did not notice pollution? If you have, why do you think the pollution level was so low?

2.   Should all pollution be eliminated? Why or why not?

3.   How would you go about determining the social costs of various types of pollution? (Remember that the cost to society is not measured by the *physical* quality of pollution.)

4.   Is there any way that pollution can be reduced without cost? If so, how? If not, why not?

1

Why Study Economics?

Preview Questions

1. With what is economics concerned?
2. Why do people have to make choices?
3. What are the benefits of specialization?
4. What are some aspects of the American capitalist system?

Definitions of New Terms

Economics: Economics is concerned with how scarce things are used, when they are used, and who uses them. It is the study of how people make choices among various alternatives.

Resource: A resource is anything available for people to use. Resources can be classified as (1) those that are useful without being processed (*natural resources*), (2) those that can produce goods (*manmade resources*), and (3) those that are present in human beings (*human resources*). Basically, the term *resources* applies to all the things that people can use to make what they want.

Scarcity: Scarcity is the condition of being in limited supply. Almost everything that exists is scarce, or limited. The problem of scarcity exists because what people want or desire is generally not available in unlimited supply.

Free good: A free good is anything to which the law of scarcity does not apply. There are few free goods. One might be air for a car engine. It is freely available.

Economic good: An economic good is any good that is scarce. An economic good always has a cost because there is a limited supply.

Specialization: Specialization is the process of having a worker do a specific job or jobs rather than doing everything required to make a product. Specialization is sometimes called *the division of labor.*

Capitalism: Capitalism is the economic system in which people decide how to use their productive talents with little interference from government. Under capitalism, individuals generally own the productive resources and are free to choose how to use them.

Private enterprise: Private enterprise is a characteristic of a capitalist system. Private enterprise stresses the freedom that individuals have to select whatever they want to do themselves or with the resources they own. (The term *free enterprise* is synonymous with *private enterprise.*)

You make choices all the time. You must decide how to spend your time when you are not in school. That is, you must choose among alternative uses of your time that compete with each other. These competing uses might be talking on the telephone, playing sports, watching television, doing homework, or reading a book.

For all people, time is a limited and valuable thing. To put it another way, time is something people want or desire. Because there is only a finite (limited) amount of time, people are forced to make choices. Making choices is what *economics* is all about.

Economics concerns situations in which choices must be made about how to use limited *resources,* when to use them, and for what purposes. Resources can be defined as the things people use to make the commodities they want.

Because economics involves examining alternatives, it can teach you some important skills. It can also provide you with knowledge that you can use to become a more informed consumer and an informed voter.

Previously you were introduced to some analysis of an important current issue—the environment. Later sections of this book will use similar analyses to examine automobiles, medical care, getting rich quick, food prices, advertising, unions, minimum wages, poverty, conservation, taxation, wage and price controls, and economic growth. Although the list could be expanded, the economics principles used remain the same. Economics is relevant and important.

This chapter introduces some key concepts that will be used throughout the rest of the book. What is useful about what you learn is that it relates to you—to how you conduct your personal life and relate to the rest of society.

The best place to begin the study of economics is to return to the initial point of this chapter: that people must always choose.

Scarcity The example about time shows that all people face the problem of *scarcity* of time. There is only a limited amount of time to do what they want to do. But what about other things? What about the products people consume? Although it may not seem apparent, the problem of scarcity arises even for the richest people.

Put yourself in the place of Nelson. *Lawrence,* or David Rockefeller—very rich individuals. What if you, as Nelson Rockefeller, wanted to buy every jet airplane in the world. Could you do it? No, you could not. You would not have enough income even though you were extremely wealthy.

What if you, as Lawrence Rockefeller, wanted to buy every building in Manhattan? Could you do it? No, because you wouldn't have enough income.

What if you, as David Rockefeller, wanted to buy every oil company in the world? Could you do it? No.

Closer to Home

In 1977 the estimated average weekly income of young people between 16 and 19 years old was $28.40. The estimated average weekly spendable income of college students was slightly higher. Thus, let's look at the average young adult with a weekly income of $30.

This young adult obviously cannot buy everything he or she desires. What can be bought is limited by the person's income. For scarcity is imposed by a limited income. What is scarce is the wherewithal—the person's money income. The young adult must, therefore, make a choice every time he or she thinks about buying something. "Should I buy this, or should I buy that? Should I put aside my money for a larger purchase, or should I spend it now?"

The Bigger Picture

If we add up all the scarcity problems facing all the people in the United States, we come to a startling finding. At any one moment, the total amount of desired things available is *fixed*. Now, what does this mean? It means that there cannot be more than what actually exists. Or, to put it another way, at any moment in the United States a fixed amount of resources is available for all the different uses people may have for them.

Therefore, scarcity imposes the same kind of problems on the United States as a nation that it imposes on you as an individual. Americans must choose between alternative uses of the available resources in the entire nation. The same could be said for the world at large. If there were no scarcity, no one would need to study economics because there would be no need to make economic choices among alternative uses. People could have as much as they wanted, of whatever they wanted, for as long as they wanted.

But people cannot have all they want. The earth does not provide people with everything desired. There are limits. Yet *human* wants or desires seem to be unlimited. Therefore economics by necessity applies to every situation in which people must decide what to do with the resources available.

What Can You Get Free?

Some things have no cost. These things are known as *free goods*. However, today there are not many free goods. In the past, air was considered a free good. But now pollution makes the air in many cities unhealthy to breathe.

Still, in many mountain areas in the United States there is clean air. In those places people can have all the clean air they want. There is no problem of scarcity. In many areas in the United States, running water is also a free good.

When clean air or water becomes scarce, as in cities, the problem of scarcity arises. During the course of the nation's history, Americans have seen many free goods, such as land for farming, become scarce as population and production increased. Scarce goods are sometimes called *economic goods.*

It is important to remember that an economic good is defined as any good that is scarce *relative* to wants. Remember, too, that a basic

You (much the same as nations) are faced daily with economic alternatives. What economic choices have you made recently? What were your alternatives?

economic principle is that human wants are unlimited and that most goods available to meet those wants are limited. In fact, almost any item you can name fits the definition of an economic good.

Often people use the term *goods* when they are really referring to *goods and services*. Goods are things. Services are activities done for other people. Butchers and bakers sell goods—meat and bread. Doctors, dentists, and auto mechanics sell services—medical and dental care and auto repair.

Choice and Exchange

It is important to realize that the economic choices people make generally involve exchanging one thing for another. For example, when you choose to buy a stereo cassette, you exchange the purchasing power of your money for the right to own the cassette.

In general, voluntary exchanges among individuals can be defined as swaps in which those concerned want to engage. By necessity, every voluntary exchange must make those involved subjectively better off. Both parties must feel that they are happier or richer after the exchange has taken place. That is, exchange is mutually beneficial.

But what about involuntary exchanges? Involuntary exchanges occur when force or power is used to alter the behavior of another person, group, or nation. When black Africans were captured and transported to America as slaves, they were forced to provide labor to their owners in return for the necessities of life. When a person is robbed, that person engages in an involuntary exchange. Although it might appear that the robber offers the victim a voluntary choice ("Your money or your life"), this choice is not one in which a person freely decides to exchange or not to exchange.

How One Becomes "Best Off"

Because people cannot have everything they want, they must decide what to do with their talents for making or producing goods. In general, people try to apply their talents to the activities that yield them the highest rewards—money (income), fame, good working conditions, personal freedom, and the like. To simplify matters here, let us consider only how much money income individuals make at different tasks.

People try to determine what they do comparatively better than others. Thus, they must look at alternatives. They then decide on those productive activities that give them the highest reward or rate of return for the time spent working. A higher rate of return means a higher income—more money. This, in turn, gives them greater command over the things they want to consume.

When people choose to do certain tasks rather than others to obtain income, they have specialized. The basic economic principle of *specialization* applies to nations or societies as well as to people. The history of economic development in the United States and elsewhere is a history of specialization. Although people have always specialized, specialization has developed enormously in modern times. For example, 200 years ago, the British economist Adam Smith was one of the first to note the importance of specialization in manufacturing when he described the making of pins:

Take the example, therefore, of a very trifling manufacture—one in which the division of labor has not very often been noticed—the trade of the pin maker. One man draws out the wire. Another straightens it. A third cuts it. A fourth points it. A fifth grinds it at the top for receiving the head. To make the head requires two or three distinct operations. To put it on is a peculiar business. To whiten the pins is another. It is even a trade by itself to put them into the paper. Thus, the important business of making a pin, is in this manner, divided into about 18 distinct operations. In some manufactories all are performed by distinct hands, though in others the same man will sometimes perform two or three of them. Ten persons, therefore, can make among them upwards of 48,000 pins in a day.[1]

Why Specialization? One of the facts that specialization through the division of labor, as outlined in Smith's example of pin making, rests on is the fact that people, communities, and even nations differ. They have different abilities to produce goods and services. Take the simplest example: if two people were exactly the same in every respect and either could do every job as well as the other, there would be no reason for specialization. One of the reasons for specialization, therefore, is the fact that the abilities and interests of people differ.

The costs of producing goods differ for workers and nations because of different available resources, production techniques, and preferences. For example, it is relatively less costly for Japan to specialize in the production of electronic equipment today than it is for the United States. That is, Japan gives up fewer alternatives by producing certain electronic equipment than does the United States. This is a field in which Japan makes more income than can other nations. The principle of specialization rests on this fact.

As an example, consider the choices of a man who is president of a large company. As an extreme example, he might type better than any company typist, file better than any file clerk, drive a truck better than any truck driver, and wash windows better than any window washer. Such being the case, his productive advantage would be *absolute* in all of these endeavors. Yet he manages the company because he is paid more for being president than for being a typist, file clerk, window washer, or truck driver.

Even if someone could do everything better than everyone else, that person would usually prefer to specialize for reasons of choice.

_____
[1]Adam Smith, *The Wealth of Nations* (New York: Modern Library, [1776] 1937), pp. 4-5.

The gasoline shortage of 1975 demonstrated the limited or fixed nature of most natural resources. How many different uses can you think of for gas other than use as a car fuel?

For example, before he became President of the United States, William Howard Taft was one of the fastest stenographers in the nation. Although he could have been the nation's best typist, he chose to seek the presidency because in that role he could get the most for his talents.

The American Economic System

Given freedom of choice, most individuals seek to make exchanges to better themselves. In so doing, they specialize, seeking out the highest-paid occupation. In general, this is how economic decisions are made in the United States. Under the American economic system, known as *capitalism,* individuals own the means of production and decide themselves how to use them.

Capitalism

The concept of capitalism is usually associated with Adam Smith. In his book *The Wealth of Nations,* Smith described a system in which the government has little to do with economic activities. He said that individuals pursue their own self-interests. In doing so, however, they are also increasing the well-being of the entire nation.

Obviously, capitalism in such a pure form has never existed. Capitalism today must be defined more realistically. Throughout this book, capitalism will be described as the economic system in which private individuals own the productive resources of the society and have the right to use these resources in whatever manner they choose *within the limits of the law.*

Basically, what this means is that people own the means of producing something or doing something to get an income. That is, they, as individuals, have a voice in how they use their labor and in how they use the things they own, such as machines, to produce income. Thus, the definition of capitalism includes the right of individuals to use their talents however they think best for themselves.

Private Enterprise

Another characteristic of the capitalistic system is the freedom of individuals to choose economic activities for whatever resources they own. This idea is called ***private enterprise.*** Private enterprise allows people to seek whatever occupations they want without restrictions. Again, this description applies purely to the theoretical aspects of a capitalist system.

In the United States, for example, people are not always free to go into any occupation they wish. Just try to become a doctor without first graduating from medical school. Or try to practice law without passing the state bar examination.

Many people view private enterprise as supporting a *laissez-faire system* (pronounced les ā. fâr). As Smith outlined in *Wealth of Nations,* a laissez-faire system lets each person go his or her own way to maximize personal self-interest. The government does not restrict a person's actions unless that person physically harms others. Thus, theoretically, in a private enterprise system productive resources are generally directed toward their best uses. For example, workers tend to work at jobs in which they can make the most money. In doing so, they contribute the most to the material well-being of society.

The Role of Government

Nevertheless, even a purely capitalistic system has a role for government. The government protects the rights of individuals, especially regarding their control over property. Smith described in some detail the role of government in a capitalist system in *Wealth of Nations.* He talked about the government's need for national defense. To pay for this, government must levy taxes.

Today the accepted role of government, even in capitalist countries, has expanded. Most governments take an active role in providing welfare for those in poverty. The government's role as the provider of education is accepted virtually everywhere. The increasing problems of pollution and degradation of the environment have brought with them increased amounts of government regulation. Much of the remainder of this book will be devoted to subjects in which the role of government has expanded since the time of Adam Smith.

Can Any System Be Perfect?

The private enterprise system of modified capitalism in the United States is by no means perfect. Even if it were, it might not be good for all the people in the system. The same could be said about other economic systems that have existed. However, it is certainly possible to improve the American system. This book will point out numerous defects in the American economic system that have caused social ills. A good example was already given in the introductory issue in the discussion about the destruction of the environment.

In the next unit, you will be introduced to some personal economics that may enable you to make more informed choices as a consumer. After all, economics begins in your wallet or purse, with how you fill it and how you empty it.

Summary

1. Almost everything in the world is scarce. That is, it exists in limited supply.

2. Because scarcity exists, people must make choices about how they use resources.

3. Although resources are scarce, people's wants are unlimited. That explains why people have problems in making choices.

4. Economics is concerned with situations in which choices must be made.

5. In any economic system, exchange takes place when individuals swap one thing for another. In most societies, money is used as a medium of exchange.

6. Because people cannot have everything they want, they tend to apply their talents to the activities that yield them the highest rewards. That is, people tend to specialize.

7. The history of economic development is a history of specialization. One reason that specialization exists is because people and nations have different abilities (resources) to produce goods and services.

8. The United States is a capitalist society. Capitalism is an economic system in which individuals own the productive resources of the society and have the right to use these resources in whatever manner they choose within the limits of the law.

9. An important characteristic of capitalism is private enterprise. Private enterprise provides people with the freedom to choose economic activities for whatever resources they own.

Important Terms

capitalism	economic good
private enterprise	scarcity
economics	free good
resource	specialization

Review Questions

1. With what is economics concerned?
2. Why do people make choices?
3. Are all things scarce? Explain.

4. What is the difference between a free good and an economic good?

5. How do goods and services differ?

6. What are the necessary conditions of a voluntary exchange?

7. What is meant by the division of labor?

8. Why do people specialize?

9. Who was Adam Smith?

10. How did Adam Smith describe capitalism?

11. What is private enterprise?

12. What is meant by laissez-faire?

Discussion Questions

1. Is there anybody in the world today who does not face a problem of scarcity? Who?

2. Imagine that the state in which you live was isolated from the rest of the nation. What goods and services could you no longer buy? Do you think there would be a significant difference in your life-style if no exchange could take place between the people who live in your state and those who live elsewhere?

3. What are the major characteristics of the American economic system? Must an economic system be laissez-faire to be capitalistic? Why or why not?

4. Why do you think the study of economics is important?

Projects

1. List some activities you think you do better than other people. Then explain whether you will continue to do these activities because you can do them better than other people or because you like to do them.

2. Obtain a copy of Adam Smith's *Wealth of Nations* from the library. Read the section on division of labor and pin making. Glance through the rest of the book. Do you find the book difficult or easy to understand? Do you think Smith's examples make the book useless for analyzing today's economic problems?

3. Interview a group of local merchants to learn how they are restricted from doing everything they might want in their businesses. Report your findings to the class. Then hold a discussion on why government regulation of business is necessary.

4. Research a simple manufacturing process, such as making a suit of clothes. In a report, describe the various steps required to make the product and explain the advantages of having different people do each step.

UNIT TWO

Practical Economics

2

Your Role as a Consumer

Preview Questions

1. What determines how much income people can make and therefore spend?
2. How do people decide what to buy?
3. What does the term *comparison shopping* mean?

Definitions Of New Terms

Consumer: Any person who buys or uses goods and services is a consumer. From birth, all people are consumers in one way or another.

Engel's law: Engel's law states that the greater the income, the smaller the percentage spent on basic commodities.

Comparison shopping: Comparison shopping is checking the types of products available at what prices from different sellers. Comparison shopping involves the use of a scarce resource—time.

Consumerism: Consumerism is a movement, the goals of which are the education and protection of the consumer.

You, as well as everyone you know, are a ***consumer.*** In fact, everybody consumes in one way or another. As consumers, people purchase an amazing variety of items—food, clothes, cars, TVs, and so on. To get an idea of what kind of numbers are involved, just look at Table 2-1, which cites the billions of dollars spent on specific categories of items that people buy.

The particular way in which Americans consume has not always been the same. Figure 2-1 shows the dramatic change in American consumption habits since the beginning of this century. The pie diagrams show that the percentage of total consumption spent for such basic items as food and housing has fallen significantly since 1900.

This observation about consumption was first made by Ernst Engel, a nineteenth-century German statistician. Engel's finding, now known as ***Engel's law,*** indicates that as a family's income increases, the percentage of income spent on basic items decreases.

Engel's law applies to nations as well as to people. As a nation, the United States has been getting richer. Therefore, the percentage of national income spent on food has fallen. On the other hand, as people or nations grow richer, spending on such luxury items as recreation would be expected to increase. In fact, Figure 2-1 shows

Table 2-1: Personal Spending in the United States (in billions)

Automobiles and parts	$ 70.6
Furniture and household equipment	62.9
Food and beverages	224.5
Clothing and shoes	75.3
Gasoline and oil	41.4
Housing services	165.8
Household operation services	71.6
Transportation	37.5
All others	329.0
Total	$1,078.6

This table shows an actual tabulation of the billions of dollars that were spent by American consumers on various categories of goods and services. (The last category, "All others," includes everything that was not listed specifically.) You can check the latest issue of the *Survey of Current Business* to find out how much personal consumption expenditures have grown since 1976. Source: *Survey of Current Business*, January, 1977.

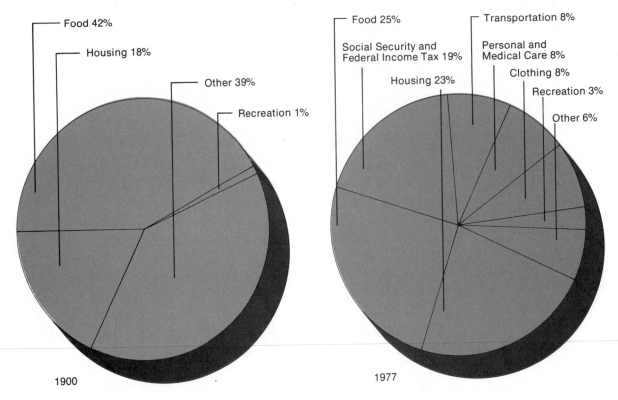

Food 42%

Housing 18%

Other 39%

Recreation 1%

1900

Food 25%

Social Security and
Federal Income Tax 19%

Housing 23%

Transportation 8%

Personal and
Medical Care 8%

Clothing 8%

Recreation 3%

Other 6%

1977

Figure 2-1. Personal spending for essential purchases in the United States.

that Americans are, indeed, spending a larger percentage of their income on recreation.

To Consume, People Must Have Income

People's role as consumers depends critically on their *ability* to consume. Their ability to consume depends on their income—that is, on how much money they have to spend. This chapter examines many aspects of the role of the consumer. But first let us look at some information about people's role as producers of income that allows them to be consumers.

Some consumers obviously have more income to spend than others. Without attempting to answer in detail why some people earn more than others, let us list some of the key factors that influence earning power. How great a person's income is might be determined by:

1. education
2. occupation
3. age
4. inheritance
5. luck

Additionally, where one lives has a bearing on income. Individuals who live in cities earn more income than those who live in rural areas.

There are also differences in income depending upon which region of the country one lives.

To get some idea of how varied the income of families in the United States actually is, look at Figure 2-2 which shows the number of American families by income category. Today, the number of families earning under $3,000 is about 1 million, while the number of families earning over $15,000 is approximately 25 million.

No matter what a person's income is, however, spending income requires that decisions be made all the time. It requires that the person as a consumer decide what to buy, how much to buy, where to buy it, and how much time to spend obtaining information about the appropriate consumer choices to be made.

Consumer Decision Making and Scarce Resources

Whenever a decision must be made about a purchase, there will always be at least two scarce resources—time and income. Scarcity of time and income presents every consumer with a problem concerning how those resources must be used.

Just think about the scarcity of time. If you are trying to decide whether to spend five dollars on a phonograph record you want or, alternatively, to go to the movies with friends, the time you spend making that decision cannot be used for doing something else.

More important, in most cases when you have made a decision about spending income, time must then be spent in obtaining information about the particular product you wish to buy. After all, there is generally a wide variety of choices among most consumer products. For example, suppose you have decided to buy a bicycle

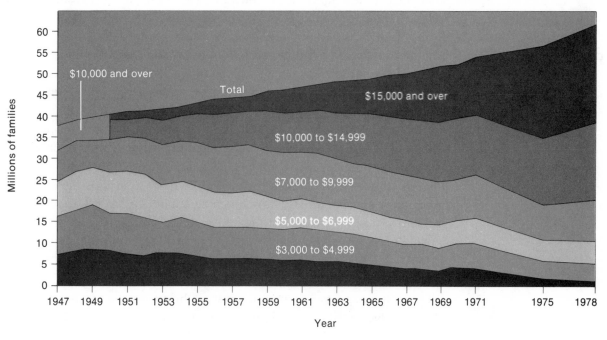

Figure 2-2. Money income in 1976 families and persons in the United States; number of families by income in 1947 to 1976. 1978 data are estimates. Source: U.S. Department of Commerce.

with your accumulated savings. There are numerous brands and styles from which to choose. Any time you spend going to various bicycle stores and checking out the available models and prices is time which you cannot spend doing something else. Thus, the time spent shopping for the bicycle is a cost to you.

The Decision-Making Process

There are many steps involved in making a decision about what to buy. Let us continue using the example of buying a bicycle. The decision-making process you might engage in could be the following:

1. deciding to buy a bicycle—that is, deciding whether or not to use up a limited income
2. deciding whether the bicycle should be new or used
3. deciding whether it should be a 1-speed, 3-speed, or 10-speed bicycle
4. deciding whether it should be light or medium weight
5. deciding which brand to buy
6. deciding which model to buy and, hence, what price to pay

Even after you have made decisions like those listed and have purchased a bicycle, you will have additional decisions to make as a consumer. You will have to decide how much time, effort, and perhaps money you want to spend in maintaining the bicycle you have purchased. A person's role as a consumer does not end after he or she has made a purchase. It continues for as long as the person has a choice about continuing to use the purchased item.

Buying Principles and Strategies

Consumer decision making can follow many different avenues. But once the consumer realizes he or she is faced with the problems of scarcity of income and time, decisions can be fitted into a set of buying principles or strategies.

Each consumer's ultimate goal is, of course, to obtain the most satisfaction possible from his or her limited time and income. In order to do this, key aspects of buying can be used. These follow from fairly obvious choices that consumers have. The first is perhaps the most important choice—namely, *how much* to spend. In reality, this is a problem of taking care *not* to spend more for an item than one is capable of paying. The problem of going into debt and the ways to stay out of debt by formulating a budget will be discussed at length in Chapter 3.

Two other aspects of consumer buying, however, are treated here. They involve getting the "right" product and the "best" deal.

Seeking out the Appropriate Product. Let us again consider the example of buying a bicycle. Once the decision about spending

Have you ever purchased something that you felt was misrepresented or defective?
What were your rights as a consumer? What did you do?

income on a bicycle has been made, you have to decide what quality to buy. You have to decide which brand and model are best for you. How do you decide? You must obtain information. The information, however, is scarce. It is scarce because obtaining it involves a cost. You must seek it out by reading advertisements, going to different stores and discussing alternative models with sales personnel, or spending time testing out friends' bicycles.

Since information is scarce, you are faced with a problem. How much information should you obtain? One specific buying principle to follow is to obtain as much information as is worthwhile. What does this mean? It means that you should try to get as much information about a product you might buy so long as the time and effort required to obtain that information does not exceed its value. In simpler terms, you would not want to go to every bicycle store in the city and spend two hours with every salesperson discussing the good and bad points of every model in the world. On the other hand, you would probably want to spend more than two minutes reading one advertisement about one brand.

Getting the Best Deal.   Once you have made a decision about what type of bike to buy, you must consider where to buy it. That decision will have a lot to do with the price you will have to pay for the desired brand and model and, hence, quality. Since you have a limited income, the more cheaply you can buy the chosen model of desired quality, the more income you will have left to spend on other things that you might want to buy. In other words, you are best off as a consumer when you are able to pay the lowest possible price for the products you want to buy once you have decided on the level of quality you desire.

How do you find out which stores are selling at the lowest prices? Some ways are to read newspaper advertisements, make telephone calls, or visit different stores. Remember, however, that finding out relevant price information about a product requires the use of your time. Thus, you probably would not want to canvass every store within a 50-mile area before deciding where to buy the bicycle you have chosen. Nevertheless, you will want to shop around.

This suggests another important buying principle. Whenever you decide to make a purchase, it is generally worthwhile to get price information from various stores in the area. Such a practice is known as *comparison shopping.* It is a principle of consumer buying that will be continually emphasized throughout this unit.

Even if you apply the principles outlined in this section to actual consumer decision-making situations, you still might find that being a wise consumer is not always easy. You live in a complex world with many sellers of many products. There are sellers who do not present complete or reliable information about their products. There are other sellers who will not stand behind the products they sell if those products turn out to be faulty. Thus, sometimes it may be worth paying more to get a reliably guaranteed product.

Helping You Spend Your Income Wisely

Today the decisions Americans face as consumers are increasingly complex. Most Americans are increasingly concerned with safety and reliability. Times have changed. The age of *consumerism* is here.

Consumerism is a relatively new movement. Its goal is to protect people against bad buying deals because they live in a society that is increasingly complex. The well-being of American consumers is the concern of many politicians, government agencies, and private consumer-oriented organizations. Active control of business practices by government has become a reality in almost every state of the nation. Business firms can no longer assume that it is the buyer's responsibility to know whether a product is safe, food is healthful, or advertising is accurate. The age of consumerism has brought a change in roles. Businesses must now make sure that their products are safe for consumption.

Consumer Rights

In 1962 President John F. Kennedy sent the first consumer protection message to Congress. In that message Kennedy stated four consumer rights:

1. *the right to safety*—protection against goods that are dangerous to life or health

2. *the right to be informed*—not only as a means to protect against fraud but also as a means to make rational choices

3. *the right to choose*—the need for markets to be competitive (many firms) and for protection by government in those markets where competition no longer exists

4. *the right to be heard*—the right to have consumer interests heard in the making of governmental business policy

To the four rights listed by Kennedy, most consumer advocates would add:

the right to redress—to obtain just compensation for damages incurred when dealing in the marketplace

Presidents Lyndon Johnson and Richard Nixon later reaffirmed the rights of consumers presented by Kennedy. The strong tide of consumer legislation at the federal level has continued ever since.

It is because people live in a world of imperfect information about products that consumerism may improve their lots as consumers. If consumerism results in consumers becoming better informed and in producers willingly providing more reliable, safer products, then most people may be able to obtain a higher level of satisfaction from the available resources in the economy.

With this goal in mind, numerous federal agencies have been set up to aid consumers. The next section describes some of these agencies.

Federal Agencies to Help the Consumer

Space does not permit a complete listing of all government agencies that have been set up to help consumers. Those cited here are some of the more important federal agencies that explicitly carry out consumer-oriented activities.

Federal Trade Commission (FTC). Congress created the Federal Trade Commission in 1914. Today the FTC has 12 regional offices, each of which has a staff of lawyers and consumer protection specialists.

A major consumer-oriented activity of the commission has been its control over advertising. Its Bureau of Consumer Protection has responsibility for "monitoring advertising, labeling, and deceptive practices and reviewing applications for complaints." Staff members closely monitor television and radio commercials, national advertising, and, through field offices, local advertising.

The FTC also enforces specific laws that cover truth in labeling; advertising of food, drugs, and cosmetics; and the sale of wool, fur, and textile-fiber products.

Food and Drug Administration (FDA). The Food and Drug Administration was established by Congress in 1906 with enactment of the Pure Food and Drug Act. That law provided for limited supervision of interstate sales of food and drugs by the new federal regulatory agency. Weaknesses in the 1906 Act led to the passage of the Federal Food, Drug, and Cosmetic Act of 1936. This law put cosmetics under the control of the FDA. In addition, it authorized the FDA to prohibit the sale of drugs until they had been proven safe for human consumption. In 1958 control over chemical food additives was granted to the commission.

The most extensive overhaul of legislation governing the FDA came with the Drug Amendments of 1962. Two major provisions of those amendments were (1) the requirement that drugs must be "effective" as well as safe, and (2) the requirement that the FDA approve the introduction of any new drug into the marketplace. The 1962 law also retained the authority of the FDA to remove any drug previously approved, if evidence should show the drug to be unsafe or ineffective.

Today the FDA has authority to require drug manufacturers to state the generic name of a product as well as its brand name in all

Federal laws now require accurate labeling. This enables a consumer to compare differences between brands. Do you make it a practice to read labels when you shop?

advertising of the product. This latest requirement is perhaps the most far-reaching from the consumer's point of view. It enables the consumer to shop for the lowest price among several brand names of the same drug.

Consumer Product Safety Commission (CPSC). The Consumer Product Safety Commission was established by Congress in 1972. It is one of the newest federal agencies designed to protect the consumer. The CPSC has sweeping powers to regulate the production and sale of potentially hazardous products. Eventually, it will have a staff of more than 1000 persons. This will make it one of the major federal regulatory agencies for consumer protection.

The CPSC grew out of a movement that began in 1953 with the Flammable Fabrics Act, designed to protect consumers from certain hazardous products. Since 1972, however, Congress has passed legislation regulating specific classes rather than broad categories of consumer products. On the other hand, the CPSC is designed to regulate all potentially hazardous consumer products. Some important causes of accidents are shown in Chart 2-1.

As stated by the Consumer Product Safety Act of 1972, the purposes of the CPSC are:

Chart 2-1: Causes of Accidents in the United States

	1976
Stairs, ramps, landings (indoors, outdoors)	543,105
Bicycles and bicycle equipment	447,279
Football-related equipment and apparel	384,502
Baseball-related equipment and apparel	355,898
Basketball-related equipment and apparel	343,973
Nails, carpet tacks, screws, thumbtacks	290,845
Chairs, sofas, sofabeds	213,286
Architectural glass	182,220
Tables (nonglass)	166,947
Skates, skateboards, and scooters	156,471
Swings, slides, seesaws, playground equipment	152,057
Beds and bunkbeds (including springs, frames)	132,270
Floors and flooring materials	101,590
Bathtub and shower structures, nonglass shower enclosures (except doors and panels)	60,467
Fuels, liquid, kindling, illuminating	59,192
Swimming pools and associated equipment (in-ground only)	57,323
Power lawn mowers	57,155
Bleaches and dyes, cleaning agents, and caustic compounds	34,844
Cooking ranges, ovens and equipment	28,148
Furnaces, floor furnaces	11,585

Source: Consumer Product Safety Commission, 1976

1. to protect the public against unreasonable risk of injury associated with consumer products

2. to assist consumers in evaluating the comparative safety of consumer products

3. to develop uniform safety standards for consumer products and to minimize conflicting state and local regulations

4. to promote research and investigation into causes and prevention of product-related deaths, illnesses, and injuries

The CPSC can formulate safety standards for consumer products. In addition, it can ban the manufacture and sale of any product deemed hazardous to consumers. For example, it has banned adhesive sprays and similar consumer items.

But on occasion the CPSC has hinted that it would ban a product and then changed its mind because of strong public opinion. In particular, a few years ago the head of the CPSC suggested that the commission had the power to ban cigarettes because they had been proven to be injurious to health. The statement caused such an uproar that nothing has been heard about the proposed ban since.

The CPSC also has the authority to require manufacturers to report information about any products that they have sold or intend to sell that have proven hazardous.

Other Consumer Protection Agencies

Several other federal agencies help consumers. Among the more important are the U.S. Department of Agriculture and the Department of Health, Education and Welfare. There are even more agencies at the state level.

On the local level, not only do many cities and towns have consumer protection bureaus, but there also are many private consumer protection organizations. The Better Business Bureau is a good example of a private agency. It is designed to help not only its commercial members but also consumers who think they have been wronged. Various complaint agencies for users of major appliances and automobiles are being formed throughout the country.

Consumers also have access to information provided by such government agencies as those previously mentioned and by such private concerns as the Consumers' Union. The Consumers' Union publishes a monthly magazine called *Consumer Reports*. The magazine has no advertising. Instead, it contains information about the characteristics of various brands of products you might wish to buy, written by experts who have no direct relationship with the manufacturers of the products. There is also useful information on health, safety, medicine, and other topics of interest to consumers.

A key to wise consuming is having adequate information about what you intend to buy. That information can be obtained from a number of sources, including those mentioned, as well as from people selling products.

Being a wise consumer goes hand in hand with being a wise spender. One way to become a wise spender, whatever your income, is to learn how to manage your income. That is the subject of the Issue 3 following Chapter 3 on debt.

Summary

1. All people are consumers. To consume, people must have income.

2. Earning power is influenced by many factors, including education, occupation, age, inheritance, and luck.

3. Consumers implicitly or explicitly go through a decision-making process every time they consider buying something.

4. All buying decisions are affected by two scarce resources—time and limited income.

5. A buying strategy involves obtaining the "right" product and getting the "best" buy.

6. Comparison shopping involves using time and energy to obtain price information.

7. Americans live in an age of consumerism. Ever-increasing attention has been given to protecting the consumer against bad buying deals. Since the 1960s, the rights of consumers have been stressed by national leaders.

8. Today there are many government agencies and private organizations that offer assistance to consumers and seek to protect the rights of consumers.

Important Terms

buying strategy
decision-making process
comparison shopping
earning power

consumer
Engel's law
consumerism

Review Questions

1. What are consumers?

2. What must people have to consume?

3. What is Engel's law?

4. What is earning power? What factors might influence it?

5. What decisions does the spending of income require?

6. What two scarce resources affect all buying decisions?

7. What does a "good" buying strategy involve?

8. What is meant by consumerism?

9. What four consumer rights were outlined by President Ken-

nedy in his 1962 message to Congress? What additional right would most consumer advocates add to Kennedy's list?

10. Who is concerned with the well-being of American consumers?

11. What are the consumer-oriented functions of the FTC, the FDA, and the CPSC?

12. What is *Consumer Reports?*

Discussion Questions

1. Why do you think Americans today are spending a smaller percentage of their income on basic necessities than did previous generations?

2. Rational decision making involves obtaining information about alternative products and the prices of those products. Does this statement mean that consumers should find out *all* information possible about a product they may want to buy? Why or why not?

3. Do you agree with the statement that "each consumer's goal is to obtain the most satisfaction possible from his or her limited time and income?" Why or why not?

4. Do you think it is difficult to be a "wise" consumer? Why or why not?

5. Consumerism in the United States is a relatively recent movement. Why do you think it came about? What reasons can you cite for its lack of support until recent times?

Projects

1. Think about a recent purchase you made. Compile a list of the steps you took in deciding what to buy, where to buy it, and how much to spend. Did you follow a buying strategy?

2. With a group of classmates, conduct a comparison shopping test for some major item, such as a 10-speed bicycle, a color TV set, or a sewing machine. Report to the class the steps the group took and the information obtained.

3. Obtain a recent issue of *Consumer Reports* and select one article on product testing on which to make a report to the class. Do you and your classmates think such test results help consumers make buying decisions about products? Is such information worth the price of a year's subscription?

4. Write to the Consumer Product Safety Commission, 1750 K Street NW, Washington, DC 20207, to obtain the latest list of most hazardous products in the United States. Take a survey of the class to find out: (1) how many members used any of the listed products, (2) if those products were known to be dangerous, and (3) if knowing that the product is considered hazardous will alter its use.

The Consumer's Advocate

Ralph Nader has been described as a public official never elected by anyone, an unmonitored watchdog accountable to no one, an institution unto himself. These observations could also describe Nader's major targets: the corporation executives, the utilities, the ineffective regulatory agencies, and the advertising media. Nader's focus for the past 10 years has been an anti-institutional one. He has attacked the paradox of "crimes" that are severely punished when committed by individuals but ignored or even subsidized when committed by corporations. His research has described the detailed way in which he feels free enterprise has become a slogan rather than an economic mode of operation.

While at Harvard Law School, Nader first became conscious of the trend for bright young lawyers to go into the lucrative fields of corporation and tax law. After receiving his degree, Nader began practicing law in Hartford, Connecticut, specializing in automobile accident cases. By 1963 he had compiled a collection of data which he thought refuted the myth that all accidents were caused by careless drivers. He discovered that the auto industry was sitting on plans for "safety cars" while pushing dangerous cars onto an unsuspecting public.

Two years later, *Unsafe at Any Speed* was published; probably few books have had as immediate and serious an impact on American industry. Its primary target was General Motors—the Chevrolet division in particular. With case studies and detailed engineering data and specifications, Nader had compiled a devastating attack. The company hired a private detective to trail Nader, and generally harassed him at every turn. But General Motors could not have selected a less vulnerable target: Nader's idea of relaxation is "sitting down to discuss anthropology." Nader then sued GM, bringing even more attention to the book, and was awarded $280,000, money he used to continue his fight against harmful corporate practices. The book and subsequent trial established Nader's reputation as an uncompromising, incorruptible, skillful fighter.

Nader has spawned a number of institutions to further his causes. The Center for the Study of Responsive Law, one Nader creation, has produced reports on many facets of industrial production, federal regulation, and state government policy in the United States. Nader, who views "citizen action as a countervailing force" to corporate and governmental injustices, has moved increasingly from exposing these injustices to lawsuits and other legal actions. Under the auspices of Public Citizen, Inc., another Nader creation, Citizen Action Groups have been formed in various parts of the country to research and organize citizens around consumer and environmental issues.

At least five major regulatory and consumer protection laws can be ascribed directly to Nader's efforts: the Motor Vehicle Safety Act (1966), a direct result of *Unsafe at Any Speed;* the Wholesome Meat Act (1967); the Natural Gas Pipeline Safety Act (1968); the Coal Mine Health and Safety Act (1969); and the Occupational Safety and Health Act (1970). Nader has also produced a series of books on some of the federal regulatory agencies; he and his staff found absenteeism, featherbedding, inefficiency, incompetence, and a lack of commitment at the highest levels of the Federal Trade Commission and other agencies.

A staff report on the state of Delaware explored the broad political and economic influence of the duPont Corporation that, in the view of the authors, completely compromises any semblance of a free market economy and electoral freedom in the state. And although it swallowed hard, the duPont Corporation spent $450 to obtain copies of the report.

The oldest argument against Nader is that he would sell the free-enterprise system down the river to a series of large agencies with absolute regulatory power. "Where is the free enterprise system?" he asks. "I'm trying to find it. Is it the oil oligopoly, protected by import quotas? The shared monopolies in consumer products? The securities market, that bastion of capitalism operating on fixed commissions and now provided with socialized insurance? They call me a radical for trying to restore power to the consumer, but businessmen are the true radicals in this country. They are taking us deeper and deeper into corporate socialism—corporate power using government power to protect it from competition."

3

Going into Debt

Preview Questions

1. What does it mean to go into debt?
2. What types of debts are there?
3. Where can consumers borrow money?
4. Why do consumers borrow?
5. What does it cost to borrow money?

Definitions of New Terms

Credit: Credit is the amount of money a person is able to borrow from another person or lending agency, such as a bank. When a person receives credit, that person is using someone else's money for a certain period of time.

Debt: A debt is the money one person or agency owes to another person or agency.

Interest: Interest is payment for the use of money. A bank pays interest on money kept in a savings account. A borrower must also pay interest on a loan. The latter is sometimes called a *finance charge*.

Installment debt: An installment debt is a debt payable in regular payments called *installments*.

Mortgage: A mortgage is an installment debt on real property, usually houses, buildings, or land.

Consumer durables: Things that consumers buy which last for a certain time, such as cars and stereos.

Purchasing power: Purchasing power is the value of money stated in terms of what that money can buy. For example, if a dollar can be exchanged for one hamburger, then the purchasing power of a dollar is a hamburger. If the price of hamburgers rises above a dollar, however, then the purchasing power of the dollar has fallen.

Suppose you are eating in a restaurant with a group of friends. When the bill comes, you find that you do not have enough money to pay for your share. What do you do? Usually you borrow from a friend, promising to repay later. Usually the friend is willing to loan you money because he or she is certain you will repay the loan. Most people borrow and lend in this friendly manner. They never give it a second thought.

But on a larger scale, the total amount of money involved in borrowing and lending in the United States is so large it boggles the mind. The economy depends on people being able to borrow for a period of time. Money borrowed this way is called *credit.* When a person loans money, that person is giving credit. On the other hand, the borrower must repay the loan. He or she owes a *debt.* The lender extends credit, and the borrower goes into debt. The lender is owed, and the borrower owes. Hence, for every debt, someone must have offered credit.

For all people in debt, the amount owed is equal to the amount someone else will receive at some future time plus any charge for borrowing. Charges for borrowing are known as *interest.* Most debts must be repaid with interest. Figure 3-1 shows the total amount of debt owed in the United States since 1950. Total debt has risen from $486 billion in 1950 to an estimated $3.5 trillion in 1977.

The Indebted Society

Obviously, the total debt in the United States means that many Americans are in debt. In fact, it is estimated that at least 50 percent of the population owes some type of debt. One of the most common debts for most American families is the *installment debt.* Many people purchase such consumer goods as automobiles, refrigerators, washers, dryers, stereos, and TV sets on an installment plan. That is, they buy the items on credit. For example, a person who buys a new car might pay 20 percent of the cost in cash and take out a loan for the remaining 80 percent of the purchase price. The loan must be repaid in equal payments or *installments* over a period of time, for example, 36 months.

The largest form of installment debt is the money people owe on homes. An installment debt owed on *real property* (houses, buildings, or land) is called a *mortgage.* Most people who owe money only for

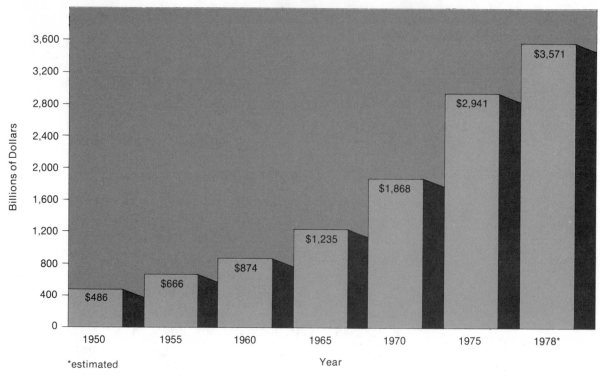

*estimated

Year

Figure 3-1. Total public and private debt in the United States. Total debt outstanding has been growing by leaps and bounds. (1978 datum is estimated.) Source: *Survey of Current Business.*

property do not consider themselves deeply in debt. They do not consider the payments on a home mortgage to be like other kinds of debt. Nevertheless, they are. Mortgages are installment debts, just like those on cars or stereos. Somebody has provided the homeowner with money to purchase the property. In return, the homeowner must repay the loan with interest in equal installments over a number of years.

Sources of Credit

When a person buys a stereo from a store, on an installment plan, that person is in effect borrowing money from the store. The store is a source of credit. In addition to stores, many other business organizations give credit to those who wish to buy something on credit. These sources of credit include commercial banks, finance companies, consumer finance companies, credit unions, and credit card companies.

Commercial Banks

The most obvious place to get a loan is from a commercial bank. Today the personal loan departments of commercial banks make almost 60 percent of all automobile loans in the United States, as well as almost 35 percent of all loans for other consumer goods. The interest rate charged by banks on installment loans is usually lower than the rate charged for installment loans from other sources of credit.

Finance Companies

Finance companies in essence "buy" installment credit from retail merchants. That is, finance companies buy loans from stores and add on a charge for their service in collecting the debt. In this way, retailers avoid the risk involved in loaning money to consumers. Finance companies supply almost 30 percent of all automobile loans in the United States. In fact, they account for nearly 35 percent of all personal loans.

Consumer Finance Companies

Consumer finance companies are really small loan companies. Generally they make loans to consumers at relatively high rates of interest. They are the finance companies that usually advertise on radio and television. They are the largest suppliers of installment cash loans—loans that consumers obtain for purposes other than buying such durable consumer goods as cars, appliances, and furniture. There are more than 25,000 licensed consumer finance offices in the United States today.

Credit Unions

Credit unions are consumer cooperative agencies. They are usually licensed by state licensing agencies and by the federal government. A person must be a member of a credit union to get a loan from it. For example, teachers in large school systems and workers in large labor organizations or companies generally belong to credit unions. Loans from credit unions account for about 13 percent of all consumer installment debt in the United States.

Credit Card Companies

Today more than half of all American families have at least one credit card not issued by a department store or a gasoline company. In fact, more than one-fourth of all American families have three or more of these cards. The most popular credit cards are BankAmericard (VISA), Master Charge, American Express, Diner's Club, Carte Blanche, and Chargex.

As with all scarce resources, credit from credit card companies has a cost. Stores that allow people to use BankAmericard or Master Charge, for example, must pay a certain percentage of all credit purchases, usually 6 percent, to BankAmericard or Master Charge. That means that the prices charged by the stores allowing the use of credit cards probably include the additional cost assessed to them by the credit card companies. In other words, the prices tend to be higher than they would be if credit card purchases were not permitted. In addition, for those people who do not pay the full balance owed when due, an annual interest charge varying from 12 to 18 percent on the unpaid balance is added to the amount owed.

Why Borrow Money?

Why or when should people borrow money? Some may answer, "There is no reason to borrow money. Pay cash for everything. Never have a debt hanging over your head." In fact, this is the

Availability of consumer credit has greatly increased since the turn of the century. In what ways does increased credit affect the economy?

attitude throughout much of Europe today. Many Europeans have a strong dislike for borrowing money to purchase the things they want.

Most Americans, on the other hand, are accustomed to borrowing money. They do not consider it wrong. In fact, at times it becomes necessary.

Let us look at one example, which usually confronts most Americans sooner or later: the decision to buy an automobile. Most people do not buy an automobile to have it sit in their garage. What they are buying is the availability of the car for use each day, week, month, and year they own it. In fact, what is really important in owning a car is the cost per amount of *service* received over a period of time.

Automobiles, houses, appliances, and other items that last a relatively long time are known as **consumer durables.** People do not consume them immediately. Rather, they obtain the services or satisfaction from such products over a period of time because these products are durable or lasting.

On the other hand, when people go to the movies, they consume the movie during the time they are in the theater. They also pay for the movie while they consume it. When people consume and pay for things at the same time, they are synchronizing the payment for the product with the *rate* at which they are consuming it.

Synchronizing payment with consumption is one reason for borrowing. Although they may not realize it, people are doing this when they borrow to buy a consumer durable such as an automobile. They do not feel obliged to pay for the item with cash because they will use it over a certain period of time. That is, when people borrow to buy a consumer durable, they are synchronizing their cash outlay to correspond more or less with the same amount of service received from the product purchased per time period.

Other Reasons for Borrowing or Going into Debt

The previous explanation for why people borrow is only one of many possibilities. If you asked people why they borrowed, you would get many answers. In fact, you could compile a long list of reasons. At the head of the list would be the explanation that people do not have sufficient cash to purchase relatively expensive consumer durables such as automobiles and color TV sets outright. Therefore, they are in some sense forced to buy these expensive items on time. They are "forced" to go into debt.

However, many people who go into debt do have a choice. They can purchase less expensive consumer durables. They can save their money until they have enough to purchase the item with cash. Or they can simply do without. As an example, many people purchase new refrigerators on credit. These people have the option of having their old refrigerator repaired or of purchasing an inexpensive used one. There are literally hundreds of thousands of used refrigerators for sale every day throughout the United States, at prices ranging from $50 to $250.

An important point can be made from this discussion. There is no denying that people have many reasons for borrowing. There is also no denying that most people give sincere and honest evaluations of their reasons for acting one way or another. Nevertheless, it is generally difficult to assess people's actual motives for their actions. This is why interviews carried on with consumers about why they borrow may not lead to any useful information. All one can do, really, is to see what consumer preferences are by how those preferences are revealed in individual actions.

Should You Buy Now or Later?

A savings and loan association once ran a very clever advertisement on purchasing an automobile in some national magazines. The ad noted that if a person were to save for 36 months to buy a car with the savings, a $5,000 car would cost that person $4,300. The remaining $700 would be made up by the interest received on the savings over the three-year period.

On the other hand, according to the ad, if the person bought the $5,000 car immediately on a 36-month installment plan, the ultimate cost would be $6,200. Not only would the person not receive interest on his or her savings, but the person would have to pay a finance charge on the installment debt. Obviously, there is a big difference between $4,300 and $6,200. According to the point of view put forth in the advertisement, it is better to save now and buy later than to buy now and go into debt.

But notice that the advertisement omitted a very crucial point. During the three years the person would be saving, the person would not be enjoying the services of the car. The person would be putting off the purchase for three years. Many people do not wish to delay buying that long. They prefer to have the services of an item immediately and pay interest. After all, interest is a payment for using somebody else's money to consume. Remember that the lender is decreasing the amount of money he or she has with which to consume at that time.

When to Borrow Money

Borrowing is really a question of whether the satisfaction the borrower gets from whatever he or she buys is greater than the interest payments the borrower must pay his or her creditor. There is no moral judgment to be made here. The question is basically one of comparing costs and benefits. The benefit of borrowing is being able to buy now instead of later. The cost is whatever the borrower must pay in interest.

The value of the benefit of borrowing is something only each person can decide for himself or herself. The cost, however, is something of which every person can become aware.

What It Costs to Borrow

You are well aware that most borrowing costs money. Of course, this should not surprise you. Few things are free. Why do people have to pay to borrow? Because lenders are giving something up. What are they giving up? Their **purchasing power,** or their ability to buy goods and services. Thus, they must be compensated. They are usually compensated with payments called *interest.*

Would you be willing to loan $100 to a person who would repay the loan in 10 years with no interest? Would you do it, even if you were sure of getting the money back? Probably not. You would have to sacrifice what the $100 could have bought. Most people will not make this sacrifice without being compensated.

It is best to think of interest on a loan as the price one pays the lender for using the lender's money. However, one cannot talk about a single interest rate or a single charge for credit. Interest rates vary, depending on the length of a loan, the risk involved, and other conditions. Generally, the greater the risk that a borrower will not repay a loan, the higher the rate of interest demanded by the creditor (or the more likely the request for a loan will be turned down).

Being a Wise Consumer— Shopping Around for Credit

As just noted, there are various interest rates charged for different types of loans. There are also a variety of places (sources) where one can get loans (credit). Thus, if you decide to borrow money, you have a job to do as a consumer.

In order to minimize the cost of going into debt, you should find the most appropriate source of credit. The shopping principle involved here is the same as that outlined in Chapter 2. You will be using two scarce resources. The first is your time in obtaining information about the various sources of credit. The second is the income that will be used up more or less rapidly, depending on whether you get a relatively low- or high-interest loan.

Basically, the person who seeks a loan must determine the appropriate source of credit. For example, a person buying a house would not go to a consumer finance company that specializes in small loans. The prospective house buyer would go to a commercial bank, a savings and loan association, or a similar institution. In each case, the buyer could then compare the various interest rates and terms that would be charged.

The purchase of an automobile perhaps allows for even greater variation among sources of credit. Most automobile dealers offer some type of credit plan. But generally, auto loans obtained through car dealers are more expensive than those obtained from commercial banks or credit unions. In fact, credit unions usually offer the lowest interest rates on auto loans.

When borrowing money for other consumer durables, such as TV sets, stereos, refrigerators, washers, and dryers, a credit union may again be the best source of credit. Other sources of credit include personal loan departments of commercial banks, consumer finance companies, the stores selling the product, and credit card companies.

A basic rule to remember when shopping for credit is: Shop for credit the same way you would shop for anything else on which you would spend income.

Determining a Safe Debt Load

Now that you have some understanding of credit, debt, and interest rates, let us examine one practical way to determine what might be a safe amount of debt. Chart 3-1 presents the basic method.

Notice that in the left-hand column of the chart all debt payments are listed and totaled. This lets one know the actual income being allotted to debt. The right-hand column presents the method for determining a safe debt load. That is, to determine a safe debt load: (1) list annual income after taxes; (2) subtract annual expenditures on housing, food, and clothing; and (3) divide the difference by 3.

By comparing the safe debt load with the actual income being allotted to debt (the total outstanding in the left-hand column), a person can tell if it is financially wise to take on additional debt.

Chart 3-1: How to Determine a Safe Debt Load

Your Debts		*Your Safe Debt Load*	
Item	Amount		
Payment for automobile	$_____	Annual Income (after	
Payment on installment		taxes)	$_____
debts (department		Less annual expendi-	
stores, etc.):		tures on housing,	
1.	$_____	food, and clothing	$_____
2.	$_____	Divide difference by three	$_____
3.	$_____	SAFE DEBT LOAD	$_____
4.	$_____		
Payments due on loans:			
1.	$_____		
2.	$_____		
3.	$_____		
4.	$_____		
Other payments:			
1.	$_____		
2.	$_____		
Payments due on			
unpaid bills (tele-			
phone, electricity,			
etc.):			
1.	$_____		
2.	$_____		
TOTAL OUTSTANDING	$_____		

To see whether you understand the method described for determining a safe debt load, apply the formula to the situation given in Chart 3-2, "American Family Finance." Do you think this family should add to its existing debt? Is its safe debt load less than the actual yearly income allotted to debt payment? (Hint: In comparing the safe debt load with the total outstanding, you must first find yearly payments. That is, you must multiply the monthly totals by 12.)

Chart 3-2: American Family Finance

Monthly Expenditures

1. Payments on 1977 Ford	$ 125.00
2. Monthly payment on Sears revolving charge account	32.00
3. Monthly payment on charge cards	40.00
4. Monthly payment on loan taken out for last year's vacation	31.00

TOTAL OUTSTANDING $228 × 12 = $2,736.00

Annual Expenditures

1. Housing	$ 4,000.00
2. Food	3,000.00
3. Clothing	1,000.00
	$ 8,000.00

*Annual Income
(After Taxes)*

Mother	
Father	$14,000.00

Obviously, not everyone in the real world operates strictly in accordance with all the principles presented in this book. Nevertheless, the safe debt load formula serves as a good rule of thumb. It is important to realize, however, that the statements and suggestions relating to consumer decision making made in this book are just that—suggestions. They are formulated by using principles of economics with some common sense. But they are tempered by the way Americans think and live. The safe debt load formula, for example, might be much different if given by a consumer expert in another country where, by custom, debt is considered differently than it is in the United States.

Summary

1. The American economy depends on people being able to borrow money for a period of time. Many Americans are in debt.

2. Today the debt in the United States is $3.5 trillion. Much of the debt is in the form of installment purchases, including mortgages on real property (houses, buildings, and land).

3. For every debt, someone must have offered credit. There are many sources of credit. Some of the more common sources include banks, stores, finance companies, consumer finance companies, credit unions, and credit card companies.

4. One reason people borrow money is to synchronize payment with consumption—that is, to match payment for a product with the rate of benefit received. The most common reason for borrowing, however, is the lack of cash to purchase expensive consumer durables (houses, automobiles, and so on) outright.

5. Most borrowing costs money. People pay a finance or interest charge on the money they borrow.

6. Interest rates vary. Reasons include the type of loan, the length of the loan, the risk involved, and the source of credit.

7. A good rule for shopping for credit is to shop for it the same way you would shop for anything else on which you would spend income.

8. It is wise to determine a safe debt load.

Important Terms

consumer durable	purchasing power
finance charge	debt
mortgage	interest
credit	real property
installment debt	

Review Questions

1. What does any act of borrowing involve?
2. What is one of the most common debts? How is it repaid?
3. What is real property? What is the name for the debt on it?
4. From whom do most people borrow?
5. Why do people borrow?
6. What are consumer durables?
7. What must people usually pay when borrowing?
8. In borrowing, what must be compared?
9. Why do interest rates vary?
10. What is a good rule when obtaining credit?
11. What is meant by a safe debt load? How is it determined?
12. What is purchasing power?

Discussion Questions

1. Is borrowing necessary? Can some people live without ever borrowing money? If so, who and how? If not, why?

2. Current debt in the United States is $3.5 trillion. Why have Americans borrowed so much? Do you think they have borrowed too much? Why or why not?

3. Some people have paid cash for a house. What is the benefit of paying cash? Are there any disadvantages? If so, what? If not, why?

4. A friend is buying a new car. What advice would you give him or her?

5. Which do you think is more important—money or purchasing power? Why?

Projects

1. Investigate the possibility of borrowing $500 for one year from a commercial bank and from a consumer finance company in your area. What requirements does each have for lending such a sum? What conditions does each place on a personal loan? Is there a difference in the rates of interest charged? If so, can you explain why?

2. Hold a discussion on family finances and debt with your parents. Explain to them the formula for safe debt load outlined in the chapter. If they agree, apply the formula to the family's situation. Does the family have a safe debt load? If not, what steps do you recommend be taken? If the family's debt is within the safe level, would you recommend adding to the debt level? Why or why not? What do your parents think?

How Do People Live Within Their Means?

Definitions of New Terms

Budget: A budget is a specific spending plan that helps a person see the limits of his or her income.

Fixed expenses: A fixed expense is one that is necessary and predetermined during a period of time. For example, car payments are a fixed expense.

Flexible expenses: A flexible expense is one that will vary over a period of time, depending on spending decisions. For example, food and clothing costs generally vary from one month to the next.

Young people are a very powerful group of consumers. In 1977, there were estimated to be about 30 million Americans between the ages of 13 and 19, spending an estimated $29 billion per year. That means, on the average, each youth spends $967 a year. Therefore, it is not surprising that advertising agencies have increasingly focused their attention on the youth market.

Many youths who are going to school receive income from their parents in the form of an allowance. Many others work at a variety of jobs on a part- or full-time basis. In addition, many youths have their own savings and checking accounts, own United States savings bonds, belong to Christmas or vacation clubs, file income tax returns, and buy insurance.

Thus, in many respects youths earn and consume just as adult members of society do.

What a Budget Can Show

All people have limited incomes. Thus, every time a person spends part of his or her income, that person must sacrifice something else. That is, if one decides to spend more money on entertainment, then one has less to spend on other things. Every spending decision a person makes involves an opportunity—the opportunity to spend income on something else.

Do you think about your decisions to spend this way? Perhaps not, unless you have a **budget**—a specific plan for spending.

When people make a budget for a given period, they write down how much income they expect to receive and how much they expect to spend during that period. Thus, a budget is a way of managing income systematically and rationally. It is not predetermined by someone else. It is a control mechanism that forces people to be aware of the decisions they make. The decisions are there, even if they may not seem an obvious part of the decision-making process.

Some people are able to determine quickly all the choices involved with each purchase they make. But most people cannot do quick or complicated computations in their heads. For them, a budget can help check undirected spending.

With this in mind, let us now examine some principles of money management. That is, let us see how budgets are made.

Making a Family Budget

Suppose a household decides to make a budget for the coming year. Where does it begin? One way is to list the family's major goals. Does the family need to have a leaky roof repaired? Does it need a car? Do new winter clothes have to be bought? Would the family members like to go on a short vacation?

After the goals have been set, the budget preparer can follow these basic steps to create a family spending plan:

1. *Use records.* Refer to last year's expenses as a guide. Old bills and receipts, canceled checks, and income tax information may help plan what to expect. Records of expenses should be kept each year to aid in planning the next year's budget.

2. *Determine what payments must be made even if they come on an irregular basis.* Some household expenses, such as insurance and taxes, not only must be made, but the cost is known in advance. These expenses are called **fixed expenses.**

3. *Determine what payments change greatly from time to time.* Some expenses, such as food and clothing, must be made, but the cost is not known. In fact, these expenses can vary greatly from one month to the next. They are called **flexible expenses.**

4. *Balance fixed and flexible expenses with available income.* If there is money left over, it can be applied to goals. If there is not enough money, then the family must reexamine its flexible expenditures and cut back on one or more.

Chart I–3–1 shows a typical form for a household budget. When you become the head of a household, you may want to use a similar form for budgeting your household's limited income.

Chart I-3-1: Suggested Family Budget Form

Cash Forecast, Month of _____

Cash on hand and in checking
account, end of previous period _____

Receipts

	Estimated	Actual
net pay	_____	_____
borrowed	_____	_____
other income	_____	_____
Total Cash Available		
During Period	_____	_____

Fixed Expenses

	Estimated	Actual
mortgage or rent	_____	_____
life insurance	_____	_____
fire insurance	_____	_____
auto insurance	_____	_____
savings	_____	_____
taxes	_____	_____
loans or other debts	_____	_____
other expenses	_____	_____
Total Fixed Expenses	_____	_____

Flexible Expenses

	Estimated	Actual
water	_____	_____
electricity	_____	_____
fuel	_____	_____
telephone	_____	_____
medical/dental	_____	_____
car	_____	_____
food	_____	_____
clothing	_____	_____
nonrecurring large payments	_____	_____
contributions, recreation, etc.	_____	_____
other expenses	_____	_____
Total Flexible Expenses	_____	_____

	Estimated	Actual
Total Payments	_____	_____

Summary

	Estimated	Actual
Total cash available	_____	_____
Total payments	_____	_____
Cash balance, end of period	_____	_____

Chart I-3-2 shows a suggested student budget. You might want to use a form similar to this to manage your money now. Notice that expenses might take roughly the same form as those a family spending unit faces. In some cases, expenditures might be the same. For example, if you have an automobile, you will have insurance and operating costs. In fact, you might pay even more for auto insurance. In general, however, you will most likely be deciding how to allocate your income among flexible items. Here is where a budget can help.

For example, suppose that you usually go to the movies once a week. But in one particular month you need to purchase a new jacket and would like to buy two new record albums. By budgeting all three items, you might find you will not have enough

Chart I-3-2: Suggested Student Budget Form

Cash Forecast, Month of _____

Cash on hand end of previous period _____

Receipts	Estimated	Actual
net pay and/or allowance		
borrowed		
other receipts		
Total Cash Available During Period		

Fixed Payments		
Christmas club		
vacation club		
savings		
loan or other debt		
room and board		
car insurance		
Total Fixed Payments		

Flexible Payments		
telephone		
transportation		
leisure		
work or school		
food		
lunches at work or school		
other		
entertainment (movies, sports events, etc.)		
recreation (club fees, hobbies, etc.)		
clothing		
other expenses		
Total Flexible Payments		

Total Payments		

Summary		
Total cash available		
Total payments		
Cash balance, end of period		

money to cover all three expenses. In this way, you will be able to decide what to cut on the basis of an actual projection of spendable income and desired expenditures.

If going to the movies once a week is really important, then you would not buy both the record albums and the jacket only to find you do not have sufficient cash to cover the cost of the movie the last week of the month. By planning a budget, you are able to spend your income (however limited it might be) on those purchases you *most* desire or need, rather than on those which come first.

Typical Family Budgets

To get an idea of how Americans actually spend their income, look at Chart I-3-3. This chart shows three typical family budgets as estimated by the U.S. Department of Labor, Bureau of Labor Statistics. The bureau collects information about the wages and incomes of various groups in U.S. society and about

Chart I-3-3: Three Typical Budgets for a Family of 4 in early 1976

Component	Lower	Intermediate	Higher
Total budget	$9,588	$15,318	$22,294
Total family consumption	7,795	11,725	16,141
Food	2,952	3,827	4,819
Housing	1,857	3,533	5,353
Transportation	702	1,279	1,658
Clothing	771	1,102	1,613
Personal care	248	331	470
Medical care	818	822	857
Other family consumption[1]	447	831	1,371
Other items[2]	436	701	1,182
Taxes and deductions	1,358	2,891	4,971
Social security and disability	577	834	841
Personal income taxes	781	2,057	4,130

[1]Other family consumption includes average costs for reading, recreation, tobacco products, alcoholic beverages, education, and miscellaneous expenditures.

[2]Other items includes allowances for gifts and contributions, life insurance and occupational expenses.

NOTE: Because of rounding, sums of individual items may not equal totals.

Source: U.S. Department of Labor

the prices they pay for the things they buy. Every year it develops a typical budget for low-income, medium-income, and high-income families based on the information it collects. Notice that the two largest items in each budget are food and housing. These items are considered essentials or necessities for everyone.

The budgets show certain differences in spending patterns for typical families with different incomes. As a percentage of total income, spending for food falls as income rises. On the other hand, housing expenditures rise as a percentage of total income as income rises. In other words, as income increases, the typical American family spends a greater proportion for housing and a smaller proportion for food.

These budgets not only allow one to see how families with different incomes spend money but also allow one to compare spending patterns. Thus they can serve as a guide for predicting changes in spending habits with changes in income. They also can guide planning reasonable allocations of income to specific budget categories.

Summary

1. Young people are a powerful consumer group. Each, on the average, spends $967 per year.

2. A budget is a way of managing income in a systematic and rational manner. It helps an individual to make reasonable spending decisions.

3. Budget making involves four steps. These are (1) keeping records, (2) determining fixed expenses, (3) determining flexible expenses, and (4) balancing total expenses with available income.

4. Learning how to budget is important, for otherwise most people can find ways to spend more income than they have.

Important Terms

budget   fixed expense
flexible expense

Questions for Thought and Discussion

1. This issue has emphasized the importance of learning to budget. Do you think there are circumstances in which it is not worthwhile to budget? If so, when? If not, why?

2. Do you agree that human wants and desires always seem to be a step ahead of the means to achieve them? Is it possible for budgeting to keep people from *wanting* to spend too much? If so, how? If not, then why is budgeting important?

3. What happens when people live beyond their means for any length of time? Does budgeting always prevent this?

4

Buying Essentials— Food and Housing

Preview Questions

1. What percentage of income are Americans spending on food?

2. How much time should be spent comparison shopping for food?

3. Are there easy ways to get information about the contents of food people buy?

4. In what types of homes do most Americans live?

5. Why have mobile homes become increasingly popular?

Definitions of New Terms

Spendable income: Spendable income is that income available for a person or family to spend. Also known as *disposable income*, spendable income is income that remains after taxes.

Cooperative: A cooperative is an apartment building in which each resident owns his or her apartment and has a share of ownership in the building and grounds.

Condominium: A condominium is an apartment building in which each resident owns his or her apartment and has a proportionate interest (but not ownership) in recreation areas and the land on which the building is erected.

Lease: A lease is a long-term contract, usually for one year, that binds both landlord and tenant to specified terms.

According to the U.S. Department of Agriculture, the typical American consumes each year 170 pounds of meat, 50 pounds of poultry, 14 pounds of fish, 41 pounds of eggs, 352 pounds of dairy products, 50 pounds of fats and oils, 80 pounds of fresh fruits, 140 pounds of fresh vegetables, 260 pounds of canned goods, 142 pounds of flour and cereal products, 120 pounds of sugar and other sweeteners, and 15 pounds of coffee, tea, and cocoa. The amount spent by Americans on food products is a staggering sum—about $250 billion annually.

Americans consume more than 30 percent of the agricultural output of the world. They buy food products at 300,000 stores, which carry thousands of different products. The number of types of foods is even greater when one considers regional specialties. In addition, each of hundreds of brands offers foods in several forms—for example, frozen whole carrots, frozen sliced or diced carrots, and frozen peas mixed with carrots.

Food and Income

Although Americans spend $250 billion a year on food, that amount represents only 16 percent of their total income. Figure 4-1 expresses food consumption in the United States as a percentage of all households' *spendable income* (income to spend after taxes) during the last 30 years. Notice that the percentage has been decreasing steadily since 1948, even though there is an occasional rise from one year to the next. The general decline should not be surprising.

How much more food do you think most people would buy if their incomes were to double? They could buy better quality food. Perhaps they would eat in restaurants more often. But there is a limit to the amount people can eat. They can eat only so much at one time. When people overeat, they tend to put on weight. In other words, eating has physical limits. If you look back at the typical family budgets given in Issue 3 (page 58) you will see that higher-income families usually spend a lower proportion of their income for food than do lower-income families.

Engel's Law Revisited

As noted in Chapter 2, German statistician Ernst Engel made some studies of family spending in 1856. Engel found that as family incomes increased, the percentage families spent on food decreased.

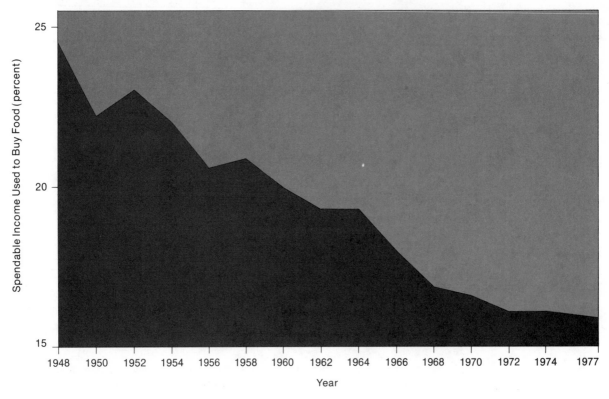

Figure 4-1. Percentage of national income spent on food by U.S. households. At the beginning of the Great Depression in 1929 and for the following 20 years, the percentage of spendable income spent on food remained between 23 and 24 percent. Starting in 1950, however, it began dropping. This percentage will probably continue to go down as real income goes up.

Engel's finding does not mean that the total amount of money spent on food decreases. It means that the proportion of total income decreases. Certainly a family of four with an income of $25,000 a year spends more money on food than a family with an income of $10,000. But the higher-income family does not spend two and one-half times as much as the other family. It might spend one and one-half times or twice as much.

Engel's law applies to nations as well as to individual families. A rich nation, like a wealthy family, spends a smaller fraction of its total income on food than a nation not as well off. Thus, it is predictable that if the United States continues to grow wealthier, the percentage of national income spent for food will fall.

Effective Food Shopping

Issue 3 pointed out methods by which you could budget a limited income. Let us assume you have budgeted a specific amount for food. You are now faced with a shopping problem: how to get the best food buys for the income available. One way you can become a more effective food shopper is by comparison shopping. This concept was explained in Chapter 3 in the discussion suggesting that you investigate alternative sources of credit when you want to borrow money. The same principle applies to shopping for food.

Remember that comparison shopping involves the use of a scarce resource—your time. People who use a car or public transportation to shop for food bargains also use another resource—transportation. Like all resources, transportation has a cost. The cost may be explicit, like a bus or subway fare, or implicit, like extra gasoline and wear and tear on an automobile.

As in all buying situations, it pays to shop around. *But only to a certain point*. It does not pay the shopper to go miles out of his or her way to shop at a store that has a few items at reduced prices. The potential savings the shopper would reap would be outweighed by the additional costs of time and transportation. Hence, most food shoppers generally confine their food shopping to a couple of stores at any one time. Going to many stores is too costly compared to the potential benefits—that is, lower food costs—that might be obtained.

With regard to the use of time for comparison food shopping, the following is a good guideline. The less valuable an individual considers his or her time, the more comparison shopping should be engaged in. Comparison shopping is most appropriate for students, who generally have relatively small incomes available for food and other things but who do have considerable "free" time. One might expect students to spend more time shopping for bargains than, say, corporation executives.

Because Americans have come to value their time more highly as the nation has become richer on average, there are differences between shopping habits in the United States and elsewhere and between shopping habits today and in the past.

Different Shopping Situations

If a person wants to buy food in a small village in Africa, Asia, South America, or another less-developed area, that person would not go to a supermarket and pick out meat in plastic-wrapped packages and frozen vegetables in freezer bags. Instead, the person would go to small stalls in an open-air market. There he or she could buy from a local merchant. The merchant might also be the person who grew the cattle or raised the vegetables being sold.

Years ago, all food shopping was done this way, even in the United States. Americans can still see some vestiges of it in roadside fruit stands along well-traveled highways in agricultural areas. But in general, most Americans do not buy food in open-air markets. They go to a supermarket or, at least, to a small store, such as a 7-11 store. Today there are some 300,000 grocery stores in the United States. A new trend in some areas is food shopping by closed-circuit television.

Shopping by Television

In Stockholm, Sweden, the Home Shop is one grocery store where a person never need go to buy food. To buy, the person simply dials an

America has not always been a land of supermarkets and fastfood chains. Scenes such as the one on the left (U.S. photo) were common at the turn of the century and did not differ from those found in other cultures such as Nigeria.

order from the store's biweekly catalog. An order can be given quickly. It is filled by a conveyor-belt system. The store delivers whatever is ordered to the person's home. Almost 4 percent of the total food bought in Stockholm is purchased from the Home Shop.

Certain self-contained living units in the United States also have food shopping for residents by closed-circuit television. Some apartments each have a closed-circuit television set. A customer dials the grocer in the building. If not busy, the grocer accepts the call. The customer uses the television set to watch items being selected. The customer indicates how large a piece of meat he or she wants, which head of lettuce, and so forth.

Shopping by television is far different from buying food in open-air markets. Compared to modern shopping, buying food in those markets may be exciting and pleasurable. In the same way, it may be fun to shop for food every day as some people do in small towns in France. But think how many hours French shoppers must spend each week to get their food.

Americans apparently do not want to spend so much time. They do not want to spend the cost in time. Thus, faster retailing methods have become common in the United States. Such trends are consistent with the voluntary choices that people make about how to spend their time. McDonald's, Kentucky Fried Chicken, and other fastfood outlets are very successful in the United States, partly because they save the consumers time. It is not surprising, then, that as people in other countries begin placing a higher value on their time, such outlets can become profitable there. Indeed, McDonald's and Kentucky Fried Chicken are becoming common in Europe and in certain major cities elsewhere in the world.

Information and Comparison Shopping

An important part of comparison shopping is the ability of people to obtain information about the products they want to buy. If there is no system of uniform grading of the quality of products, then comparison shopping becomes more difficult. In this setting, shoppers find potential usefulness for government standards and methods of grading produce, meat, and other food staples that they buy.

Government Inspection and Labeling

The federal government has established a system of inspection and labeling designed to aid the consumer in making wise choices about the food products he or she buys. The government inspects meat-packing houses and various food-processing establishments to see that the food is processed in a clean, healthful environment. The Food and Drug Administration, for example, periodically determines what it considers an *acceptable* amount of insect residue in peanut butter! The Federal Trade Commission attempts to enforce fair packaging and labeling laws.

In addition to meat inspection and establishing labeling requirements for canned or processed foods, the U.S. Department of Agriculture (USDA) marks various grades of meats and fresh produce to indicate their quality to consumers. All fresh meats, with the exception of pork, are labeled by grade. The grading marks on fresh meats are usually stamped on the meat in purple ink.

The USDA also grades such other food products as poultry, eggs, and milk, as well as fresh fruits and vegetables that come pre-packaged. Unfortunately, the grading of produce can often be misleading. Table 4–1 lists some of the grades for produce. As you can see, it certainly is not sufficient to look for "U.S. No. 1" as a guide to quality. In some cases, "U.S. No. 1" represents the third grade.

Despite the government's attempts to provide consumers with information about the quality of the products they buy, it seems obvious, at least from the point of view of produce labeling, that consumers still must take time to figure out the quality of what they buy. They cannot simply look at the U.S. grade and know the quality immediately. This is just one example of many in which the consumer cannot take for granted the meaning of the information given.

Another Important Purchase— Housing

As indicated by typical family budgets (page 58), food and housing are the two largest items in most people's spending patterns. Thus, it seems appropriate to look at certain characteristics of the housing market and to explore why some people prefer to rent rather than to purchase a home to satisfy their shelter needs.

Table 4-1: U.S. Department of Agriculture Produce Grades.

Commodity	Top Grade	Second Grade	Third Grade	Fourth Grade
Apples (all states but Washington)	U.S. Extra Fancy	U.S. Fancy	U.S. No. 1	U.S. Utility
Apples (Washington)	Washington Extra Fancy	Washington Fancy		
Grapefruit (all states but Arizona, California & Florida)	U.S. Fancy	U.S. No. 1	U.S. No. 1 Bright	U.S. No. 1 Bronze
Grapefruit (Arizona & California)	U.S. Fancy	U.S. No. 1	U.S. No. 1	U.S. Combination
Grapefruit (Florida)	U.S. Fancy	U.S. No. 1	U.S. No. 1 Bright	U.S. No. 1 Golden
Onions	U.S. No. 1	U.S. Combination or U.S. Commercial	U.S. No. 2	
Oranges (all states but Arizona, California & Florida)	U.S. Fancy	U.S. No. 1	U.S. No. 1 Bright	U.S. No. 1 Bronze
Oranges (Arizona & California)	U.S. Fancy	U.S. No. 1	U.S. Combination	U.S. No. 2
Oranges (Florida)	U.S. Fancy	U.S. No. 1 Bright	U.S. No. 1	U.S. No. 1 Golden
Pears (Summer & Fall)	U.S. No. 1	U.S. Combination	U.S. No. 2	
Pears (Winter)	U.S. Extra No. 1	U.S. No. 1	U.S. Combination	U.S. No. 2
Potatoes*	U.S. Extra No. 1	U.S. No. 1	U.S. Commercial	U.S. No. 2
Tomatoes (fresh)	U.S. No. 1	U.S. Combination	U.S. No. 2	U.S. No. 3

*Potatoes are also sold as unclassified, meaning ungraded.

Figure 4-2 shows that the number of housing units in the United States has steadily increased throughout the twentieth century. Today there are more than 50 million houses in the United States. There are over 20 million apartments and 4 million mobile homes. In any one year, the number of new houses built generally exceeds 1 million. Americans also like to remodel existing homes, as shown by the $30 billion spent every year for additions, improvements, and the like.

The data on housing can be deceptive, however. It is one thing to build 1 million one-bedroom apartments, and another to build 1 million four-bedroom houses. Why, after all, do people buy apartments, houses, or mobile homes? They buy them for the satisfaction

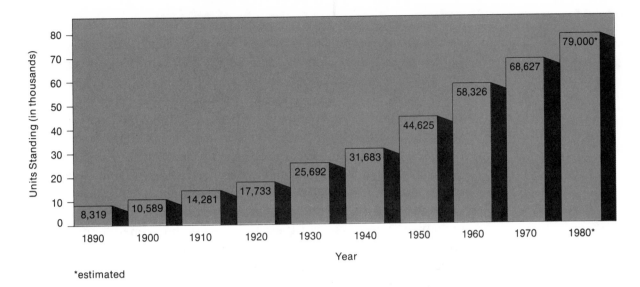

Figure 4-2. Housing in the United States. The increase in the number of housing units in the United States has risen from a little over 8 million in 1890 to 79 million in 1980. Source: United States Department of Commerce.

or utility these residences render over time, just as they buy clothes, cars, or anything else that lasts. A home is a consumer durable. Someone who buys an apartment, a house, or a mobile home expects to reap a payoff in the form of housing utility for many years to come.

Utility from a House

When people buy a house, they are buying not only the building but also the pleasure they expect to receive from living in it. That pleasure depends on how large it is, how well it conforms to the needs of the family, and so on. The reason there is "no place like home" is that most people try to make their homes as special as possible in order to get as much satisfaction from them as possible.

Owning Various Types of Housing

It is important to distinguish among various kinds of housing. Most people are familiar with a single-family dwelling—a house usually owned by the people who live in it. Many people, however, are less familiar with multiple-family dwellings, such as *cooperatives* and *condominiums.* In addition, in recent years there has been a rise in the ownership of mobile homes in the United States.

Cooperatives.   Cooperative apartment buildings look like most other apartment buildings. In a cooperative, each apartment dweller owns a share in a nonprofit company that owns the building and the land on which the building is built. The apartment dweller also has a long-term lease on his or her unit. All operating costs, such as real-estate taxes and maintenance, are divided proportionately among the owners.

Much cooperative housing has been produced for middle-income families. But recently it has become more popular with higher-income families in such cities as New York and Miami. According to 1977 estimates, there is more than $5 billion worth of cooperative housing in the United States, for over 75,000 families.

Condominiums.   Condominiums are a newer form of apartment ownership than cooperatives. Here, apartment dwellers own the apartment in which they live. In addition, the apartment owners have a proportionate interest in such common areas as stairways, swimming pools, and the *lot* (land). But they do not usually own the common areas, as in the case of cooperatives. In other words, condominium owners own their apartments, but generally do not own the outside facilities. These are usually owned by the builder of the condominium or some other corporation.

Ownership rights in a condominium are similar to those in a single-family house, with some exceptions. Owners are free to decide on all maintenance expenditures within their apartment. External repairs, however, are determined either by a majority vote of all apartment owners (an apartment association) or by the owner of the condominium complex.

Condominiums have become especially popular in resort areas where owners do not plan to live year-round. They are becoming more popular with younger, unmarried people.

Mobile Homes.   Figure 4-3 shows the increase in the construction of mobile homes since 1963. Mobile homes are one of the most popular forms of low-income housing in the United States today. One reason they are so popular is favorable tax treatment. In some states, mobile homes are taxed as motor vehicles rather than as real estate.

Another reason for their popularity is expense. Most mobile homes are less expensive to buy and maintain than conventional houses. A consumer may get more housing per dollar because many mobile homes are built on an assembly-line basis. This method enables builders to produce mobile homes for less money than regular houses would cost to produce.

Renting a Place to Live

Until recently, many people looked down on renters. They considered renters to be people who were unable to manage their money correctly. The supposed proof of poor money management, of course, was the lack of home ownership. This attitude has been changing, however. Today many people rent apartments or houses from choice, even though they could buy.

There are several reasons why people may prefer to rent.

1.   Renters have greater mobility than those who own homes.

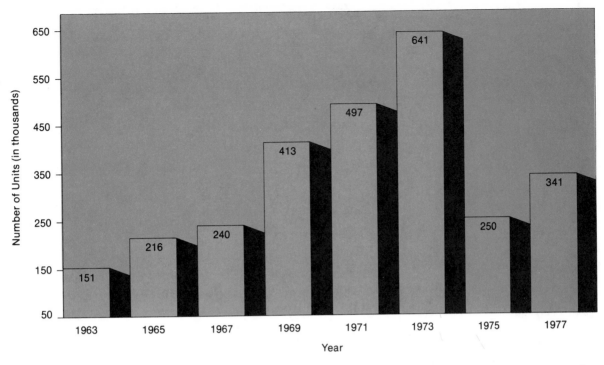

Figure 4-3. Mobile homes built each year. The growth in mobile homes over the past sixteen years has been startling. This rapid growth shows that many home-buyers are finding mobile homes a better buy than conventional housing. (Datum for 1977 is estimated.) Source: Federal Reserve Board of Governors, and Mobile Home Manufacturers Association.

2.   Renters are not required to make a down payment or go through a rigorous credit check to secure a mortgage.

3.   Renters are free from the maintenance tasks that homeowners must face.

4.   Renters can easily estimate their cost of housing.

Most apartments or houses are rented on a monthly basis with the rent payable in advance. The renter or tenant automatically gets the right to live in the dwelling for the next month. In this type of landlord-tenant relationship, the contract may be ended by either party with a 30-day notice in writing. The rent can also be raised at any time when a proper 30-day notice is given. The tenant can be asked to leave with the same advance warning.

There are advantages and disadvantages to this short-term arrangement. A renter can move when he or she wishes without giving notice long in advance. But a renter also has the uncertainty of being asked to leave on short notice or of finding the rent raised.

As an alternative, renters may obtain a *lease.* A lease is a long-term contract that binds both landlord and tenant to specified terms. Most leases are for one year. They require one month's rent in advance. A sum equal to one month's rent may also be required as a cleaning deposit.

Providing for food and housing is probably not your greatest concern at this time. On the other hand, many young people either own their own cars or contemplate buying them. Chapter 5 is about transportation and the automobile.

Summary

1. Americans spend approximately $250 billion per year on food. This represents about 16 percent of their income.

2. As one's income rises, the percentage of that income generally spent on food falls. This principle applies to nations as well as to individuals and families.

3. There is value in doing some comparison shopping when buying food. Remember, however, that comparison shopping has certain costs—time and transportation expenses.

4. Americans can increasingly buy food without spending much time. Gone are the days when people would go to open-air markets or shop each day for that day's meals.

5. One of the newer methods of buying food is shopping by television.

6. The federal government has established a system of inspection and labeling of foods designed to aid the consumer. Care must be taken, however, because some grades have different standards for different items.

7. Today there are more than 75 million housing units in the United States. More than 1 million new dwellings are built each year.

8. People buy housing for the utility rendered to them over time.

9. The most common housing units for sale are houses, cooperative apartments, condominiums, and mobile homes.

10. Some people prefer renting to owning housing. Common reasons are greater freedom of mobility, lower cost, and less responsibility.

Important Terms

cooperative   lease
residence   condominium
spendable income

Review Questions

1. How much food do Americans consume? At what cost?

2. Who spends the greatest percentage of their income on food—low-, medium-, or high-income families? Why?

3. What is the purpose of comparison food shopping?

4. What resources are involved in comparison food shopping?

5. How does shopping for food in the United States differ from that in less developed countries?

6. How does the government assist shoppers in making wise choices about food products?

7. Why can't a shopper look at a U.S. grade and know the quality immediately?

8. What are usually the two largest items in people's expenditure patterns?

9. Why do people buy housing?

10. What are the most common types of housing?

11. What is the basic difference between ownership of a cooperative apartment and of a condominium?

12. Why do some people prefer to rent?

Discussion Questions

1. To what extent should people apply the principles of comparison shopping when buying food? Are there limits? If so, what? If not, why?

2. Why do you think Americans generally spend less time shopping for food than people in many other countries?

3. Do you think most shoppers are aware that the federal government has specific grades for many food products? Why or why not?

4. Would you expect to be happier owning or renting housing? Why?

5. Why do you think some people prefer to buy apartments or mobile homes rather than houses?

Projects

1. With a group of students, interview homeowners in the area to learn what they believe are the advantages and disadvantages of owning property. Report your findings to the class. Is there any correlation between people's personal situations (age, occupation, marital status, etc.) and their opinions about the value of owning property?

2. Write to the U.S. Department of Agriculture, Agricultural Marketing Service, Fourteenth Street and Independence Avenue SW, Washington, DC 20250, to obtain copies of the latest Meat Grades information sheet. Ask whether the system of grading is the same today as it was 10 years ago. Hold a class discussion on why grades of beef marked "prime" cost more than other grades. Do you think most Americans prefer prime beef? Why or why not?

3. If there is a mobile home dealership or mobile home park in your area, visit it to obtain information about the types of models available, the costs, and so on. Report your findings to the class. How do houses and mobile homes differ? In what ways are they alike?

5

The Automobile and Its Problems

Preview Questions

1.   What costs are involved in owning and operating a car?

2.   Why is automobile congestion a problem in so many cities?

3.   What might happen if motorists were charged higher rates during rush hours than they were charged at other times in crossing city toll bridges?

4.   What alternatives are there to automobiles to solve the nation's transportation problems?

Definitions of New Terms

Peak-loading: Peak-loading is the large use of a resource, such as use of a street or bridge at rush hours that results in congestion.

Peak-load pricing: A system of increased prices to those who use a resource such as a road or bridge during a peak-load period.

Subsidies: Subsidies are direct or indirect government payments for part of the cost of doing something. When a person drives an automobile, that person does not pay directly for all the costs associated with driving. For example, the person does not have to pay the full cost of parking on city streets.

The twentieth century could be called "The Age of the Auto." Although cars were already being manufactured in the late 1800s, they were considered luxury items for the rich. "The Age of the Auto" did not begin until Henry Ford developed the means to mass-produce cars at low cost. By using assembly-line production, in 1916 the Ford Motor Company was able to reduce the price of a "Tin Lizzie" to $360. The benefits of cheap transportation were quickly recognized.

By the mid-1970s, 85 percent of all American families owned cars. Some families own two, three, or more automobiles. Figure 5–1 shows the trend in ownership of two or more cars since 1957.

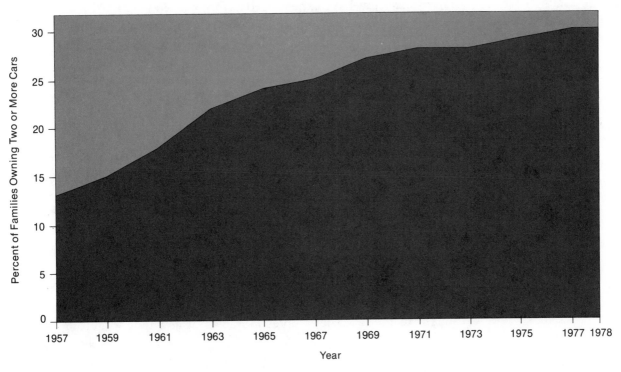

Figure 5-1. Multiple car ownership. The trend in multiple car ownership is continuing to increase. In 1957, only 13 percent of the families in the United States had two or more cars. In 1977, the estimate is 30 percent. Source: Mandell, Lewis, *et al., Survey of Consumers,* Institute for Social Research. Ann Arbor: The University of Michigan, 1975.

Mass produced cars such as the "tin Lizzie" (pictured here) ushered in inexpensive personal transportation. How many different ways can you think of that the costs of owning and maintaining an automobile have changed in the last fifty years?

The Private Cost of Driving

Driving a car does not just involve making a monthly payment. In addition to payments on a car loan, the personal costs of owning an automobile include such items as repairs, depreciation, gas and oil, taxes, and insurance. Table 5-1 shows the estimated cost of operating an automobile as given by the U.S. Department of Transportation. According to 1976 estimates, the total cost to run a standard size car came to about 14¢ a mile.

Social Costs and Congestion

Many Americans have experienced automobile congestion firsthand. For example, you may sometimes be late for school if caught in rush-hour traffic. In many cities, regardless of the number of new streets and expressways built, congestion continues to be a problem.

The congestion problem is sometimes overwhelming. People can do little when stuck in a traffic jam. If they abandon their car, they will get fined. They are stranded.

In most cities, congestion occurs only during certain hours each weekday. For example, people usually can drive anywhere they want at 3 A.M. in most cities in the world without running into traffic problems. Congestion generally limits itself to peak or critical periods of street use. It is a problem of *peak-loading,* of overusing city streets during morning and afternoon rush hours.

Individual drivers are given very little incentive to change the congestion situation. One reason for this is that individuals must pay only the private costs of their driving. Most are not aware of the social costs—time, aggravation, and so forth. Nor do they give much thought to the fact that congestion costs others time in getting to work or to school. In addition, there are costs imposed on all those who want to drive but do not because they know the streets are congested.

As yet, there is no way that drivers can be rewarded for staying off the road so that congestion is eliminated. On the other hand, drivers cannot offer to stay off the streets for a price, either. Any such

Table 5-1: Estimated Cost of Driving an Automobile

	Suburban Based Operation Cents Per Mile				
	Taxes	Gas & Oil	Depreciation	Maintenance	Total
Standard Size	1.6¢	3.3¢	4.9¢	4.2¢	14.0¢
Compact Size	1.2¢	2.5¢	3.8¢	3.4¢	10.9¢
Subcompact Size	0.9¢	1.8¢	3.2¢	3.1¢	9.0¢

Source: U.S. Department of Transportation, Federal Highway Administration, 1976.

agreement would be difficult to create and enforce. Is there a way out of this dilemma? One solution is to make private costs equal to social costs. This is called ***peak-load pricing.***

Peak-Load Pricing

To understand the theory behind peak-load pricing, let us take the example of a typical toll bridge into a city. The bridge is crowded perhaps 4 hours each day. During those hours, cars creep along at 4 to 5 miles per hour. It may take half an hour or more to cross the bridge. This is a typical peak-load problem. During the other 20 hours of the day, the bridge is not crowded. The nonpeak crossing time is quick, perhaps 5 or 10 minutes at most. Thus, one might wonder if there are ways to discourage drivers from using the bridge during peak periods.

One way to discourage use involves an added charge for use during peak-load times. If the cost during off-peak hours were 25¢, then the cost at peak hours might be 50¢ or higher. In this manner, drivers would face a truer representation of the cost of using the bridge during peak periods. That cost involves preventing other drivers from getting on the bridge and slowing down those already on it. Toll bridges are not usually priced in this manner, however.

Reverse Peak-Load Pricing

Many cities with toll bridges charge a *lower* price for peak use. They sell special commuter tickets at reduced prices. Most commuter tickets are purchased by workers who use the bridge mainly at peak hours.

Commuter tickets are an example of *reverse* peak-load pricing. The decrease in cost actually encourages more use. More people use the bridge at peak periods than would without a system of lower-priced commuter tickets.

On the other hand, if the price for peak-period use of the bridge were raised sufficiently, users would be likely to change their transportation habits. Many commuters would be more apt to join car pools. Some businesses would allow their employees to come and leave in nonpeak hours, thereby saving the employees the added toll charge. People going into the city over the bridge on a more

Lower tolls (reverse peak load) encourages additional commuter use of bridges into major cities. Increasing tolls during this same period (peak load pricing) is one way to reduce traffic. Can you think of other ways that would be effective?

irregular, casual basis would alter their schedules to avoid peak periods. As a result, the peak-load problem could be greatly reduced, if not eliminated.

What People Can Afford

Some people might say that commuters who must cross the bridge at peak periods are those least able to afford the added charge. This criticism may, in fact, be true. Remember, however, that the higher peak-load price reflects the true, higher cost of using the bridge at rush hour.

The discussion so far has been exploring methods of eliminating congestion around urban areas. The object is to discover the best use of available resources—the example being a bridge. A peak-load pricing system will discourage use of the bridge during peak periods. Those concerned that some people will not be able to afford a price increase are concerned with the fact that some people lack sufficient income. This is a separate issue from how to use a resource.

Some economists like to separate problems of *how to use resources* from problems of *how to distribute income*. If one devises a system that uses resources best, there will usually be more income to redistribute to poorer people than if one tries to redistribute income merely by altering the use of existing resources. In other words, attempting to improve the conditions of poor people by keeping down the prices of the products they buy will generally result in an inefficient use of resources.

Alternatives to Automobiles

Many alternatives to the automobile have been suggested as another means of eliminating congestion. Almost all methods involve providing mass transportation in the form of subways, railroads, or bus lines. But the future of mass transportation does not appear bright.

Mass transit systems such as BART have been installed in many major cities in an attempt to reduce traffic congestion and pollution. These systems have not been as effective as hoped for. Can you suggest ways in which people can be encouraged to make use of rapid transit?

In the first place, most subway systems that have been installed have cost much more than anticipated. In addition, many systems have not worked well during the initial years of their existence. This is particularly true regarding BART, the integrated rapid transit network of the San Francisco Bay area. It cost more than three times its original estimate, and it took almost a decade longer to build than first promised. In addition, it had numerous operating problems during the first few years it was functioning.

More basic, however, is the fact that mass transportation may never effectively replace the automobile and stop congestion as long as the government continues to subsidize drivers of private automobiles.

Subsidizing the Auto

Automobiles are certainly in competition with mass transit systems. Mass transportation may never be able to make it on its own as long as motorists are subsidized to the extent they are. **Subsidies** are direct or indirect government payments for part of the cost of doing something.

Motorists who do not live in the city (such as commuters) pay little, maybe only one-third, of the true cost of driving their cars in the city. For example, they do not directly pay for street repairs and maintenance, street cleaning, traffic signals, snow removal, or traffic police. Most of these costs are incurred by city dwellers, who pay the property taxes from which most city revenue is obtained.

In addition, motorists who park on the streets use land for which they pay no rent or property taxes. In most cities they do pay a parking meter fee, but this fee is generally low. And when city officials decide to improve streets and highways, they often borrow funds. The federal government often subsidizes the interest costs on such loans.

Until motorists are less heavily subsidized, most people will not respond to the mass-transit attempts of public authorities. Americans are so wedded to the automobile as the chief means of local transportation that it is most difficult to induce them not to use it. Perhaps the best way to induce people not to use their cars is to make doing so more expensive and to make mass transit more enticing.

Plans to Make Mass Transit More Enticing

Attempts have indeed been made to make forms of mass transit more enticing. Seattle offers a free in-town bus service, as does Los Angeles on Sundays. In 1973 Pennsylvania initiated free fares for senior citizens, financed from state lottery income. The Chicago Transit Authority temporarily canceled fares for local riders in Evanston and Willamette. A bill proposing to phase out all transit fares in New York by 1980 has been stalled in the state legislature since 1971. The bill suggested a 10 percent surcharge on state income taxes of individuals and corporations, to be returned to various transportation districts based on transit use.

All of these attempts at enticing people onto mass transit have value. Nevertheless, one might ask: Why continue to subsidize motorists? Some argue that this is where the solution to urban traffic congestion should begin. Yet, given the problem of urban crime, people may still prefer to use their cars rather than take subways and buses.

Summary

1. After Henry Ford developed the means to mass-produce cars at low cost, the automobile quickly became the most popular mode of transportation in the United States.

2. Today 85 percent of all American families own cars. In fact, over 30 percent own two or more cars.

3. There are both *private* and *social* costs to owning automobiles. Private costs include repairs, depreciation, gas and oil, taxes, and insurance, as well as payments on an auto loan.

4. One of the major social costs resulting from the use of automobiles is traffic congestion.

5. One method of reducing traffic congestion in cities is to adopt a system of peak-load pricing for such toll facilities as bridges, tunnels, and so on.

6. Commuter tickets for toll bridges are an example of reverse peak-load pricing: Cheaper cost actually encourages more use.

7. Another alternative for solving the problem of traffic congestion is the development of rapid mass transit systems. To date, however, the success of mass transit has been quite limited.

8. As long as motorists are subsidized heavily by government, the probability of traffic congestion being eliminated by increased use of mass transportation appears low.

Important Terms   mass transit   peak-load pricing
                       subsidies   peak-loading
                       reverse peak-load pricing   traffic congestion

Review Questions   1. Why can the twentieth century be called the "Age of the Auto?"

                       2. What are the private costs of owning an automobile?

                       3. How are social costs involved with driving?

                       4. Why would peak-load pricing help to reduce traffic congestion?

                       5. Why is reverse peak-load pricing counterproductive?

                       6. Why does the future of mass transportation not appear bright?

                       7. How effective is mass transit in reducing traffic congestion?

                       8. How are motorists subsidized by the government?

                       9. What effect does heavy subsidization of motorists have on mass transportation?

                       10. What types of enticement have cities attempted to stimulate use of mass transit systems?

Discussion   1. Why do you think the automobile has become the most popular
Questions   mode of transportation in the United States?

                       2. Do you think there should be a law against owning more than one automobile? Why or why not?

                       3. What recommendations would you make to solve the problem of traffic congestion in urban areas?

                       4. Do you think people profit from government subsidy of motorists? If so, who and how? If not, why?

Projects   1. Prepare a report on BART, the San Francisco Bay Area Rapid Transit system. Information on BART is available in articles listed in the *Reader's Guide to Periodical Literature*. What problems arose during BART's construction? What benefits have been or may be realized from the system? Compare the benefits with the costs.

                       2. Contact the mass transit system of a large city in your area to learn what transit officials are doing to stimulate increased use. How effective are their attempts? Report the findings to the class.

                       3. Prepare a debate on one of the following propositions:

                       a. *Resolved*, all non-city residents should be barred from driving within city limits during the hours of 7 A.M. to 10 A.M. and 3 P.M. to 6 P.M.

                       b. *Resolved*, all drivers residing in areas outside of metropolitan cities (cities with populations over 250,000) should pay a special licensing tax to be used to defray the expenses those cities incur in servicing motorists.

You and the Automobile

Definitions of New Terms

Depreciation: Depreciation is the amount of value a product loses over a period of time (also, the process of losing that value, for one reason or another).

Liability insurance: Liability insurance covers the financial obligations that a person might incur if that person is responsible for injuring or destroying another's property or life.

Collision insurance: Collision insurance covers the repair costs to a driver's car resulting from an accident.

Deductible: The amount of damages a person agrees to pay for in case of an accident is deductible from the amount of total damages. Typical deductibles for auto insurance are $0, $25, $50, $100, and $250.

Chapter 5 noted some of the major *private* costs of operating an automobile. These included maintenance and repairs, depreciation, and insurance. This issue will treat these private costs in more detail.

The Auto Repair Industry

The automobile repair industry is huge. Americans spend about $20 billion a year on auto repairs. More than 210,000 garages and 220,000 gas stations do repairs in the United States.

Labor costs for car repairs have increased rapidly in the last few years. Therefore, it is important for a car owner to find a reputable repair shop. This is not always easy. Friends and acquaintances are usually willing to tell where they have gotten good repair work done. And regular customers usually are treated better. Thus, it is advisable to use the same garage for all repair service once one is satisfied with the quality of the work.

If repair firms could run profitably for any length of time on *new* customers whom they have gypped, then one might have less confidence in the value of repeat business. But profitable auto repair firms (as well as most businesses) generally remain profitable only so long as customers keep coming back. Of course, the only way to keep customers coming back is to keep them satisfied. Thus it is not a bad idea for a person to make it clear to an auto repair shop that he or she would like to engage in what might be called *continuous dealing* (coming back again and again). This increases one's chances of getting high-quality

Car maintenance and repair is very expensive. Because of this it is important to find a quality repair shop. What maintenance and repair costs can you avoid by making them yourself?

work done at reasonable prices.

Many consumer experts believe preventive maintenance is the key to avoiding large repair bills. Although this is generally true, one needs to take account of the maintenance costs themselves. Sometimes it may be cheaper not to keep a car in perfect condition. That is, it may cost less to let things wear out and then replace them or to trade the car. Some state governments buy a fleet of cars on which they do no servicing for a year and then trade them in for new cars. This arrangement seems to be cheaper than trying to maintain the cars.

As the price of repair services continues to rise faster than other prices, this type of behavior will become more practical. What this means is that car owners will have two choices: (1) to buy a car they expect to keep for only a short period of time without servicing it, or (2) to buy a car with a reputation for very low service requirements.

Each year, the April issue of *Consumer Reports* contains information on the repair needs of various makes and models of cars. Such information is important to a consumer who is trying to assess the annual cost of operating an automobile. But no matter how well one maintains a car, it is going to wear out sooner or later.

Depreciation

One buys a car to use it for a while. It is a consumer durable good, just like a house. And like most consumer durables, a car **depreciates.** That is, it loses its value over time.

A person who buys a car one year and sells it the next year

cannot sell it for as much as he or she bought it for. The difference between the price the person paid when buying and the price he or she gets when selling represents the amount of the car's depreciation. Depreciation is determined by two things—physical wear and tear and obsolescence. Obsolescence is caused by the availability of newer, better, more stylish, or technologically superior competing cars.

Adequate repair and maintenance will reduce the amount of physical deterioration of an automobile. But there is little the car owner can do to avoid obsolescence. One thing he or she might do is to buy a car whose design does not change drastically from year to year. The Volkswagen is a good example. Its depreciation is due mainly to physical wear and tear, rather than to model changes. Table I–5–1 presents some U.S. Department of Transportation information on depreciation of automobiles.

Insuring Against Disaster

A person can reduce physical depreciation of a car by regular maintenance and corrective repairs and by driving less erratically. However, sometimes there are accidents that one cannot avoid. These accidents may involve substantial damages to a person's car, to another's car, or to someone else's property. Even worse, someone may be injured or killed.

How do people take account of such potential disasters? They buy insurance that protects them in case they are at fault in an automobile accident. Certain types of auto insurance also cover medical expenses that drivers or passengers may incur from an accident. Before discussing auto insurance in the United States in more detail, let us first look at how insurance works.

The Principle of Pooled Risks

Suppose there are 1,000 people driving cars in a given area. All of them know that a certain fraction of them—say 5 percent—will be involved in an auto accident each year. Each driver, therefore, has good information about the *average* number of automobile accidents in the group each year. Moreover, there is good information about the total cost due to automobile accidents for the group. Yet no one driver has good information about whether

Table I-5-1: Average Depreciation Rates of Cars

	1st year	2nd year	3rd year	4th year	5th year
Standard	75.1%	59.7%	46.6%	37.0%	30.0%
Compact	86.0%	73.0%	61.5%	51.0%	41.0%
Subcompact	88.0%	77.0%	66.0%	55.3%	45.0%

Source: U.S. Department of Transportation, Federal Highway Administration

"IT WAS A PECULIAR CIVILIZATION, DEPLETING ALL ITS FUEL RESOURCES WORSHIPING THIS STRANGE MACHINE..."

or not he or she will be involved in an accident. Rather than risk the chance of paying a substantial cost for damage, repairs, and injury resulting from an accident, each of the 1,000 drivers may be willing to share or pool the costs. That is, each driver may be willing to pay a proportionate share of the total cost of accidents each year in the form of an insurance premium.

Let us say that the total cost of automobile accidents for the 1,000 drivers is $100,000 a year. If they share all of the risk, each would pay 1/1000 of the cost. That is, each would pay a yearly insurance premium of $100,000 divided by 1,000, or $100 per person.

This is basically how auto insurance works. A person pays a premium to an insurance company. The company has good information on the total cost of accidents for drivers in the area according to age, class, and so on. Of course, each insuree pays somewhat more than his or her proportionate share of the total cost of accidents because the company has to make a profit on doing business. Most insurance works basically this way. The principle of shared, or pooled, risk is the same for insuring against fire or theft in homes or medical expenses due to illness or inury.

Auto Insurance Coverage

When a person buys a car, one of the first things that person has to do is to obtain insurance. Generally, very few people drive without automobile insurance. In fact, certain coverage is required by law in some states. Whether or not an owner's coverage is adequate is another matter.

Most people buy auto insurance to cover several different types of risks—liability, medical expenses, collision, and fire and theft (sometimes called *comprehensive insurance*). Each kind of risk has its own premium (or rate). **Liability insurance** is divided between bodily injury and property damage. It covers the financial obligations that a driver incurs for damage or injury resulting from an accident in which he or she is at fault. **Collision insurance** (usually bought with a **deductible** clause) covers the cost of repairs to a driver's car resulting from an accident.

When buying auto insurance, a person need not purchase all of the various types of coverage. It is advisable, however, to obtain those listed here. As previously noted, some states require liability coverage for an automobile to be *registered* (licensed for use on public roads in the state).

Auto Insurance Companies

The automobile insurance industry consists of many different companies. A person may often find different prices charged for the same amount of insurance from different companies. Comparing services can be misleading, however. Different insurance companies may offer different amounts or qualities of service. One company may be stingy or slow about paying off claims, for example. Information about the quality of service and the promptness to pay can best be obtained by asking people who have needed help from their insurance companies.

Insurance companies offer different rates to different classes of drivers. Why? Simply because the probability of an accident occurring is different for various classes. Competition has forced insurance companies to find out which classes of drivers are safer than others and offer those classes lower rates. Statistics indicate, for example, that unmarried males of age 16 to 25 have the highest accident record of all drivers. Hence, young, single males pay a higher premium for auto liability insurance than other drivers. Statistics also indicate that female drivers generally have fewer accidents than male drivers. Thus, it is not unusual for women to pay lower insurance rates for those cars they alone use.

Shopping Around for Insurance

The principles of comparison shopping apply to buying insurance as well as to anything else. One must take time to engage in such a task, however. Not only does it take time to talk to different insurance agents, but it takes time to figure out the differences in policies and services offered. Sometimes it is difficult to compare service information from various automobile

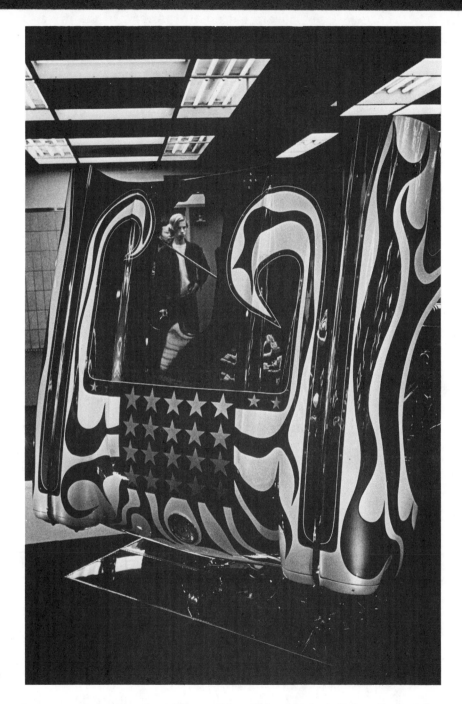

Insurance rates are generally higher for an unmarried male under 26 years old. Because of this it is important to comparison shop for the best rate possible. What factors account for differing rates for the same coverage from one insurance company to another?

insurance companies. Thus, it is advisable to talk to others who have used various insurance companies to learn which ones to avoid.

Reducing Auto Insurance Costs

One definite way a person can reduce the amount he or she pays annually for automobile insurance is to request a high **deductible** on collision coverage. As noted earlier, collision insurance covers the cost of repairs to the driver's car resulting from an accident. If a person is willing to pay an initial portion of the cost—say, the first $100 of damage (the deductible)—then the insurance rate will be much lower than if that person does not have to pay anything for repairs.

The deductible clause of a policy is, therefore, an important consideration when buying insurance. Each person should compare the rates for $0, $25, $50, $100, and $250 deductibles. Remember, the higher the deductible, the lower the cost, since the deductible eliminates claims less than that amount.

The consumer should also be acquainted with other aspects of auto insurance policies. Just remember, shopping for insurance is no different from shopping for any other product. The cheapest policy may not always be the best one.

Summary

1. The auto repair business in the United States is huge. There are more than 400,000 garages and service stations providing repair service at a cost of approximately $20 billion per year.

2. Like all businesses, auto repair shops depend on repeat customers. Doing business with a reputable garage on a regular basis generally provides satisfactory work at reasonable cost.

3. Automobiles, as well as most other consumable durables, depreciate because of physical wear and tear and obsolescence.

4. Like most insurance, auto insurance is based on the principle of pooled, or shared, risks. That is, a group of individuals agree to pay a premium that covers each one's share of the cost of accidents for the entire group each year.

5. Most people buy auto insurance. Several different types of coverage are available, including liability (bodily injury and property damage), collision, comprehensive (fire and theft), and medical expenses. Each coverage has a separate rate (premium).

6. Competition among insurance companies generally leads them to charge rates that reflect different costs for insuring different groups. Hence, drivers in high-risk categories pay more than others.

7. The principles of comparison shopping apply to buying auto insurance.

Important Terms

collision insurance
liability insurance
depreciation
comprehensive insurance

deductible
continuous dealing
pooled risk
premium

Questions for Thought and Discussion

1. Why is the auto repair business so extensive in the United States? Does its size mean that Americans are poor drivers?

2. This issue has emphasized the importance of finding a reputable auto repair shop with which to do business. How would you go about finding a reputable auto repair garage or service station?

3. As noted, automobiles depreciate because of physical wear and tear and obsolescence. How might one combat depreciation? That is, in what ways can the rate be slowed? Is it always best to fix everything in a car that malfunctions? Why or why not?

4. Single males between the ages of 16 and 25 are usually charged more for auto insurance than other drivers. Do you think this is fair? Why or why not?

6

Savings and Life Insurance

Preview Questions

1. Why is it advisable to save?
2. What is the nature of compound interest?
3. What kinds of savings institutions are there?
4. What is the difference between term and whole life insurance?
5. What is the value of life insurance?

Definitions of New Terms

Compound interest: Compound interest is interest earned on both the original amount saved and the interest already earned.

Time deposits: A time deposit is a bank deposit for which the depositor is required to give notice before withdrawing money. Time deposits are usually called *savings accounts*.

Board of trustees: A board of trustees is a group of people who serve as the overseers or supervisors of some institution.

Death benefits: Death benefits are the funds paid to the beneficiary of a policy when the policyholder dies—that is, the benefits paid on death only.

Policy: A policy is an insurance contract telling the policyholder the conditions under which he or she can expect to receive payment.

Premiums: Premiums are the payments a policyholder makes to an insurance company for the policy he or she has purchased.

Cash value: The cash value of a whole life insurance policy is whatever money the policyholder can get by canceling the policy.

Living benefits: Living benefits are the funds paid in lump sum or installments to a policyholder while he or she is still living.

Suppose you work after school each day and earn $40 per week. You want to buy a stereo that costs $160. To do so, you could save four weeks' earnings.

Perhaps you save all the time. Perhaps you do not spend all of your income, whether it is from a part-time job, an allowance, or gifts from relatives and friends. You put money aside to spend later. This is what saving is about.

Saving is the nonuse of income for a period of time so that it can be used later. The saving you do now may only be for purchases that require more money than you usually get at one time. When you are self-supporting and have additional responsibilities, you will probably save for other reasons. For example, you might save to have a source of money to fall back on in emergencies, such as losing your job, and to provide income for retirement. Although such considerations may not be important to you now, most Americans who save do so expressly for emergencies and retirement. People save during their working years to have income during their nonworking years. They save to even out their ability to spend throughout their lifetime.

This chapter will look at how much people save and why. It will also examine more closely two general ways for providing for the future—saving and buying life insurance.

The Tendency to Save

Throughout most of human history, people have saved. In the United States, the percentage of income Americans have saved has been more or less constant for the last several decades. Year in and year out, they save an average of 10 percent of their income. Figure 6-1 shows how many billions of dollars Americans have been saving over the last quarter century.

Saving is a way to spread one's consumption over a lifetime. It is a way to even out income, which may fluctuate. Even very poor people who are barely making a living know that sometime in the future they may no longer be able to work. When people reach retirement age or become unproductive so that no one will hire them, their earning power ceases. Unless children, government, or private charities are willing to care for them, they could face starvation if they have not accumulated savings.

Therefore, as a working adult, one must decide how much of his or

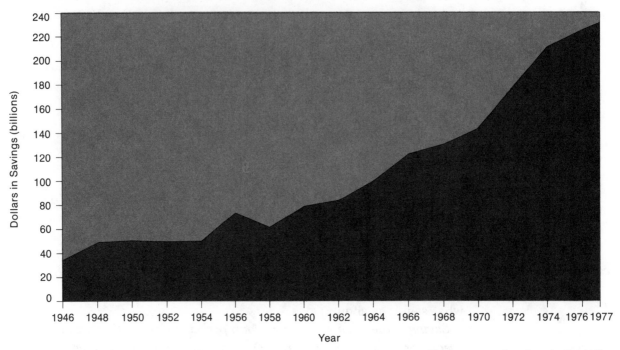

Figure 6-1. What Americans save every year. These are total savings in the U.S., including that done by business. (1977 datum is estimated.) Source: United States Department of Commerce.

her current income to set aside now for those years when he or she can no longer work. Unless a person would literally starve by reducing his or her current level of consumption, that person would be well advised to try to save a portion of current income, no matter how small the amount. Without saving, the person could face severe problems of survival when he or she is no longer able to work.

Saving Among the Poor

Many Americans believe that poor people in less-developed nations cannot save because they are barely subsisting. Yet anthropologists who have studied small villages in such countries as India have found that saving does take place. However, it often takes forms that Americans would not recognize in a money economy. In some places, for example, saving involves storing dried foods. Look at the worldwide rates of savings shown in Table 6-1. You will find that even the poorest nations save.

A Reward for Saving

Generally, when people think of saving, they think of putting their money in a savings bank or some similar institution. That money earns interest. Our earlier discussion of interest, in Chapter 3, centered on the payment a person must make to obtain credit—that is, the money one pays to use someone else's money. Interest is also the payment people receive if they loan money. That is, it is the reward (payment) one gets for letting someone else use one's money.

In general, people expect to be rewarded if they allow someone else to use a portion of their income. That reward is the interest they

Table 6-1: Saving Rates for Selected Nations

Country	Total personal savings as a percent of National Income
Malaysia	8.4
Panama	9.2
Jamaica	9.8
Honduras	10.1
Philippines	10.2
Denmark	10.3
United Kingdom	11.5
Portugal	11.8
Canada	12.0
Ireland	12.3
Korea	12.5
Luxembourg	13.4
South Africa	13.4
Sweden	14.9
Italy	15.1
Spain	15.2
Venezuela	15.7
Fiji	16.0
Norway	16.4
Belgium	16.7
Germany, Fed. Republic	17.5
France	17.9
Australia	18.3
Netherlands	18.8
Switzerland	18.9
Finland	20.1
Japan	20.4

The saving rates for different nations do not vary that greatly. A relatively poor nation such as Korea saves at about the same rate as a relatively rich nation such as Canada.

Source: United Nations

receive. Try to find out what interest rate a savings bank is offering on savings. The rate will vary from 5 to 8 percent, depending on how much money is invested and how long one has agreed to leave it in an account.

A person gets interest on a savings account for as long as that person leaves money in the account. For example, if a person puts $100 into an account that pays 5 percent interest yearly, at the end of one year the account will have grown to $105. If this money is left in the account, it will total $110.25 at the end of two years. Each additional year it will continue to grow, paying interest not only on the original $100 but on each year's interest as well. This is what is known as earning **compound interest**.

The Nature of Compound Interest

Whenever people want to find out how much savings they will have accumulated at the end of a specified time period, they must compound the interest. In the previous example, $100 was put into a savings account paying 5 percent interest yearly. At the end of the first year, $5 would have been paid in interest. Accumulated savings would thus be $105. At the end of two years, however, 5 percent interest is paid on $105, or .05 × $105 = $5.25. The savings have then grown to $110.25. At the end of three years, 5 percent interest on $110.25 would be .05 × 110.25 = $5.51. Savings would then have accumulated to $115.76. Since doing the computations for many years would get tedious, people can use tables that show compound interest at certain rates for certain amounts.

The Power of Compounding

The power of compound interest is, indeed, amazing. Table 6-2 shows $1 compounded from 1 to 50 years at various interest rates. At an interest rate of 8 percent, for example, the $1 would accumulate to $46.90 after 50 years.

Suppose a person inherited $20,000 when he or she was 20 years old and invested it at 8 percent interest compounded annually. When that person reached 70 years of age, he or she would have $938,000! How can one figure that out? Look at the column under 8 percent in Table 6-2. Find the row for 50 years. In 50 years, $1 compounded at 8 percent each year equals $46.90. In this example, the person inherited $20,000. By multiplying $20,000 × $46.90, one gets $938,000.

Table 6-2: One Dollar Compounded at Different Interest Rates

Year	3%	5%	6%	8%	10%	20%
1	1.03	1.05	1.06	1.08	1.10	1.20
2	1.06	1.10	1.12	1.17	1.21	1.44
3	1.09	1.16	1.19	1.26	1.33	1.73
4	1.13	1.22	1.26	1.36	1.46	2.07
5	1.16	1.28	1.34	1.47	1.61	2.49
6	1.19	1.34	1.41	1.59	1.77	2.99
7	1.23	1.41	1.50	1.71	1.94	3.58
8	1.27	1.48	1.59	1.85	2.14	4.30
9	1.30	1.55	1.68	2.00	2.35	5.16
10	1.34	1.63	1.79	2.16	2.59	6.19
15	1.56	2.08	2.39	3.17	4.17	15.40
20	1.81	2.65	3.20	4.66	6.72	38.30
25	2.09	3.39	4.29	6.85	10.80	95.40
30	2.43	4.32	5.74	10.00	17.40	237.00
40	3.26	7.04	10.30	21.70	45.30	1470.00
50	4.38	11.50	18.40	46.90	117.00	9100.00

Here is shown the value of the dollar at the end of a specified period after it has been compounded at a specified interest rate. For example, if one took $10 today and invested it at 10 percent, it would yield $11 at the end of the year. At the end of 10 years, it would be equal to $25.90. At the end of 50 years, it would be equal to $1170.

Chart 6-1: Comparing Simple and Compound Interest

If a person had invested 1¢ at 5 percent *simple* interest yearly at the time Jesus Christ was born, that person would have almost $1 in interest in 1977.

However, if 1¢ was put in a savings account at Christ's birth in which interest was paid at 5 percent interest *compounded* yearly, savings would have accumulated to nearly $6,730 followed by 36 zeros, or $6,730,000,000,000,000,000,000,000,000,000,000,000,000.

Perhaps this helps to explain how some people become millionaires. A person does not need to be smart or have a lot of business ability to get an 8 percent return on investment over a *long* period of time. A number of people inherit moderate amounts of money when they are quite young. If this money is invested wisely and left to compound itself, it can grow to very large amounts after 30 or 40 years. Hence, one should be careful about envying the cleverness and foresight of elderly millionaires. They might merely have invested a reasonable sum of money at a young age.

Getting the Highest Interest on Savings

To be a wise saver, one has to shop around to get the highest possible interest for your savings. This is the same principle that has already been emphasized on a number of occasions, particularly in the discussion on credit. When you want to get the best credit arrangement, you try to get the lowest interest rate. Now the tables are turned. You become, in effect, the lender. Thus, you want to obtain the highest interest rate possible.

Savings Institutions

There are several types of savings institutions. Although most savings institutions pay lower interest rates than some other forms of investment, one's money is quite safe. In fact, it is virtually impossible to lose it.

Even though the money is safe, one can compare the different interest rates that are offered by the various savings institutions in the area when opening an account. In some cases, savings institutions offer a higher rate of interest on savings left in for a longer period of time.

Currently, savings in most savings accounts are insured to a maximum of $40,000 by the federal government. This means that a person cannot lose money put into an insured account even if the savings institution goes out of business.

Commercial banks.   One of the chief institutions in which people have savings accounts is the commercial bank. Commercial banks offer what are called **time deposits.** In principle, time deposits are accounts for which savers must allow time between the day they ask to withdraw their savings and the day they receive them. Commercial banks generally pay the lowest interest rates on savings.

Savings and Life Insurance   **93**

Savings banks.   A second savings institution is the savings bank. The main purpose of a savings bank is to get money from depositors and to lend money to reliable borrowers at higher rates of interest than it pays depositors. Most savings banks provide a safe place for small depositors to invest their money.

Savings banks are regulated by the states in which they are authorized to do business. They usually pay slightly higher interest than commercial banks. Like commercial banks with time deposits, however, they are legally permitted to (but seldom do) require that notice be given before money can be withdrawn from an account.

Among the various types of savings banks, the two most important are *stock* savings banks and *mutual* savings banks. A stock savings bank is organized and conducted for profit by its owners. In effect, the depositors pool their savings, which are invested by a **board of trustees** (overseers) and a hired manager. Depositors are not paid a fixed rate of interest on their deposits. The deposits represent shares of ownership. Whatever earnings result from the bank's investments belong to the depositors and are divided among them in proportion to their deposits.

Savings and loan associations.   Savings and loan associations are a third type of savings institution. They offer depositors accounts at varying interest rates, depending on the time the money is deposited. At the same time, they use part of their deposits to make loans to homeowners. Savings and loan associations are called by different names in different parts of the country. In some places, they are called *cooperative banks* or *building and loan associations.*

Credit unions.   A fourth type of savings institution is the credit union. Credit unions are the fastest-growing savings institutions in the United States. They are owned by their membership. They have three purposes: (1) to enable members to borrow money for valid reasons at lower than market interest rates, (2) to help members save, and (3) to educate members in money management. In effect, credit unions are cooperative small-loan banks that lend money to their members at reasonable rates and that pay interest on deposits.

There are yet other avenues for savings. Chapter 7 will discuss investing in stocks and bonds. Now, however, let us talk about another way in which a person may save as well as provide for his or her family in the case of death—that is, life insurance.

Life Insurance as a Form of Saving

There has already been some discussion about buying insurance. You know that you can insure a car for collision or theft so that if the car is wrecked or stolen the insurance company will pay to repair or replace it. But you can also insure your life. Life insurance is one of the largest industries in the United States today.

There are many different places you can safely save your money. Interest rates differ according to services and the length of time savings are left in deposit. What kind of savings account would be best for your needs?

There are many different types of life insurance policies. Two of the most common are *term* life insurance and *whole,* or *ordinary,* life insurance. These will be the types discussed here.

Term Life Insurance

Suppose you want to insure your life in a way that will make money available to your dependents immediately on your death. One method is to buy term insurance, so called because the insurance is in effect for a specified period of time—usually five years. During the term, you pay a constant yearly premium for the insurance.

Most term insurance has no "saving" dimension to it. It is solely protection in case of death. That is, it pays a **death benefit,** which is the amount of the insurance bought, in the event of the insuree's death.

When people buy life insurance, they receive a **policy,** a contract telling them the conditions under which they can expect to receive payment. They make regular payments, called **premiums,** to the insurance company.

Premiums for term insurance commonly increase every year or every five years. The larger premiums reflect the greater probability of death as people get older. When a person is 25 years old, the cost of term insurance is relatively low. By the time that person becomes 60 years old, however, premiums will have risen dramatically.

Most people who buy term insurance do so when they are young. They buy it as low-cost insurance to maximize protection for their family. When they grow older and their children are well on the way to supporting themselves, they generally reduce the amount of term insurance they carry and so reduce the premiums they pay.

Whole Life Insurance

Suppose a person does not want life insurance that pays only a death benefit. Instead, the person wants protection that includes a savings plan. That person might buy whole life (also called *straight life* or *ordinary life)* insurance. Whole life insurance allows one to save while at the same time insuring against death.

The premiums for whole life insurance are the same throughout the life of a policy. As a result, the policyholder pays more than is necessary to cover the insurance company's risk during his or her younger years and less than necessary during his or her older years. The premiums that a person pays for an ordinary life insurance policy depend on the person's age when he or she buys the policy. The younger one is, the lower the price. The older he or she is, the higher the price.

Compared with term insurance, whole life insurance is relatively expensive. It costs more because it is a form of savings as well as protection. The savings feature is known as the policy's **cash value.** The cash value is the amount of money that the insurance company will pay if, at any point in time, a person wants to cancel his or her policy. One can cancel a whole life policy at any time and be paid the cash value.

Some people "cash in" their whole life policies when they retire, taking the cash value either as a lump sum or in installments. These are the benefits that the policyholder, rather than his or her survivors, may enjoy. They are called the **living benefits** of a whole life policy, those benefits received when the policyholder is still alive. In any one year, about 60 percent of all insurance payments are in the form of "living" benefits.

Getting the Best Insurance Deal

As with all goods, one must shop around to get the best insurance deal. Shopping around is difficult because insurance is a complex product to buy.

Many insurance experts claim that term insurance is the best deal. They point out that, with term insurance, a person buys pure protection—nothing else. On the other hand, with whole or straight life insurance, one buys a savings plan. Yet the rate of return on this savings plan is often less than what one could get from a savings institution. That is, the interest rate paid on the cash value of a whole life policy in the form of a dividend is low.

Thus, one thing one might do when buying life insurance is to purchase term insurance in the amount desired. Then the difference between the premiums for term insurance and the premiums for the same amount of whole life insurance could be put into a savings institution. Remember that this is only a suggestion. The decision is up to each individual. What is given here is a framework for insurance decision making.

Summary

1. Saving is the nonuse of income for a period of time so that it can be used later.

2. On the average, most Americans save about 10 percent of their income for emergencies and retirement.

3. Even in the poorest countries today, people save for the time when they will not be able to work.

4. Money put into an account in a savings institution earns interest. Most savings interest is compounded.

5. Compound interest can grow to phenomenal levels over a period of time.

6. There are many types of savings institutions. Some of the more common are commercial banks, savings banks, savings and loan associations, and credit unions.

7. People buy life insurance to provide for the financial needs of their dependents in case of their death and to save for the future.

8. Two of the most common forms of life insurance are term and whole life.

9. Term life insurance provides pure protection. It has no savings provision.

10. Whole life insurance has a cash value. The cash value is the savings portion of the policy. Interest, in the form of dividends, is paid on it.

Important Terms

board of trustees
living benefits
savings
cash value
policy
term life insurance

compound interest
premiums
time deposits
death benefits
whole life insurance

1. Why do people save?

2. How much do Americans save, on the average?

3. What is the reward for saving?

4. How does compounding work?

5. What would be the compound interest at 6 percent on $10,000 at the end of 30 years?

6. What are the common types of savings institutions?

7. What is the difference between a stock and a mutual savings bank?

8. What are the purposes of a credit union?

9. How might a person save other than depositing money in a savings account?

10. Why do people buy life insurance?

11. How do term and whole life insurance differ?

12. How might one get the best deal in buying life insurance?

Discussion Questions

1. Even poor people in less-developed countries save. How might their savings differ from those of Americans? Do you think the rate of saving in a less-developed country is considerably lower than in a highly industrialized nation? Why or why not?

2. Different savings institutions pay different interest rates on different types of accounts. How would you decide what type of an account to open and in which savings institution?

3. Do you think it is important to have life insurance? Why would a person with no dependents purchase life insurance?

4. The premiums on term insurance are generally much less than those for the same amount of whole life insurance. This being the case, who do you think would purchase whole life insurance? Why? Which type of policy would you buy? Why?

Projects

1. Canvass various savings institutions in your area to learn the interest rates they pay and the types of accounts they offer. Report the findings to class. Have the class decide where it thinks is the best place to open an account.

2. Invite an insurance agent to the class to give a talk on life insurance. Have him describe some of the various plans available, the premiums for each, and the rates of interest paid on the savings portion. Are the rates of interest lower than those available from a savings institution? If so, what reason does the agent give for purchasing that type of policy?

3. Prepare a report on savings institutions in other countries. Information can be obtained from reference books in the library.

Perhaps the manager of a savings institution can give you some advice as to sources of information.

4. Write to the Federal Deposit Insurance Corporation, 550 Seventeenth Street NW, Washington, DC 20429, to obtain information on its functions and the ways it protects the deposits of individuals in various savings accounts.

7

Investing in the Stock Market

Preview Questions

1. What is the stock market?
2. What is the difference between stocks and bonds?
3. Why do people buy stocks?

Definitions of New Terms

Market: A market is the place where buying and selling of goods takes place. The physical extent of a market may be large. It encompasses the area in which the price of similar products tends toward uniformity.

Stock market: The stock market is that market in which shares of stock in companies are bought and sold.

Over-the-counter market: Over-the-counter markets are the smaller stock markets that exist around the country. There is a national over-the-counter market and regional over-the-counter markets.

Broker: A broker is the person responsible for bringing together buyers and sellers of stock.

Stock: A stock is the legal document that gives its owner the right to a certain portion of the profits of the company that issued it. In other words, it represents part ownership of the company.

Bond: A bond is the evidence of a debt that a company owes the bond's owner. Bonds usually pay interest at a certain percent every year.

Principal: The principal is the amount of money loaned to a company in exchange for a bond.

Common stock: Common stock is stock by which its owner has ownership rights in a company. It includes voting power and may be paid dividends when the company is profitable.

Preferred stock: Preferred stock gives its owner a claim against the company's money that is placed ahead of that of common stockholders. Preferred stocks generally earn a specified rate of interest every year.

Dividend: A dividend is the interest that any stock, preferred or common, pays the owner.

Capital gain: Capital gain is the increase in value of something owned.

Capital loss: Capital loss is the decrease in the value of something owned.

Profits: Profits are the monies a company has left after all expenses are paid.

When people save, they usually want to invest their savings to earn interest. In that way they can increase their savings and therefore will be able to consume more in the future.

Chapter 6 discussed one way to invest savings—depositing money in savings institutions. Savings institutions offer a certain rate of return, even if the interest rate may be low. Moreover, money put into a savings account is almost impossible to lose because it is insured. Some people, however, may not be satisfied with the rate of return offered by savings institutions. They may be willing to take more risk to obtain a higher return. Thus, they are interested in other types of investments.

One of the most common areas for investment is the *stock market*. Before discussing what stocks are and how people buy and sell them, let us first look at what a **market** is.

What Markets Are All About

When most people think of going to the market, they think of going to a store where one buys food. But the term market has a more general meaning. A market is a place where individuals buy and sell various things. In past times a market was clearly defined in terms of

Like markets of all types, the stock market is designed to bring buyer and seller together. The New York Stock Exchange (pictured here) is the largest stock market in the U.S. and, despite appearances, is highly structured and well organized.

a physical marketplace. For example, buyers and sellers would come together at medieval fairs once a year to trade their wares.

Today, however, most countries have widespread communication networks. Markets therefore usually extend beyond physical limits. For example, suppose a person wants to buy a particular book. The person is not limited to what is available at the local bookstore. The person can write to the publisher and have the book mailed directly. Or the person can telephone a bookstore in another town or even in another state and have the book sent. Therefore, the market for books extends throughout the United States (indeed, to some extent, throughout the world, because a person can send away for books printed in foreign countries).

An important aspect of a market is the fact that *within a market, the price of similar products tends toward uniformity*. The book that a person might want to buy will probably cost the same whether that person buys it in his or her home town or from a city 1,000 miles away.

The Stock Market

One of the best-known markets is the **stock market.** It is the market in which shares of stock in companies are bought and sold.

The largest stock market in the United States is the New York Stock Exchange in New York City. The second largest is the American Stock Exchange, also in New York City. These two stock markets account for about 70 percent of the value of all stock transactions carried out in the United States. In addition to the New York and American exchanges, there are regional markets, such as the Midwest Stock Exchange in Chicago and the Pacific Coast Stock Exchange in San Francisco. Then there are what are known as **over-the-counter markets.** These are stock markets in which the stocks of smaller, less well-known companies are traded. There is a national over-the-counter market as well as numerous regional ones.

In all stock markets, those people who want to buy or sell stocks work through **brokers.** The broker is the person responsible for bringing together buyers and sellers of stocks. Brokers can be found in the thousands of brokerage firms throughout the United States. Issue 7 will discuss how much help a broker can provide in deciding which stocks to buy or sell.

The stock market is very well-organized. One can easily obtain information about the price at which to buy or sell any stock that is listed. Moreover, one can generally buy or sell a stock merely by calling a broker and placing an order. Finally, information is available about past prices of stocks as well as about the number of stocks that were traded on any one day.

The Different Types of Stocks

A *stock* is a legal document giving its owner the right to a certain portion of the profits of the company that issued it. Why would a company want to give away part of the rights to profits made in the future? Let us look at an example to see why.

Suppose a woman owns Cosmo, a cosmetics company worth $1 million. She wants to raise $200,000 for expansion. To obtain the money, she is willing to sell stock. She has 100,000 shares of Cosmo stock. Thus, to raise $200,000, she would have to put 20,000 shares of her stock on the market. That is, she would have to sell 20,000 shares at $10 a share. If all the stock were sold, she would get the money for expansion, and the people who bought stock (called *stockholders* or *shareholders)* would receive stock certificates for the number of shares they purchased. As part owners, they would collectively have a claim to one-fifth of whatever profits the Cosmo Company earned.

Bonds as an Alternative

The woman who owned Cosmo could have also raised money to expand in another manner. She could have sold bonds to someone who wanted to invest in her company. A **bond** is a promise to pay a specified amount of money every year for a specified number of years and then to repay the total amount of money that was loaned. In other words, the bondholder is guaranteed a specific rate of return every year and a repayment of the amount of money he or she has loaned.

The amount of money loaned is generally called the **principal** of the bond. The payment each year is interest. The bonds that a company issues for investors to buy are part of the debt of the company. Chart 7-1 lists some differences between stocks and bonds.

Chart 7-1: How Do Stocks and Bonds Differ?

Stocks	Bonds
1. Stocks represent ownership (except preferred stocks).	1. Bonds represent debt.
2. Stocks do not have a fixed dividend rate (excluding preferred stocks).	2. Interest on bonds must always be paid, whether or not any profit is earned.
3. Stockholders can elect a board of directors, who control the corporation.	3. Bondholders usually have no voice in or control over management of the corporation.
4. Stocks do not have a maturity date. The corporation does not usually repay the stockholder.	4. Bonds have a maturity date. The bondholder is to be repaid the face value of the bond.
5. All corporations issue or offer to sell stocks.	5. Corporations are not required to issue bonds.
6. Stockholders have a claim against the property and income of a corporation after all creditors' claims have been met.	6. Bondholders have a claim against the property and income of a corporation that must be met before the claims of stockholders.

Common versus Preferred Stock

People buy two types of stocks: *common* and *preferred*. Common stock is the most commonly bought and sold. It makes its owner a part owner of the issuing company. In addition, it includes voting rights in the election of the company's board of directors and in other matters brought before the ownership in a yearly meeting.

Common stock does not, however, guarantee its owner a return on investment. Nevertheless, there are two ways people make money on common stocks. One is through *dividends*, which the company may declare at one or more times during a given year. Dividends are equivalent to the interest a person might receive on a bond. But dividends on common stocks are not automatically guaranteed. They are only declared to be paid when a company has made a profit. If a company is not profitable, it will not declare dividends. Hence, the common shareholder will not receive any return. The second way people make money on common stock is by selling it for more than they paid for it. Before discussing the sale of stock, however, let us describe preferred stock.

Preferred stock is not necessarily "preferred" by prospective buyers. Rather, it is stock that guarantees a specified amount of interest or dividend each year for a certain number of years. When a company is really doing badly, however, preferred stockholders may not be paid this interest or dividend. Thus, preferred stock is actually a type of bond that pays a guaranteed dividend (or interest) except in very bad years for a given company.

Another difference between preferred and common stock arises if a business goes bankrupt. Preferred stockholders have a preferred claim on whatever value is left in the company. Moreover, preferred stockholders must be paid their dividends before any dividends can be paid to common stockholders.

Capital Gains and Losses

One of the ways a person can make money on common stock (and preferred stock) is to sell it for more than he or she paid for it. When the value of a stock rises, and a person sells it, that person has made a *capital gain.* That is, the person has had an increase in his or her capital, or wealth.

Suppose a person buys a stock at $20 and sells it for $30. That person makes a profit of $10 for each share of stock he or she bought and then sold at the higher price. This profit is a capital gain.

It is possible for the value of stock to fall. When it does, a person can suffer a *capital loss.* For example, if one bought stock for $20 and sold it for $10, that person would suffer a capital loss of $10 for each share of stock he or she bought and then sold at the lower price.

What Affects the Price of Stock?

A stock that sells for $5 today may sell for $10 or $2 next week. What makes people willing to pay more or less for it? Some observers believe that only people's psychological, or subjective, feelings matter. In other words, if people think a stock is going to be worth more in the future, they will bid up the price. If they think it will be worth less, then they will bid the price down. However, this is not a very satisfactory theory.

What is the basis for people's psychological feelings? Usually, such feelings are based on ***profits,*** that is, what is left over after all costs are paid. Whenever people expect a company's profits to rise, the value of the stock generally rises. That is, people bid up the price of the stock. Thus, any information about future profits is valuable in assessing how the price of a stock will react.

Reading Stock Quotations

One can find out what is happening in the stock market by looking at the financial pages of a daily newspaper. Chart 7-2 shows some of the information that is generally given about the stock market and explains how to read it. Armed with this ability, you will be able to read any information presented in a newspaper about what is happening to the stock market in general and to any given stock in particular.

Chart 7-2: Reading the Financial Page

Partial List of New York Stock Exchange Securities Traded

A	*B*	*C*	*D*	*E*	*F*	*G*	*H*	*I*	*J*
High	*Low*	*Stocks*	*Div.*	P-E *Ratio*	Sales by *100s*	*High*	*Low*	*Close*	Net *Change*
2½	1	Instit	InvTr	..	1	1¾	1¾	1¾	–⅛
9⅝	7	Integon	.36	6	31	9	8⅞	8⅞	–¼
48⅜	38⅝	Interco	1.66	8	42	45½	44¾	44¾	–¼
8⅞	3⅞	Interctl	Div	..	6	5⅞	5¾	5¾	–¼
42½	25⅝	Interlak	2.20	6	13	38⅞	38⅝	38⅞	+⅜
288½	223⅜	IBM	9	18	771	272	268	269	– 2¼
28⅜	19	IntFlavF	.44	23	1195	21⅝	21¼	21⅜	+⅛
33⅛	22⅜	IntHarv	1.85	5	446	32¼	32	32	–¼
42¼	32¾	IntMinC	2.40	6	219	40½	40⅛	40⅛	–¼
14⅞	6⅛	IntMng	.40e	6	26	14⅛	13¾	13¾	–¼
19½	15⅝	IntMulti	.85	7	45	19⅜	19⅛	19⅜	+¼
79¾	57⅝	IntPaper	2	10	1768	66⅜	61	62	– 3½

The above stocks and prices are excerpted from a page in the *Wall Street Journal.* Below you will find definitions of the abbreviations used and explanations of the columns.

A. High: This is the highest price paid for the stock to date this year.
B. Low: This is the lowest price paid for the stock to date this year.
C. Stocks: This is the name of the company, usually abbreviated.
D. Div.: This is the most recent annual dividend for each share.
E. P-E Ratio: This is the ratio of the current selling price to the earnings per share.
F. Sales in 100s: This is the number of round lots (100 shares each) sold that day. The odd lots, which are less than 100 shares each, are not listed.
G. High: This is the highest price paid for the stock the day it is listed.
H. Low: This is the lowest price paid for the stock the day it is listed.
I. Close: This is the price of the stock at the end of the trading day.
J. Net Change: This is the difference between the closing price of the stock the day it is listed and the closing price of the stock at the end of the previous trading day.

Who Should Invest in the Stock Market?

Some 35 million Americans own shares of stock in American businesses. Should you now, or at some time in the future, be one of the 35 million? That depends on (1) whether or not you have any savings, and (2) how much risk you want to take when you invest those savings. After all, if you invest in stocks, you may find that the price for which you can sell those stocks later is less than the price you paid. You may find that you will have less savings after investing them in the stock market for a while than if you had left them in a savings institution.

On the other hand, over a *long* period of time, you can make a higher rate of return by investing your savings in the stock market than in a savings institution. But the long run may be long indeed. It may mean that you will have to leave your savings in the stock market, without touching them, for many years. If your long-term goal is to provide for retirement, then perhaps at least part of your savings should be invested in the stock market.

Many people who have savings do have some of their savings in the stock market. They may also have a percentage of their savings in bonds, in cash, or in savings accounts. The more easily and quickly one wants to be able to draw on his or her savings without worry about loss, the smaller the percentage that should be kept in the stock market. But this type of decision is not one that one person can make for another. It is a decision that each one must make in accord with his or her own needs.

Summary

1. A common method of saving is investing in the stock market. The stock market is one of the best-organized markets in the world.

2. In investing in the stock market, people may buy either common or preferred stock. Each stock has certain advantages and disadvantages.

3. Another kind of investment is bonds. Stocks and bonds have several differences.

4. One way to make money on stock is by dividends. Dividends are paid when a company shows a profit.

5. A second way to make money on stock is to sell it at a higher price than the price at which it was bought. When stock is sold at a higher price, the owner has a capital gain. If it is sold at a lower price, the owner has a capital loss.

6. Prices of stock vary according to investors' ideas about the companies' ability to make profits.

7. In the long run, the rate of return from investment in the stock market can be greater than that from savings put into a savings institution.

Important Terms   bond   common stock
                      principal   broker
                      dividend   profits
                      capital gain   market
                      stock   capital loss
                      over-the-counter markets   stock market
                      preferred stock

Review Questions

1. What is a market?

2. Do markets have physical limits? Explain.

3. What are the two largest stock markets in the United States?

4. Why is the stock market considered to be well organized?

5. What kinds of stock are there? How do they differ?

6. How do stocks and bonds differ?

7. What is a capital gain? a capital loss?

8. What determines the price of a stock?

Discussion Questions

1. Many people invest in the stock market. Do you think investing in stocks is a smart thing to do? Why or why not? What are the advantages? the disadvantages?

2. Suppose you had $10,000 to invest in the stock market. Would you buy common stock or preferred stock? Why?

3. There are significant differences between stock and bonds. Which do you think is a better investment? Why?

Projects

1. Look at the market quotations cited in Chart 7-2. Look up the market quotations for the same companies in a current newspaper. Calculate the capital gains and/or losses you would have made on 10 shares of stock for each company. Assuming that the figures on the chart represent prices one year ago, what is the annual rate of return on the total investment?

2. Invite a broker to speak to the class on the operation of the stock market. Have the broker explain the fees and commissions involved in buying and selling stock. What advantages to owning stock does the broker cite? Does he or she point out any disadvantages? If so, what? If not, why?

Can People Get Rich Quick in the Stock Market?

Definitions of New Terms

Public information: Public information is any kind of information that is widely available to the public.

Inside information: Inside information is any kind of information that is available only to a few people, such as the officers of a company.

Random walk: The term *random walk* refers to the situation in which future behavior cannot be predicted from past behavior. Stock prices follow a random walk.

A dream that many people have is to become rich. Some will be rich when they are older because they will inherit wealth. That is, they will inherit or be given stocks, bonds, homes, valuable paintings, and other kinds of property that their parents or relatives own. Most people, however, are not so fortunate. For them to become rich, they must work hard and put their savings into wise investments.

A distinction must be made here between putting savings into wise investments that will pay a steady rate of return year after year and schemes in which one puts savings to make a "killing" over the course of a few months or a year. The latter is the kind of investing that some individuals try as a means to get rich quick. Most people, however, do not gamble with their accumulated savings. Rather, they put their savings in a savings account, long-term bonds, a pension plan, and/or the stock market. Furthermore, they leave much of the money they invest for 20, 30, or even 40 years before taking it out to live on during retirement years.

In this Issue you will see that long-term investment is generally best. It is the most secure and allows a better retirement. The truth of this principle might be attested to by looking more closely at "get-rich-quick" schemes involving the stock market.

One of the most popular "get-rich-quick" schemes involves picking the "right" stocks to buy at the "right" time. But what are the right stocks? Obviously, they are stocks whose price is low when bought and extremely high when sold. The mechanics of buying and selling stocks were discussed in Chapter 7. However, Chapter 7 did not explore the probability of always making gains in the buying and selling of stocks, nor did it discuss the length of time it takes to have a reasonable gain.

Finding Out About the "Right" Stocks

Perhaps your parents deal in the stock market—that is, buy and sell stock. If so, you have probably heard some strange words about "the market" in their conversations. They may talk about "hot" tips, reasons why the market might rise or fall, or about a broker's forecasts about stock prices.

When one wants information about an illness, for example, he or she generally consults a doctor. The person may even go to a specialist. If one wants information about how to repair a car, he or she may go to another type of specialist—an automobile mechanic. Thus, when one wants information about the stock market, reason would seem to suggest that he or she should go to a stock specialist—a broker.

This reasoning is partly accurate. A stockbroker can provide information about how the stock market runs and about the costs of buying and selling stocks. The broker can also lead the investor away from very risky stocks that have a small chance of making a huge gain and a large chance of losing everything. The broker can explain the right combination of stocks and bonds and of different types of stocks for the investor's particular investment needs, in terms of security and income in the future. But the broker is generally not the person who can make the investor rich quick. The broker cannot tell the investor with absolute certainty how to invest his or her dollars in the market.

An Experiment with a Specialist

Look in the yellow pages of the telephone book under "Stock and Bond Brokers" and pick a name at random. If you were to call a brokerage firm, you would speak with a broker. (A broker is a salesperson, but he or she may have the title of "account executive.") The following is what would probably happen.

When you got the broker on the phone, you would tell him or her that you have $5,000 to invest, and ask for advice. Before the broker tells you anything, he or she will ask you what your goals are. Do you want income from your investment of $5,000? Do you want growth stocks that will provide a reasonable capital gain in the future?

After you tell the broker the strategy you want to take, he or she will probably advise you which stocks are the best to buy and whether the stock market will go up or down in the next few months. The broker's opinion will sound very informed and authoritative.

Nevertheless, strange as it may seem, the broker's advice on how to invest your money generally is not any better than anyone else's advice. In fact, *the chances of the broker being right are no greater than the chances of you being right!* Does this sound improbable? Perhaps. Yet the fact remains that economists, statisticians, and investors have examined and tested this proposition from numerous angles. And all have reached the same conclusion.

Your Guess Is as Good as Anyone Else's

You have probably never studied investing before. How can you guess about what the stock market will do? Or about how profitable a company may be in the future?

The stock market is one of the most competitive markets in the world. Although Chapter 9 will discuss the nature of competition more specifically, you already have some understanding of it. When people are competing for something, each person tries to do better than the others.

In the stock market, the name of the game is to make money. Competition among investors means that all investors try to do as well as they can. In doing so, each investor must compete with all other investors. Every investor cannot get rich on every deal. Some people lose, and some people gain. Each investor's efforts to gain are what make the stock market highly competitive. It is more competitive than most other markets because literally millions of investors trade in it. In addition, it is still more competitive because of the availability of information about it.

Market Information

Most Americans can use almost any daily newspaper to find information about the price of stocks on the New York, American, and certain regional stock exchanges. Stock price quotations are published daily in the financial section of the newspaper. In addition, current stock price information is available from most brokerage firms. These firms have electronic equipment or ticker-tape machines that receive price changes for various stocks almost as fast as they are announced, even though the firm may be 3,000 miles from the stock exchange.

Information about a specific company also rapidly becomes widely known. As soon as a company announces its profits, literally thousands of people learn about it. Such information is not as readily available as the prices of listed stocks, but it flows quite freely within the American economy.

The point is that by the time one investor reads about what a company, an industry or, for that matter, the national economy is going to do, most other investors have also read it. The information is **public information**—information available to anyone and everyone. Public information cannot help one very much in a plan to get rich quick.

Public Information

To understand why public information will not help, let us look at an example. Suppose a company in your neighborhood has discovered a substitute for gasoline. You read about the discovery in the newspaper. After reading the article, you decide that the company's stock would be an excellent purchase because the company should make a great deal of money from its discovery.

But think about the idea more carefully. Will not everyone else think the same way? In fact, will not many people who learned

There is nothing magical about the stock market. More often than not your guess as to the best stock to buy is just as good as a trained stockbroker. Do you know someone who owns stocks? Ask them why they bought a particular stock.

about the discovery before you also realize that the company stands to make higher profits? Certainly they will. Some will already have started to buy stock in the company. As they bid against each other to buy stock, the price of the stock will start to rise. By the time you read about the discovery, competing investors will have *already* bid up the price of the stock. Hence, by the time vital information becomes public, it is essentially useless to someone trying to get rich quick.

Inside Information

The only useful information in a person's quest to get rich quick is information that is not yet public. This information, known only among a small group of people, is called **inside information.** Here is an example of how one might get inside information.

Suppose a lawyer meets with an executive of the International Chemical and Drug Company, in the executive's office. When the executive steps out of the office for a moment, the lawyer looks down in the wastebasket and sees a crumpled memo that reads, "Success! We've done it!" Recently, the lawyer has noticed several news items about a miracle drug on which the company is working. Now the lawyer has some inside information.

Assuming that the corporate officers at International Chemical and Drug Company do not announce the discovery immediately, the lawyer has some very valuable information. No one outside the company knows about the discovery. If the lawyer were to buy as many shares of International Chemical and Drug Company as he could, then he might be able to get rich quick. The probability is high that the stock would be bid up when the inside information became public and investors anticipated higher profits in the company.

A Random Walk

Suppose someone asked you to walk at random in a room. What would you do? You might close your eyes and walk in any direction, back and forth, diagonally, or around various objects in the room. If you have studied physics, you will recognize the similarity between such activity and the Brownian motion of molecules.

According to Brown's theory of motion, molecules jump at random. It is impossible to predict where a molecule might move next by knowing where it is or has been. In other words, when something follows a **random walk,** it takes directions that are totally unrelated to its past movements. Hence, no amount of information about the past is useful for predicting the future.

Because the stock market is so highly competitive and because information flows so freely, it follows a random walk. The market as a whole has trends, such as the general upward trend from its beginning that reflects the growth in the American economy. The prices of specific stocks and the average of all stock prices, however, exhibit a random walk. Any examination of past stock prices will not yield useful information for predicting future prices. Years of academic research have left little doubt that the stock market follows a random walk.

If a person were to find out otherwise, he or she could get rich quickly. But a stock is not like a dog. It will not eventually come home to its former price. Lacking mind or purpose, a stock does not even know where its home was.

Is There No Way to Get Rich Quick?

Figure I–7–1 shows the Dow Jones industrial stock average for 1920 to 1977. The Dow Jones is an average of 30 large companies' stock prices. It is thus an indicator of stock prices.

Looking at the graph, you will see many movements up and down. But the general trend is upward. Obviously, anybody who could buy stocks at the times when prices were low and sell

While fortunes can and have been made in the stockmarket, the chances of this actually happening are extremely small. Under what circumstances would you invest your money in the stock market?

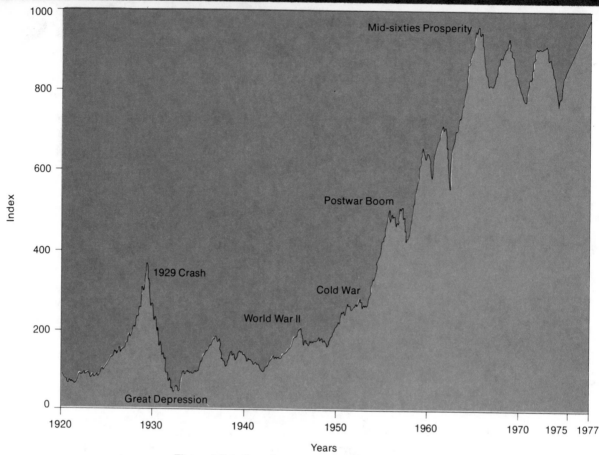

Figure I-7-1. Dow Jones Industrial Averages, 1920–1977.

them at the times when prices were high would become rich. But no one knows how to do that with any certainty.

Thus, when you have money to invest in the stock market, a wise course to follow might be to buy a random selection of major companies' stock and hold the stock for many years. The return on such an investment has historically been between 8 and 15 percent. But for any given short period, it can be much less.

Most people find this is difficult to accept. Many think they can outsmart the stock market. Yet the facts are irrefutable. In the words of economist Paul Samuelson, a Nobel Prize recipient:

Even the best investors seem to find it hard to do better than the comprehensive common-stock averages, or better on the average than random selection among stocks of comparable variability. *

---
*Paul Samuelson, *The Bell Journal of Economics and Management Science*, Autumn 1973, Vol. 4, No. 2, pp. 369–374.

Summary

1. Many people dream of getting rich quick by investing in the stock market. In reality, however, few do.

2. Brokers can advise investors about many things regarding the stock market. Nevertheless, their guesses about stocks that might produce a quick profit are no better than anyone else's.

3. Public information is of little value to a person in a plan to get rich quick. Inside information, on the other hand, can lead to quick wealth under certain circumstances.

4. Generally, the stock market follows a random walk.

5. In the United States, the long-range trend of the stock market has been upward. Therefore, stocks in major companies held for a period of years are usually good investments.

Important Terms

inside information	public information
random walk	

Questions for Thought and Discussion

1. This issue has emphasized the idea that "get-rich-quick" schemes generally fail. Do you agree with this point of view? Why or why not? Why is it difficult to get rich quickly by investing in the stock market?

2. Do you think most brokers would agree that their guess about which stocks might result in a quick profit is no better than anyone else's? Why or why not? Why, then, do people consult them?

3. What is a random walk? How does it apply to a person's ability to predict the future price of a specific stock? Do you think the principle applies to predicting gain from other types of investments, such as land? Why or why not?

4. What is the current Dow-Jones industrial average? How has it changed in the last year? What reasons can you give to explain the changes? Do you think the changes were predictable? If so, how? If not, why?

UNIT THREE

Markets, Prices, and Types of Business

8

Supply and Demand

Preview Questions

1. What determines the price of what people buy?

2. Why do people buy more of something when its price is lowered?

3. Why do people buy less of something when its price is raised?

4. Do manufacturers of products want to sell more or less when the price of the product goes up?

Definitions of New Terms

Relative price: Relative price is the price of an item relative to the price of something else. More generally, it is the price of an item relative to the index or the average of all other prices.

Law of diminishing utility: The law of diminishing utility states that the additional satisfaction a person gets from consuming one more unit of a product falls or diminishes as he or she consumes more and more.

Law of demand: The law of demand states that as the relative price of a product goes up, a smaller quantity will be demanded; as the relative price of a product goes down, a larger quantity will be demanded.

Demand curve: A demand curve is a graphic representation of the law of demand.

Law of supply: The law of supply states that at higher relative prices, suppliers of a product are willing to supply more than they will at lower relative prices.

Supply curve: A supply curve is a graphic representation of the law of supply.

Equilibrium price: The equilibrium price is the price that will prevail for a good or service. It is determined by the balance of the forces of supply and demand. In graphic terms, it is located where the supply and demand curves cross.

When people decide to buy a consumer durable, they generally shop around and then buy what they think is the best deal. Let us assume that you want to buy a 10-speed bicycle. What do you do? You might look in the newspaper at the ads for bicycles. You can go to local department stores and bicycle shops. You can also look in mail-order catalogs from Sears and Roebuck, Montgomery Ward, and other mail-order businesses. You probably look first at the prices of different models and brands. In most cases, you assume that the seller's price is fixed. That is, you do not usually think of bargaining to get the price of a particular model lowered.

When you bought something, have you ever wondered why the price is what it is? Many times you may have felt helpless, thinking you have no influence whatsoever on the price you pay for anything you buy. To be sure, few individual consumers do. On the other hand, all consumers collectively have a great influence on the relative price of everything bought and sold in the economy.

Relative Price

When one refers to the *relative price* of an item, the stress is on the word *relative*. What is important is how expensive is one good or service as compared with, or relative to, another. In deciding what and how much to buy, people generally make decisions about one good or service based on its price compared with the price of an alternative good and service. A simple example will illustrate this point. Let us look at the prices for eight-track stereo cartridges and four-track stereo cassettes over two years:

	8-track stereo cartridge	4-track stereo cassette
Year 1	$ 5.00	$ 5.00
Year 2	$10.00	$ 7.50

What has happened to the prices from year 1 to year 2? The prices of both cartridges and cassettes have risen. The relative price has also changed. In year 1, cartridges and cassettes cost the same amount. In year 2, however, the price of cartridges rose relative to cassettes. On the other hand, the price of cassettes fell, relative to cartridges. In year 1, the relative price of cartridges compared with cassettes was $5/$5. In year 2, the relative price of cartridges compared with cassettes was $10/$7.50.

© Chronicle Publishing Co. 1977

"We'll bring those coffee producers to their knees!"

Perhaps now you can understand why it is important to compare relative prices. This is particularly true when the economy is prone to inflation (rising prices), as it is now. Just because the price of something has gone up does not mean it is a poor buy. What one needs to find out is whether its price has risen faster or slower than the prices of other goods one may wish to purchase. In other words, one has to look at relative prices.

What Determines Relative Prices?

The question still remains, What determines the relative prices of goods? Why would a stereo cartridge cost more than a stereo cassette? Why does an essential item such as water cost so little and a nonessential item such as a diamond ring cost so much?

Perhaps the best way to find an answer is to look at how people decide what to buy and how people who want to sell those things decide how much to sell and at what price.

How do people determine what to buy and how much they are willing to pay? One way is to look at how useful people think a good or service is. In other words, what people buy and how much they are willing to pay is determined by how much satisfaction or use they think they will get from what they buy.

Pizza Utility

To explore this idea, let us look at an example. Suppose a friend offers you as many slices of pizza as you care to eat. Assume that you like pizza and that the pizza has been well prepared. Certainly you will get much satisfaction from eating the first slice. But how much satisfaction will you get from eating the second? Probably a lot, but not as much as from the first. What about the third, fourth, and fifth slices? Most likely, the satisfaction (or utility) you receive from each *additional* slice will be less than that from the previous one. In other words, the amount of satisfaction or utility will diminish as you eat additional slices.

This concept is useful in predicting how a consumer will react to different prices of goods and services. The principle is called the ***law of diminishing utility.*** Actually, it should be called the law of diminishing *additional* utility—for as long as you do not get sick, you will have a higher level of total satisfaction from eating more slices of pizza. What happens, however, is that the *additional* satisfaction you get from each slice you eat is less.

Diminishing Utility and Willingness to Buy

Let us go back to the pizza example and make it more realistic. Let us suppose that each slice of pizza costs $.50. How many will you buy? Assuming you have money and like pizza, you will buy at least one slice. Will you buy a second? a third? a fourth? That depends on the additional utility or satisfaction you expect to receive when you buy another slice.

At some point, however, you will stop buying additional slices. At that point you value the satisfaction you receive at less than $.50, the price you must pay for a slice. It is obvious that you will stop buying when the value you place on the additional satisfaction from the next slice is less than the price you must pay.

Diminishing Utility and the Law of Demand

The previous analysis can be used to form what is called the ***law of demand.*** This law deals with how people usually react to a change in the (relative) price of something they buy.

Again let us look at the pizza example. At a price of $.50 per slice, let us assume that you have had enough pizza after buying three pieces. That decision means the value you place on additional satisfaction from a fourth slice would be less than $.50, perhaps $.40.

What would happen if the seller suddenly informed you that the price of a slice of pizza today would be $.35 rather than the $.50 you anticipated? Would you buy more? Unless three slices were all you could eat, you would probably buy at least one additional slice.

This brings us to a very important observation. Generally, as the price of something people want to buy goes down, they will purchase more. Based on the analysis of utility, the reason is clear. People will continue to buy something up to the point where the value they place on the satisfaction received from the last unit bought is equal to the price. Then people will not buy any more.

But what happens when the price of whatever they are enjoying falls? Now they can justify buying more. Even though the satisfaction or utility from each additional unit is less—that is, the value is less—the lower price will induce people to purchase more. Thus, they will continue to buy to the point where satisfaction received again falls below price.

The Law of Demand

The previous section has outlined the law of demand. Simply put, the law of demand states:

As the relative price of an item falls, a larger quantity will be bought. As the relative price of an item rises, a smaller quantity will be bought.

The law of demand tells us, for example, that as the price of imported automobiles rises relative to domestic cars, the quantity of imports demanded will fall. The law of demand will also allow us to predict that as the relative price of calculators falls, the quantity demanded will rise. You can probably think of many examples of the law of demand. Still, one does not need to rely on the analysis of diminishing utility to come up with the law of demand. The law of demand exists because no person has unlimited income.

The Law of Demand and Incomes

All people face one universal problem: No individual will ever be able to buy everything that he or she wants to buy. This problem faces men and women everywhere, at all times, and in every way.

As a nation, the United States will never have unlimited natural resources. Individuals realize they have a constraint on, or a limit to, spending. That limit is their income. Income constrains each person's purchasing habits. Suppose that you want something very much—so much that you consider it a necessity. If its relative price rises and rises, eventually you will not be able to keep buying the same quantity no matter how much you want it. Why? Because at some point you will be reaching beyond the limit of your available income.

Long before people reach the limit of their financial resources, most would cut back on consumption, or purchase, of whatever they once considered essential. That is, they would *substitute* something else for it. The limitation of financial resources forces people to reevaluate how much they want something. There is no way that they can keep buying the same quantity of a good if its price rises while nothing happens to their income. Even if all other prices stay the same, they would need to reduce the purchase of other things to keep buying the item whose price keeps rising.

Thus, what is involved is a trade-off. For example, suppose the money you have to spend each week remains the same, but the price of Big Macs keeps rising. There is no way that you can keep buying a Big Mac every day and still buy the same amount of other things. It is impossible. In order to keep eating a higher-priced Big Mac every day, you will have to give up something else.

At some point you will no longer be willing to cut back on your purchases of other things if the price of Big Macs continues to rise. What you will do is cut back on your purchase of Big Macs, perhaps buying one every other day. This example illustrates the law of demand. As the relative price of an item goes up, the quantity demanded falls.

Showing the Law of Demand

If you understand the law of demand, you should have little difficulty with the next example. It will help to explain the relationship between the quantity demanded of an item and its price. Remember, whenever the word *price* is mentioned, think of the word *relative*. Until the discussion of inflation in Chapter 20, this book always refers to relative prices.

Let us now continue the example of Big Macs and add some numbers. Table 8-1 shows how many Big Macs might be sold at prices ranging from 50¢ to $2.00.

What can be learned from this table? The table points out that as the price of Big Macs increases, fewer Big Macs are sold. Conversely, as the price decreases, more will be sold.

The table also points out another important aspect of the law of demand. It is a projection, or estimate, made for a certain period of time. In this particular table, the second column shows the quantity demanded, or purchased, *per year*. It could have been for half a year or a month, and the numbers could have been adjusted accordingly. What is important is that the estimate covers a *definite* and *specific* period.

Table 8-1 can also be made into a graph showing the combinations of prices and quantities demanded at points on a line called a **demand curve.** The line is a representation of the law of demand. A demand curve is another way of saying: As the price of an item falls, the quantity demanded rises. As the price of an item rises, the quantity demanded falls.

Figure 8-1 shows the information of Table 8-1 in relation to two lines called *axes.* The horizontal axis represents the quantities demanded, marked off at equal spaces along a line. The vertical axis

Table 8-1: Quantity of Hamburgers Demanded at Various Prices

Price per Hamburger	Quantity of Hamburgers Purchased Per Year
$0.50	7 million
$0.75	6 million
$1.00	5 million
$1.25	4 million
$1.50	3 million
$1.75	2 million
$2.00	1 million

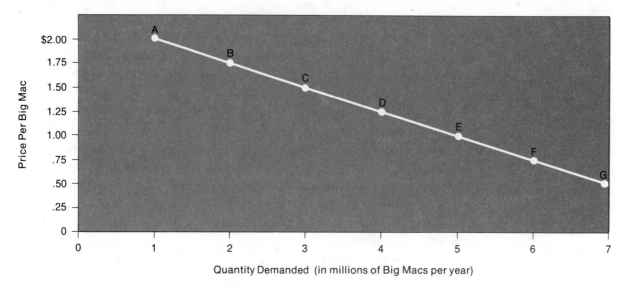

Figure 8-1. Quantity demanded at various prices.

represents the prices per Big Mac. How are the facts in the table shown as a graph? To find out, look first at the table. At a price of $2.00, the quantity of Big Macs demanded is 1 million. Now look at the graph. A dot has been placed at the point that represents the price, $2.00, and the quantity demanded, 1 million. That point is labeled *A*. Each entry in the table has a corresponding point in the graph, labeled *B, C, D,* and so on.

When the points are connected by a line, that line forms a demand curve. The demand curve shows the relationship between the quantity of Big Macs people will buy and the various prices at which they are sold.

What to Remember About the Law of Demand

Whether one states the law of demand in words or shows it with numbers in a table or graph, it is important to remember that the law of demand represents only the relationship between price and quantity demanded for a specific period of time with income remaining constant. Remember that other factors also affect price and quantity demanded.

Perhaps the most important factor is income. As income increases, people will purchase more of an item even though its price does not decrease. Thus, when a demand curve is drawn, it is assumed that income remains constant. That is, it is assumed that everyone's income remains the same over the period in question.

A second factor that affects price and quantity demanded is the relative price of alternative items. For example, what do you think might happen to the sale of hamburgers if the relative price of hot dogs dropped 90 percent during the same period? Certainly the total of Big Macs sold would be smaller. Some people would purchase more hot dogs and fewer Big Macs. Thus, a demand curve also assumes that the price of competing, or substitute, products is constant during the period. Although there are other assumptions, these two are perhaps the most important to remember in demand analysis.

Demand Is Not Enough

The law of demand alone is not enough to explain what determines the price of things people buy. It states only that at lower prices, people will purchase more than they will at higher prices. It does not explain the given price for an item and why that price may change.

In order to complete the picture, it is necessary to look at the opposite side of demand. That side is concerned with the individuals who provide things people want to buy. Those individuals are producers or suppliers. Hence, let us now turn to the supply side of the analysis.

Suppliers and Supplies

Assume that you are the owner of all the McDonald hamburger stands in a given area. How do you supply Big Macs to people who want to buy them? You must have land on which to build the stands. You must hire employees to service your customers. You must purchase meat, buns, and sauces. You must have grills, refrigerators, and other equipment. You must pay taxes and insurance. You must pay for the repair and upkeep of each stand and all its equipment.

Assume for the moment that the price you are charging for Big Macs covers all your costs and gives you a profit. What would happen if you decided to raise the price? According to the law of demand, the number of hamburgers you would sell would fall. But you would want to sell more to make a higher profit. Thus, at the higher price, you might be willing to build new stands, to hire additional workers, and to buy additional equipment.

In other words, at a higher price for each Big Mac, you would be willing to supply more than you supply at a lower price. At a higher price, you can afford to take on any higher costs per hamburger in order to increase the quantity supplied (sold).

Discussion to this point has presented the essential basis of the *law of supply.* The law of supply states:

At higher prices, suppliers are willing to supply more than at lower prices.

Perhaps you might better understand the law of supply by looking not at one supplier, but at many suppliers who either are or could be in an industry. Let us consider the entire fast-food hamburger stand industry. At a higher relative price for all hamburgers sold in hamburger stands, *potential* operators—that is, those who do not run them now—might be attracted into the business. At a higher price, they see the opportunity to make larger profits than they could have made before the price of hamburgers went up.

Why were not the potential operators already in the business?

They were not because at the lower price and the degree of efficiency they thought they would have operating a stand, the business did not look profitable. Therefore, as the price of an item goes up, the lure of profit causes less efficient producers to enter the industry.

To summarize, at higher prices, present producers, or suppliers, will increase their supplies. Thus, *potential* suppliers will become *actual* suppliers. Both will add to total output. Perhaps you now see why the law of supply is as logical and useful as the law of demand to explain what happens in the economy.

Showing the Law of Supply

The law of supply can be shown by a table, just as the law of demand was shown. Let us use the same numbers that were used in Table 8-1. Notice, however, that there is a difference. The quantities supplied at each price will not be the same as before. Table 8-2 shows that at a price of $2.00, the largest quantity will be supplied, and at a price of $.50, the smallest quantity will be supplied. Remember that the law of supply states that, as the price goes up, the quantity supplied also goes up. Notice, too, that a specific time period is indicated for the quantity supplied—in this case, one year.

The data in Table 8-2 representing the law of supply can also be shown as a graph. Figure 8-2 shows a supply graph. The **supply curve**—the line connecting points *A, B, C, D,* etc.—looks like a demand curve. But it goes in a different direction. The direction is different because, according to the law of supply, the quantity supplied and the selling price go in the same direction; whereas, for the law of demand, the quantity demanded and the selling price go in opposite directions. Thus, what one should remember about a supply curve is that the quantity supplied of an item and its relative price move up or down together.

With this in mind, let us now look at how price is determined for the things people buy. To do so, we must combine the law of demand with the law of supply.

Table 8-2: Quantity of Hamburgers Supplied at Various Prices

Price per Hamburger	Quantity of Hamburgers Purchased Per Year
$2.00	7 million
$1.75	6 million
$1.50	5 million
$1.25	4 million
$1.00	3 million
$0.75	2 million
$0.50	1 million

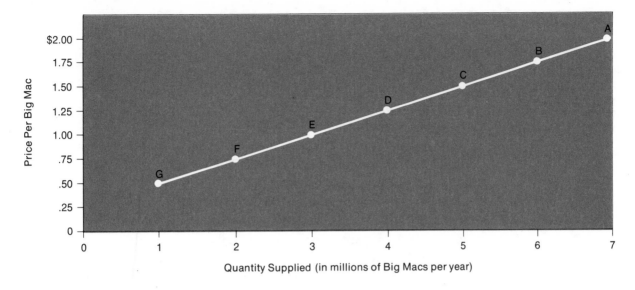

Figure 8–2. Quantity supplied at various prices.

Putting Demand and Supply Together

As the price of a good or service goes down, the quantity demanded rises, and the quantity supplied falls. As the price goes up, the reverse is true. This being the case, does it not seem plausible that at some point these two opposite tendencies might mesh? Or, to put it another way, is there a price at which the quantity demanded and the quantity supplied meet? The answer to this question is yes. The price of any good or service will find a level at which the quantity demanded and the quantity supplied are the same. That level is called the *equilibrium price.* At the equilibrium price, quantity demanded and quantity supplied are in balance and have no tendency to change unless something else changes.

The concept of equilibrium is easy to understand. It operates around you all of the time. Let us look at an example. Suppose in a given week you engage in a certain amount of physical and mental activity. During the same period, you consume the number of calories equal to the calories you use in physical and mental activities. Your weight will remain constant. It reaches an equilibrium, or balance, as your activity and eating habits stabilize.

But what if you get a jolt? You could get out of equilibrium. For example, should you get more physical activity, your weight could go down. Should you eat more, your weight could go up. Nonetheless, you will be tending toward some sort of equilibrium at all times.

Another point to note about equilibrium is that sometimes it is stable. Other times it is not stable. For example, take the case of a pencil with a new eraser. If you stand the pencil on end, it is in a special kind of equilibrium—one that is not stable. The equilibrium is not stable because the pencil cannot return by itself to its upright position if knocked over. Contrast this with a ball hung on a string from a light fixture. No matter how often you push the ball away from its vertical position, it will eventually return to the same position. That vertical position, then, is one of stable equilibrium.

Equilibrium Price and Quantity

One way to visualize equilibrium price is to put together the graphs of the law of supply and the law of demand. Figure 8–3 combines the two previous figures. Its horizontal axis measures both the quantity demanded *and* the quantity supplied. The vertical axis still measures the price per Big Mac.

Can you pick out the equilibrium price on the graph? Is it $2.00? No. At $2.00, demanders want to purchase only 1 million Big Macs while suppliers want to provide 7 million.

What about a price of $.50? The reverse is true. Demanders want 7 million Big Macs, but suppliers are willing to supply only 1 million.

Only one price satisfies both demanders and suppliers. That price is $1.25. At $1.25 for a Big Mac, the quantity demanded is 4 million Big Macs, and the quantity supplied is the same. At that price, there are neither too many nor too few Big Macs in the economy. If nothing changes, the price will prevail. So will the quantity. It is the equilibrium price.

What Determines Price?

Can it be said that supply and demand determine all (relative) prices? Yes and no. Certainly it is a concise way of indicating that supply and demand are important aspects of the economy, and that they affect the price of things people buy.

Prices are not really determined by supply and demand, however. Instead, they are determined by the *forces,* which in turn determine supply and demand. What are those forces? Many forces determine supply and demand. On the demand side, they include such things as people's tastes, preferences, values, and customs. On the supply side, they include such things as natural resources, the ability to produce,

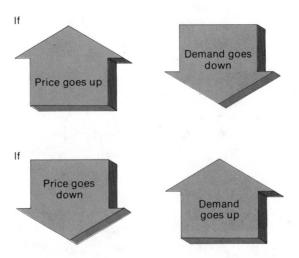

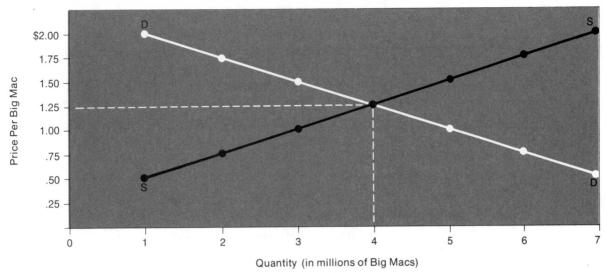

Figure 8–3. Finding the equilibrium price.

and the costs of production. Just remember that when someone says price is determined by supply and demand (or where the supply curve intersects the demand curve), what that person means is that the forces *underlying* supply and demand determine price in the marketplace.

Then, too, the interworkings of supply and demand do not always determine price. Many prices in the economy are fixed by legislative or government rules. In some cases, one must distinguish between a legal and an illegal price of a good. If there is a complete ban on some good, such as heroin, there is no legal price. And the illegal price will tend to be quite high.

Throughout the remainder of this book, you will have occasion to use the concepts of supply and demand. You must be careful to determine whether other factors are also affecting relative prices. You must realize that the forces of supply and demand set prices only in a private enterprise system. In a command economy, such as in the Soviet Union or Communist China, government planners set many prices. These planners may have to give in to the forces of supply and demand eventually, but they try to counter them in the short run.

Summary   1.   In deciding what and how much to buy, people generally make decisions on the basis of relative price.

2.   Collectively, consumers greatly influence the relative price of everything bought and sold in the economy.

3.   As people obtain more and more of a particular thing, they value each additional unit less and less. This principle is known as the *law of diminishing utility.*

4.   Because of the law of diminishing utility, people will stop buying a particular item when they believe the satisfaction or utility received is of less value than the item's cost.

5. Generally, as price decreases, demand increases. As price increases, demand decreases. This principle is known as the *law of demand*. It is an important factor in determining relative price.

6. Generally, as price increases, supply increases. As price decreases, supply decreases. This principle is known as the *law of supply*. It, too, is an important factor in determining price.

7. Both the law of demand and the law of supply can be shown by a table or a graph, as well as described in words. The line connecting prices and quantities is known as a *(demand or supply) curve*.

8. By combining supply and demand, one can find the equilibrium price that will prevail in the marketplace. The equilibrium price is found at the intersection of the supply and demand curves.

9. Prices are not really determined by supply and demand, but by the forces that determine supply and demand. These forces include many things, such as people's tastes and the ability to produce.

10. Although the forces of supply and demand generally determine prices in a private enterprise system, some prices might be set by legislation.

11. Most prices in a command economy are set by government planners.

Important Terms

demand curve	law of demand
relative price	equilibrium price
law of diminishing utility	supply curve
law of supply	

Review Questions

1. What is meant by relative price? Why is it important?

2. What is the law of diminishing utility? Why should it be called the law of diminishing *additional* utility?

3. How does the law of diminishing utility affect the willingness to buy?

4. How is demand affected by price? By income?

5. How may the law of demand be shown?

6. What does the law of demand represent?

7. What assumptions are basic to demand analysis?

8. How is supply affected by price?

9. What induces potential suppliers to become actual suppliers? Why were they not in business already?

10. How may the law of supply be shown?

11. How does a supply curve differ from a demand curve? How are the two curves similar?

12. How is an equilibrium price determined?

13. What is the difference between stable and unstable equilibrium?

14. What is the relationship between equilibrium price and quantity?

15. What factors determine price in a private enterprise system? Cite some examples.

Discussion Questions

1. How do you find the relative price of an item when all prices seem to be rising? Is an item's price important in helping you to decide whether or not to buy it? What other factors enter into your decision?

2. Do you think all things are subject to the law of diminishing utility? If so, why? If not, why not?

3. In theory, the laws of supply and demand suggest that supply will adjust to demand to reach a point of balance—the equilibrium price. Still, supply of or demand for a product can change. What factors do you think cause such change? What are the immediate effects of such change?

4. As noted in the chapter, not all prices are determined by the forces that determine supply and demand. In a command economy, prices are set by central planners. What effect do you think setting prices has on demand and supply? Do, in fact, the laws of supply and demand ultimately affect the prices planners set? Why or why not?

Projects

1. Interview a local merchant to learn what effect a recent price change on a popular item has had on its volume of sales (quantity demanded). Does this tend to support the theory of the law of demand? Why or why not? Ask the owner the reasons for the change in price. Do the reasons support the principles of supply-demand analysis? If so, how? If not, why not?

2. Construct a demand curve and a supply curve for skateboards, based on the data provided in the following tables.

Price per skateboard	Quantity demanded per year
$ 75	3 million
$ 50	6 million
$ 35	9 million
$ 25	12 million
$ 15	15 million
$ 10	18 million

Price per skateboard	Quantity supplied per year
$ 75	18 million
$ 50	15 million
$ 35	12 million
$ 25	9 million
$ 15	6 million
$ 10	3 million

What is the equilibrium price? What is the quantity supplied and demanded?

Founder of Modern Economics

In 1776 the Declaration of Independence was drafted by the Second Continental Congress in Philadelphia. This document was an eloquent statement setting forth a doctrine of political freedom for the American colonies. In the same year, *An Inquiry into the Nature and Causes of the Wealth of Nations* was published. Its author was Adam Smith. Like the Declaration of Independence, Smith's work stressed freedom—economic freedom.

Adam Smith was born in Scotland and went to college at Oxford University in England. Apparently not satisfied with his education in the English university system, Smith acquired much of his knowledge from out-of-class reading. He was not just interested in economics. His interests ranged from physics and astronomy to literature and the arts.

After leaving Oxford, Smith became a lecturer in literature and philosophy at the University of Glasgow in Scotland. Eventually he was appointed professor of logic and philosophy—at that time economics was taught under the name of *moral philosophy.*

Smith was the first major advocate of economic freedom. He talked in terms of "free" or "unrestricted" market actions in the economy. He believed the self-interest of people would lead them to do what was not only best for themselves, but also best for the economy and society as a whole. This idea underlies Smith's doctrine of the "invisible hand." According to Smith, the economy is guided as if by an invisible hand when all individuals are allowed to do what they want to improve their standard of living. Since the invisible hand is at work at all times, there is no need for government help to make things run smoothly.

Another term used to describe Adam Smith's basic theory of economics is *laissez-faire,* a French term that means "do not interfere." To be sure, Smith recognized that government should do certain things for the people. It should provide for national defense, domestic tranquillity, and the like. But it should not hinder activities in the economy in any way.

Smith did not write solely about *laissez-faire* policy. He also wrote about industrialization and the production process, especially about the division of labor. He was one of the first to understand the advantages of having individuals specialize in particular jobs. He pointed out that if individuals specialize in particular productive activities they can pool their talents to produce more and thus consume more.

Most economists consider Adam Smith the founder of modern economics. He pointed out the benefits from unrestrained competition in an economy free from government interference. And he pointed out the benefits of specialization or the division of labor. His writings eventually convinced many people that governments should not only stay out of domestic economic activities but also should refrain from involvement in international economic dealings.

9

Business Organization and Competition

Preview Questions

1. How does a person start a business?
2. What risks do businesses take?
3. Are all businesses organized in the same way?
4. How do businesses compete?

Definitions of New Terms

Money capital: Money capital is money that an individual or individuals have invested in a business venture.

Inventory: Inventory is a supply of whatever items are used in a business, such as raw materials, parts, or goods for sale.

Short-term working capital: Short-term working capital is money that a businessperson needs for a short period of time and plans to pay back after selling the goods or services created by it.

Entrepreneur: An entrepreneur is an individual who takes a risk by investing money in a business venture in which there is no guarantee that a profit on that money will be made.

Proprietorship: A proprietorship is a business owned by one person.

Liability: Liability is the amount of debt or responsibility that a person has. Limited liability is an aspect of corporate ownership. Under limited liability, a stockholder's financial liability is limited to the amount his or her shares cost. In other words, the stockholder cannot be personally held liable for additional debts or suits against the corporation in which he or she owns shares.

Partnership: A partnership is a business owned by two or more individuals.

Corporation: A corporation is a business made up of an association of stockholders. The corporation itself is considered to be an artificial being (a legal entity) by the courts.

Articles of incorporation: The articles of incorporation are a set of rules for and a description of a corporation. They include the corporation's name, purpose, and address, its board of directors, and its original capital funding.

Corporate income tax: Corporations must pay a corporate income tax to the government on their profits.

Profit maximization: Profit maximization is the assumption that businesses seek to make as much profit as possible.

Competition: Competition is vying with others for a goal or prize.

Perfect competition: Perfect competition is a model in which so many firms are selling, or supplying, a particular product and so many buyers are buying that no one seller or buyer could influence the price.

Mixed economy: A mixed economy is one in which there is both private enterprise and government ownership and/or regulation of economic activity.

Suppose that you have been tinkering with electronic equipment since the age of seven. By now you can take apart and reassemble radios and television sets without difficulty. In fact, you are so good at repairing electronic equipment that you have been fixing your friends' portable radios and old television sets. Thus, the idea comes to you: Why not make some money? Why not do electronic repairs for other people and charge for your work? That is, why not start a business? How can you begin?

Starting a Business

To start a business, you need to make potential customers aware that your services are available for a fee. One way to do this is by word of mouth. That is, you tell your friends and relatives, who tell their friends that you are in the repair business. Another way to make your business known is to print business cards and distribute them in the area. Yet another way is to buy advertising space in the local newspaper. A three- or four-line advertisement in the classified section will probably not cost more than a few dollars a week. You can also run what is called a *space ad* in a nonclassified section of the paper. But that costs more.

Once you get customers, information about your business will spread if they are satisfied with your work. Satisfied customers will tell their friends about your work and what it cost. Information gets around. Nevertheless, you can help it along by using advertising.

Buying Equipment

As the number of your customers increases, you may want to buy more sophisticated equipment to handle more complex problems and to do work faster. To buy new equipment, you will need money. Perhaps your parents or a friend will lend you ***money capital***—the cash you need to buy equipment to increase the income you earn from your business.

You will also need replacement parts. At first, you might buy parts as you need them for a specific job. But if you need certain parts for many jobs, you may want to have some ***inventory***. That is, you may want a supply of parts on hand so that you do not have to go to a supply shop for each job. When you have inventory, you have money tied up in it. Of course, your customers will repay you for the parts as you use them.

When starting a new business, there are many ways of advertising to attract customers. Some types of advertising may be more effective than others, depending on the nature of the business. Can you give some examples of this?

Sometimes you may find you need major parts for a repair job. These parts may take more capital than you have on hand. Again you might face the problem of obtaining ***short-term working capital***—the money you need only until you have finished the job and the customer has paid.

If you had a well-established business, you might get a bank loan. Instead, why not ask the customer whose radio or television needs major repair to pay in advance? But this might not be convenient for the customer. In addition, most of the other electronic repair shops in the area probably do not require prepayment for major repairs. For you to do so would put you at a competitive disadvantage.

Hence, you look for short-term working capital from whoever will loan it to you. Some friend might agree to do so if you are willing to pay him or her interest. Obviously, the cost of borrowing is a business expense.

Keeping Records

From the start of your business, you need to keep records. You need to know how much money you are making and how much taxes you may owe. Of course, you may not be making enough profit to owe taxes. Nevertheless, you need a record of all of your expenses and receipts. Basically, your profits are the difference between your expenses and receipts.[1]

Taking Risks

As a combination repairperson and businessperson, you are taking many risks. They may not seem big, but they exist nonetheless. For

[1]Actually, not all of the difference is profit. After all, your time is worth something. You could be working for somebody else and making income. Therefore, you should pay yourself a wage equal to what you could earn elsewhere. This can be counted as part of the cost of doing business. If you add it to your other expenses and subtract the total from receipts, you get a truer measure of what economists call *(economic) profit.*

example, if you spend part of your savings to pay for advertising and equipment, you are risking money. You may not get sufficient business to cover these costs. Whenever you buy inventory, you are taking a risk. Your business could drop off so that you never use them, or you could be forced to sell them at a loss. Whenever you buy a major part for a repair job, you are taking a risk. Suppose you do the repair job but your customer refuses to pay the bill. Even if you are left with the radio or television set, you may not be able to sell it or get enough money to cover your costs.

You are even taking a risk with the time you spend to set up the business. That is, it will take you time to think about what to do, to write the ads, to set up the bookkeeping. That time has a value. You could have used it to do something else, including working for someone else for a wage.

Notice that if you work for somebody else, you take essentially only the risk of not being paid. As a worker, you take little risk. As an **entrepreneur** (a businessperson), you take many risks. However, you expect to make a profit as a reward for taking them.

Types of Businesses

A Sole Proprietorship

The business just described has the most basic type of business organization, the **proprietorship.** A *sole* proprietorship, also called an *individual* proprietorship, is a business owned by one person. It is the oldest form of business organization. It is also the most common. Today there are more than 10 million sole proprietorships in the United States. You may know of hundreds in your area—beauty parlors, fruit stands, repair shops, drugstores, hobby shops, liquor stores, etc. Many doctors, dentists, lawyers, and accountants also practice as sole proprietors.

Advantages of a sole proprietorship.   There are many advantages to operating a sole proprietorship. Here are a few.

1. *The proprietor receives all profits.* As sole owner, the proprietor gets all the profits because he or she takes all the risks.

2. *Pride of ownership.* Because a proprietorship is owned by one individual, that person has full pride in owning it. The person is his or her own boss and makes the business whatever it is.

3. *Ease of starting a business.* Since the proprietor makes all decisions, starting a proprietorship is less difficult than types of businesses that require agreement with the people involved.

There are many risks to owning your own business. Do you know people who own their own business? Are their reasons for wanting to be sole proprietors different from the advantages listed here?

4. *Freedom from corporate income taxes.* A proprietor does not pay corporate income taxes, which will be discussed later. Of course, he or she does have to pay personal income taxes on profits. These taxes may be lower than those for a different type of business organization, however.

Disadvantages of a sole proprietorship. Obviously, a proprietorship has disadvantages. They must be less than the advantages, however, or proprietorships would not be so widespread in the United States.

1. *Responsibility for all losses.* As sole owner, the proprietor bears the risk of all losses.

2. *Limited capital.* The proprietor is limited by his or her own funds and those that others will lend. This is perhaps the greatest disadvantage. It is very difficult for a business to grow with little capital.

3. *Unlimited liability.* The proprietor has **liability,** or legal responsibility, for all debts and damages incurred in doing business. For example, if the proprietor of a repair service wired a television set incorrectly and it blew up, he or she could be held responsible and sued for damages. If someone were injured, the legal responsibility might extend to all of the proprietor's personal wealth.

Taking on a Partner

Let us now suppose that your repair business is doing very well. You find that your workload has increased to the point where your studies are suffering. You find that you do not have time to see your friends or go to the movies. You have several choices. You could refuse to take on more business. You could discourage business by charging higher prices. Or you could expand your business.

One way to expand is to take on a partner (or hire an employee). You also want to buy more sophisticated equipment. So you look for somebody who has skills similar to yours and who has money to put into business expansion. When you find this person, you make a proposal to share ownership of the business. That is, you offer to form a *partnership.*

A partnership is any business that two or more individuals own and operate for profit. A written agreement is usually drawn up when a partnership is formed. You probably know of numerous partnerships in your area. Many lawyers, doctors, and dentists, as well as small retail stores, are partnerships.

Advantages of a partnership.   Partnerships are formed because they offer advantages not found in a sole proprietorship.

1.   *More capital.* A partnership combines the capital of two or more people. It makes more money available to operate a larger and perhaps more profitable business. If each partner has a good credit rating, the partnership can generally borrow more money than a sole proprietorship.

2.   *Greater efficiency.* Partnerships are usually more efficient than proprietorships. They allow each partner to specialize in certain aspects of the business, thereby making it more efficient.

Disadvantages of a partnership.   A partnership also has disadvantages. You can decide whether a partnership has more or fewer disadvantages than a sole proprietorship.

1.   *Unlimited liability.* Complete legal responsibility is a major disadvantage in a sole proprietorship. As a partner, however, one is responsible for the debts of other partners as well as his or her own. As a partner, one may have an even greater legal responsibility for debts than if that person owned a business alone.

2.   *Profits must be shared.* Obviously, since partners share the risks of the business, they also share the profits.

3.   *Possible disagreement.* In partnerships, disagreements regarding necessary decisions can lead to severe problems in running the business.

The number of small businesses—that is, businesses with liabilities under $100,000—changes daily. In the last four years, small businesses accounted for 80 percent of all business failures. In 1953, Congress passed the Small Business Act to assist small business firms. This act created the Small Business Administration (SBA). The SBA counsels, assists, and protects the interests of small businesses. It also makes loans to small businesses.

The Corporate World

In terms of the volume of business transacted in the United States today, by far the most important type of business operation is the corporation. Corporations provide most of the goods that people buy. Although they constitute only 10 to 12 percent of all business firms, they collect almost 75 percent of all business receipts.

The corporate form made possible large-scale business. It was a key to the development of American industry and to the growth of the nation as the most industrial in the world.

A *corporation* is an artificial being. It has a separate and distinct existence from those of the human beings who control it. That is, it enjoys many of the same legal powers, such as the rights to buy and sell property, enter into contracts, and sue or be sued. In other words, it is a legal entity.

Forming a corporation.   Let us continue our supposition about your repair business. Your business has grown until you have several partners, and you have converted your garage into a workshop. But still you are not satisfied. You think that you are more efficient than many other firms in the city. You want to expand again. In fact, you would like to rent a store so that your business would be more visible. You would like to buy the latest automated repair equipment, charge a little less than similar businesses, and capture a larger share of the market. But you do not have the capital to do all these things.

What you want are financial backers who would let you use their money and would not bother you about how you ran the business. You do not want more partners, because then you would have to consult with them about every detail of business.

Therefore, what you want to do is form a corporation. **That** is, you want to sell shares of stock in the business to raise capital. The shares represent ownership rights to a certain proportion of the profits of a corporation. Here are two things you must do to start a corporation and sell stock.

1. *Register the corporation.* State and federal laws govern the formation of all corporations. Most state laws are similar, although they vary according to the type of corporation to be formed. People who are forming corporations generally need to consult a lawyer to have him or her draw up ***articles of incorporation.*** These articles include four items: (a) the name, address, and purpose of the corporation, (b) the names and addresses of the initial board of directors, (c) the number of directors, and (d) the amount of capital to be put into the

Corporations make up a small percentage of business firms in the United States but account for a large part of the business receipts. Why do you feel this is so?

corporation. The articles of incorporation and an application for a charter (or certificate) of incorporation are sent to the appropriate state or federal agency. If the articles comply with the laws, a charter will be granted.

2.   *Choose a board of directors.* Every corporation must be controlled by a board of directors. The board is elected by the stockholders, the people who own the corporation. The bylaws of the corporation govern the election. The bylaws describe a time and place of the stockholders' meeting at which the board of directors is elected. The directors are responsible for supervising and controlling the corporation. However, they do not generally perform daily business operations. Rather, the board selects company officers—a president, vice-president(s), secretary, and treasurer—to run the business. Figure 9-1 shows a typical major corporate organization.

Stock in a corporation.   Chapter 7 discussed the various types of corporate stock sold on stock exchanges. Basically, shares of stock represent ownership rights to the profits of a corporation. You could sell shares of either common or preferred stock in your new repair service corporation. If your corporation became large, you might find that its stock would be traded in a local over-the-counter stock market and listed in the local newspapers. Should it continue to grow, it would be traded on a regional exchange and might eventually be traded on one of the national exchanges.

Other ways to raise capital.   Selling stock is not the only way for a corporation to raise capital to develop or expand. A corporation can

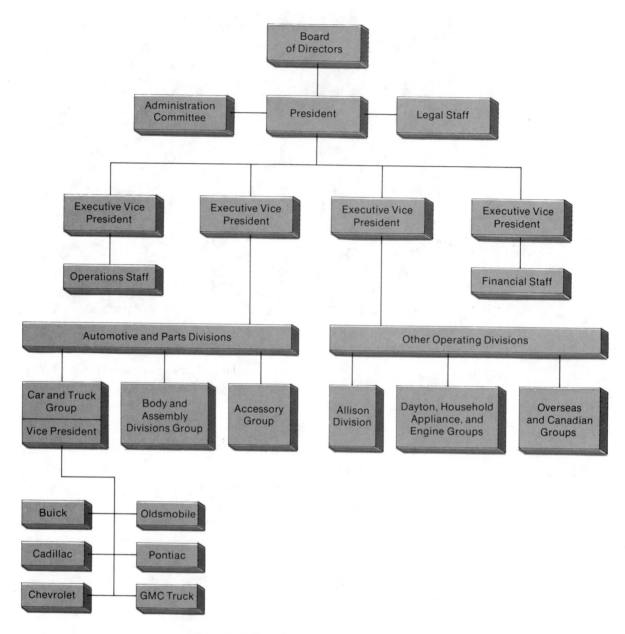

Figure 9-1. Organization chart for General Motors Corporation.

also sell debt. That is, it can issue bonds. It also can reinvest some (or all) of the profits in the business rather than distributing them among the stockholders.

Advantages of a corporation.   There are three major advantages to the corporate form of business.

1. *Greater capital.* Ownership shares in a corporation are sold to people who risk only their investment. A corporation can raise more capital than either a sole proprietorship or a partnership because of the stockholders' limited risk.

2. *Limited liability.* A stockholder in a corporation generally limits his or her liability to the money invested. Many people consider limited liability to be the major advantage of the corporate form of business. If a corporation goes bankrupt or is sued, stockholders generally cannot be asked to pay more than the value of their stock. They pay by having the market value of their stock reduced or eliminated.

3. *Unlimited life.* When the owner of a sole proprietorship dies, his or her business ceases to exist. When one partner in a partnership dies, the partnership ceases to exist. It must be reformed. The existence of a corporation can continue indefinitely if it continues to be profitable. The life of the corporation is not affected by the death of owners, because the shares are transferable.

Disadvantages of a corporation.   The corporate form of business has two chief disadvantages.

1. *Federal and state taxes.* The federal income tax on corporations is a problem that proprietorships and partnerships do not face. The **corporate income tax** is levied on the profits of all corporations. In addition, some states and localities tax corporation profits or property. A state may also tax a corporation for the right to carry on business within its boundaries.

2. *Increased government control.* Since corporations are chartered by government agencies, these agencies are generally more concerned with corporate activities than with those of other forms of businesses. Therefore, there are numerous laws and enforcement procedures that affect corporations but not partnerships or proprietorships.

The advantages of a corporation far outweigh its disadvantages. Corporations dominate the business scene in the United States today. Some of them are larger than the economies of many nations. Table 9-1 lists the 10 largest corporations in the United States. You may already be familiar with most of them. Some of them employ a virtual army of workers and control a kingdom of assets. The financial pages of most daily newspapers will give the latest stock quotations for these corporations.

Other Forms of Business Organizations   There are several other forms of business organizations. Space does not permit a detailed discussion of them, however. One of the more common forms is the cooperative, which is owned by its members who share any profits. Perhaps the most popular cooperatives are consumer and farmer cooperatives.

Table 9-1: Top Ten Corporations in the United States

	Total Number of Employees	(000) Assets	(000) Sales
1. Exxon	137,000	$36,331,346	$48,630,817
2. General Motors	681,000	24,442,400	47,181,000
3. Ford Motor Company	416,120	15,768,100	28,830,600
4. Texaco	75,235	18,183,818	26,451,851
5. Mobil Oil	71,300	18,767,450	26,062,570
6. Standard Oil of California	38,801	13,765,397	19,434,133
7. Gulf Oil Company	52,100	13,449,000	16,451,000
8. IBM	288,647	17,723,326	16,304,333
9. General Electric	375,000	12,049,700	15,697,300
10. Chrysler	217,594	7,074,365	15,537,788

Source: *Fortune,* May 1977, "The *Fortune* Directory of the 500 Largest U.S. Industrial Corporations."

Government-owned and government-operated corporations are another type of business organization. Examples include the post office and many public utility (water, gas, and electric) companies.

Competition and How It Works

At least in theory, the private enterprise system is based on competition among businesses. Regardless of its form, each business attempts to capture as large a share of the market as possible.

In talking about competition, one assumes that most business owners prefer higher profits to lower profits. This assumption should not be too surprising. Observation of the real world confirms the theory of *profit maximization*—that individuals in business try to make as much profit as possible.

To describe profit maximization is neither to condemn nor condone the behavior. Economics is amoral, because it is a science. That is, there is no morality involved in economic analysis, although it deals with many issues that have moral aspects. To assume profit maximization on the part of businesspersons is merely to make a convenient assumption, no more and no less.

How does a businessperson attempt to maximize profits? He or she tries to make a product or offer a service that appeals to a sufficiently large number of people to get a market. Once that market is established, the businessperson will attempt to expand it, thereby increasing profits. The businessperson will look for ways of improving the product or service so that it will appeal to new customers as well as to keep present customers. Various means will be tried to reduce cost in order to lower the price. Lower price helps to induce more customers to buy.

Generally, much competition in the business world can be analyzed as one would analyze competition in a sporting event or a classroom. *Competition,* vying with another for a goal or prize, takes various forms. Nevertheless, it is basically the same throughout society.

Competition as a Model

Discussion to this point has outlined how competition works in the real world. Some observers of the economy, however, like to talk about the model situation of *perfect competition.* Perfect competition never has and most likely never will exist. Still, it is interesting to compare the real situation with a model.

Perfect competition could exist only in a very special situation. If there were literally thousands of sellers of a product, one seller could not possibly change the price of the product. It is all the sellers together who determine the supply of the product. The supply, in turn, interacts with the demand so that an equilibrium price is reached. Each individual seller accepts that price. Perfect competition involves such large numbers of sellers that none of them individually affects anything.

Alternatively, on the demand side, perfect competition requires a large number of informed buyers. They all know exactly what the going price is. These buyers would never buy the product at a higher price. Yet the sellers would never sell at a lower price.

Competition in the American Economy

Although there is much competition in the American economy, there are a number of industries that are dominated by large corporations. In such cases, those industries are anything but perfectly competitive. In fact, most people talk more about the economy in terms of industries that are *not* competitive. Chapter 10 discusses such noncompetitive situations.

Moreover, once a person realizes that perfect competition does not exist, then that person expects to see competition taking on forms other than changes in prices. That is, he or she expects to see businesses vying with each other on the basis of changes in the quality of products. These changes may involve nothing more than packaging or advertising. One must also realize that, since the goal of businesses is to maximize profits, some firms try to maximize profits by buying up smaller firms, thereby eliminating competition. This topic will also be discussed in Chapter 10.

In the United States, there is one market with nearly perfect competition. This is the agricultural market. A product such as corn or wheat is so highly uniform that information about it can be obtained quickly. Information about its price and quality is readily available. Further, there are literally tens of thousands of farmers (sellers or suppliers), so that no one farmer can affect the selling price.

Issue 9 examines competition in agriculture. It describes how effective the forces of supply and demand are in that industry. It also looks at ways government can influence price. When government enters into the economic picture, a capitalist economy moves to what today is called a ***mixed economy.*** A mixed economy has both private enterprise and government ownership and/or regulation of economic activity.

Summary

1. In order to start a business, a person needs capital.

2. A person in business must keep records.

3. Being in business means taking risks.

4. There are three major types of business organizations—proprietorships, partnerships, and corporations.

5. Each type of business organization has distinct advantages and disadvantages. These center on capital, liability, ease of starting, decision making, and taxation.

6. A corporation must be registered in at least one state. Each state has its own rules about chartering corporations.

7. Every corporation has a board of directors.

8. When businesses attempt to expand or to enter existing markets, they compete with other businesses.

9. Businesses try to maximize profit.

10. In a system of perfect competition, there are so many sellers and buyers that no one seller or buyer can influence the price of a good or service.

Important Terms

articles of incorporation	inventory
partnership	competition
liability	perfect competition
corporate income tax	mixed economy
profit maximization	corporation
money capital	proprietorship
entrepreneur	short-term working capital

Review Questions

1. What does a person need to start a business?

2. What is short-term working capital? Who needs it? How can it be obtained?

3. Why is it important to keep accurate records when in business?

4. Who are the people who take risks in the business world? Explain why and how.

5. What is a proprietorship? What are its advantages and disadvantages?

6. What is a partnership? What are the advantages and disadvantages of them?

7. What is a corporation? What are its advantages and disadvantages?

8. What is necessary to form a corporation?

9. In addition to proprietorships, partnerships, and corporations, there are other types of business organizations. Can you name any?

10. What do all businesses attempt to do? How?

11. Why does perfect competition not exist?

12. What is a mixed economy?

Discussion Questions

1. In the business world, inventories can consist of many things, including raw materials, parts, and finished goods. Why do you think some firms maintain inventories of finished goods? What firms would not be able to have large inventories?

2. Some people believe the corporate form of business is the most important in the United States. Do you agree? Why or why not? If you were in business, what kind of business organization would you prefer? Why?

3. Many Americans are in business for themselves. Would you prefer to own your own business instead of working for someone else? Why or why not? What are the advantages? the disadvantages?

4. One goal of businesses and businesspersons is to maximize profits. What other goals may they have?

Projects

1. Invite a local merchant to speak to the class on the advantages and disadvantages of owning one's own business. Is the merchant a sole proprietor or a partner in a partnership? Which type of business organization does the merchant favor? Why?

2. Visit an office of the U.S. Internal Revenue Service (IRS) in your area to obtain information on the corporate income tax. Report what you learn to the class. Does the rate seem high? Who pays it?

3. Several government and private organizations exist to serve the interests of business and businesspersons. Two of the most important are the Small Business Administration, a government agency that assists and protects the interests of small business, and the National Federation of Independent Business, a nonprofit private business association. Write to one of these organizations to find out how it assists the small businessperson; report your findings to the class. The addresses for the two organizations are as follows:

a. Small Business Administration, 1441 L Street NW, Washington, DC 20416

b. National Federation of Independent Business, 150 West 20th Avenue, San Mateo, CA 94403

ISSUE 9

Competition and the Agricultural Industry

Definitions of New Terms

Price supports: A price support is a price maintained by the government on basic farm products through various kinds of programs. Historically, price supports have been greater than the equilibrium, or competitive, price of the farm product.

Price insensitivity: Price insensitivity exists when variations in relative price do not result in much change in quantity demanded.

Surplus: Surplus is the difference between a higher quantity supplied and a lower quantity demanded.

If you have ever gone shopping for food, you know that the prices for some food sometimes seem "too" high. You might even complain about how expensive bread, coffee, sugar, and meat have become. Despite high prices, however, you probably have noticed that some food items have lower prices at certain times of the year. Specifically, fruits and vegetables are cheaper in warmer months than in colder months of the year.

Why does this occur? Why does the price of produce fall in summer and rise in winter? It is easier to grow fruits and vegetables in warmer months than in colder months. Thus, the total quantity available is much greater in summer. Given the amount that people demand, the only way produce suppliers can sell all of the available supply is by lowering the price. If you recall the law of demand, people buy more of something at a lower price than they do at a higher price. Thus, it seems reasonable that with an increase in supply, the only way to get people to buy that greater supply is for the suppliers to lower the price. And, indeed, they do lower the price of produce in summer.

An Example— The Wheat Market

Basically, the prices of agricultural products in the United States are determined by the interaction of supply and demand. Let us look at one example of this.

There are literally thousands of wheat farmers in the United States. All of the wheat farmers collectively determine the amount of wheat that is put on the market for sale each year. Each individual wheat farmer contributes such a small part of the total quantity, however, that in fact no one farmer has any significant influence on price.

148 Markets, Prices, and Types of Business

The demand for most food products does not change significantly regardless of variations in price. What other products could be called price insensitive?

The price of wheat is determined by the interaction of supply and demand. The supply is the total supply produced by all farmers raising wheat. The demand is the total demand for all uses of wheat in making bread, cakes, pastries, and other wheat products. The equilibrium price is the price at the point where supply and demand are equal.

Individual wheat farmers have to accept the going market price. For example, if the going price of wheat is $5 per bushel, that is what each farmer has to accept. Farmers who attempt to raise their price above $5 per bushel will find that no one will buy their wheat. Hence, the individual farmer takes the price of wheat as given and cannot influence it. This is a characteristic of a highly competitive market. In fact, the wheat market approaches very closely the idea of perfect competition discussed in Chapter 9.

The Demand for Wheat

The demand for wheat is somewhat different than the demand for many other products. People's demand for wheat is relatively unresponsive to changes in price. That is, even if the relative price of wheat falls dramatically, not much more wheat will be sold. A major reason for this is there are only so many uses to which people can put wheat. Moreover, people can only eat so much wheat. After that, even a much lower price does not induce them to eat more.

Food in general has a demand that is relatively **price insensitive.** That is, variations in the relative price of food do not result in much change in the quantity of food demanded. Table I–9–1 shows the price responsiveness of the demand for food. For wheat, a 1 percent increase in price will only bring about a 0.08 percent decrease in the quantity demanded.

Table I-9-1: How Food Buyers React to Changes in Food Prices

Commodity	If price goes up by 1%, then the quantity demanded falls by
Beef	0.92%
Sugar	0.31%
Corn	0.49%
Cotton	0.12%
Hay	0.73%
Wheat	0.08%
Potatoes	0.31%
Oats	0.56%
Barley	0.39%
Buckwheat	0.99%

Source: H. Schultz, *Theory & Measurement of Demand* (Chicago: University of Chicago Press, 1938).

The relative price insensitivity for wheat has implications for variations in the price of wheat over time because of variations in the supplies of wheat. After all, consumers are not going to buy much more wheat, even if the price falls. If there happens to be a huge crop one year, the only way wheat farmers will be able to get rid of most of the crop is by lowering price drastically. But when they drastically lower price, they will get lower incomes. Naturally, they will not be happy about that outcome. Farmers are really at the mercy of weather conditions.

The Supply Side of the Wheat Market

The supply side of the wheat market is relatively unique, as is the supply side of most agricultural markets. The supply of agricultural products is highly dependent on conditions—such as variations in the weather—over which farmers have little control. Moreover, a new type of crop disease or crop-destroying insect can wipe out entire crops.

These variations in the determinants of the supply of wheat and other agricultural products mean that farmers may have a huge bumper crop one year because the sun and rain were right and there were no pests or diseases. The next year, they may have a poor harvest, no matter how hard they work, because of insufficient sun, an early freeze, and many insects.

Therefore, people expect to see widely fluctuating supplies of wheat and other goods in the agricultural market. One year there may be a good crop; next year there may not be. In the absence of any restrictions on price, people also expect large fluctuations in the price of an agricultural product, such as wheat, as compared to other goods. In fact, in those situations where there are no government controls on the price that farmers charge, there are large fluctuations. That is why, during the Great Depression of the 1930s, a government program was begun to even out the fluctuations in the prices of wheat, corn, cotton, barley, tobacco, and many other agricultural products.

Yet, given a knowledge of the laws of supply and demand, one could suspect that attempts to even out price fluctuations might create problems. And there have been problems. In fact, some have caused embarrassment to the United States government. Before turning to that subject, however, let us take a brief look at attempts to help out the agricultural sector in the American economy.

Agricultural Program in the United States

In 1933, Congress passed the Agricultural Adjustment Act, which created the Agricultural Adjustment Administration (AAA). The AAA's purpose was to keep the prices of farm products from dropping further, in order to keep the income of farmers up. The AAA attempted to stabilize farm prices by putting restrictions on the amount of wheat, corn, and other basic agricultural crops that could be offered for sale. This makes sense, according to the law of demand. The only way to get rid of a large amount of wheat, for example, is to offer it at a lower price. Hence, if wheat farmers offer a much smaller quantity, the price that will "clear the market" can be much higher. In other words, a restriction on the supply allows farmers to charge higher prices and not have any wheat left over.

The AAA was rather unsuccessful, however, in keeping farmers from producing "too much" wheat and corn. Thus, another way to keep the price of those products up was devised. It involved **price supports.** Since the 1930s, price supports have been paid for such agricultural products as wheat, feed grains, tobacco, cotton, rice, peanuts, soybeans, dairy products, and sugar.

Price Supports

A price-support system is precisely what the name implies. The government supports, or fixes, the price of an agricultural product at a particular level. That level is usually higher than would exist without government support. That is, the price support is set at a level that exceeds the market price that would be determined by the interaction of supply and demand.

Price supports produce two contrary effects. On the one hand, consumers react to relatively higher prices by buying less of a product than they would buy at lower prices. On the other hand, suppliers (farmers) react in the opposite direction by producing more. As you know, at relatively higher prices, it is more profitable to produce more.

As a result of these effects, at price-support levels that exceed an equilibrium price, there is a difference between the quantity supplied, which is relatively larger, and the quantity demanded, which is smaller. The difference is often called a **surplus.** But a surplus cannot exist very long without government support, because farmers would ultimately be forced to accept lower prices to get rid of their huge inventories.

Under the program that was in effect for many years, the federal government allowed farmers to sell "surpluses" to the Commodity Credit Corporation (CCC). In principle, the CCC was only giving each farmer a kind of loan. That is, the farmer would give the CCC all of the wheat or corn on which he or she wanted to "borrow money." The CCC, in turn, would "loan" the farmer the support price times the number of bushels of wheat or corn that the farmer gave to the CCC.

Surpluses Grew

Whenever a price support was set high enough, farmers produced and sold to the CCC immense quantities of surplus price-supported agricultural products. By the mid-1950s, the CCC had begun to stockpile ever larger inventories of surplus farm products it had purchased.

Throughout most of the 1960s, the government's stockpiles grew. Meanwhile, new programs to have farmers reduce production by reducing acreage planted did not meet with great success. Through technological developments, farmers were able to get ever-increasing yields per acre.

Finally, however, the world demand for food became so great that the price at which the quantity supplied equaled the quantity demanded for some products—especially wheat—was higher than the support prices. Thus, the government got rid of all of its "surpluses" in 1973. That year saw numerous crop failures elsewhere in the world. Many countries thus turned to the United States to obtain needed agricultural products. This increased demand for American agricultural products drove the price up. For a couple of years, then, the price-support program for many agricultural commodities was actually inoperative. The price-support level was below the prices that actually prevailed in the world agricultural markets.

Whether price supports will again become effective is uncertain at the moment. Starting in 1975, bills were presented in Congress to raise the price-support levels. One thing is certain, however: **whenever the market price falls below the price-support price, people can expect to see "surpluses" again.**

Summary

1. In general, agriculture in the United States is a good example of a highly competitive market.

2. For most basic crops such as corn or wheat, there are thousands of farmers (suppliers).

3. No one farmer can generally affect the market (equilibrium) price. Each must sell his or her crop at the going price.

4. Since the 1930s, there have been special federal programs to help keep farmers' incomes up.

5. Price-support programs have existed for many agricultural products. Usually the price-support level is higher than the market price that would be determined by the interaction of supply and demand.

6. Whenever the price-support level is higher than the market equilibrium price, surpluses result.

7. World market demands in recent years have resulted in great reductions in government surpluses in agricultural products, especially wheat.

Important Terms

price insensitivity   surplus
price supports

Questions for Thought and Discussion

1. The agricultural sector of the economy is considered to be highly competitive. Why? What kind of control do farmers have over supply? What problems does this create?

2. What are price supports? How do they work? Who wants them? Why?

3. Since the 1930s, the federal government has had price-support programs for farmers. What are the arguments in favor of helping farmers this way? Do you approve of this kind of federal assistance? Why or why not?

4. Is it important that the price of a particular farm commodity remain stable? Why or why not?

10

Monopolies and How to Control Them

Preview Questions

1. How does one form a monopoly?
2. Why would one want to be a monopolist?
3. What forms do monopolies take?
4. How are monopolies regulated?
5. What is the government's antitrust policy?

Definitions of New Terms

Monopoly: A monopoly exists whenever there is only a single seller or supplier of a product.

Barriers to entry: A barrier to entry is any situation or condition that prevents potential competitors from entering a profitable industry.

Oligopoly: An oligopoly exists whenever there are only a few sellers or suppliers of a product.

Monopolistic competition: Monopolistic competition exists whenever there are many sellers of slightly differentiated products.

Antitrust policy: Antitrust policy consists of laws and regulatory activity seeking to prevent the formation or continuation of monopolies.

Injunction: An injunction is a court order to cease and desist from a certain activity.

When you turn on lights to read, you are using the output of the electric power company in your area. How many companies offer to sell you electricity? Only one, right? Because there is only one power company from whom you can buy electricity, that company is a **monopoly.** The word *monopoly* comes from the Greek words *monos* meaning "one" or "single," and *pōlein*, meaning "to sell."

Most electric power companies are monopolies because an agency of the government has granted them monopoly power. That is, the government has given various electric power companies the sole rights to operate in certain geographical areas. You and your friends could not pool your money, buy a small generator, and sell electricity to people in your neighborhood. That would be illegal, because government regulations do not allow it.

When you talk on the telephone, you are using the services of another monopolist. In most areas of the country, telephone service is provided by a Bell company of the American Telephone and Telegraph system. Until recently, the telephone you used was also produced by a single supplier.

When you mail a letter, you are using the services of a government

Your phone service is one example of a monopoly. How do monopolies such as this affect you as a consumer?

monopoly. Various groups are testing the legality of the federal government to restrict first-class mail service to the U.S. Postal Service. Nevertheless, at this time first-class service remains a government-owned and government-controlled monopoly.

How to Become a Monopolist

How is a monopoly formed? Can an individual become a monopolist? It is not easy. Although there are many ways to become a monopolist, few work in the long run. In the first place, a monopoly implies that there is little or no competition. Thus, there must be some reason why other people are barred from setting up competing companies. These obstacles to competitors are called *barriers to entry*.

Barriers to Entry

One barrier to entry is government regulation. It is impossible to enter the electric utility business where another is already operating because the government does not permit it. The government creates the barrier to entry. One cannot start a telephone system, because the government will prevent it. The most obvious barriers to entry, therefore, are legal ones.

Another barrier to entry is the cost of getting started. Setting up an electric power company—building a dam, buying generators, stringing power lines—is so costly that it does not pay to compete with an existing firm. The same is true regarding telephone service. The amount needed for start-up expenses to produce a competing phone system is immense. In other words, this barrier to entry is excessive *capital* costs. Raising sufficient money to purchase the necessary equipment, resources, and the like is difficult and unlikely.

Ownership of essential raw materials can also provide a barrier to entry. A classic example is the diamond industry. The DeBeers Company of South Africa controls the export of nearly all of the world's diamond mine output. An example from the past is the Aluminum Company of America (ALCOA). At the turn of the twentieth century, it controlled almost all of the basic sources of bauxite, the major ore used to produce aluminum. For many years, ALCOA was able to retain its near monopoly in aluminum because it would not sell bauxite to any potential competitor.

Why Be a Monopolist?

Why would anyone want to be a monopolist? To answer this question, let us continue discussing the supposition begun in Chapter 9—that you own a small electronic repair business.

Suppose your business was in a very small town. At the time you began your business, there were no other repair services. You would be a monopolist. Then suddenly, someone who knew as much as you did about the repair business moved into your area and started another repair service. How would that person attract customers? One of the easiest ways is to offer the same quality of service at a

As suggested by this early cartoon, large businesses can and have used their power to drive smaller competitors out of business.

lower price. This would induce some people to give business to the new entrant.

For a short time, you would probably not notice much change. But eventually you would find your profits decreasing as customers went to your lower-priced competitor. To regain a competitive advantage, you then would lower your prices. This could lead to a price war. The lowering of prices could continue to the point at which neither you nor your competitor could afford to lower prices further. That is, the price war could continue until neither you nor your competitor were able to cover the costs of doing business. To lower prices further would mean that it would not pay to stay in business.

To avoid this type of competitive situation—making less profit than you made when you had the only repair service—you would obviously want to reach an agreement with your competitor. You would want to form a new monopoly in which both you and your competitor agreed to raise prices and not undercut each other. If the agreement was kept, the total profits made by you and your competitor would be greater than if you were competing. But such arrangements usually do not last long.

Let us again ask, why be a monopolist? In simple terms, a monopolist generally makes higher profits than competitors do.

Forms of Monopoly

When a business has a true monopoly selling a good or service, that business is, by definition, an entire industry. There are few pure monopolies. Nevertheless, there are several less pure forms of monopoly in the United States today. These less stringent forms of monopoly have more than one seller of a good or service. Economists call the two most common forms *oligopoly,* meaning few sellers, and *monopolistic competition,* meaning many sellers, each selling a slightly different product.

Oligopoly

An oligopoly is a market structure characterized by a few firms that depend on each other. Presumably, each firm makes its own pricing policies with an eye to how rival producers will react. The main characteristic of an oligopoly is that any change in one firm's output or price influences the profits and sales of its existing competitors. Thus, an oligopolist will attempt to anticipate changes in pricing and output policies of other firms before changing its policies.

Perhaps you can name some oligopolies. The automobile industry is dominated by three large corporations—General Motors, Ford, and Chrysler. Although the steel industry has numerous firms, the four largest account for more than 60 percent of the industry's steel ingot capacity each year. Economists maintain that these firms must take into account the reactions of the others each time they contemplate a price change. One of the most basic observations about an oligopolistic industry is that when one firm changes its prices, others generally follow suit immediately.

Table 10-1 shows a number of industries in which the four largest

Table 10-1: Industry Concentrations

Industry	Percent of Industry Output Produced by Four Largest Firms
Primary aluminum	100%
Passenger cars	99
Locomotives and parts	97
Steam engines and turbines	93
Sewing machines	93
Electric lamps (bulbs)	92
Telephone and telegraph equipment	92
Gypsum products	84
Synthetic fibers	82
Cigarettes	80

Source: United States Senate, Subcommittee on Antitrust and Monopoly Concentration Ratios in the Manufacturing Industry, 1973.

firms produce more than 80 percent of the total industry output. The firms in all of these industries are oligopolies. The fact that the four largest in each industry produce most of the industry's output does not necessarily mean the situation should be changed. In fact, a surprising aspect of the general criticism of oligopolies is that often little proof is given about the harmful effects of such an industry structure. To define an industry as oligopolistic says nothing about an *alternative* market structure and what the *costs* of getting such an alternative might involve.

Monopolistic Competition

In the 1920s and 1930s, economists became increasingly dissatisfied with talking only about the extremes of market structure—perfect competition and perfect monopoly. They started to develop some theoretical and practical research on some sort of middle ground. The most popular and best-received theory was that of monopolistic competition. Edward Chamberlin, a Harvard economics professor, presented the principles in *The Theory of Monopolistic Competition* in 1933.

Chamberlin defined monopolistic competition as a situation in which a relatively large number of producers offer similar but slightly different products. Obvious examples are such brand name items as toothpaste, cosmetics, and gasoline. Each firm within the industry has some special product identity, even though the differences between its products and its competitors' products may indeed be very small. Nonetheless, Chamberlin presumed that each producer selling its differentiated product was a partial monopolist.

In monopolistic competition, each producer has such a small part of the industry that it faces neither the total industry demand nor even a *large* part of it, as an oligopolist does. Still, each monopolistic competitor has some control over the price of its product. That control is slight, however, because many substitutes—other brand name products—are available.

Chamberlin found it useful to group together all firms producing similar products. He called them a *product group*. The way to combine firms into various product groups is well defined. But no way exists to decide how much alike substitutes must be in order to be included in the same product group. In other words, it is hard to define a product group accurately.

Regulating Monopolies and Oligopolies

One reason that many economists and legislators oppose monopolies is that monopolies generally charge a higher price than would prevail in a competitive situation. People pay more for products furnished by a monopolist than they would for those furnished by competitors. People also buy less of such products.

The federal and state governments have not been content to let monopolies form or, once formed, charge high prices. Through the years, these governments have established regulations and regulatory agencies to force monopolies and oligopolies to act in certain ways in the public interest. They have also passed laws that attack monopolies directly. This legislation is called *antitrust, trust* being another word for *monopoly*. **Antitrust policy** is concerned with preventing new monopolies from forming with and breaking up those that already exist.

Antitrust Policy

One of the many aims of government in the United States is to foster competition in the economy. To this end, many laws have been passed in opposition to business practices that seem to weaken greatly competition or destroy it. Let us now briefly examine the two major federal antitrust acts in operation today.

The Sherman Antitrust Act

The first major antitrust law passed by Congress was the Sherman Antitrust Act of 1890. The most important provisions of the act are:

Section 1: *Every contract, combination in the form of trust or otherwise, or conspiracy, in restraint of trade or commerce among the several states, or with foreign nations, is hereby declared to be illegal.* Section 2: *Every person who shall monopolize, or attempt to monopolize, or combine or conspire with any other person or persons to monopolize any part of the trade or commerce . . . shall be guilty of a misdemeanor.*

Notice how vague the wording of the act actually is. No definition is given for *restraint of trade* or *monopolize*. Despite its vagueness, however, the act was used to prosecute the Standard Oil Trust of New Jersey.

In 1906, Standard Oil was charged with violating Sections 1 and 2 of the Sherman Antitrust Act. At that time, Standard Oil controlled more than 80 percent of the nation's oil-refining capacity. Among other charges, Standard Oil was accused of cutting prices to drive competing companies out of business. It was also accused of obtaining preferential price treatment from the railroads for transporting its products. This enabled Standard Oil to cut prices.

Standard Oil was first convicted in a U.S. district court. The company then appealed to the U.S. Supreme Court. The Supreme Court ruled that Standard Oil's control of and power over the oil market created an obvious "presumption of intent and purpose to maintain dominancy . . . not as a result from normal methods of industrial development, but by means of combination." The court's reference to *combination* meant taking over other businesses and obtaining preferential price treatment from railroads. The Supreme Court forced the Standard Oil Trust to break itself into many smaller companies.

The Supreme Court ruling came about because the justices believed that Standard Oil had used "unreasonable" attempts at restraining trade. The court did not rule against monopoly in itself. The fact that Standard Oil had the major share of the oil market did not matter. Rather, the problem was the way in which Standard Oil had acquired its share.

The Clayton Antitrust Act   The Sherman Act was so vague that a new law was passed to sharpen its antitrust provisions. This second law was the Clayton Antitrust Act of 1914. The Clayton Antitrust Act prohibits or limits a number of specific business practices that were viewed as "unreasonable" attempts at restraining trade. Some of the more important sections of the act are:

Section 2: *It is illegal to discriminate in price between different purchases (except in cases where differences are due to differences in selling or transportation costs).*
Section 3: *Producers cannot sell on the condition, agreement, or understanding that the . . . purchaser thereof shall not use or deal in the goods . . . of a competitor or competitors of the seller.*
Section 7: *Corporations cannot hold stock in another company where the effect . . . may be to substantially lessen competition.*

Notice that these provisions outlaw practices that tend to lessen competition "substantially." Because it is not clear what *substantially* actually means, the courts have a difficult time interpreting the law.

Antitrust Enforcement Today

Vigorous antitrust enforcement is still a goal of the U.S. Department of Justice and the Federal Trade Commission. In recent years, several large companies have been prosecuted for attempts at restraining competition. IBM has had an antitrust suit against it. The three major car-rental firms—Hertz, Avis, and National—have also been prosecuted.

Periodically, one will see in the newspaper or hear on news broadcasts that another large company has had an antitrust suit filed against it. Such suits are usually brought by the government acting in the public interest. Occasionally a competitor will file suit, seeking an ***injunction*** (a cease and desist order) against certain practices that the competitor contends are illegal, noncompetitive, and harmful.

Summary

1. Many monopolies are formed with the help of government regulations and laws. The government has also expressly created some monopolies, such as the U.S. Postal Service.

2. To maintain a monopoly, one must set up barriers of entry to prevent potential competitors from entering the industry.

3. A monopolistic business can make higher profits than it could make in a competitive situation.

4. There are numerous oligopolies in the United States. These are industries (markets), such as exist for automobiles and steel, that are controlled by a few major suppliers.

5. Monopolistic competition involves an industry or market in which there are many sellers of slightly differentiated products.

6. One of the many aims of government in the United States is to foster competition in the economy.

7. The federal government has enacted antitrust legislation to prevent monopolies and monopolistic practices considered to be in restraint of trade. The two major antitrust laws are the Sherman Antitrust Act of 1890 and the Clayton Antitrust Act of 1914.

8. Over the years, many large companies have been prosecuted by the government for violating antitrust laws.

Important Terms

antitrust policy	monopolistic competition
barriers to entry	monopoly
injunction	oligopoly

Review Questions

1. What is a monopoly?

2. Why would a business want to be a monopoly?

3. What are three common barriers to entry in certain industries?

4. How does an oligopoly differ from a pure monopoly?

5. How is monopolistic competition distinguished from pure competition?

6. What is antitrust legislation?

7. What are the two principal federal antitrust laws in operation today? What are their chief provisions?

Discussion Questions

1. Generally a monopoly can make higher profits than it could make in a competitive situation. Why? Is a business that is a monopoly guaranteed high profits? Why or why not?

2. There are barriers to entry in business. When barriers to entry exist, are such industries monopolistic? Explain.

3. Which businesses do you think have the greater advantages—oligopolies or monopolistic competitors? Why?

4. Antitrust legislation makes restraint of trade illegal. What is restraint of trade? What business practices do you think would be viewed as being in restraint of trade?

5. Do you think that the government should promote or prevent the formation of monopolies? Why?

Projects
1. Visit or call the local office of the telephone company or electric power company to obtain information on how it is regulated by the government. Can it change any rates it so chooses? How are rates set?

2. In addition to the Standard Oil Trust case, there have been other historically famous antitrust cases, such as the Northern Securities case of 1904 and the American Tobacco case of 1911. Research one of these cases at the library and report on it to the class.

3. Make a list of industries that you think are characterized by monopoly. In a report, describe how one of these industries evolved into a monopoly. Do you think that the industry should be a monopoly? Why or why not?

4. Make a list of industries you think have the characteristics of monopolistic competition. Are there more than you might list as competitive? What does this indicate about American business?

Robinson

Ward

Women in Economics

Joan Robinson is considered one of the world's most important contemporary economists. Born in England, she attended St. Paul's Girls School in London and Girton College in Cambridge. She has taught for more than 40 years and today is a professor of economics at Cambridge University.

Robinson has written and lectured widely on economic theory. Her important books include *Introduction to the Theory of Employment, The Accumulation of Capital, Economic Philosophy,* and *Freedom and Necessity: An Introduction to the Study of Society.*.

Joan Robinson believes the main fact behind most economic thought is that "the pursuit of self-interest by each individual rebounds to the benefit of all." This means everyone can benefit if each person has concern for his or her own well-being and advantages.

In *Economic Heresies: Some Old-Fashioned Questions in Economic Theory,* published in 1971, Robinson wrote that the growth of monopolies is inherent in the nature of competition in capitalist society. "The majority of businesses are either growing, being forced to close down because of the growth of other businesses, or being absorbed into some larger organization."

Barbara Ward was also born in England. Today she is one of the world's most widely read economic writers. She is the author of *Faith and Freedom, The Interplay of East and West, Five Ideas that Changed the World,* and *India and the West.*

Both as a writer and a speaker, Ward is known for the clearness with which she can make complex issues understandable to the layperson. She has lectured extensively in the United States and has contributed numerous articles to *Foreign Affairs, Harper's, New York Times Magazine,* and *Atlantic.*

In 1949 Ward became one of only two women to have addressed the New York State Chamber of Commerce. She was a visiting scholar at Harvard University from 1958 to 1968 and became an Albert Schweitzer Professor of International Economic Development from 1968 to 1973. She has received honorary doctorate degrees from Smith, Fordham, Columbia, and Harvard universities.

Besides being an author and lecturer on political and international economic affairs, she has been a governor of the British Broadcasting Company and of London's Old Vic Theater.

Why Do Businesses Advertise?

Definitions of New Terms

Competitive advertising:
Competitive advertising attempts to persuade consumers that the products being advertised are different and superior. It is really defensive advertising used to prevent other firms from taking away customers.

Informative advertising: Informative advertising gives information about the product. In most cases, informative ads are considered to benefit consumers.

When you turn on the radio, you will more than likely hear a commercial. When you travel, you will see advertising all around you—billboards, posters on buses, and so on. If you watch TV, you will again be bombarded with commercials. If you read a newspaper or magazine, you will see advertisements on most pages. In fact, it seems that few phases of American life escape advertising.

Figure I–10–1 shows the average amount, in dollars, spent in the United States on advertising *per capita*—that is, for every man, woman, and child. In 1935, $13.28 per person was spent on advertising. By 1978, that figure had risen to an estimated $190. Part of the increase in spending for advertising can be accounted for by the general rise in prices. But even correcting for rises in prices, the figure has steadily increased. The total amount of advertising in any one year is now in excess of $40 billion.

Why Use Advertising?
There must be a good reason why Americans are subjected to so much advertising and why advertising is increasing each year. Look at it from the advertiser's point of view. Most businesspersons are in business for one reason—to make money. They would not advertise if they did not think that advertising could make them more money or help them keep their current sales and level of profits.

Chapter 9 discussed various types of business organizations and competition. A market in which there was perfect competition would not need advertising. In perfect competition, any business is such a small part of the market that it has no effect on the market and no control over what price can be charged for a product. There would be no need to advertise in such a market because, by definition, the perfect competitor can sell all of its output at the market price.

The world is not perfect, however. Perfect competition is not what people see around them. What they see are various grades of imperfect competition in which businesses find that it pays to advertise products, prices, and various positive features of service.

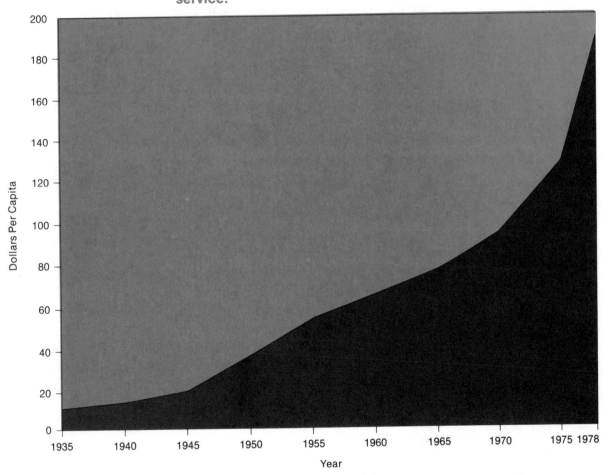

Figure I-10-1. Advertising expenditures per capita in the United States. Expressed in purchasing power of dollars that actually existed in each year, per capita advertising expenditures have been rising quite rapidly in the United States. The estimate for 1978 is almost $190 per every American. Source: McCann-Erikson Advertising Agency, Inc., for *Printer's Ink* Publications, New York, 1935–1966. *Market Communications,* 1966–1969. After 1970, *Advertising Age* (Crain Communications).

The question might then be asked: How do businesses justify all the advertising they are doing? From a common sense point of view, they must believe that the additional sales generated by advertising will at least cover the costs of advertising. In this sense, advertising can be treated like most other expenditures (a variable cost of business). If advertising does not pay for itself, it will be reduced. If it more than pays for itself, it will be expanded.

In monopolistic competition, advertising helps to establish the differentiated product. People in such businesses have recognized this fact, and it is they who have brought on the advertising explosion. They believe that more advertising yields more than enough additional sales to justify the expense. When one looks at advertising in this way, one also comes to a stark realization about who ultimately pays for it.

Who Pays for Advertising?

Since business people are out to make money for themselves, they certainly do not plan to lose money by advertising. It is only when they err about the profitability of a particular advertising campaign that they take a loss on that expenditure. In general, the cost of advertising is built into the price of the products people buy.

This statement should not be a surprise. After all, the costs of labor and raw materials are built into the price of all products people buy. So are the costs of buildings, machines, and resources. Why should not the cost of advertising be built into the price of advertised products?

Is Advertising "Good" or "Bad"?

Advertising exists on a grand scale in the United States. Since businesses advertise only to the degree that it pays, increased advertising must at least pay for the costs of that increased advertising. But for society as a whole, is advertising good or bad? A definite answer cannot be given; it is a value judgement. Nevertheless, to many, advertising does have good and bad points.

To the extent that advertising is informative, consumers benefit from it. They can learn about the existence, prices, and qualities of various products they might want to buy without necessarily expending much time or effort. Advertising can provide information about products to consumers at a relatively low cost.

To the extent that advertising intensifies competition among sellers (suppliers), consumers also benefit. As you know, competition often leads to lower prices. If several competing sellers make information about themselves well known through advertising, then consumers will have more information to choose the best deal. People will go to the seller that gives them the best deal. That means advertising can prevent sellers from selling a product at a higher price than competitors.

Not all advertising, however, leads to information that consumers can use. Nor does it necessarily lead to lower prices for the things people buy. Some advertising seems to have little information content whatsoever. A common example cited by advertising critics is cigarette advertising. Those ads do not seem to say anything of value about the product. In fact, most cigarette ads are representative of the type of advertising known as **competitive advertising,** as opposed to **informative advertising.** Competitive advertising does not attempt to provide consumers with useful information to make them more rational shoppers. Its chief purpose is to promote products in a manner that allows those in an industry to keep selling the same amounts that they have always been selling. Thus, competitive advertising does not carry with it the beneficial side effects that informative advertising does.

Summary

1. Advertising is a common aspect of American life. Over $40 billion is spent in advertising every year.

2. Businesses advertise because they believe that advertising will promote additional profits exceeding its costs.

3. Consumers ultimately pay for advertising in the form of higher prices for advertised products.

4. Advertising can be informative or competitive.

Important Terms

competitive advertising   per capita
informative advertising

Questions for Thought and Discussion

1. In what types of industries would you expect to see more advertising—highly competitive industries or monopolistic industries? Why?

2. Why do you think oligopolists advertise?

3. What is the difference between informative and competitive advertising? Can one always draw the line? Explain.

4. If you were in charge of deciding if an advertisement was informative or competitive, how would you make your decision? Would your criteria be any different if you knew that your decision would determine whether the ad in question would be allowed or banned by law?

UNIT FOUR

Labor and Production

11

Labor and Its Wages

Preview Questions

1. What determines the wages workers receive?
2. What determines the supply of labor?
3. Why has the average work week in the United States become shorter in the last 50 years?

Definitions of New Terms

Labor force: The labor force of a society consist of all of the people who are classified as employed or unemployed. That is, the labor force is made up of all of the people who could work, whether or not they are working.

Wages: Wages are the price paid for labor services.

Employee: An employee is a person who works for another and is paid a wage.

Employer: An employer is a person or agency who pays another to work for him or her.

Productivity: Productivity is the ability to produce goods or services. The greater a worker's productivity, the more that worker produces in any period of time.

Participation rate: Participation rate is the percentage of the working-age population in the labor force *or* the percentage of a specific group employed.

When you finish school, most likely you will look for work. (Some of you probably work already.) You will find that there are numerous jobs you could take. More important, you will find that different jobs pay workers different wages. One job may pay $4 per hour, while another job may pay $6 per hour.

The wage rates offered to people in the labor force are not determined mysteriously, however. Wage rates are determined by supply and demand, just like the prices for the things people buy. The only difference is that the item bought is labor, not hamburgers.

Before exploring in more detail what determines wage rates, let us first take a brief look at the American labor force.

The American Labor Force

The American labor force is composed of about 90 million workers. Almost everyone in the United States who works is part of the *labor force.* Officially, the civilian labor force includes all civilians who are classified as employed or unemployed. Members of the military services are not included, however. People under 16 and those in prisons, mental institutions, homes for the aged, or similar institutions are also not counted. Retired persons, some seasonal workers, and full-time students are also excluded much of the time.

Changes in the Labor Force

The size and makeup of the American labor force has changed dramatically in the 200 years since the nation's birth. Figure 11-1 shows how the size of the labor force has grown.

As the civilian labor force has grown, it has also changed dramatically. When the nation began, more than 95 percent of all workers were engaged in agricultural pursuits. Today only 4 to 5 percent of the nation's workers are in agriculture. As manufacturing became dominant, during the latter part of the nineteenth century, the United States became a less agriculturally oriented society.

In recent years, there has been a steady shift away from both manufacturing and agricultural work to the service sector of the economy. The service sector includes the work done by such individuals as auto mechanics, repair technicians, barbers and beauticians, teachers, and the like. Service workers do not produce goods as the result of their efforts. Figure 11-2 shows that the United

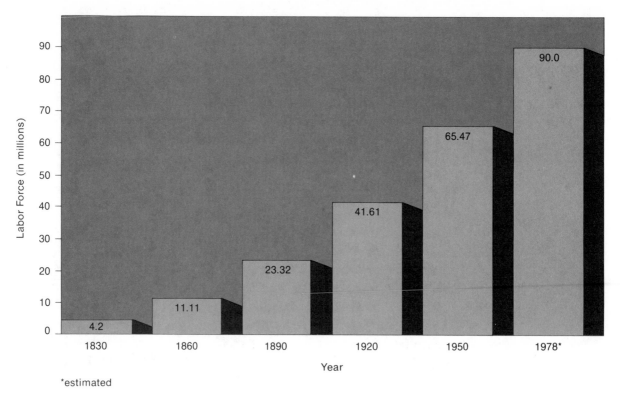

*estimated

Figure 11–1. Growth in the U.S. civilian labor force. Source: Bureau of Labor Statistics.

States is rapidly becoming a service economy as fewer members of the labor force work in manufacturing and agriculture.

Changes in Working Conditions

Not only has the composition of the labor force changed, but so have working conditions for most workers. Americans no longer take jobs in "sweat shops" or crowded factories with poor heat and ventilation and inadequate safety devices, where they work 10 to 12 hours a day, seven days a week. Except in a few cases, these job conditions have not existed for many years. They were not unusual, however, when this nation first became industrialized.

The possibility of a worker being injured on the job today is much lower than it was in the days of the 70-hour work week. Working conditions are much more pleasant. Today's factories are well lighted, evenly heated in winter, and often air conditioned in summer—all luxuries that no one dreamed of only 50 years ago.

What Determines How Much Workers Are Paid?

If you were offered a job at $2 per hour or at $5 per hour, which wage would you accept? Undoubtedly you would choose to work for $5 per hour. That wage would give you more income to do with as you wish. Generally, however, most workers never get a job that pays them as much as they want. No matter what the wage, it is normal to want a relatively higher wage.

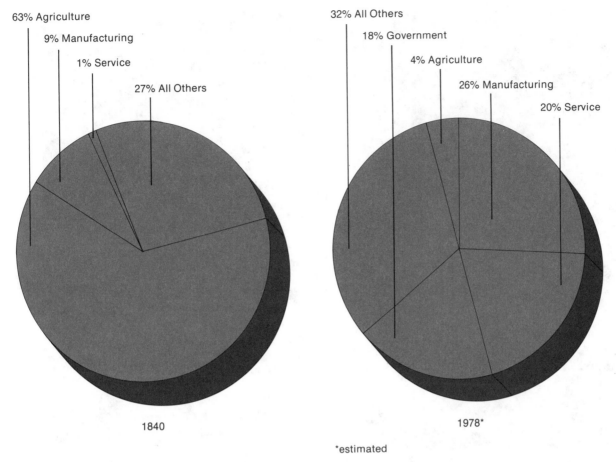

63% Agriculture

9% Manufacturing

1% Service

27% All Others

32% All Others

18% Government

4% Agriculture

26% Manufacturing

20% Service

1840

1978*

*estimated

Figure 11–2. Make-up of the American labor force. Source: Bureau of Labor Statistics.

Does this mean that workers are at the mercy of an impersonal marketplace? No; most American workers are paid a living wage. How the wage rate a worker receives is decided may seem a mystery, but it is not.

There is good reason why a restaurant worker, for example, may be offered $2.50 per hour instead of $1.00 or $5.00 when he or she applies for a job. In Chapter 8, you learned that there was a good reason why a product was offered for sale at a certain price. That chapter examined the ways that the basic forces underlying supply and demand establish an equilibrium price for all goods and services bought and sold. Supply and demand go a long way toward explaining how relative prices are determined in the economy.

The workings of supply and demand also apply to the price paid for labor. The demand and supply of labor can be treated just as the demand and supply of anything else—bicycles, cars, or razor blades. **Wages,** the price paid for labor services, are determined by the supply and demand of labor. The only real difference between the labor market and other markets is in the underlying factors that determine supply and demand.

As evidenced in these scenes, there have been many changes both in the type of work and the working conditions over the last 200 years for American labor. Do you think countries other than the U.S. will similarly change as they develop? Why or why not?

The Demand for Labor

Chapter 9 examined the problems of owning an electronic repair shop. Let us suppose that now you need some additional help. Therefore, you plan to hire a worker, an *employee.* What determines how much you as an *employer* will be willing to pay an employee? Assume for the moment that you are going to base your decision on very explicit, objective criteria. That is, you are not going to be influenced by any potential employee's personality, sex, age, or social standing. You are going to look only at how much to pay a potential employee for work done.

From this point of view, what is the *maximum* amount you would be willing to pay a worker? Here is one way to make your decision. First, interview each possible worker to find out what his or her qualifications are. Then try to estimate how well that worker would fit into your operation—what job skills the worker has. Basically, you determine how much additional repair servicing the business might do. Now you have an idea of the potential worker's *productivity*— that is, how much additional output the worker would generate as an employee. Of course, a worker's productivity is not the total indication of how valuable that person might be as an employee.

To measure fully the benefit of employing a worker, you, as an employer, must know how much the worker's output is actually worth to you. The only way you can find this out is to look at the selling price for the output. Assuming that you have had the repair service for a while, you know how much you can charge and receive in payment for repair services. Thus, you determine how many additional repair jobs can be done if you hire a worker and total up their respective prices. This figure gives you the additional productivity value that a worker would add to your business. It also represents the absolute maximum wage you should be willing to pay a worker. If you paid more than this amount, the wage would be more than the value of the employee to you.

Increasing Productivity

The demand for labor depends on two important items: How productive a worker is, and the price at which the worker's product can be sold. The latter is a function of market supply and market demand for the product.

A worker can control productivity. However, he or she has little control over the price at which products can be sold. The fact that workers can increase their productivity has some bearing on your current behavior. By going to school, you are increasing your potential productivity. Among other ways to increase potential productivity are receiving on-the-job training, or learning skills on your own. A worker's productivity will also be increased if he or she has larger, more efficient, and more sophisticated machines to use. But this is not a condition over which most workers have much control.

The fact that American workers can use many machines to increase productivity is probably the chief reason why they are paid more than workers in other nations. The average worker in Asia or Africa has far less machinery capable of increasing productivity at his or her disposal than the average worker in the United States. Thus, the higher productivity and standard of living of American workers reflects the technology available to them. Chart 11-1 compares the American standard of living, in terms of the amount of labor required to buy goods, with those in Great Britain and the Soviet Union.

The Supply of Labor

What determines how many hours per week and how many weeks per year a person is willing to work? Because so many psychological factors affect a decision of this kind, it is very difficult to suggest a complete analysis of a person's desire to work or not to work. Nonetheless, we can examine some of the factors that determine how many Americans, of those who actually could work, want to work at any one time. The proportion of those in any group able to work who want to work is called the *participation rate.*

Chart 11-1: Comparative Standard of Living

Commodity	Washington, D.C.	London	Moscow
White bread (1 kg.)	21 minutes	10 minutes	20 minutes
Hamburger meat, beef (1 kg.)	34 minutes	76 minutes	3.5 hours
Apples, eating (1 kg.)	16 minutes	24 minutes	5.4 hours
Sugar (1 kg.)	9 minutes	15 minutes	65 minutes
Milk (1 liter)	7 minutes	11 minutes	21 minutes
Eggs (10)	10 minutes	13 minutes	97 minutes
Vodka (0.7 liters)	67 minutes	3.4 hours	9.8 hours
Cigarettes (2)	10 minutes	27 minutes	23 minutes
Soap, toilet (150 grams)	5 minutes	10 minutes	72 minutes
Lipstick	31 minutes	54 minutes	7.8 hours
Men's shoes (black, leather)	6.7 hours	7.7 hours	36 hours
Man's business suit	25 hours	40 hours	106 hours
Refrigerator, small (150 liters)	47 hours	50 hours	168 hours
Color TV set, large (59cm. screen)	3.9 weeks	5.5 weeks	19.5 weeks
Small car (Fiat or Zhiguli)	6.9 months	11.1 months	3.1 years

Approximate worktime required for average manufacturing employee to buy selected commodities in retail stores in Washington, D.C., London, and Moscow. Source: National Federation of Independent Business, 1976.

Participation Rates

For the United States as a whole, some people who are not working will decide to enter the labor force when wage rates increase. In other words, as wages are raised, participation rates increase for groups who may not otherwise choose to be employed. These groups include homemakers, students, and retired people. Table 11-1 shows participation rates of certain groups at various times.

Numerous studies have attempted to explain such phenomena as the entry of women into the labor force during some phases of the business cycle but not during others. A major determinant has been found to be higher wage rates during boom times and lower wage rates during recessions. Higher participation rates are typical during boom periods.

From a psychological point of view, one might expect most people to put a positive value on leisure time. Therefore, in order to induce more people to work, employers must pay higher wages. Higher wage rates will induce more people to give up more of their leisure.

Another way to look at the choice of leisure or labor is to consider the cost of *not* working. The true cost is the highest value for the alternative use of a person's time. Suppose that the after-tax wage rate rose from $2 to $3 per hour and that a person not working has the opportunity to work at the higher wage rate. The true cost of *not* working now becomes $3 per hour instead of $2.

Table 11-1: Labor Force Participation Rates

The participation rates expressed here are percentages of the total population actually in the labor force. Thus, in 1960, 59.2 percent of the entire population was actually in the United States labor force. We see that the projection through 1985 shows almost no change in the participation rates for the total population.

Race and Sex	Participation Rates (Percent)					
	1960	1965	1970	1975	1980	1985
Total	59.2	58.8	60.3	60.1	60.5	60.8
White	58.8	58.5	60.2	60.0	60.3	60.6
Male	82.6	80.4	79.7	79.4	79.4	79.8
Female	36.0	37.7	42.0	41.8	42.5	42.7
Negro and other	63.0	62.1	61.1	61.4	61.6	62.0
Male	80.1	77.4	74.7	77.0	77.5	78.7
Female	47.2	48.1	48.9	47.4	47.1	46.9

Source: Department of Labor, Bureau of Labor Statistics

Combining Supply and Demand

Chapter 8 explained how demand for and supply of a good or service interact to reach an equilibrium price. The demand for labor and its supply also interact to set an equilibrium wage rate in the economy. This principle is greatly simplified because there are, in fact, many types of jobs at various wages. However, one can use supply and demand to discuss various submarkets within the entire labor market. One can also use supply and demand to generalize about what might happen on the average in the United States.

Summary

1. Until the latter part of the nineteenth century, most Americans were employed in agricultural work. Today, however, agricultural workers make up only 4 to 5 percent of the labor force.

2. Over the years, working conditions have improved greatly. The vast majority of workers no longer toil under unsafe conditions in crowded factories that are poorly ventilated. Nor do they work 10 to 12 hours a day for six or seven days a week at a subsistence wage.

3. The willingness of an employer to pay a worker a specific wage depends on the worker's productivity and on how much consumers value the worker's output.

4. Workers can influence their own productivity. The more productive they become, the more they can expect to earn, given any level of consumer demand for their output.

5. The supply of labor depends on several factors, including the relative wage rate. The higher the wage rate, the greater the number of people willing to work.

6. The participation rate of various classes of workers has changed. A higher percentage of women are working today than 50 years ago.

7. The wage rates in the economy are determined by the interaction of market demand for labor and market supply of labor.

Important Terms

employee
employer
labor force

participation rate
productivity
wages

Review Questions

1. How has the labor force in the United States changed since the nation's birth?

2. How have working conditions changed since the turn of the century?

3. What determines how much workers are paid?

4. How might one increase his or her productivity?

5. Why are American workers paid more than workers in most other nations?

6. What effect does productivity have on living standards?

7. What is the participation rate?

8. Why does the participation rate go down during a recession?

9. How are wage rates determined in the economy?

Discussion Questions

1. In recent years the percentage of workers employed in the service sector of the economy has steadily increased, while the percentages employed in manufacturing and agriculture have declined. What reasons can you cite for this trend?

2. Besides worker productivity and consumer demand for a worker's output, what other factors do you think have a bearing on a worker's value? Explain.

3. What reasons can you give for changes in participation rates? How is the participation rate affected by the status of the economy?

4. Most people work to earn income. What other reasons are there for working? Is the wage one will be paid always the most important reason for accepting a specific job offer? Explain.

Projects

1. With a group of students, conduct a survey on the wages and salaries of people in the area. Ask each participant why he or she thinks some workers are paid more than others. Report the findings to the class. Do the responses to the question on wage difference agree with the analysis in the chapter? If not, how do the answers differ?

2. Research the monthly participation rates for the past year for the various groups of workers listed in Table 11–1. The data on rates can be obtained from the U.S. Department of Labor's publication,

Monthly Labor Review. Do the rates change significantly during the year? If so, what reasons do you think account for such changes? If not, why?

3.   Organize a panel discussion on how a decline in employment (the participation rate) might be offset in periods of recession. In other words, how might unemployment be lessened or avoided?

Poverty and the Demand for Labor

Definitions of New Terms

Poverty: Poverty is relative. Currently it is defined by the U.S. Bureau of Census statistics on the costs of essentials for families of various sizes.

Welfare programs: Welfare programs are one means of providing purchasing power to the poor to buy essentials.

In-kind benefits: In-kind benefits are public assistance benefits, or welfare payments, such as food stamps and Medicaid.

Negative income tax: A negative income tax is a system of income transfers. Individuals who earn less than a certain level of income are taxed negatively—that is, paid money—by the government.

Work disincentive effect: A work disincentive effect results from any program that tends to make people who could work decide not to work.

From the founding of the nation until World War II, extreme differences in income narrowed remarkably. During the 1940s and 1950s, however, the percentage of income going to the lowest 20 percent of American wage earners changed very little. Because most Americans were earning more and living better, they thought **poverty** no longer existed in the United States.

A book published in 1962 changed that view. It also provided the incentive for President Lyndon B. Johnson's War on Poverty. The book, *The Other America,* was written by Michael Harrington.

Harrington lived among the poor in order to gather data about poverty. In *The Other America,* he wrote about a world of slums, of desolation, bitterness, discrimination, and hopelessness. He wrote about old people living alone in run-down tenement rooms. He stressed the need to use sociology as well as economics in order to reach a better understanding of poverty and poor people.

Harrington contended that the poor live in a subculture all their own. He also pointed out that most poor believe no one cares about them. Their world is isolated from the mainstream of American life. Harrington claimed that the poor are totally alienated from the values of middle-class America. Because the poor are mainly concerned with day-to-day survival, they are not inclined to try to understand or to integrate themselves into middle-class society.

What Is Poverty?

Because it can be defined in many ways, poverty is a *relative,* not an absolute, concept. Who is poor and who is not poor can be defined only in relative terms. The poor person today often has more income than a rich person had 200 years ago. Moreover, what is considered poverty in the United States today is considered luxury in many less-developed nations.

Thus, this book uses the definition of poverty established by the Bureau of the Census of the U.S. Department of Commerce. That specific definition changes every year, depending on the costs of essentials of life for families of different sizes. Table I–11–1 cites the bureau's definition of poverty for 1976. For a family of two adults and two children living in a city, the poverty line is $5,500. According to the bureau's definition of poverty, approximately 26 million persons could be classified as poor in 1976.

Who Are the Poor?

Specific, well-defined groups in the United States tend to have incomes below the poverty line. Those groups include members of racial and cultural minorities, the aged, the very young, rural residents, and female heads of households. Some people fit into more than one category. Chart I–11–1 describes some pertinent facts regarding these groups.

The Demand for Labor and Income Differences

One way to analyze the problem of poverty is to discover why there are such extreme differences in income among households in the United States. Today the bottom fifth (20 percent) of all wage earners gets only 5½ percent of the money income in the United States, whereas the top fifth gets about 40 percent. If there were no differences, the bottom fifth would earn one-fifth of all income, the next fifth would earn one-fifth, etc.

The Demand for Labor

The price of labor—wages—is determined like the price of most things in the economy, assuming, of course, there are no restrictions in the labor market. The price of labor is determined by the interaction of the supply of and the demand for labor. Basically, the demand for labor is a function of how productive each worker is. A worker's productivity is affected by intelligence, schooling, experience, and training. These factors are more fully described in Chart I–11–2.

One reason why some people are poor is they are not as productive as other individuals. They may lack innate charac-

Table I-11-1: Poverty Levels for Various Family Sizes 1976

Number in Family	Non-Farm	Farm
1 (14–64 yrs.)	$2,797.00	$2,396.00
1 (65 & older)	$2,581.00	$2,196.00
2 (where head of household is 14–64 yrs.)	$3,617.00	$3,079.00
2 (where head of household is 65 & older)	$3,257.00	$2,772.00
3	$4,293.00	$3,643.00
4	$5,500.00	$4,695.00
5	$6,499.00	$5,552.00
6	$7,316.00	$6,224.00
7 or more	$9,022.00	$7,639.00

Source: U.S. Census Bureau

teristics that would cause them to be more productive. They may have been denied adequate schooling or training. Or they may simply choose not to be productive. Other individuals are poor because they have been denied job opportunities that others in the society receive. In other words, racial or sexual job discrimination can prevent a worker from being paid according to his or her productivity.

The Supply Side

The price of anything is determined not only by demand but also by supply. The supply of workers who have few skills—those who are classified as unskilled—is quite large relative to the demand. This means that the price unskilled workers can charge for their

---

Chart I-11-1: The Disadvantaged in Our Society

Racial and cultural minorities. Minority groups composed mainly of blacks and individuals with Spanish surnames have a high incidence of poverty. Black families have a poverty rate more than three times that of white families. Rates for native Americans and Chicanos are even higher.

The aged. Families headed by individuals over 65 years old frequently have low levels of income. One out of every five poor families is headed by an elderly person. Many of the aged own their homes, so they spend less on this essential.

The young. The young, especially black teenagers, suffer from high rates of unemployment. One of the main causes of these high rates is the minimum wage law. The young, who are generally undertrained and undereducated, do not have high levels of productivity. As a result, they are not valued enough to be paid the minimum wage required by law.

Rural residents. Poverty is more common among families in rural areas than among families in urban areas. Families living on farms have poverty rates almost twice those of families living in cities. Data on farm incomes may be misleading because many farm families grow much of their food. Thus, they need to spend less for this essential.

Families headed by women. Almost 40 percent of all families headed by women with children are defined as poor. Among nonwhite women with children, the figure is nearly 60 percent.

Chart I-11-2: Factors Affecting Productivity

Factor influencing productivity	How this factor influences productivity	How individual can alter this factor
Intelligence	Allows worker to learn faster, grasp more complex ideas, etc.	Some believe that intelligence is purely innate; others believe it can be changed by environment.
Schooling	The more education a worker has, the more functions he or she can perform for an employer. An educated person will, therefore, be of more value to an employer.	Enroll part- or full-time in a vocational school, college, university, or adult education program to acquire more education.
Experience	An experienced worker will be able to apply knowledge gained by working at similar tasks. He or she will, therefore, work more efficiently and quickly. Hence, the worker will be more productive.	Learn as many aspects as possible of employer's firm or business by taking on new tasks when possible.
Training	On-the-job training in specific tasks, such as operating machinery or filling out forms, is often as important as formal schooling in increasing a worker's productivity.	When accepting a job, a worker should try to undergo as complete a training program as possible for the specific work he or she has been assigned to do.

services is relatively small. Hence, one reason many poor people earn such low wages is because they lack the skills that are in high demand. That is, they have only skills that are in great supply. The equilibrium wage rate for these unskilled workers is low, so they are classified as poor.

The Elimination of Poverty

The previous analysis suggests several ways in which poverty might be eliminated. The first, obviously, is to improve the productivity of poor people. This is being done by manpower training programs, job corps where unskilled poor people are given new skills, job retraining programs for those who have outmoded skills that can no longer be used, and improved educational opportunities for minority groups.

These are the direct ways of influencing the future productivity and earning power of relatively poor people in American society. To the extent that they are successful, they allow retrained workers to make higher incomes year in and year out. But what happens in the interim? What about the poor who cannot be retrained? What about women who have many children and no income-earning husband? How can they be helped? Many are helped, at least partially, by existing **welfare programs.**

Welfare Programs

Welfare programs are one means of providing purchasing power to the poor to buy essentials. Most welfare payments are made through programs that are partly or largely federally funded. Approximately 10 to 12 million Americans receive some form of welfare each month.

Welfare payments are not given out to just anyone, however. In fact, many poor people do not receive welfare. They cannot pass the so-called means tests. These tests are used by welfare agencies to compare a budget plan with the potential resources of those who apply for aid. Furthermore, in the past, many poor could not obtain public assistance because they failed to meet state or local minimum residency requirements. However, these requirements were recently voided by the U.S. Supreme Court as unconstitutional. Then, too, many poor do not know they are eligible. Others turn away because they feel shame at taking what they view as charity.

How Successful Has Welfare Been?

A poverty line has been established. If the line is not changed, "poverty" will ultimately be eliminated because all incomes in the United States are growing. But the poverty line does not stand still. Poverty is a relative concept. In 1985, when poverty by today's definition will have been eliminated in the United States, many Americans will still think there are a large number of poor. The difference will be that times will have changed and the definition of poverty will be different.

Even the most disgruntled taxpayer will agree that certain forms of poverty should be eliminated. For example, people unable to support themselves because of physical disabilities should be assisted. Many Americans cannot justify poverty in a nation of plenty. They want a more comprehensive program for redistributing income from the rich to the poor, even if the poor are working. Today's complex, often ineffective system frequently fails to help those in need. In fact, it assists many who are not in need.

Few economists will agree on a "correct" approach to income redistribution, however. Even fewer will admit that current income redistribution programs have had much effect. Nevertheless, some recent studies have shown that the relative standard of living of the lowest 20 percent of American wage earners has changed dramatically since World War II. While it is still true that this group receives only 5½ percent of money income, the figures change when the so-called in-kind benefits are included. In-kind benefits include food stamps, Medicare, Medicaid, public housing, education, and so forth. When a family receives food stamps, it receives an increase in its real income. When a family receives free medical care, it receives an increase

The term poverty has different meanings to different people. Ask a friend to define poverty. Do your definitions agree? Why or why not?

in its real income or standard of living. Professor E. K. Browning of the University of Virginia estimates that the lowest 20 percent of American wage earners actually receives 12.6 percent, rather than 5½ percent, of total income.[1] His results, of course, do not indicate that the battle against poverty has been won. Rather, his data point out that some headway in helping out the relatively poorest members of American society has been made.

Nonetheless, there can be improvements in public assistance programs. It appears that they have to some degree perpetuated a class of welfare recipients who are encouraged to remain unemployed. Other alternatives to the current welfare confusion must be found. Inescapably, any plan will cause some deterioration in the incentive to work. This is the cost society must bear for any type of income redistribution—a goal the society considers worthwhile.

Negative Taxes

One alternative to the present welfare system is a **negative income tax.** The negative income tax is not a tax, but a government payment to certain citizens. It uses the personal income tax system to make up the difference between the income of poor families and the income that society stipulates as the poverty line. The money would be paid to these citizens by

[1]Edgar K. Browning, "The Trend Toward Equality in the Distribution of Net Income," *Southern Economic Journal* (July 1976).

the U.S. Treasury according to a schedule based on family size and actual income earned. The plan would not require setting up a new system. It could be an extension of the fully computerized system that already exists.

The Case for a Negative Income Tax

Many economists favor a negative income tax. They point out that the negative income tax would not require the massive bureaucracy that now exists for administering public assistance, food stamps, and other programs. A negative income tax system might also restore dignity to the poor. Most welfare recipients must now fill out endless forms and generally submit to the snooping of a not altogether benevolent welfare bureaucracy. Furthermore, a negative income tax would free many of the resources now spent for the huge bureaucracy that runs various welfare programs. These resources could then be spent on other priorities, or used to provide the negative taxes (the government payment) to needy families.

The Case Against a Negative Income Tax

On the other hand, many economists oppose a negative income tax. They point out that a negative income tax might cost "too" much. In particular, if such current welfare programs as food stamps and subsidized housing cannot be dismantled, then the negative income tax would merely be an additional part of the welfare system. These critics contend that it would not really simplify the existing bureaucracy.

They also point out that any effective negative income tax would have a strong **work disincentive effect**. That is, the payoff for returning to work would be so small with an effective negative income tax program that many who could work would decide not to work.

Summary

1. According to sociologist Michael Harrington, the poor in the United States live in a subculture of their own. They are isolated from the mainstream of American life and are alienated from the values of middle-class America.

2. Poverty is a relative concept that can be defined in many ways. Poverty in the United States is defined by Bureau of Census statistics on the cost of essentials for families of various sizes.

3. According to the Bureau of Census definition of poverty, 26 million Americans could be classified as poor.

4. The ranks of the poor are made up largely, though not exclusively, of members of racial and cultural minorities, the aged, the very young, rural residents, and female heads of households.

5. One underlying cause of poverty is extreme differences in incomes among segments of a society's population.

6. One reason why incomes differ significantly in the United States is that individual productivity affects individual wages.

7. Productivity is affected by intelligence, schooling, experience, and training.

8. Some people are poor because they are not as productive as other individuals. Others are poor because they have been denied opportunities that many in the society receive.

9. One way to eliminate poverty is to improve the productivity of poor people through various types of job skill training programs.

10. The welfare system of the United States consists of a maze of programs.

11. Approximately 10 to 12 million Americans receive some form of welfare each month. Many poor, however, do not receive welfare, for various reasons.

12. Many economists support a negative income tax system as an alternative to some of the existing welfare programs. Other economists oppose the idea.

13. Some economists contend that many welfare programs have a built-in incentive for people not to work.

Important Terms

in-kind benefits
negative income tax
poverty

welfare programs
work disincentive effect

Questions for Thought and Discussion

1. Can poverty be eliminated completely? If so, how? If not, why?

2. How might discrimination cause increased income differences?

3. How would you define poverty? Do you agree that it is a relative concept? Why or why not?

4. Do you agree that in-kind benefits received should be considered part of a person's income in determining a person's standard of living? Why or why not?

5. Do you favor or oppose the adoption of a negative income tax system? Why?

12

Unions and the Labor Market

Preview Questions

1. What types of restrictions exist in the labor market?
2. What is the history of the labor movement?
3. How can labor unions help their members?
4. How can a labor union get wages raised?

Definitions of New Terms

Union: A union is an organization of workers whose goals are to improve working conditions and wages. The union bargains for the workers as a group to achieve their goals.

Collective bargaining: Collective bargaining is bargaining by union representatives for all workers in a company or industry. Such bargaining covers wages, fringe benefits, and working conditions.

Craft guild: Craft guilds were the original occupational associations formed during the Middle Ages to advance and protect the interests of members.

Craft union: A craft union is a labor organization of skilled workers in a specific craft or trade, such as shoemaking or printing.

Industrial union: An industrial union is a labor organization of all workers, skilled and unskilled, in an industry, such as all workers in the automobile industry.

Right-to-work law: A right-to-work law makes it illegal to require a person to be a union member in order to get a job in a particular firm.

Strike: A strike is a deliberate work stoppage by workers to force an employer to give in to their demands.

Picketing: Picketing is the practice of setting up lines to keep actual or potential workers from working for an employer during a strike.

Would you like to become a doctor, a dentist, a plumber, a carpenter, or a musician? If your answer is yes to any of these choices, you may find that desire alone is not enough. Many occupations in the United States are not freely open to anyone.

Certain restrictions in the labor market prevent people from casually entering professions, trades, or industries they might like to try. State or federal regulations may bar entry into a particular occupation. Some jobs and professions require specific study, practice under supervision, passing an examination, and paying a fee for a license. Other limitations are laws, such as the minimum wage statutes. Minimum wage laws can, in effect, reduce job opportunities for people who are young and inexperienced or who want to work temporarily or part-time.

A second restriction is discrimination. Discrimination by race or sex prevents many people from receiving wages equal to their worth or productivity. In some instances, it prevents them from entering certain occupations at all.

Union membership and union regulations are a third kind of restriction on the labor market. A labor or trade **union** is an

Unions in one form or another have existed since the middle ages. Today unions are not just limited to the craftsman or industrial worker but include service and professional workers.

association of wage earners organized to maintain or further their interests by bargaining as a group with their employer or employers. This is aptly called **collective bargaining.** To understand how unions function today, let us first look at how they began.

History of Unions

The concept of unions dates to the **craft guilds** of the Middle Ages. The medieval craft guilds, the first occupational associations, were formed by artisans in a particular field. Although the guilds were unable to obtain a monopoly over trade (each city had many crafts), they did restrict membership by requiring a long training period.

The training began with the apprenticeship of a boy to a guild master. After a successful training period, an apprentice became a journeyman—a free worker paid by the day. The journeyman was expected to save money to open his own shop. He was also required to work many years to provide proof of his technical competence before becoming a master craftsman.

The Labor Movement in the United States

The labor movement in the United States, like that in Europe, started with local associations of skilled workers called **craft unions.** Craft unions are organizations made up of workers in a specific trade, such as baking, shoemaking, or printing. The organizing efforts of many early craft unions were defeated by unfavorable court judgments. Table 12-1 shows the growth of union membership from the 1830s to the present.

With the rise of industry after the Civil War, the movement to organize labor on a national basis began to grow. In fact, the first permanent union on a national scale was formed in 1852. That union still exists as the International Typographical Union.

The Knights of Labor. The first important national labor organization was the Knights of Labor. It was formed in 1869 under the leadership of Uriah Stevens, a Philadelphia garment worker. By the late 1880s, its membership of both skilled and unskilled workers had grown to nearly 800,000. Although many of its demands, such as the eight-hour work day, were eventually to become accepted, the Knights of Labor rapidly lost popularity when it engaged in a number of violent, unsuccessful strikes. Its decline and ultimate demise was also hastened by the rise of the American Federation of Labor.

The American Federation of Labor (AFL). The American Federation of Labor (AFL) was formed in 1886 under the leadership of Samuel Gompers. Unlike the Knights of Labor, the AFL was a decentralized federation of independent national trade unions. Its membership was limited solely to skilled workers.

Through the strong leadership of Gompers, membership in the AFL steadily grew. In 1900, it had more than 500,000 members, and

Table 12-1: Union Membership in the United States

	Union Membership (Thousands)	Labor Force (Thousands)	Percent Organized
1830	26	4,200	.6
1860	5	11,110	.1
1870	300	12,930	2.3
1880	50	17,390	.3
1883	210	.—	—
1886	1,010	—	—
1890	325	23,320	1.4
1900	791	29,070	2.7
1910	2,116	37,480	5.6
1920	5,034	41,610	12.1
1930	3,632	48,830	7.4
1940	8,944	56,290	16.6
1945	14,796	65,600	22.6
1950	15,000	65,470	22.9
1960	18,117	74,060	24.5
1965	18,519	77,177	23.9
1970	20,689	85,903	24.1
1975	22,750	94,793	24.0
1977	23,257	96,104	24.2

Until 1900, union membership never exceeded 3 percent of the United States labor force. Union membership as a percentage of the labor force reached its peak in 1960 and has since slowly declined.

Source: L. Davis, *et al., American Economic Growth* (New York: Harper & Row, 1972), p. 220; and U.S. Department of Labor, Bureau of Labor Statistics.

on the eve of World War I, it had more than 2 million. A major reason for its growth was its acceptance of the capitalist system and its concentration on practical economic objectives—higher wages, shorter hours, and improved working conditions. Under Gompers' leadership, the AFL did not attempt to push a variety of social reforms or to engage directly in politics.

Although the AFL could claim that it spoke for the vast majority of organized labor, union membership began to decline in the 1920s. One reason for the decline was the antilabor attitude of many businesses that refused to recognize unions as the bargaining agents for workers. This attitude carried over to the courts, which ruled against such labor activities as picketing and boycotting. Still another reason was the fact that no national organization represented the hundreds of thousands of unskilled workers employed in industry.

The Congress of Industrial Organizations (CIO). It was not until the depths of the Great Depression that the unskilled workers of industry acquired union representation. A group of dissident AFL

leaders, headed by John Mitchell, recognized the need to organize labor on lines other than a craft basis. In 1935 they formed the Congress of Industrial Organizations (CIO). Unlike the AFL, the CIO organized all workers in an industry, skilled and unskilled.

With the emergence of *industrial unions,* union membership grew rapidly. By 1955, when the AFL and CIO merged into one national labor organization, organized labor had over 17½ million members. One of the major underlying causes of this growth was government support of labor, which began with a series of laws passed by Congress during the Great Depression.

Federal Legislation

In 1929 the Great Depression began. It lasted throughout the 1930s. A desperate nation looked for a new leader. In 1932 Franklin Delano Roosevelt was elected President. Roosevelt felt that one way to combat depression was to get rid of "wasteful, cut-throat competition." He wanted to allow management organizations to join together to decide industrywide prices and quantities. He also wanted to encourage organizations of workers.

The National Industrial Recovery Act. During the early days of Roosevelt's New Deal administration, Congress passed the National Industrial Recovery Act. This act was originally intended to apply only to large industries, which were to draw up codes of fair practice. But the National Recovery Administration (NRA) became ambitious and soon established a national code, known as the President's Reemployment Agreement. The NRA was supposed to grant "justice to the worker."

The Wagner Act. The National Industrial Recovery Act was declared unconstitutional by the Supreme Court in 1935. Section 7a of that act had given workers the right to organize. This right was promptly reaffirmed by the passage of the National Labor Relations Act (NLRA), otherwise known as the Wagner Act. The Wagner Act was based on the argument that the bargaining power of workers as individuals was not equal to that of large businesses.

Among other rights, the Wagner Act guaranteed workers the right to engage in collective bargaining and to belong to any union. The Wagner Act, which openly encouraged labor and the growth of unions, has been called labor's Magna Carta.

The Taft-Hartley Act.   With the Wagner Act, the power of organized labor grew. After World War II, the nation was rocked by a series of strikes. Many Americans began to demand that the government exert some control over unions and their practices. That demand led to the Taft-Hartley Act of 1947, also called the Labor-Management Relations Act.

Union sympathizers have called the Taft-Hartley Act the "Slave Labor Law." This nickname refers to the fact that the Taft-Hartley Act allows individual states to pass right-to-work laws. A *right-to-work law* makes it illegal to require union membership as a condition of employment.

In general, the Taft-Hartley Act aimed to reduce the power of labor. Perhaps its best-known feature is the provision that allows the President to obtain a court injunction to delay for 80 days any strike thought to threaten national safety or health. Presidents have used this provision on occasion, much to the anguish of unions.

The Labor-Management Reporting and Disclosure (Landrum-Griffin) Act.   This act was passed in Congress in 1959. It is an amendment to the Taft-Hartley Act. Among other things, the Act forbids all agreements between unions and employers in which the employer agrees in advance not to do business with a firm in which there is a strike in progress. Further, the Act restricts picketing for the purpose of winning membership for a particular union. It also requires annual detailed reports to be given to the Secretary of Labor by all union officials in charge of union finances.

What Unions Do for Workers

The constitution of the AFL-CIO states the goals of the organization. These include:

1. improving working conditions
2. getting better wages and better hours
3. allowing employees to realize the benefits of unrestrained collective bargaining

The services that unions provide for their members include:

1. providing information about alternative job opportunities

2. helping workers improve their skills

3. verifying that insurance, retirement, and other fringe benefit payments are carried out according to contract

4. reducing the cost of certain fringe benefits by buying them for all members

5. helping members obtain loans from union credit agencies

How Unions Get Their Strength

Unions are strong only when they represent the majority of workers in a firm or an industry. Moreover, unions are stronger when individual workers cannot negotiate separately with an employer about wages or working conditions. In other words, for a union to remain in power, it must be the *sole* bargaining agent for most or all of the workers involved.

A union engages in collective bargaining (a process by which workers, labor management, and business management work out their differences) with an employer for wages, fringe benefits, and working conditions. In a sense, the union sets a minimum wage for each classification of workers. The employer is not allowed to pay less than that minimum wage, and the worker is not allowed to accept less. Collective bargaining is a positive process by which workers, labor management, and business management work out their differences.

How Unions Get Higher Wages

Throughout the history of the United States, all personal incomes have risen at various rates, except during depressions or recessions. Wages rise even without unions, and in industries where unions are weak or do not exist. For the union to improve conditions, it must set a wage rate above the amount that the employer would pay without collective bargaining.

Without a union, supply and demand, as influenced by many other factors, determine wages. Then how can a union get a higher wage rate? After all, if supply and demand are working, the employer could obtain other workers at the competitive wage rate determined by supply and demand. This would be true except for one powerful tool of unions—the *strike.* Without the strike, unions could not function as they do today.

The strike.   Workers in the United States have not always had the right to strike. In some nations today, including the Soviet Union and Cuba, strikes are still illegal.

When employees strike, they stop working for their employer. More important, they use such activities as *picketing* to prevent other workers from competing for the jobs they have temporarily left. Herein lies one restrictive aspect of union behavior. When union workers are on strike, they immediately set up picket lines. The pickets attempt to prevent all actual or potential workers from crossing the line to work for the employer.

In some recent years, unions in the United States have resorted to strikes a lot. Figure 12-1 shows the number of work days lost to strikes since the end of World War II.

The Effects of Higher Wages

When unions successfully raise wage rates above those that would result from a competitive market, they then face a difficult task. At the higher union wage rate, more workers are willing to work than employers are willing to hire. Thus, unions find a surplus of workers available for a limited supply of jobs. The union must ration jobs among applicants.

One very effective way to ration jobs is to restrict entry into a particular labor market. Entry is restricted for merchant seamen, electricians, teamsters, butchers, barbers, and other occupations.

Entry may be restricted by requiring a long and costly apprenticeship. During apprenticeship, the worker is not paid the normal union wage. In some cases, a person must be nominated by three union members to become an apprentice. When such a requirement exists, members generally nominate only relatives of those already in the union.

Who Loses and Who Gains from Unionizing?

The argument is made that the activities of organized workers benefit all workers and hurt employers. If this claim is true, then the share of all income going to workers in the United States would have to grow at the expense of employers. However, available evidence

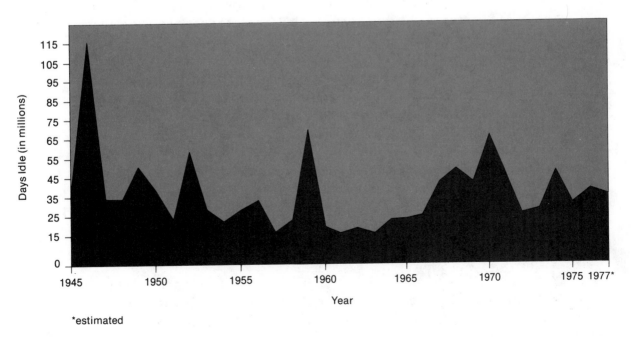

*estimated

Figure 12-1. Work days lost to strikes. Source: Bureau of Labor Statistics.

The most effective bargaining tool unions have is the right to strike. Do you agree or disagree with this right? Why?

does not strongly support this claim. The share of all income going to workers has remained constant (between 70 and 75 percent) during the last 50 years. The remainder goes to people as profit, interest, and dividends.

Who gains and who loses as a result of union activities? Analysis suggests that as union workers obtain wages, fringe benefits, and working conditions greater than those that would otherwise exist, the quantity of labor demanded from this group declines. As a result, some members are unable to get employment. Herein lies the rationing problem previously discussed. Eventually, some of the unemployed union members find that they must accept work in the unorganized sector of the economy. Many then work at lower wages than they had before. Some economists, therefore, contend that union workers benefit at the expense of those who are working in the nonunion sectors of the economy.

Summary   1.   Restrictions in the labor market can result from government regulations and laws, discrimination, and union practices.

2.   The American labor movement began with local craft unions. It

was not until the rise of industry following the Civil War that major national labor organizations appeared on the scene.

3. Organized labor made its greatest gains in membership after gaining government support during the 1930s.

4. The National Labor Relations Act (Wagner Act) guaranteed workers the right to belong to unions and to engage in collective bargaining.

5. Following World War II, many Americans thought organized labor had become too powerful. The Taft-Hartley Act was passed in 1947 to curb some of labor's power.

6. Unions benefit their members by providing information about job opportunities, helping them to improve their skills, and, most importantly, negotiating with employers for higher wages and better working conditions.

7. The basic strength of unions lies in their ability to bargain collectively for all workers and thus to set a minimum wage for each classification of workers.

8. The strike is a major tool that unions use to get wages raised or conditions improved.

9. Higher union wages can result in a surplus of workers, forcing unions to find ways to ration jobs among members.

10. Some economists contend that organized labor benefits union workers at the expense of workers in the nonunion sectors of the economy.

Important Terms

craft guild	picketing
craft union	right-to-work law
collective bargaining	strike
industrial union	union

Review Questions

1. In what ways can a person be restricted in his or her choice of occupation?

2. When did the idea of unionism begin?

3. How did the labor movement develop in the United States?

4. What have been the important national labor organizations in the history of American unionism?

5. What prompted the great growth of unionism beginning in the late 1930s?

6. Why can the Wagner Act be called labor's Magna Carta?

7. Why do some union sympathizers consider the Taft-Hartley Act the "Slave Labor Law"?

8. Why would unions oppose right-to-work laws?

9. What are the goals of unions?

10. What services do unions provide members?

11. On what is union strength based?

12. What is the major weapon of unions in forcing employers to meet workers' demands?

13. What can be the effect of higher union wages?

14. How do unions restrict certain jobs?

Discussion Questions

1. Certain restrictions in the labor market prevent people from casually entering professions, trades, or industries they might like to try. Do you think this is right? If so, what restrictions and for what occupations? If not, why?

2. During the late nineteenth and early twentieth centuries, considerable industrial strife took place as unions sought to gain recognition and to promote the rights of workers. Why do you think unionism met such stiff opposition from business? Was business's opposition to unionism justified? Was labor justified in resorting to violent tactics? Explain.

3. Franklin D. Roosevelt thought the Great Depression was, in

part, caused by "wasteful, cut-throat competition." What do you think he meant?

4.   Although the Taft-Hartley Act curbed some of organized labor's powers, many Americans believe that unions today still have too much power. Do you agree? If so, how would you restrict them? If not, why?

Projects   1.   In the history of the labor movement in the United States, certain strikes have had a significant impact on the rise or fall of unions. Two of the most important strikes were the strike against the McCormick Harvest works, which led to the Haymarket Square Riot in 1886 and to the Anthracite Coal strike of 1902. Research one of these strikes and report your findings to the class.

2.   Organize a debate on one of the following topics:

   a.   *Resolved,* that unions should be prohibited by law.

   b.   *Resolved,* that union membership should be required for all American workers.

3.   Interview a group of union members in the area to find out how they think unions have benefited them. What kind of differences are there among various unions? What benefits are common?

4.   Over the years, decisions of the U.S. Supreme Court have had a significant impact on the rights of labor and the power of unions. Some of the landmark cases in the history of American labor include: *Adair* v. *U.S.* (1908), *Loewe* v. *Lawler* (1908), *Duplex Printing Press Co.* v. *Deering* (1921), *Wolff Packing Co.* v. *Court of Industrial Relations* (1923), *NLRB* v. *Jones and Laughlin Steel Corp.* (1937), and *Wilson* v. *Newspaper and Mail Deliverers' Union of New York* (1938). Research one of these cases and report your findings to the class.

Does Labor-Market Discrimination Affect Wages?

Definitions of New Terms

Employment discrimination: To the extent that a person is treated differently in the job market because of age, sex, race, or religion, that person has suffered from employment discrimination.

Racism: Racism is discrimination because of race.

Sexism: Sexism is requiring workers to be of a specific sex for a specific job or paying a person of one sex less than that of another sex when all other aspects of the job are the same.

Suppose you apply for a job that is advertised in the newspaper. When you go to the place of employment, you find that there are five other applicants. You and the others fill out applications and are interviewed. During the course of your interview, you learn that your qualifications are better than those of the other applicants.

How would you feel if you did not get the job? Disappointed, no doubt. Perhaps even angry, if you thought you were turned down on the basis of sex, race, or religion. To the extent that an employer decides not to hire an applicant because of the applicant's sex, race, or religion, that person has suffered from **employment discrimination.** Employment discrimination can result from several causes—the personal dislikes of the employer (employer discrimination) or the employer's concern over the dislikes of employees (colleague discrimination) or customers (customer discrimination).

Discrimination and Wage Rates

Discrimination in the labor market does not simply mean that those who are discriminated against may not get a job. Discrimination can also affect the wages of individuals in the labor force. Discrimination exists when two workers of different sex, race, or religion are paid different wages for doing the same job although they have the same qualifications. This type of discrimination is clearest in terms of **racism** and **sexism.** Race and sex are group characteristics. They cannot be changed or, in most cases, hidden. A look at average income differentials according to race and sex illustrates the degree of discrimination that exists in American society.

White males earn the highest income. In every occupational category, white males make more than any other group. Black males are second, then white females, and finally black females.

Why Do Women and Minority Group Members Earn Less?

It is not enough to say that women and minority group members earn less because they are discriminated against. We should be able to find out more specifically how they are discriminated against. One way to do this is to look at several factors that affect wage differences among different classes of workers. These factors include education, on-the-job training, and occupational choice.

Education.   Whites, on average, receive more education and higher quality education than do minority groups. Most white males, for example, have more than 12 years of formal schooling, whereas black males average less than 10. The gap is narrowing, however, and the amount of discrimination in schooling among whites and minority groups will be less in the future. Hence, schooling will have less effect on income differences.

Why do not minority group members remain in school as long as whites? One theory suggests that white students stay in school because of the lure of increased job opportunities in the

Discrimination comes in many different forms. Recently, increasing attention has been drawn to the fact that women in American labor are being treated unequally. What reasons caused this to be?

future. If job opportunities are limited because of discrimination—in terms both of job availability and of wage rates paid—then we can assume that discrimination in the job market does affect the amount of schooling minority group members undertake. Furthermore, because of family financial difficulties, minority group students are more likely to quit school to help support the family unit.

An examination of higher education shows evidence of discrimination against females. On the average, females complete more years of schooling than males. But, according to some educational experts, substantial evidence of discrimination against women exists in college. Female high school graduates, for example, have only half the chance of getting into college with a *C* average that males do. At the graduate school level, this differential treatment of men and women is even more pronounced. Apparently, women are not expected to pursue independent careers.

On-the-Job Training.   One reason why more experienced workers get paid more is the on-the-job training they receive while working. On-the-job training is an alternative to formal education. One study of on-the-job training found that minority group members receive less than whites. The amount of money spent by employers for on-the-job training for females is only one-tenth of that spent on males.

Occupational Choice.   For the typical minority group member and female worker, the choice of occupation seems to be more limited than that for white males. That is, minority group members and women find themselves in lower-status occupations.

Looking at the jobs women hold, for example, one finds that more than 40 percent are in clerical and sales occupations. It has been estimated that men experience roughly one-third of the occupational restriction confronting women. To a lesser extent, the same occupational restrictions confront minority group members.

Trends in Discrimination   Looking at the differences in earnings between males and females and between whites and blacks, one finds that the differences narrowed during the 1960s but widened again in the 1970s. Table I–12–1 shows average earnings by sex and average family income by race for a number of years. The male-female differential has not changed significantly. On the other hand, the black-white differential fell by more than 10 percent between

Table I-12-1: Average Earnings by Sex and Average Family Income by Race for Selected Years

Average Earnings by Sex	1958	1962	1966	1969	1976
Male	$4,068	$4,814	$5,809	$6,899	$10,142
Female	1,593	1,812	2,238	2,564	4,112
Female as percent of Male	39.2%	37.6%	38.5%	37.2%	40.5%
Average Family Income by Race					
White	$5,300	$6,237	$7,792	$9,794	$14,630
Black	2,711	3,330	4,674	6,191	8,779
Black as percent of White	51.2%	53.4%	60.0%	63.2%	60.0%

Source: Statistical Abstract of the United States.

1958 and 1969. Since 1969, however, it has begun to widen again.

What Does Discrimination Cost the Nation?

Individual workers who are discriminated against in the job market certainly bear the major cost of discrimination. However, the nation also bears some cost. Any discrimination reduces the amount that can be produced in the country for all Americans to share.

To the extent that minority groups are denied access to education and on-the-job training, they are prevented from developing their productive ability fully. Hence, they produce less, and the average real standard of living in the United States is lower. Furthermore, to the extent that discrimination prevents an individual from utilizing his or her training, that individual's contribution to the output of the economy is lessened.

Attempts have been made to estimate the cost of racial discrimination in terms of lost national production. In the 1960s the President's Council of Economic Advisers estimated the loss at about 2 percent. In the 1970s, the loss was estimated to be less, but it may still have exceeded 1 percent. That is not a small number; it represents almost $20 billion annually.

Neither of the studies included any national costs of discrimination against groups other than women and blacks. The national costs of all discrimination might reach as high as 4 percent of national production.

What does all this mean? It means that if, in the long run,

One of the principal reasons for job discrimination against minorities is said to be lack of education. Some suggest minorities leave school earlier to provide needed financial support for the family. What other reasons might there be?

society is able to eliminate discrimination in the labor market, living standards will rise. How Americans go about eliminating such discrimination is, of course, not an easy question to answer.

Summary

1. Employment discrimination takes several different forms. Workers may not be able to get certain jobs because of employer, colleague, or customer discrimination.

2. Discrimination may account for differences in wage rates between whites and minority group members and between males and females.

3. Areas that affect differences in wage rates include education, on-the-job training, and choice of occupation. Discrimination due to race or sex also affects wage rates.

4. The differential in earnings between whites and blacks narrowed during the 1960s but began to widen again in the 1970s. The differential between males and females, however, has remained relatively constant.

5. Discrimination has been estimated to cost the nation from 1 to 4 percent of its total output annually.

Important Terms

employment discrimination sexism
racism

Questions for Thought and Discussion

1. Is it possible to distinguish between discrimination in hiring practices resulting from employer discrimination and from colleague dislikes? If so, how? If not, why?

2. How might employment discrimination be reduced or eliminated? That is, what do you recommend be done about employment discrimination?

3. In what ways are minority group members discriminated against in the educational process? What do you recommend to change such practices?

4. How does discrimination reduce total output in the society?

5. "The differential in earnings between whites and blacks narrowed in the 1960s because blacks were able to migrate from relatively low-paying jobs in the South to relatively higher-paying jobs in the North and West." Do you agree with this statement? Why or why not?

13

Land, Energy, and Entrepreneurship

Preview Questions

1. What other productive factors are there besides labor?
2. What determines the rent on land?
3. What is the role of profit in the economy? Who earns it?

Definitions of New Terms

Commercial rent: Commercial rent is payment to an owner of a resource according to a written or verbal contract.

Use value: The use value of a resource is the highest return from its use.

Derived demand: Derived demand is the demand for a resource that is ultimately based on the demand for a consumer product using that resource.

Economic surplus: Economic surplus is payment for a resource above what is necessary to keep the same quality and quantity of that resource in existence.

Capital goods: Capital goods are manmade tools, equipment, and machines used to produce commodities.

Entrepreneur: An entrepreneur is a person who is willing and able to take risks in a business. An entrepreneur puts up the money to start a new business or to expand an old one.

When you eat an apple, you know that labor alone did not produce it from a seed in the ground to fruit in the refrigerator. Obviously, other productive resources were involved—land, for example.

When you buy a ballpoint pen, you know that labor alone did not produce it. Such raw materials as iron ore to make steel and petroleum by-products to make plastics went into producing it.

When you use an aluminum skillet, you know that labor and raw materials alone did not make it. To make aluminum, great quantities of electrical energy were needed.

To provide the goods and services people use daily, labor must be combined with other productive resources. This chapter examines these resources, particularly land. It also looks at why people are able and willing to take on the risks of going into business.

Land and Production

In the past many economists considered land to be the ultimate productive resource. Without land, they said, nothing else could exist. This argument is true. Nevertheless, the same could be said for any item used to produce things. For example, nothing could exist without labor, either.

No matter how important land is in most production processes, its importance is not helpful in understanding what land is. We can define it as the productive resources from which we obtain our raw materials and on which we grow our crops and live. Another approach is to consider how more surface land could be produced.

The Supply of Surface Land

Surface land is often considered as the only fixed productive resource. In other words, the total amount of existing land cannot be increased. Actually, this is not completely accurate. Total surface land area has been expanded by landfill. Swamps and tideflats have been filled to extend the amount of usable land surface in the United States and elsewhere. The total land area that has been created without human labor, however, is indeed in fixed supply.

Land can be used for many purposes—for farming, housing and factory sites, parks, airports, wilderness areas, recreational facilities, etc. The number of uses of land is infinite. For any specific land use, such as agriculture, however, the supply of land is not fixed. If farming should become more profitable tomorrow than it is today,

Location is always important in determining the value of land. What factors might make one location better for housing and another better for farming or industry?

for example, then more land will be used for farming and less for recreation. On the other hand, if farming becomes less profitable tomorrow, less land will be used for farming and more for other purposes.

The key to understanding the use of land is to realize that land will be used for whatever purposes yield the highest income to land-owners. The income landowners receive is called *rent*.

Rent on Land

The term *rent* has many meanings. People speak of renting a car, a farm, or a house. This type of rent is called **commercial rent,** or *contract rent*. Commercial rent is payment to an owner of a resource according to a written or verbal contract.

What Determines Rent on Land?

Land is necessary for the production of almost every good and service. It is also necessary for building sites for homes and businesses. What determines how much commercial rent people are willing to pay to use land and how much landlords can charge?

Land can be treated like any other resource. Its demand is determined by the uses to which it can be put and by the amount available. For example, the central district of a city usually has a limited amount of land that can be used as the site for a multistory office building to accommodate hundreds of businesses and thousands of workers. The potential income from this use of land—that is, its **use value**—is extremely high. The demand for the land is also very high. As one might expect, the price for this land is relatively high. Hence, the rent one must pay to use it is also high.

Alternatively, land in the middle of the desert has fewer uses. Hence, it has a lower price and rent. Land in the desert may sell for as little as 1/100,000 of the price of land in the center of a large city.

As a productive resource, land has a demand that is derived from

The value of the land is also dependent upon its use. If the land pictured here was used for farming, would the derived demand be more or less than it is now? Why? Can you think of any situations that could change the value of this land? Why?

the demand for the final product that the land allows a producer to provide. In the case of an office building, the final product is whatever goods and services the companies in the building provide. In the case of agricultural land, the relationship is even more obvious. As the market price of agricultural products rises or falls, the ***derived demand*** for land will rise or fall accordingly. Thus, the demand for land is a *derived* demand, as is the demand for labor. One hires labor because it produces a product that some consumer wishes to buy. If the product is no longer desired, labor to make it is no longer demanded.

Do All Landowners Earn an Economic Surplus?

Some economic observers contend that landowners are "leeches on society" because they possess a God-given resource that they did nothing to create. Hence, any rent they obtain is in some sense unearned income, or *economic surplus.*

Economic surplus arises whenever more money is paid to the owner of a productive resource than is necessary to keep that resource in its present activity. Because land cannot be disposed of, it is sometimes argued that all of the income earned from the owner-ship of land is economic surplus. However, different parcels of land have different qualities. Indeed, the varying commercial rents, or prices, that can be gotten for different parcels of land dictate how land will be used. Thus, the fact that landowners receive income from land does not mean anything. In a sense, land is no different from any other productive resource. Landowners must be rewarded for hav-ing their land in a particular productive activity, whether it be for agriculture, commercial building sites, or homesites.

Economic Surplus for Other Productive Factors

Economic surplus does not apply only to land. Many athletes and entertainers receive it. They possess unique skills that few can imitate. In an extreme situation, only one person may possess a particular skill. Only one surgeon, for example, may know how to do a very complicated operation.

Because only one person may have a particular skill, its supply is strictly limited. No matter how much money is offered its owner, he or she cannot do or give more than is humanly possible. At the other end of the scale, there is a floor to the possible lowest wage rate that the person will accept. That floor is the next-best alternative employment.

For many superstars, alternative occupations would offer a com-paratively low wage rate. In the case of a rock singer, for example, the next-best alternative might be working as another rock singer's manager. A top recording artist may earn $1 million a year, even though his or her next-best alternative employment may pay only $15,000 annually. The difference between what this person receives and the value of his or her alternative occupation is economic surplus. In this case, the difference would be $1 million minus $15,000, or $985,000.

Why Does Personal Economic Surplus Exist?

Why is a superstar paid $1 million a year, if his or her next-best alternative employment might be valued at only $15,000? The reason is demand.

A record company may calculate that an album by a particular superstar will make a profit of at least $1 million. Of course, the record company would like to hire the singer for less, but it cannot. The reason is that other record companies are making similar calculations about the star's value. They will keep bidding the price up until it reaches a figure close to $1 million. Thus, to obtain the services of the star, a record company must pay the higher wage.

The Role of Capital

In economics, *capital* does not refer only to money. The term also refers to all things except labor used to produce goods and services—that is, all manmade tools. Specifically, the term is **capital goods,** or *producer goods.* Capital goods are the machines and equipment used in the production process.

The supply of capital goods has certain special characteristics. For one thing, capital goods cannot be increased instantaneously. If more are desired or required, buyers of capital goods (producers of consumer products) must give manufacturers of capital goods time to make them.

Also, capital goods have a tendency to wear out. Wearing out is called *depreciation,* a concept first discussed in Issue 5. As capital goods depreciate, they must be repaired or replaced in order for the supply of capital, at a very minimum, to remain constant.

Like other factors of production, the amount of capital goods in existence depends on demand and supply. If business is booming and future profits look good, the demand for capital goods increases. More orders are placed. On the other hand, if business is bad and future profits look low, the demand for capital goods falls.

Taking Risks and Earning Profits

In a capitalist society, those who take risks by starting and operating businesses are called **entrepreneurs.** The word *"entrepreneur"* is derived from the French, meaning "someone who undertakes a venture." An entrepreneur is also a capitalist—a person who provides money for a business.

The persons providing capital, or money, to start a business are taking a risk. They could lose all of that money or get less reward than they might get in some other business venture. Entrepreneurs expect a reward. Otherwise, they would not engage in a risky activity. Their reward for taking risks in starting businesses is profit.

Profits and Parasites

Many critics of capitalism have claimed that capitalists are parasites on society, whose parasitic rewards are profits. How valid is this interpretation of the economic role of entrepreneurs? To understand the problem, ask yourself whether you would loan money to a person to start a business if you were not promised a reward. After all, you could lose your money if the business failed. You might be willing to loan money for a short period with no reward. But then you would be worse off. You could have spent the money on something you wanted, or earned interest on it in a savings account. Thus, you can see why entrepreneurs in society must earn a reward in the form of profits.

In fact, the lure of relatively higher profits directs entrepreneurs to invest their money in areas in the economy in which individuals want more goods and services. The lure of increased profits also causes areas in the economy to decline when consumers no longer consider an industry's product to be desirable. It did not take brains to stop entrepreneurs from investing their capital in the horse carriage trade when the automobile became popular. They were willing to invest capital in the automobile industry because it offered the lure of relatively high profits.

A Basic Rule

A basic rule that can be applied to the analysis of all productive resources—labor, land, raw materials, money capital, and entrepreneurship—is that the laws of supply and demand apply uniformly and at all times. If a person finds a situation in which a critical "shortage" or an unnecessary "surplus" of a productive resource exists, that person can ask what has been left out of the analysis. Is some outside force preventing supply and demand from interacting to change price and to make the quantities supplied equal the quantities demanded?

Generally, some external force prevents price from changing to reflect changing supplies and demands. For example, Issue 9 pointed out that agricultural surpluses were caused by government price supports. For many years, the United States has had "shortages" of natural gas. But the selling price for natural gas has been set by government well below what would have prevailed without intervention. Hence, at the artificially low prices, more natural gas was demanded than could be supplied by owners of natural gas wells.

Using this analysis, let us take a closer look at a problem that people have faced for centuries, namely lack of food. Issue 13 looks at the interaction of supply and demand and the way land is used for agricultural purposes.

Summary

1. Productive resources include labor, land, raw materials, capital goods, and entrepreneurship.

2. Some productive resources are in relatively fixed supply, such as surface land.

3. Economic surplus arises whenever more money is paid to the owner of a productive resource than is necessary to keep that resource in its present quantity or quality.

4. The demand for a resource is generally related to its use value. The higher its use value, the higher the demand and thus the higher the price (wage, rent) that can be obtained for it.

5. Capital goods have certain special characteristics. They cannot be increased instantaneously. They also wear out.

6. Profit is the reward that entrepreneurs receive for the risks they take in investing in business ventures.

7. The lure of increased profits directs entrepreneurs to the ventures in which they will invest.

Important Terms

capital goods
commercial rent
derived demand

economic surplus
entrepreneur
use value

Review Questions

1. What does the term productive resources include?

2. Is the supply of a resource such as land fixed? Why or why not?

3. What determines the specific use of a resource such as land?

4. What determines its commercial rent?

5. What affects derived demand?

6. How does economic surplus arise?

7. Why are top recording stars paid so much money?

8. What are capital goods?

9. What kind of people take risks by starting and operating businesses? Why do they take these risks?

10. What determines in which areas these people will invest their money?

11. What is the basic rule that can be applied to the analysis of all productive resources?

Discussion Questions

1. In the past, many economists have considered land to be the ultimate productive resource. Why have they thought so? Do you agree with their thinking? Why or why not?

2. Some economic observers have contended that landowners are "leeches on society." Why do you think people would make such a claim? Do you agree with their thinking? Why or why not?

3. If the earning of profits were to be barred from the economy, how would resources be directed to new uses?

Projects

1. Each year *New York Magazine* publishes a list of people who earn the greatest income in the United States that year. Research the current year's list and report your findings to the class. How much of their income do you think is economic surplus?

2. Organize a debate on the following issue:
Resolved, earning of profit should be barred from the economy.

3. Survey commercial rent costs (price per square foot) for office space in your area. Undoubtedly you will find a significant variation. How would you account for such variation?

The Single Tax

Henry George was born and raised in Philadelphia. After quitting school in his early teens, he worked at different jobs until he went to sea for two years. In 1856 George moved to California. There he spent the next few years trying to find work, while living on the edge of poverty. Eventually he joined the staff of a San Francisco newspaper and was quickly promoted from printer to editor. He helped found the *San Francisco Post* in 1867, but the paper folded in 1873.

In 1879 George published *Progress and Poverty.* In this book George argued that people who owned land were receiving substantial "surpluses." That is, most landowners got too much payment for the use of land and improvements, simply because their land happened to be in the right spot, not because they were working for the money. George claimed that since land is given to everyone by nature, the unfairness to the people who do not own land becomes greater when the value of land increases and the owner profits. To solve the problem, he contended the government should take away the "extra" money by setting a *single* tax on land.

Under George's plan, the public would benefit whenever any land increased in value. The money obtained from taxing the increased value of land would be sufficient to pay all government expenses. Beside encouraging trade and industry, it would also enable workers to pay less taxes on production and consumption.

Although George at first had difficulty finding a publisher for *Progress and Poverty,* the book became extremely popular. In fact, it sold millions of copies throughout the world and today is considered one of the most successful popular economics books ever published. But although it brought George considerable recognition, it brought him little money.

In 1886 George ran as the unsuccessful candidate of the Labor and Socialist parties for the mayor of New York City. He became a candidate again in 1897. Due to the strain of that campaign, he died shortly after.

Henry George's proposal of a single tax poses two questions. Did the proposal have merit? Economists have been debating the issue ever since. Some conclude that despite major flaws, a single tax may be as good as other, more complicated taxing systems.

If this is the case, why has the idea never been put into effect? In the settling of America, many people acquired wealth by accumulating land. To the settler, finding and "working" land was of primary importance. Obviously, over time the landowners grew in number, and many became powerful because of their wealth. So one can see why George's theory did not catch on!

Nonetheless, Henry George did make an original and lasting contribution to economic theory: The value of land is not necessarily tied to its fertility. Rather, the growth in population in an area and the increase in productivity of that society can have a substantial effect on land value. In other words, those who acquire land where future growth is likely to occur stand to profit handsomely. One example of this is the Orlando, Florida, area. The people who purchased land prior to the building of Disney World have seen land values increase many times over since the building of that tourist attraction.

Will the Land Stop Giving Us Food?

Definitions of New Terms

Malthusian theory: Malthusian theory suggests that a society's population increases until the food supply is outstripped. Then famine or disease occurs, reducing the population, and the cycle starts again.

Real income: Real income is income translated into purchasing power, the ability to purchase whatever people want.

Law of diminishing returns: According to the law of diminishing returns, a point is reached at which additional output from an additional worker will not be as much as that added by the previous worker.

Less than 10 years ago British author C. P. Snow stated that millions of people in underdeveloped nations were facing starvation. Snow felt that the most important questions on earth were: How soon? How many deaths? Can they be prevented? Can they be minimized?

At the time Snow made this charge, most food experts dismissed it as that of an alarmist. After all, they said, miracle seeds and fertilizers had created a global green revolution. They talked of such chronically hungry nations as India becoming self-sufficient in their food supplies.

However, the 1970s saw a change in attitude. Concerned people throughout the world began predicting massive food crises, particularly in underdeveloped countries. According to biologist J. George Harrar, unless present trends are somehow reversed:

Millions of people in the poor areas will die of starvation. But the affluent societies—including the United States—will experience dramatically reduced standards of living at home.

During the mid-1970s, food shortages did affect much of the underdeveloped world. The sub-Saharan nations of Africa suffered widespread misery and starvation. In 1973 and 1974, an estimated 250,000 people in that area died of starvation. In addition, nutritionists now think that half of the world's nearly 4 billion people live in continuous hunger.

But worries about recurrent food crises in the world are not new. Many years ago in England, Thomas R. Malthus advanced a theory that continues to haunt people today.

Malthus' Theory of Population

In 1798 Thomas R. Malthus, an English clergyman, published *An Essay on the Principle of Population, as It Affects the Future Improvement of Society.* In this essay, Malthus noted that "population, when unchecked, goes on doubling every 24 years or increases in the geometric ratio." A geometric increase doubles each generation: 2, 4, 8, 16, 32, 64, and so on. According to Malthus, food production, or the means of subsistence, can increase only in an arithmetic ratio. An arithmetic increase would be 1, 2, 3, 4, 5, 6, and so on. Figure I–13–1 points up what Malthus meant about geometric and arithmetic rates.

In Figure I–13–1 the heavier line represents population, which rises at a geometric rate. Notice how the line starts upward slowly and then quickly gets steeper. Compare this with the lighter line, which represents increases in the food supply. This line, increasing at an arithmetic rate, remains at the same angle throughout its path.

When Malthus was growing up, industry was replacing production taking place in people's homes. Nevertheless, he was a product of traditional Europe, of the preindustrial society. He believed, as did Adam Smith, that economic life depends on the productivity of land—that ultimately, land determines the level of material well-being. He was convinced that people breed as long as there is enough food to feed a growing family.

Figure I–13–2 shows Malthus' theory of population growth and decline. It is known as the **Malthusian theory.** Population is shown on the horizontal axis. What people can buy with their

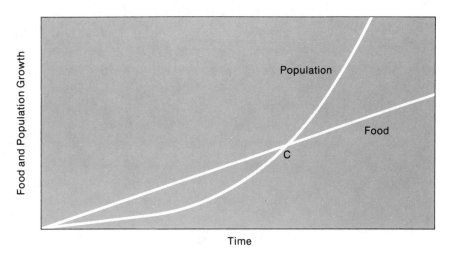

Figure I–13–1. The Malthusian Prediction. Population increases at a geometric rate, whereas food production increases only at an arithmetic rate. At point C there is a crisis. Population cannot grow anymore for lack of food.

Figure I–13–2. The Malthusian Theory. Population is shown horizontally. Real income or standard of living is shown vertically. The heavy horizontal line indicates the subsistence level of real income that people must receive to survive. At first, real income will increase as population grows. After all the good agricultural land is used, as population continues to increase, income will decline to point D. At that point, checks such as famines and pestilence cause the total population to decrease.

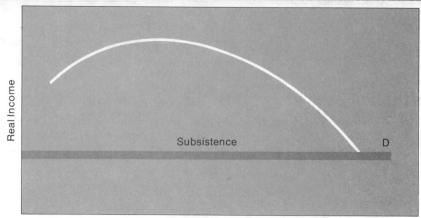

incomes is shown on the vertical axis. Income expressed as the ability to purchase goods and services is called **real income.** That is, real income is whatever income will buy stated in terms of goods and services, such as food and clothing.

Real income is adjusted to allow for general changes in the level of prices. It is a way of looking at income in terms of what it can purchase rather than how it is counted. For example, if all prices and everyone's income increase 100 percent, then no one is better off. All real incomes remain the same.

The shaded line in Figure I–13–2 shows the level of real income people need to live. This is the subsistence level of real income—the income to survive. Presumably, if a person did not obtain at least a subsistence level of real income, his or her children would die because they could not be fed or clothed.

Once the population reached Point D in Figure I–13–2, widespread famines would occur. At this point, many people would die, according to the Malthusian doctrine. Therefore, society would experience a period of "positive" checks on population, causing it to decline. These positive checks include disease, famine, war, and an increase in vice. According to Malthus, these checks result in fewer births.

Malthus and History

Malthus' theory is considered a relatively accurate description of the life cycle in Europe over many centuries prior to his writing of the essay. For example, there had been recurrent periods of widespread starvation and disease.

The doctrine can be used to describe life during feudal times. To break into the cycle, population would begin to increase on a *manor,* a large estate headed by a lord. The population would continue to grow until the land could no longer support any additional workers, or *serfs,* as they were called. What happened to the lord and his serfs may be something like the following example:

The lord knows that he has a fixed amount of land with a given fertility. He also has a fixed number of plows. He has a fixed number of seeds and whatever else is necessary to grow crops. The only element that can vary is the number of serfs working on the lord's land. After a certain point (for example, 10 serfs) the lord no longer has a plow for each. Thus, the eleventh serf will take turns using someone else's plow instead. When the twelfth serf comes to work, that serf must also share a plow. So must the thirteenth, and so on.

Finally, if there are more than 20 serfs, each will be able to use a plow less than half the time. With a fixed amount of land and tools to work, the time comes when each additional worker contributes less to total production. This is because returns are diminishing.

According to the **law of diminishing returns,** a point is reached at which adding more workers causes the productivity of each additional worker to be reduced when the amount of land and technology is set or fixed. That is, the additional output from an additional worker will not be as much as that added by the previous worker.

What Was Malthus' Mistake?

When Malthus stated his theory, he assumed a fixed technology. Hence he concluded that the law of diminishing returns would lead to reduced productivity per worker as population grew. Starting in the seventeenth century, however, the technological capacity of society increased. Thus, industrial society was more productive.

Malthus ignored the possibility that the curve of real income shown in Figure I–13–2 could rise. Figure I–13–3 (see next page) gives three curves showing low, medium, and high productivity. These increases in productivity result from increases in technology. If the curves shift up fast enough, the real income of people can rise even though the population is growing.

Malthus' second assumption was that population size depended only on real income. Although the survival rate of children may increase as real income rises, birth rates can fall—or at least not rise as fast as income—in many situations. Stable populations, such as those of Japan, France, and the United States, are not unknown today. One characteristic of many industrial societies is the leveling off of their population growth rates.

Malthus' description of conditions before his time was accu-

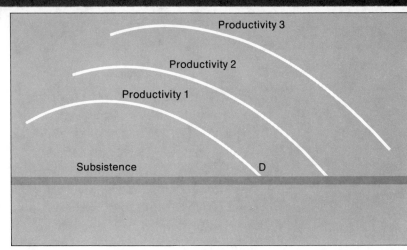

Figure I–13–3. The Malthusian Cycle and improved technology. This diagram uses the same level of subsistence and real income as Figure I–13–2. As technology improves, productivity increases. This is shown by two additional curves labeled Productivity 2 and 3. If productivity rises fast enough, real income will not fall to subsistence levels, even if the population increases.

rate. Perhaps similar conditions do exist in certain less-developed countries today. However, Malthus was wrong in assuming that technology would never change and that real income alone determines the size of a society's population.

Can Food Crises Recur?

To predict exactly what will happen is often impossible, particularly when the topic is as important as food. It is interesting, however, to use the principles of economics to see how they might help predict the future.

There seems to be little threat of a food crisis in the United States. If food were to become relatively more scarce, food prices would rise. Thus, work related to agriculture would become more profitable. More capital would flow into agriculture and less into other areas of the economy. The output of agriculture would then increase, and the relative scarcity of food would decline to some equilibrium.

It would be nice if this analysis could be applied to the less-developed nations that suffer the most from food problems. In many cases, however, these nations have numerous restraints on improvements in agricultural output. Equipment and products requiring a highly developed technology to manufacture are not allowed to enter these nations freely. Many less-developed nations have placed restrictions on the importation of the machinery needed to make agricultural pursuits more productive. Therefore, food production in these nations will not rise as rapidly as it could.

Summary

1. In recent years, many food experts have become increasingly concerned over the possibility of widespread starvation resulting

from massive food shortages, especially among the less-developed nations of the world.

2. Concern over food crises is not new. In 1798 Thomas R. Malthus stated that population cyclically outstrips food supply.

3. The Malthusian theory assumes that population increases at a geometric rate and food production increases at an arithmetic rate.

4. Malthus claimed that when real income (food) fell below a subsistence level because of increased population, population would decline from famine, pestilence, war, and the like.

5. Malthus based his theory on the law of diminishing returns. That law states that at a certain point additional output from an additional worker is less than that added by the previous worker, if the amount of all other productive resources (land, tools, etc.) are fixed.

6. When Malthus developed his theory, he assumed a fixed technology. He also assumed that population's size depended only on real income. Malthus was wrong in both of these assumptions.

7. There seems to be little threat of a food crisis in the United States resulting from increased population.

8. The food problems faced by the less-developed nations of the world are caused, in part, by numerous restraints these nations have placed on improvements in agricultural production.

Important Terms

arithmetic ratio
geometric ratio
law of diminishing returns

Malthusian theory
real income

Questions for Thought and Discussion

1. What does it mean that population increases at a geometric ratio and food production increases at an arithmetic ratio? Do you agree with this assumption? Why or why not?

2. How does the law of diminishing returns work? Was Malthus correct in basing his theory on this law. Why or why not? Does the Malthusian theory apply to the food crises of present times? If so, how? If not, why?

3. What are the implications of Malthusian theory for today's public policy?

4. What do you think underdeveloped nations should do to combat food shortages they might be experiencing? That is, how might such nations overcome potential food crises?

UNIT FIVE

The National Economy

14

How to Measure the Economy's Performance

Preview Questions

1. What does gross national product measure?

2. During a period of inflation, does one have to take account of rising prices to measure the nation's income?

3. Should one take account of the taxes people pay before estimating their spendable income?

4. For what can national economic figures on income be used?

Definitions of New Terms

Gross national product: Gross national product (GNP) is the total value of all final goods and services produced in the economy during a one-year period.

Constant-dollar GNP: Constant-dollar GNP is GNP corrected for price changes.

Constant dollars: Constant dollars are dollars corrected for price changes. They can be contrasted with current dollars, which express value without considering price changes. Constant dollars relate to a base period.

National income and product accounting: National product income and product accounting is the study of GNP.

Net national product: Net national product (NNP) is equal to GNP minus wear and tear on business machines and equipment (depreciation).

National income: National income (NI) is the total of all wages and salaries paid employees, incomes earned by self-employed individuals, all rents, all corporate profits, and interest payments received by individuals.

Personal income: Personal income (PI) is all income received by individuals before personal taxes are paid.

Disposable personal income: Disposable personal income (DPI) is personal income minus the personal taxes that are paid.

Transfer payments: Transfer payments are welfare and other payments made by the government to individuals.

From an economic standpoint, people can measure how successful they are by looking at how much income they make. The more they make working, the more successful they seem to be in the work they are doing. If they change jobs to make more income, they generally consider that they have improved their economic situation.

Individuals can determine their level of economic performance by looking at how much income they make, but how do people measure the nation's economic performance? How can they tell if the nation's economy is running too slow, too fast, or just right? There are several ways, of course. They can ask businesspersons how they think the nation is doing. They can look at the rate of unemployment or the rate of inflation. People can look at a whole host of indicators of economic performance.

The one indicator that stands out above all others, however, is the measure of the total value of output in the economy over a one-year period. That figure tells people how much American workers have produced in the given year. It provides a way of comparing what has been produced in one year with what was produced any other year.

Measuring the Value of Total Output

Almost everyone knows that a person cannot add apples and oranges together. There is no way to add up the *physical* quantities of items that are not the same. Then how do people measure the total output produced in the nation in one year when that output consists of tens of thousands of different items? There is a common measure of value in the United States—the *dollar*.

Generally, people assume that something costing $5 is worth half as much as something that costs $10. The fact that the value of things produced and bought can be expressed in terms of money makes the task of measuring how much has been produced in the nation in any one year much easier. All statisticians have to do is add up the total value of all goods and services produced in any one year in the United States.

Actually, to measure the economy's performance accurately, statisticians add up only the value of all *final* goods and services produced. This avoids *double counting*. After all, it makes little sense to add to the price of a transistor radio the price of the transistors that went into it. Their price is included in the final price.

When one adds up the value of final goods and services, he or she gets what economists call ***gross national product,*** or GNP. Gross national product is the leading indicator of a nation's economic performance. But we must then look at GNP per capita, or per person. The reason that we must use per capita GNP as the measure of well-being is that GNP must be related to population to tell us how much each citizen's well-being is improving, on the average. If per capita GNP goes up, then generally the nation's material well-being (the standard of living) is rising. If per capita GNP declines or stagnates, then in most cases the standard of living is not improving.

In order for you to have a precise definition of GNP, let us define it as follows:

Gross national product, or GNP, is the sum total of all expenditures on final goods and services produced in the United States during a one-year period.

Looking at GNP

Figure 14-1 shows the rise in the GNP in the United States from 1929 through 1977. It has grown dramatically since the Great Depression in the 1930s.

One has to be careful about looking at the dollar value of goods and

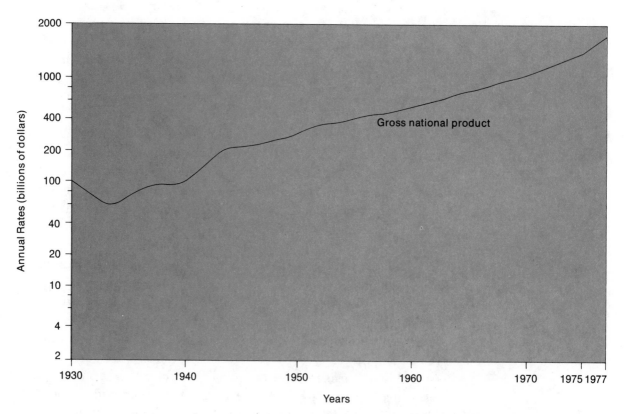

Figure 14–1. GNP over time. Except during periods of depression and recession, GNP has been rising in the United States. 1977 is an estimate. Source: United States Department of Commerce.

services produced in the United States in any one year. Obviously, the prices of the things people buy seem to go up year in and year out. Whereas last year a hamburger may have cost $1.00, a hamburger may cost $1.10 this year. The physical output—the hamburger—has not changed. Only the *money* value has changed. To measure the nation's economic performance, one has to take into account price changes for things people produce and buy. Price changes do not always reflect a change in the total amount of output available for use.

Correcting GNP for Price Changes

To correct GNP for changes in prices, one finds an index or indication of how prices have changed in the economy and then applies that index to the dollar values of GNP in any one year. Essentially, one tries to standardize GNP for any change in prices, on an average. In doing this, one gets what is called **constant-dollar GNP.** The dollars are constant only in the sense they are expressed in terms of a base year. The base year that the federal government uses in calculating GNP price indexes is 1972. GNP expressed in constant, 1972 prices and dollars is shown in Table 14-1.

Figure 14-2 shows GNP in both current and **constant dollars.** In recent years, much of the GNP's growth in current dollars has really been the result of a growth in prices, not a growth in total output available for use. This type of increase in GNP has little bearing on material well-being. Price rises do not help society. They do not constitute an increase in the available amount of goods and services that people can consume.

Other Measures of the Economy's Performance

While GNP is the most widely used indicator to measure an economy's performance, other measures can be used. Occasionally you might see them in newspaper and magazine articles. Of course, if you continue studying economics, you will encounter the concepts frequently.

The study of GNP and its components is called **national income and product accounting.** The name comes from the fact that such study deals with the income and the product of the economy from an accounting point of view.

Table 14-1: Correcting GNP for Price Changes, Using 1972 as the Base Year

1966	$ 981.0	Billion	1972	$1,171.1	Billion
1967	1,007.7		1973	1,235.0	
1968	1,051.8		1974	1,214.0	
1969	1,078.8		1975	1,191.7	
1970	1,075.3		1976	1,265.0	
1971	1,107.5		1977	1,302.9	

When we correct for price changes, GNP doesn't always go up.

Source: Dept. of Commerce. (1977 is an estimate.)

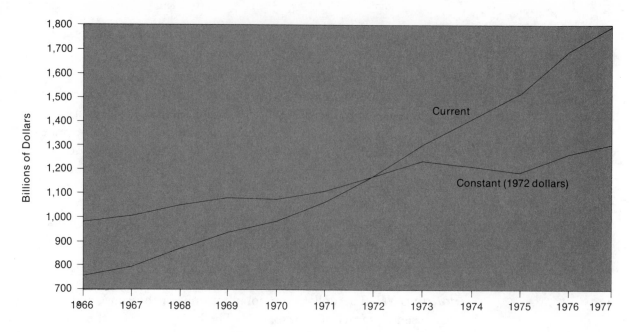

Figure 14–2. Current and constant-dollar GNP over time. Current GNP rises much faster than inflation corrected GNP. Source: United States Department of Commerce.

Net National Product

GNP is a measure of *gross* national product. As such, it overlooks the fact that some output in the economy is used merely to replace machines and equipment that have worn out. In this sense, GNP overstates the amount of material well-being that is produced. The replacement of worn-out machines does not provide consumers directly with the things they want to buy.

You know that a car must be repaired occasionally to keep it running. That is, a car depreciates through normal wear and tear. So, too, do the machines that businesses use to produce the goods and services people want to buy. In order for those machines to be kept in operation, they must be repaired. At some point, they may even have to be replaced. The expenses of maintaining the amount of machines, tools, and the like in the economy are called *depreciation.* When depreciation is deducted from gross national product, one gets **net national product,** or NNP. NNP is equal to GNP minus the depreciation of business machines, equipment, and tools.

National Income

In compiling GNP figures, one measures output by adding up all expenditures made on final goods and services. Alternatively, one could add up the income received by everyone who produces in the economy. By doing this, one gets **national income.** National income, or NI, is defined as follows:

NI is equal to the sum of all the wages and salaries paid employees, all of the incomes earned by self-employed individuals, all of the rental incomes of individuals, all corporate profits, and net interest received by individuals.

National income goes to the owners of productive resources, which were discussed in Unit 4. Look at Figure 14-3. It shows that the owners of labor—workers of all sorts—receive three-fourths of national income.

Personal Income

Personal income, or PI, is all of the income received by individuals. It includes not only all income noted in the definition of NI but also welfare payments and any other supplements that are given to individuals by government. These are called *transfer payments.* They add to income but do not represent payments for any current productive effort. Personal income also differs from national income with respect to what is *not* available for individuals to spend. Individuals cannot spend that part of corporation profits that is taxed. Nor can they spend such things as employer contributions to

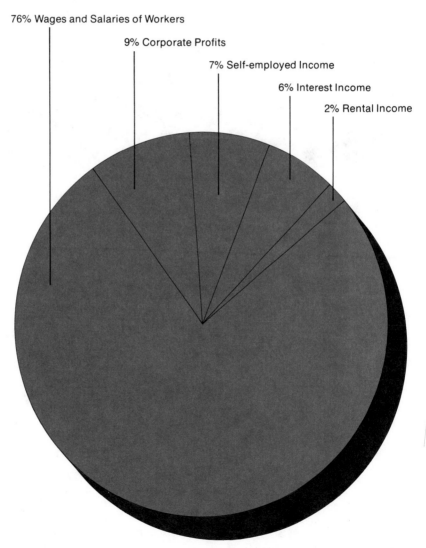

76% Wages and Salaries of Workers

9% Corporate Profits

7% Self-employed Income

6% Interest Income

2% Rental Income

Figure 14–3. Shares of national income, 1976. Labor income accounts for three-fourths of the national income in the United States. Source: *Economic Indicators,* March 1977, U.S. Government Printing Office, Washington, D.C.

Disposable personal income may be spent in any manner an individual chooses.

social insurance, which are not directly given to the employee. In short,

personal income is equal to all money income received by individuals before personal taxes are paid.

Disposable Personal Income

Individuals can seldom keep all of the money they earn. Most must pay a portion in taxes to the federal and state and sometimes local governments. Deducting personal taxes from personal income gives *disposable personal income.* Disposable personal income is the income available to an individual for immediate purchase of goods and services.[1]

Figure 14-4 shows GNP and its components for 1976. You can find out what the GNP is today by going to your school or public library and looking at some of the many government publications. You might try the *Survey of Current Business,* the *Federal Reserve*

---

[1]This was referred to as *spendable income* in Chapter 4.

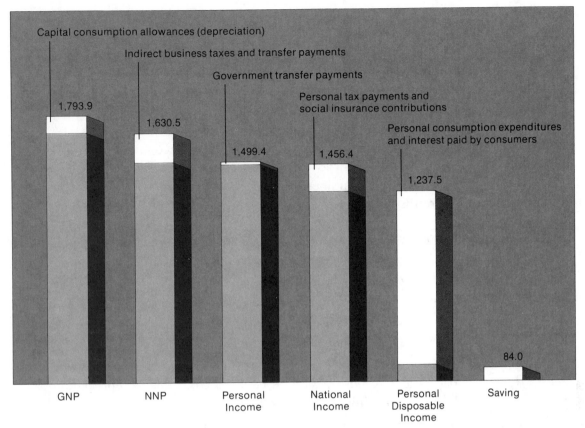

Billions of Dolllars (1977)

Capital consumption allowances (depreciation)

Indirect business taxes and transfer payments

Government transfer payments

Personal tax payments and
social insurance contributions

Personal consumption expenditures
and interest paid by consumers

1,793.9

1,630.5

1,499.4

1,456.4

1,237.5

84.0

GNP   NNP   Personal   National   Personal   Saving
               Income   Income   Disposable
                                      Income

Figure 14–4. GNP and its components—1976. Shown in descending order are the individual components of the national income and product in the United States. Source: Adapted from *Economic Indicators,* March, 1977.

Bulletin, or the *Business Conditions Digest.* If you have any trouble finding them, ask the librarian.

The Usefulness of National Income and Product Accounting

You have read a brief overview of how people measure the nation's economic performance. Let us now briefly discuss how these measures are used.

In the first place, measures of GNP indicate changes in total economic activity. That is, the GNP is an indication of how well an economy is performing relative to its potential. The American economy has a potential growth rate of about 4 percent of the standard of living per year. If GNP corrected for price changes is growing only at 1 percent, then policymakers know that something is wrong. They will take such information as a signal that policy should be changed to get the economy growing again.

Moreover, certain economists are concerned with helping policymakers make the right decisions about what to do to keep the economy from overheating or from slowing down. These economists must know what is happening and what has happened in the past when various policies were tried. Unfortunately, unlike biologists and physicists, they cannot control all the variables of experiments to test their ideas about how the world works. Economists must rely on available information about what has happened. Much of this information is given in national income accounts.

The available information is expressed in terms of dollars. In the American system, the dollar is the unit of accounting. But dollars also serve other purposes. These purposes are discussed in Chapter 15, which also examines the American banking system—the guardian of the dollar.

Summary

1. The nation's economic performance can be measured by numerous indicators. The leading indicator is GNP.

2. GNP measures the total value of all final goods and services produced in the economy for a one-year period.

3. Since prices change frequently, GNP is measured in constant dollars to determine changes in the living standard.

4. A more accurate reflection of the existing standard of living is net national product. NNP is equal to GNP minus depreciation of business machines, tools, and the like.

5. Other indicators of economic performance include national income, personal income, and disposable personal income.

Important Terms

constant dollars	gross national product
constant-dollar GNP	national income
current dollars	net national product
disposable personal income	personal income

Review Questions

1. What is considered the leading indicator of the nation's economic performance? What does it measure?

2. In what terms is GNP expressed in the United States?

3. Why are *final* goods and services stressed in measuring GNP?

4. How can the GNP be corrected for changes in prices?

5. What is the difference between GNP and NNP?

6. What makes up national income?

7. How does personal income differ from national income?

8. How does personal income differ from disposable personal income?

9. Why is it important for policymakers to know the rate of growth of constant-dollar GNP?

Discussion Questions

1. Which indicator of the nation's economic performance is most important to you as an individual? Why?

2. Who do you think would be most concerned with GNP figures? Why?

3. In recent years, the GNP of the United States has been growing at about 7 percent per year. Do you think this indicates good growth in the material well-being of Americans? Why or why not?

4. Figure 14–4 shows the various indicators discussed in this chapter for 1976. Why do you think the figures vary? That is, why is NI less than NNP but greater than PI?

Projects

1. Figures on GNP, NNP, NI, PI, and DPI are given in numerous publications, including *The Economic Report of the President, Statistical Abstract of the United States, Survey of Current Business,* and *Business Conditions Digest.* Research current figures for each indicator and compare the figures with those for the previous year. Has there been much growth? What do you think accounts for this?

2. This nation's GNP has been increasing in recent years at a rate of about 7 percent per year. How does this rate compare with the growth rate of the economies of such western European nations as Great Britain and West Germany, such less-developed countries as India and Nigeria, and such communist states as the Soviet Union and Cuba? Statistics on the GNPs of other countries are available in a variety of publications published by the United Nations. Ask the librarian to help you find the information. Report your findings to the class. Which nations seem to have the highest growth rate? Does this mean they have the highest standard of living? Explain.

15

Money and the Banking System

Preview Questions

1. What is money? Why do people use it?
2. What are the different types of money?
3. How does the banking system operate?
4. How is the supply of money controlled?

Definitions of New Terms

Currency: Currency consists of bills and coins.

Money: Money is anything that serves as a medium of exchange, a store of value, and a unit of accounting. In the United States, it consists of currency and checking account balances.

Barter: Barter is the act of exchanging one commodity for another without using money.

Legal tender: Legal tender is money that must be accepted as fulfillment for a debt or obligation or in payment for goods or services.

Fiduciary: Fiduciary is paper currency that is founded on trust and not backed by some valued commodity such as gold or silver.

Fractional reserve banking system: In a fractional reserve banking system, each bank holds only a fraction of its deposits on reserve for immediate withdrawal by depositors and uses the rest for lending and investment purposes.

Reserve requirement: Reserve requirement is the percentage of deposits that by law must be kept on reserve. For members of the Federal Reserve System, required reserves are kept on deposit in Federal Reserve Banks.

Discount rate: The discount rate is the rate of interest that the Federal Reserve charges its member banks to borrow in order to meet their required reserves.

When people get paid for the work they do, they are paid with *currency* (bills and coins) or with a check. If they are paid with a check and want to have currency, they generally go to a bank to cash the check. Or they might exchange it with the seller of a product they want to buy. The seller then deposits the check in a bank.

In one way or another, most Americans deal with banks and with money in the form of currency and checks. As you will see, the nation's banking system is very influential in affecting the amount of money and credit available in the economy, and hence the amount of business activity that exists. Before turning to a description of the banking system, however, let us examine what money is and why people have it.

Money makes economic transactions much easier.

Money, Money, Money

The dictionary defines **money** as "anything customarily used as a medium of exchange and measure of value, such as sheep, wampum, gold dust, etc." Most Americans have a good idea of what money is in their society. They constantly use bills, coins, and checks as money.

Nevertheless, have you ever asked yourself why money exists? Why do people engage in almost all economic transactions using money—currency or checks? The major reason they use money is because they do not receive their income at exactly the same time they want to buy things they would like. Take an example. Many working people get paid once a week. Yet they buy things each day of the week. What do they do? They keep part of their income in the form of currency and spend only a portion of it at a time.

Obviously, then, the use of money allows people to receive income at one time and spend it at another time. It facilitates transactions. Just think how society would be if people had to **barter** for everything—that is, exchange goods for goods.

For example, suppose you had a part-time job working in a grocery store. If there were no money, the grocer would have to pay you in groceries. To obtain something you wanted, you would have to exchange some of the groceries for that item. Things could get very complicated. In fact, in economies based on a barter system, people spend tremendous amounts of time and effort making transactions. They waste much potential output by engaging in barter transactions instead of using money.

Why Use Money?—A Recap

Let us summarize the reasons people use money. People use money because:

1. It facilitates economic transactions and exchanges. That is, money serves as a medium of exchange.

2. It is a temporary store of purchasing power. That is, money allows people to purchase things at a future date.

3. It is a convenient unit of accounting.

Why is money a convenient unit of accounting? People need some unit to measure the value of various things if they want to keep records of what is owed, how much income is made, how much income is saved, and so on. It would be inconvenient to use, say, bushels of wheat as a unit of accounting and express everything in terms of bushels of wheat, even though that could be done. The easiest thing is to use money as the unit of accounting. Everything is measured in terms of dollars in the United States, in marks in Germany, in francs in France, and so on.

Now let us look at the different types of money that have existed and exist today.

Different Types of Money

If you look at a dollar bill, most likely at the top of the face side it will say, "Federal Reserve Note." On the left it will say, "This note is legal tender for all debts, public and private." Nowhere is there any indication that the bill can be exchanged for a certain amount of gold or silver. It merely states that it is **legal tender.** This means that in the United States the bill has to be accepted in exchange for all debts owed. To summarize, the dollar bill is not *backed* by anything. The only reason it is useful is that people have trust in it.

People have trust that its value—in terms of what it will buy—will not fluctuate dramatically. They also have trust that others will accept it in exchange for debts owed. In technical language, money of this kind is called **fiduciary.** Fiduciary money is currency that people trust but that is not backed by any particular commodity.

Americans have not always used Federal Reserve Notes like those now in use. They have, for example, used gold and silver as circulating currency. Some societies have used other things. Chart 15-1 shows some examples of the many types of money that have been used in the United States.

It is important to understand that money can take many forms. It can be a commodity currency, as cigarettes were in some combat areas during World War II. Or it can be bills and coins. Whatever its form, all money serves the same basic purpose. It is a store of purchasing power, a standard of value, and it facilitates transactions by negating the need to barter.

Checks as Money

In the United States, something else is also used as money. Checking account balances on which people can write checks to pay for the things they buy are considered a form of money.

Undoubtedly you have seen many checks. Most adults use them to pay bills. Figure 15-1 shows a sample check. Notice that it is blank. In writing a check, a person fills in whom it is to and the amount and signs his or her name. Then it becomes money, just like dollar bills.

The reason that checking account balances are another form of money is that they serve all three purposes of money. They are a medium of exchange; they provide a temporary store of purchasing power; and they use a convenient unit of accounting.

To understand how checks work, one must understand the nation's banking system. To understand the banking system, one needs to know something about the central bank that controls the amount of money and credit in the United States.

The Early Development of Banks

Hundreds of years ago, rich moneylenders had strong vaults and tough guards. People who had valuables but no means of protection began to ask the moneylenders if they could leave their valuables with them for safekeeping. Undoubtedly the moneylenders charged a small fee for this kind of banking service.

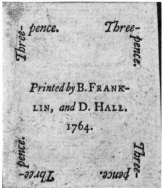

Chart 15-1: Different types of money that have been used in the United States at varous times.

Figure 15–1. A sample check.

Finally it dawned on a few moneylenders that many of the people who were keeping valuables in their vaults kept the valuables there for awhile. In fact, the valuables might be left for months, even years. As the number of clients and the amounts deposited grew, the owners of the vaults realized that only a small fraction of clients would ask for their deposits at any one time. Thus, to meet the demands of those clients, the vault owners needed to keep only a relatively small fraction of the total deposits on reserve.

Now if you were a vault owner and knew that only a certain percentage of deposits would be demanded at one time, you could loan the rest out at interest and make additional income besides the fee for use of your vault. This, theoretically, is how banks grew up as part of a *fractional reserve banking system.* All commercial banks operate on this principle in the United States today.

It may surprise you to learn that if you deposit $100 in your checking account, your bank is not legally obliged to keep that $100 on reserve. It can, and does, loan a certain percentage of its deposits to other people, or it buys bonds and other investments that earn income.

Depositors as a whole will not demand more than a small percentage of any given bank's total deposits in any one day. The bank can be assured that it will have sufficient reserves available for net withdrawals. The fact that it loans out the rest means there is more credit available in the economy. That credit allows people to buy now and pay later, when they have more income.

Now that you understand the idea of a fractional reserve banking system, let us look at the guardian of the nation's banking system—the Federal Reserve.

The Federal Reserve System

The Federal Reserve System was established in 1913 by the Federal Reserve Act. According to the Act's preamble, its purpose was "to provide for the establishment of Federal Reserve Banks, to furnish an elastic currency, to afford means of rediscounting commercial paper, to establish a more effective supervision of banking in the United States, and for other purposes."

Currently, the Federal Reserve System consists of 12 Federal Reserve Banks with 24 branches, a seven-member board of governors whose members are appointed by the President to 14-year terms, a Federal Open Market Committee, and other less important committees. The basic system is outlined in Figure 15-2.

Required Reserves

The ***reserve requirements*** for member banks are set by the board of governors of the Federal Reserve. The approximately 5,700 member banks must keep their reserves in the Federal Reserve Banks. Not all banks, however, are members of the Federal Reserve System. The reserves of the nation's banking system are, therefore, made up only of deposits of the member commercial banks of the Federal Reserve. Additionally, commercial banks are allowed to count as reserves any currency kept in their own vaults.

Changing the Supply of Money

The key function of the Federal Reserve is to control the amount of money in circulation in the United States. It controls the amount of money in circulation in order to provide an adequate amount for the expanding needs of business in a growing economy. Another of its goals is also to prevent an oversupply of money in circulation, which would overheat the economy and cause inflation. (This topic will be discussed in Chapter 20.) The Federal Reserve can affect the amount of money in circulation in several ways.

Changing Reserve Requirements

If the Federal Reserve should decide to raise reserve requirements, what do you think would happen? Let us look at an example. Suppose a bank has $1 million in deposits, and the reserve requirement is 20 percent. That bank can, therefore, loan out $800,000. It must keep $200,000—the reserve requirement—on deposit with the Federal Reserve. Of course, when the $800,000 is loaned out, that money eventually finds its way into other banks. These banks, in turn, can loan out 80 percent of $800,000, or $640,000. The $640,000 will then find its way to other banks, which can loan out 80 percent of it, and so on down the line.

What happens then if the Federal Reserve raises reserve requirements to 40 percent? The bank with $1 million in deposits would now

Figure 15–2. The Federal Reserve System. At the top of the system is the Board of Governors. The Board sets policy for the 12 Federal Reserve Banks, which have 24 branches throughout the country. There are about 5,700 member commercial banks which are part of the Federal Reserve System.

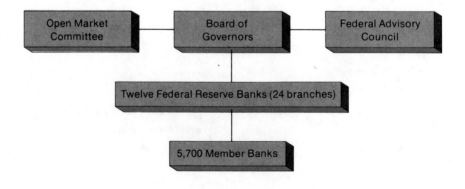

have to have $400,000 on reserve. Thus, it would have to call in $200,000 in loans, or at least not renew that amount as loans came due, in order to build up its reserve position to meet the legal requirement. Obviously, this would contract the amount of money in circulation in the economy, because not only would that bank loan less money, but so, too, would all other banks.

In recent years, the reserve requirements have not been used often to change the money supply in the United States.

Changing the Discount Rate

If a bank does not have enough reserves to meet its reserve requirement, it has to borrow the portion needed, at least temporarily. One of the ways it may do this is by calling the Federal Reserve and asking for a loan. The Federal Reserve does not make this type of loan for free. It charges interest. In banker's talk, this interest is called the *discount rate.*

If the Federal Reserve raises its discount rate, it will discourage some member banks from borrowing reserves. Therefore, a change in the discount rate is also a way to affect the total money supply.

Affecting Reserves Directly

The most powerful and often used means by which the Federal Reserve affects the supply of money in circulation is by changing reserves directly. It does this by buying and selling U.S. government bonds from and to the public or banks.

To understand how this works, let us look at an example. Suppose the Federal Reserve buys a $1,000 bond from a member bank. How does it pay for the bond? It does something that individuals cannot do. It credits $1,000 to the reserve deposit account of the bank from which it purchases the bond. What does this mean? It means that bank now has one less bond and $1,000 more in reserves. Therefore, that bank can loan additional money because its reserves are now

When a bank borrows money from the Federal Reserve to make you a loan, would this affect the amount of interest you paid for your loan? Why or why not?

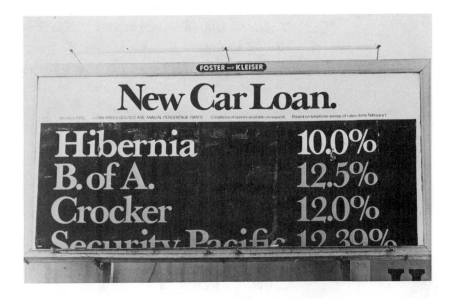

higher than before. In this manner, the Federal Reserve can increase the money supply.

When the Federal Reserve wants to decrease the money supply, it merely sells a bond to a member bank. The bank pays for the bond by having its reserve deposit account lowered by the amount of the bond. The bank then can loan less money.

Figure 15-3 shows how the money supply can be increased or decreased.

Chapter 18 examines how changes in the money supply can affect the amount of economic activity in the nation. Right now, let us look at another major function of the Federal Reserve—acting as a clearinghouse for checks.

A Clearinghouse for Checks

The Federal Reserve System has greatly simplified the clearing of checks. This is the method by which a check that has been deposited in one bank is transferred to the bank on which it was written.

Again, let us look at an example. Suppose John Smith, who lives in Chicago, writes a check to Jill Jones, who lives in San Francisco. When Jill Jones receives the check in the mail, she deposits it in her bank. Her bank then deposits the check in the Federal Reserve Bank of San Francisco. In turn, the Federal Reserve Bank of San Francisco sends the check to the Federal Reserve Bank of Chicago. The Federal Reserve Bank of Chicago then sends the check to John Smith's bank. There the amount of the check is deducted from John Smith's account. Figure 15-4 is a schematic diagram showing how this is done.

Issue 15, which follows this chapter, looks at another function of banks—lending people money.

Summary

1.   Money is anything that serves as a store of purchasing power and as a standard of value, facilitating transactions and negating the need to engage in barter.

2.   In the United States money consists of currency and checking account balances.

3.   Currency in the United States is legal tender. It must be accepted for all debts owed and as payment for things purchased.

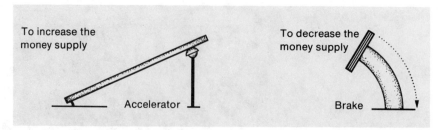

Figure 15-3. How the money supply can be changed.

To increase the money supply — Accelerator
1. Reduce member bank reserve requirements.
2. Reduce discount rate that member banks must pay to borrow reserves.
3. Buy bonds in the open market.

To decrease the money supply — Brake
1. Increase reserve requirements.
2. Raise discount rate.
3. Sell bonds in the open market.

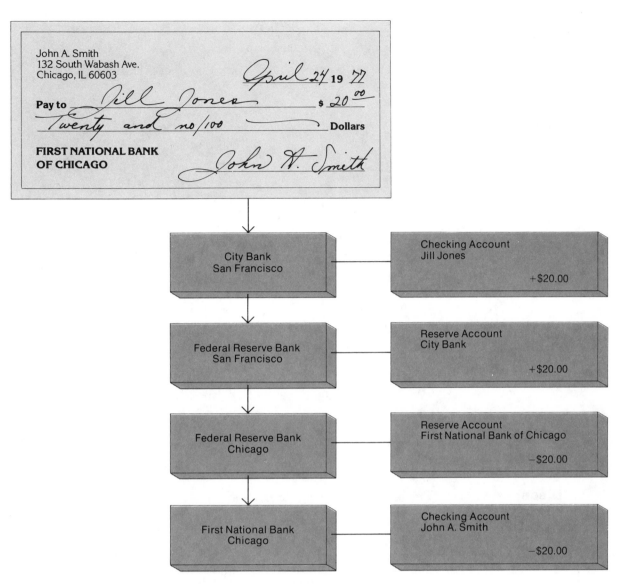

Figure 15–4. How a check is cleared.

4. Today U.S. currency is not backed by gold or silver. Its value is based on public trust and confidence.

5. The commercial banking system of the United States is controlled by the Federal Reserve System.

6. The Federal Reserve System consists of a seven-member board of governors, 12 Federal Reserve Banks with 24 branches, some 5,700 member banks, a Federal Open Market Committee, and several other, less important committees.

7. Banks generally are required to keep a specific amount of reserves on deposit. These reserves are expressed as a fraction of the total deposits that a bank has.

8. The Federal Reserve has three ways to change the supply of money in circulation in the United States. It can change the reserve

requirements or the discount rate. It can also buy and sell U.S. government bonds on the open market.

9. The Federal Reserve also operates as a clearinghouse for checks.

<table>
<tr><td>**Important Terms**</td><td>barter</td><td>fractional reserve banking system</td></tr>
<tr><td></td><td>currency</td><td>legal tender</td></tr>
<tr><td></td><td>discount rate</td><td>money</td></tr>
<tr><td></td><td>fiduciary</td><td>reserve requirement</td></tr>
</table>

Review Questions

1. What is money?

2. Why do people use money?

3. Why are checking account balances considered part of the money supply?

4. What is meant by legal tender?

5. What backs U.S. currency today?

6. What is a fractional reserve banking system?

7. What is the guardian of the nation's banking system

8. What is the makeup of the Federal Reserve System?

9. What functions does the Federal Reserve perform?

10. How can the Federal Reserve control the supply of money in circulation in the United States?

Discussion Questions

1. Throughout most of the nation's history, U.S. currency was backed by gold (also silver during some periods). Until 1968, the Federal Reserve was required to hold gold certificates equal to no less than 25 percent of the Federal Reserve notes in circulation. In that year Congress removed the requirement. Why? Do you think U.S. currency should be backed by some commodity such as gold or silver? Why or why not?

2. In the United States today, money consists of currency and checking account balances. Is there any other thing you think should be considered part of the money supply? If so, what? If not, why?

3. Should banks be required to have a larger percentage of their total deposits available for withdrawal? Why or why not?

Projects

1. The Federal Reserve System was created by the Federal Reserve Act in 1913 as part of Woodrow Wilson's "New Freedom" program. Research the background history of the act to learn why Wilson advocated the establishment of the system. Why was banking reform necessary at that time?

2. Obtain from the school or public library a copy of the current issue of the *Federal Reserve Bulletin*. Research the current reserve

requirements and the discount rate. When was each last changed? For what reasons? How does the discount rate compare with other interest rates?

3. Invite a representative from a local bank to speak to the class on how banking policies are affected by the Federal Reserve. Ask the bank representative to cite the advantages and disadvantages of being a member bank of the Federal Reserve System.

4. Write to the Board of Governors of the Federal Reserve System, Twentieth Street and Constitution Avenue NW., Washington, DC 20551, to find out what the requirements are to become a member bank and what functions the Federal Reserve Board performs in addition to those listed in the chapter.

Can We Get Banks to Charge Less for Credit?

Definition of New Term

Usury: Usury is the practice of charging rates of interest that exceed those set by law.

One of the major functions of commercial banks and the banking system in general is to make loans, or extend credit, to individuals and businesses. Banks, of course, are not the only institutions in the economy that extend credit. People can also get credit from credit card companies, retail stores, and credit unions. They can get credit from savings and loan associations, particularly for the purchase of a house. As a matter of fact, there are hundreds of thousands of places where people can go to purchase credit.

The Why and Wherefore of Usury Laws

There have always been restrictions on interest rates, both for the lender and the borrower. Many people seem to think that moneylenders have some special monopolistic power over others. In fact, moneylenders have been attacked so much in the past that dominant ethnic groups have historically shunned the profession, leaving it to minority people. And, for that matter, during the Middle Ages, the Catholic Church made laws against usury—the lending of money at "unreasonable" rates.

Today most states have passed laws prohibiting lenders from charging borrowers interest that exceeds a specified rate. The persistence of state legislation affecting the lending of money indicates that widespread suspicion of moneylenders still exists. Today most people are in favor of legislation limiting the amount of interest that can be charged on consumer loans. Since no action is cost free, however, one should be aware of both the benefits and the costs of usury laws.

One way to approach the issue is to remember that the selling of credit is no different from the selling of anything else. If usury laws are valid, then so, too, are government controls on other prices in the economy. Price control is too complex an issue to discuss here. Nevertheless, some of the unpredicted effects of usury laws can be pointed out by looking at two examples.

Washington State Usury Laws

Until 1968, interest on consumer loans from credit card companies and on revolving credit accounts from retail stores was generally 18 percent per annum (year), or 1.5 percent per month, in the State of Washington. Many people thought this rate of interest was much too high. They claimed that poor people were not able to afford credit at such a high price.

At that time, commercial banks making personal loans to customers were charging interest at rates as low as 9 percent. Poor people who did not qualify for bank loans at that low interest rate were supposedly being discriminated against. Therefore, many had to forego the benefits of buying on credit. A political movement was begun to get legislation passed against such "usurious" interest rates.

In 1968, a motion was put on the ballot to set the maximum interest rate on consumer loans at 12 percent per annum. It was felt that lowering the interest rate from 18 percent per annum would benefit those who could not afford that high rate. The measure passed by a wide margin. All credit card companies and stores doing business in Washington state were forced to lower their rates to 1 percent per month, or 12 percent per year.

Banks generally lend money at a lower interest rate than pawn shops, credit card companies and other lending institutions. Why do you suppose there are differences in lending rates?

What would you predict the results to be? Lower-cost credit? To be sure. But it turned out that the people benefited by the lower rate were not necessarily those the backers of lower-cost credit had in mind. Two professors, John J. Weatley and Guy G. Gordon, did a study of the effects of the law one year after it went into effect. Their conclusions were startling:

Low-income people who are marginal credit risks seem to have suffered the most from the enactment of the law because of the general tightening of credit.[1]

What, in fact, did creditors do? They raised some prices, adjusted credit practices and merchandise assortment, and raised the charges on special services, all in an effort to make up the lost revenues from their credit accounts. You must realize that there was a tremendous amount of competition for consumers' credit dollars, both before and after the change in the interest rate. In fact, according to a study made of the profits of credit institutions, the 18 percent rate did not lead to above-normal profits. This meant that it generally reflected the true costs of providing credit with a reasonable rate of return, or profit, to the lending companies. Thus, the reduction in rate to 12 percent forced creditors to adopt policies to offset the lost revenues. One way of doing this was to raise prices. Another, of course, was to eliminate risky debtors.

The Case of Arkansas

For many years, Arkansas has had a maximum interest limitation of 10 percent. In the face of high rates of inflation, the 10 percent rate of interest has been insufficient to induce many retailers and credit companies to provide credit in Arkansas. One need only visit the city of Taxarkana on the Texas-Arkansas border to verify this.

The main street of Texarkana is the dividing line between Arkansas and Texas (where interest rates on consumer loans are generally the same as in most other states). On the Texas side, there are numerous finance companies, used-car dealers, and TV and appliance stores. On the Arkansas side there are few, if any. Data on the number of credit purchases per person in Arkansas show that there are few compared to the credit purchases in Texas. Why? Simply because the usury law is too restrictive. Suppliers of credit prefer not to do business in Arkansas.

---

[1]John J. Wheatley and Guy G. Gordon, "Regulating the Price of Consumer Credit," *Journal of Marketing,* Vol. 35 (October 1971), pp. 21–28.

Are the people of Arkansas better off because of the 10 percent limitation on interest rates? Some are—those lucky enough to get credit at the 10 percent interest rate. But many are not. They must go to other states or forego credit purchases altogether. Or they may, in fact, end up borrowing from loan sharks outside the law when they think they need money desperately.

Many economists believe usury laws tend to be detrimental to the general welfare of the people who are supposed to be helped.

Summary

1. In most states today, there are restrictions on the rates of interest that lenders can charge.

2. The maximum rates are set by usury laws.

3. Usury laws are not new. The Catholic Church made laws against usury—the lending of money at unreasonable rates— during the Middle Ages.

4. Although most people favor setting limitations on interest rates, usury laws do have some disadvantages.

5. When rates of interest are set too low, they can lead to higher prices, tightening of credit practices, and the like.

6. Low-income people often benefit the least from highly restrictive usury laws.

Important Term   usury

Questions for Thought and Discussion

1. What is a "reasonable" rate of interest for a loan?

2. Why do you think creditors are less likely to grant credit to low-income people if interest rates are reduced?

3. Corporations are often exempt from usury laws. Why would they be exempt?

4. Do you favor usury laws? Why or why not?

16

The Government Spends, Collects, and Owes

Preview Questions

1. What has been the growth of government in the past?
2. What can Americans expect government to do in the future?
3. What are the various aspects of the federal government's budget?
4. What are some types of taxes?
5. What is the national debt?

Definitions of New Terms

Fiscal year: Fiscal year is the financial year on which a government or a business works. The federal government's fiscal year starts on July 1 and ends on June 30.

Proportional taxation: Proportional taxation is a system whereby every dollar earned is taxed at the same rate.

Progressive taxation: Progressive taxation is a system whereby more must be paid in taxes on each increment of income earned. In other words, the rate of taxation goes up as a person makes more income.

Regressive taxation: Regressive taxation is the opposite of progressive taxation. That is, as a person's income goes up, the average tax paid goes down.

The national debt: The national debt is the amount of debt that the federal government owes to private citizens, firms, and foreigners.

Deficit spending: Deficit spending occurs when government expenditures are greater than government revenues—that is, when government takes in less than it spends.

What Governments Do

Most likely, you are already familiar with many things that governments do. You know that government provides for schooling, roads, fire and police protection, and the like. You also know that many people work for the government, doing many different kinds of jobs. The government buys many things, from pencils to aircraft carriers. In recent years the cost of government has grown considerably.

The Growth in the Cost of Government

Figure 16-1 expresses total government purchases of goods and services as a percentage of GNP from 1890 to the present. Notice that in recent years there is a definite trend upward. Until the Great Depression and World War II, government purchases of goods and services exceeded 10 percent of GNP only during World War I. Just before the Great Depression government purchases were only 8.2 percent. At the beginning of the twentieth century, they were closer to 6 percent.

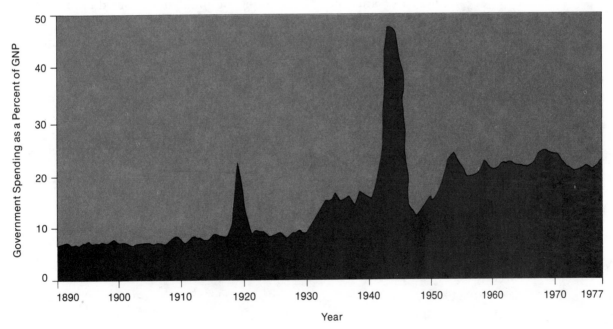

Figure 16-1. Rising government activity. This graph shows government spending at all levels—federal, state and local—on goods and services as a percentage of total gross national product. The big jump occurred during World War II, and there has been a continued upward trend ever since. 1977 is an estimate. Source: United States Department of Commerce.

Where Government Is Growing the Most

Table 16-1 breaks down the growth in the cost of government among the three levels in the United States. Notice that both the state and local levels are growing faster than the federal government. In particular, local and state expenditures on sewers, roads, schools, and welfare assistance to the poor have increased dramatically. However, both local and state governments are more than overshadowed by the federal government. This was not the case before World War I.

Prior to 1917, local government was the most important level of government. The federal government did little more than pay for national defense, finance a few public works projects, and pay the salaries of members of Congress, judges, and the few thousand employees who worked in such executive departments as the U.S. Post Office. Local governments performed most government functions at that time. They depended primarily on property taxes for their revenues. The property tax will be discussed in depth in Issue 16 on financing education.

The Federal Government Budget

Issue 3 provided the means by which one could set up a personal budget. That budget consisted of how much is spent and how much is earned. It broke down earnings into income from work, savings, and so on. It broke down expenditures into housing, food, insurance, etc. The same thing can be done for the federal government.

The federal government is the largest business in the world. It is difficult to comprehend the size of the numbers involved in federal expenditures. Whereas people customarily talk in hundreds or thousands of dollars, the federal government deals in millions and billions of dollars. In one-dollar bills laid end to end, a billion dollars would stretch around the world at the equator four times.

The 1978 federal government budget estimate is $480 billion. Table 16-2 presents the 1977 federal budget. Notice that it is based on a *fiscal year* rather than a calendar year. That is, expenditures

---

Table 16-1: Growth in Government—Federal, State, and Local. Total Outlays of Governments as a Percent of GNP (Including Government Welfare Payments)

Year	Federal	State	Local
1950	15	4	6
1955	18	4	7
1960	18	4	8
1965	17	5	8
1970	19	6	9
1976	22	8	10
1978*	23	10	11

*estimated

Source: U.S. Bureau of the Census

are figured for a year's period from July 1 of one year through June 30 of the next year. Chart 16-1 provides some information on federal expenditures according to category.

Now that the expenditure side of government has been discussed, let us see how government obtains money. The main way it obtains its revenues, of course, is by taxation.

How the Government Taxes

There are many types of taxes in the American economic system, including property taxes, personal and corporate income taxes, Social Security taxes, sales taxes, excise taxes, gift taxes, and inheritance taxes. Space does not permit an in-depth study of all these taxes, but the main features of income taxes will be pointed out. Before discussing those specific taxes, however, it is important to understand that there are essentially three ways to tax.

Table 16-2: Federal Budget—Fiscal 1977

	Billions
Income Security (Soc. Sec, SSI, etc.)	$137.2
Health Care	35.0
Interest on Debt	42.0
Nat. Resources + Energy	13.7
Revenue Sharing	7.4
Veterans Benefits	17.2
Education	16.6
Commerce + Transportation	16.5
International Aid + State Dept.	6.8
Defense	102.0
Agriculture	1.7
Total	$396.1

Source: U.S. Department of Commerce

Chart 16–1: Categories of the Federal Budget

Category	Purpose
National Security	Expenditures for all items that the government deems necessary to defend the United States against external aggression (e.g., payment of Army, Navy, Air Force, Marine salaries and equipment, etc.).
Veteran's Benefits and Services	Payments for past wars, essentially. These involve all of the benefits to the men and women who fought in World Wars I and II, the Korean War, and in Vietnam.
Interest on the Public Debt	Interest payments that must be made to individuals, firms, or foreigners who loaned money to the government.
International Affairs and Finance	Expenditures concerned with all of the international dealings that the government engages in, both politically and economically.
Space Research and Technology	Includes all payments for space shots and space activities.
Natural Resources and Environment	Payments for the support of land and natural resource conservation programs, control of air and water pollution, etc.
Agriculture and Agricultural Resources	Basically, all of the payments that go to the farming community for price supports and research that leads to increasing agricultural productivity.
Health, Labor, Welfare, and Education	By far the largest item in the federal budget today. It includes welfare aid to the aged, needy, handicapped, the family assistance program, the poverty program, Medicare, and health, education, and welfare expenditures.
Commerce, Transportation and Housing	Expenditures for highways, the regulation of interstate transportation, and public housing projects.
Revenue Sharing	Payment to the various states and localities of a percentage of taxes collected at the federal level to be spent by the state and local governments as they wish.
General Government	The cost of running Congress, the courts, and all of the expenses of the executive branch.

Ways to Tax

In terms of their relationship to the income of the taxpayer, taxes can be levied in three ways. Any specific tax can be put into one of these categories.

Proportional Taxation.   In *proportional taxation,* taxpayers pay a fixed percentage of every dollar they earn. When their income goes up, the taxes they pay go up. When their income goes down, the taxes they pay go down. If the proportional tax rate is 20 percent, then the taxpayer pays 20 cents in taxes out of every dollar he or she earns.

Progressive Taxation. Like a proportional tax system, a *progressive tax* system requires the taxpayer to pay more taxes as his or her earnings increase. The one difference is that the percentage of tax—that is, the tax rate—increases as income increases. Chart 16-2 gives an example showing how a progressive tax works.

Regressive Taxation. *Regressive taxation* is the opposite of progressive taxation. That is, under a regressive tax system a smaller and smaller percentage of additional income is paid as tax as income rises. As an example, suppose that all government revenues were obtained from a 50 percent tax on food. Since the percentage of income spent on food falls as total income rises, the percentage of total income paid in taxes under such a system would likewise fall with rising income. This would be a regressive tax system.

Kinds of Taxes

There are several different kinds of federal taxes. Some of these are progressive. Some are not.

The Personal Income Tax

The personal income tax at the federal level is a progressive tax. To some degree, however, the current system of allowable deductions diminishes the effective progressiveness of this tax.

Table 16-3 presents a portion of the 1978 federal tax schedule. Notice that as income rises, the tax rate on the last bracket of income increases. The rate applicable to the previous lumps of income, however, is less.

Many people think that a person in the 50 percent tax bracket pays 50 percent of all income to the federal government in taxes. This is not the case. That person pays a 50 percent tax only on taxable income in excess of $32,000 on a single return or $44,000 on a joint return. Income up to those amounts is taxed at lower rates. In fact, people in the 50 percent bracket may pay as little as 32.6 percent of their taxable income in income taxes to the federal government.

The Corporate Income Tax

Corporations pay income taxes, too. They are taxed on the difference between their costs of doing business and their total receipts.

In 1901, the corporate tax rate was a mere 1 percent of total taxable corporate profits, and corporations were given a $5,000 exemption.

Chart 16–2: A Progressive Tax System

Income	Tax Rate Applying to Each Jump in Income	Tax	Average Tax Rate
$10	10%	$1	$\frac{\$1}{\$10} = 10\%$
$20	20%	$1 + $2 = $3	$\frac{\$3}{\$20} = 15\%$
$30	30%	$1 + $2 + $3 = $6	$\frac{\$6}{\$30} = 20\%$

Table 16-3: Federal Personal Income Tax for a Childless Couple, 1978

Here we show the different income brackets and the marginal tax rates along with the average tax rates. As you can see, the marginal tax rates go up to a maximum of 70 percent. However, if income qualifies as being "earned," the maximum is 50 percent. All wages are considered earned income, but interest on bonds or dividends from stocks are not.

NET INCOME BEFORE EXEMPTIONS (BUT AFTER DEDUCTIONS)	PERSONAL INCOME TAX	AVERAGE TAX RATE PERCENT	TAX RATE ON INCOME SHOWN BETWEEN CUTOFF POINTS
Below $ 1,500	$ 0	0	0
2,000	70	3.5	14
3,000	215	7.2	15
4,000	370	9.2	16
5,000	535	10.7	17
10,000	1,490	14.9	22
20,000	3,960	19.8	28
50,000	16,310	32.6	50
100,000	44,280	44.3	60
200,000	109,945	55.0	69
400,000	249,930	62.5	70
1,000,000	669,930	67.0	70
10,000,000	6,969,930	69.7	70

Source: Internal Revenue Service

In 1932 the exemption was eliminated. By then the rate had also increased to 13.8 percent.

Although individuals had a progressive tax schedule since the adoption of the personal income tax in 1913, corporations did not have a progressive tax schedule until 1936. Since 1950, corporations have had to pay a standard tax on the first $25,000 of profit. Profits in excess of $25,000 were charged a surtax in addition to the regular tax. Today corporations pay 22 percent on the first $25,000 of profits and 48 percent on any profits in excess of $25,000.

The National Debt

Whenever government spends more than it receives, it has to go into debt. The federal government goes into debt by borrowing money from American citizens, and sometimes from sources abroad. When it borrows money, it increases the **national debt.** When it increases the national debt, it increases the interest that must be paid to the people who loaned it money.

The national debt has grown steadily since World War II. Yet if one corrects for changes in the price level and increases in population, one will find that the per capita, inflation-corrected national debt in the United States has actually been falling in recent years. Figure 16-2 supports this.

In recent years, there has been a great deal of debate over **deficit**

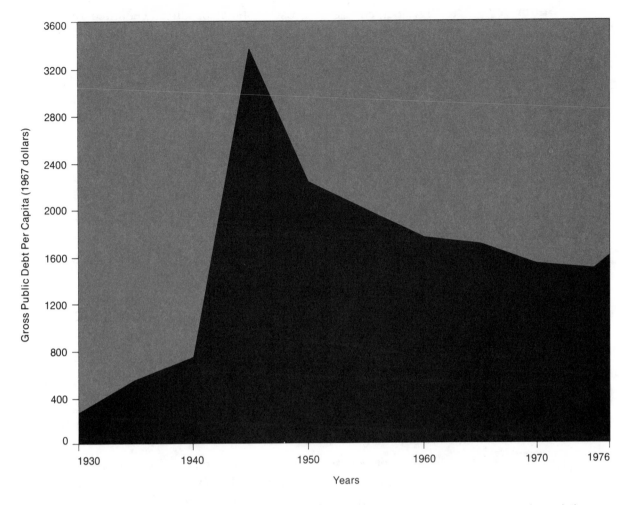

Figure 16–2. The public debt over time corrected for inflation and population. We incurred our biggest public debt fighting World War II. Since then, it has actually fallen, if we correct it for inflation and population increases. (In the very recent past, the figure has started to rise, though.) Source: U.S. Treasury Department.

spending—spending more than is taken in through taxation and other channels. Those opposed to increasing the national debt claim that it is spending future generations' money today. In other words, future generations will have to pay for much of what is being spent now. It is not unusual for newspaper editorials to decry the increase in the debt. However, the same newspapers will run advertisements promoting the purchase of U.S. savings bonds—an increase in the national debt!

Summary

1. The percentage of gross national product accounted for by government purchases of goods and services has risen steadily since World War II.

2. Today government purchases account for almost 30 percent of total spending in the economy.

3. The cost of government is growing faster at the state and local levels than at the federal level.

4. The federal budget can be broken down into eleven general categories. By far the largest category today is expenditures for health, education, welfare, and labor.

5. The main way governments raise revenue (income) is by taxation.

6. Basically there are three types of tax systems—proportional, progressive, and regressive.

7. The federal government levies several different taxes, including income taxes, excise taxes, sales taxes, gift and inheritance taxes, and Social Security taxes.

8. The federal personal income tax is a progressive tax.

9. The federal corporate income tax is 22 percent on all profits to $25,000 and 48 percent on all profits over $25,000.

10. Whenever the federal government borrows money, it increases the national debt.

11. If one corrects the national debt for changes in population and price levels, he or she will find that it has fallen in recent years even though it has steadily risen in absolute numbers.

Important Terms

deficit spending	fiscal year
national debt	progressive taxation
proportional taxation	regressive taxation

Review Questions

1. What is the trend in government spending?

2. Government spending is growing the fastest at what level?

3. How large is the federal budget?

4. What is the largest component of the federal budget in expenditures today? Has this always been so?

5. What is the main way government raises revenue?

6. What are the three types of tax systems?

7. What kind of tax is the personal income tax? The corporate income tax?

8. From whom does the federal government borrow?

9. Is the national debt growing? Explain.

10. Why are some people opposed to increasing the national debt?

Discussion Questions

1. Why do you think government grows so much during wartime periods?

2. Do you think a limit should be placed on government spending? If so, what limit? If not, why?

3. Do you favor reforming the federal tax system? If so, what recommendations regarding reform would you make? If not, why?

4. Does it matter how large the national debt is? Why?

Projects

1. Many Americans complain about the high taxes in the United States. Research the taxes paid by citizens in such countries as Great Britain, Sweden, and Italy. Do you think Americans are taxed too much? Why or why not?

2. Obtain copies of Form 1040 and instructions for filing a personal income tax from the nearest branch of the Internal Revenue Service. With a group of students, prepare a set of data that can be used for a class exercise on making out a tax return.

3. Obtain copies of the most recent federal budget. What are the major sources of revenue? Which source is the most important? Which source seems to be increasing the fastest in terms of percentage? What do you think accounts for this?

4. Hold a class debate on the following issue: *Resolved,* all taxes in the United States should be progressive in form.

How to Tax and How to Spend—The Case of Education

Definitions of New Terms

Public education: Public education is a system of education financed by taxes.

Tuition: Tuition is a direct payment to a school made for the privilege of attending that school.

Property tax: A property tax is a tax on real property (residences and places of business). It is generally computed on a percentage of the value of the property.

When most people go to a movie, they usually pay for their admission directly at a ticket counter. When they buy groceries, they usually pay for the groceries directly at the cashier's stand. When young people go to public school, however, their parents do not pay the school directly.

The vast majority of young people in the United States go to public schools. Public schools, in essence, are owned by the citizens of the community and are administered by the board of education of the district. Public schooling is not paid for directly. It is paid for out of taxes collected from various sources. Chapter 16 discussed taxes in general and briefly examined federal income taxes. This issue will focus on the type of tax used to finance **public education** at the primary and secondary levels.

Public Versus Private Schooling

When you go to a public school, to you it appears "free." Yet nothing that is scarce in this world comes free of charge. Public school teachers earn salaries. Money is required to build and maintain public school buildings. The books you use in class cost money. The electricity to light classrooms must also be paid for. In short, providing "free" public education certainly does not come at a zero cost.

What is the difference between "free" public education and "expensive" private education? After all, many Americans do go to private schools, and private schooling is costly. Those families who send their children to private schools must bear the *full* cost of their children's education. They make tuition payments directly to the school. Those parents who send their children to public schools, however, do not pay a direct **tuition.**

Public schools are paid for by taxes. Thus, parents whose

Public education is not free. Do you feel the present method of financing public schools through property taxes is adequate and fair? Why or why not?

children attend public schools pay for schooling indirectly through the taxes they pay. Thus, public education is not free. It is merely paid for in a different manner than most goods and services that people buy.

The Way Public Schools Are Financed

Generally, public schools are financed by a **property tax**. A property tax is a tax on the real property (residences and places of business) in a particular geographical area. A property tax is usually paid every year on the basis of some percentage of the value of the property taxed.

Since homeowners pay the bulk of property taxes, it is they—rather than just those who have children attending public school—who pay most of the costs of public education. Families with a large number of children attending public schools benefit more from the property-tax system of financing schools than families with few children. Of course, the direct benefit to families with no children, or to those whose children attend private schools, is essentially quite small. They partake in few, if any, of the services of public education. They do, however,

The costs of private education are paid directly by those who attend. Through property taxes many of these same people indirectly support public education.

receive indirect social benefits from a literate, educated group of young people.

Families who choose to send their children to private schools, in effect, pay twice for education. They pay property taxes that go to finance public schools. They must also pay tuition to the private schools their children attend.

Some Problems with Property Taxation

In general, under the current system of property taxation, school districts composed mainly of low-income families having low-valued property collect less taxes for public education than school districts where property values are high. In recent years, this situation has resulted in a number of suits challenging the legality of the present public school financing method. Most suits charge that a particular school system is discriminating against its students because it spends less per student than other districts in the area. The difference, of course, is due to the fact that districts that spend less per student are generally poor, having low property values and hence a small base on which to assess property taxes.

Solutions to the Property-Tax Dilemma

Because of the great variation in the amount of revenue available per pupil for school districts, a number of critics have suggested alternative ways of financing education. Most proposals involve a sort of equalization of per pupil expenditures from district to district. The idea, of course, is to bring the lower districts up to the level of the higher districts, closing the gap from the bottom rather than pushing down the top. Note, however, that this means spending more money on education. Generally, it is impossible to increase expenditures per pupil at the low end of the scale without collecting more revenues to pay for those increases.

The public is therefore faced with the question of how much should be spent on education. This is no easy question to answer. The appropriate amount of expenditures on any public service is not infinite. No doubt young people are better off if they get a better education. Yet the dollars that are spent on education cannot be spent on other priorities. Thus, the question remains, what is the appropriate amount to spend on education?

That question must be answered not only on the basis of the additional benefits to be derived from additional expenditures on education, but also in terms of comparison with the benefits that might be derived from alternative spending. All individuals make decisions of this kind when they are faced with how to spend their income. (Scarcity and decision making were discussed in Chapter 2 and Issue 3.)

The choice does become somewhat more complicated when the individual who is purchasing the service of education does not pay for that service directly. The decision becomes political—that is, it is ultimately made by the electorate. The majority of voters will set the level of expenditures for education for all families in a particular district through the candidates they elect to the school board, or the position they support on school bond issues. From past voting records, one can see that those families with several children generally tend to vote for increased expenditures on education, whereas those families with few or no children tend to vote against increased expenditures.

Can the Issue Be Solved?

Eliminating the property tax and imposing an alternative method for financing local expenditures for public education will not solve the problem of differences in expenditures per pupil throughout the country. That problem might only be solved by the federal government forcing a uniform standard for per pupil expenditures for the entire country and using federal tax dollars to make up any differences that might result.

In any event, many improvements in education for those in disadvantaged areas will require more revenue. This means that some increase in taxation will most likely have to be made. The government cannot obtain better schooling without somehow raising additional money to pay for it. This involves an art. As Jean Baptiste Colbert, the French Minister of Finance during the reign of Louis XIV, once said, "The art of taxation consists in so plucking the goose as to obtain the largest possible amount of feathers while provoking the smallest amount of hissing."

Summary

1. Public education is not free. It is paid for by taxes.

2. Most public schools are financed by property taxation.

3. Under the present method of financing public education, there are great variations in school expenditures per pupil from one district to the next.

4. In recent years, there have been many suits involving the financing of public education. Most suits charge that the current system discriminates against low-income areas.

5. There have been attempts in some states to equalize per pupil expenditures from district to district.

6. The only way to make education better is to spend more money on it. Increased expenditures most likely mean increased taxation.

Important Terms   property tax   public education
                         tuition

Questions for   1. How do you think education should be financed?
Thought and
Discussion   2. Do you think private schools should receive some revenue
                      raised from educational tax dollars? Why or why not?

                      3. Should families who send children to private schools get a
                      tax credit on their property taxes? Why or why not?

UNIT SIX

Managing the Nation's Economy

17

The Ups and Downs of Economic Activity

Preview Questions

1. Does business activity in the United States operate smoothly all the time?
2. What is a business cycle?
3. What is unemployment?
4. What are some reasons for unemployment?

Definitions of New Terms

Business cycle: The business cycle is made up of the changing phases of business activity in any economy. A business cycle usually has ups and downs.

Recession: A recession is a period of insufficient economic activity, characterized by higher than normal rates of unemployment.

Depression: A depression is a period of major reductions in economic activity characterized by large amounts of unemployment.

Theory: A theory is a belief, policy, or procedure proposed or followed as the basis of action. Much of what people believe to be true about the world is based on theories about the way the world works.

Sunspot theory: The sunspot theory holds that sunspots cause changes in weather, which cause changes in agricultural output, which cause changes in the output of the entire economy.

Innovation: Innovation is the adaptation of an invention to some actual production technique.

Innovation theory: The innovation theory suggests that innovation causes fluctuations in the desire to invest, which causes ups and downs in business activity.

Psychological theory: The psychological theory proposes that waves of optimism and pessimism cause changes in business activity.

Unemployment rate: The unemployment rate is the percentage of workers in the labor force who are out of work and are seeking jobs but cannot find them.

Full employment rate: The full employment rate is the level of unemployment that is considered acceptable. Today the acceptable level of unemployment is considered to be 5 percent.

Frictional unemployment: Frictional unemployment is unemployment caused by imperfect information in the job system.

Cyclical unemployment: Cyclical unemployment is unemployment associated with the recessionary stage of the business cycle.

Structural unemployment: Structural unemployment is unemployment associated with structural changes in the economy that put individuals permanently out of work.

Automation: Automation is the replacement of human labor by machines.

Seasonal unemployment: Seasonal unemployment is unemployment resulting from the seasonal nature of some work.

Have you ever worked at a job only to have your boss tell you there was not enough business to keep you on? If that has happened, you know how it feels to be laid off or fired from a job because business is down. You have experienced that feeling of helplessness and anger. Your plight as a student laid off from a job is certainly important to you, even if your parents provide for you. Millions of American workers are fired or laid off from their jobs each year including breadwinners, who must take care of themselves and others who depend on them.

Changing levels of business activity can greatly affect the lives of millions of Americans. They especially affect the lives of those who have difficulty finding jobs because there is little demand for their skills or services. To be sure, even when business activity is on an upward path, some people find themselves unemployed for any of a variety of reasons.

Chapter 14, in the previous unit, talked about how to measure the economy's performance. A person does that generally by looking at

The depression of the 1930s was the worst in American history. Ask a friend or relative who lived through this period what it was like. Do they feel it could or couldn't occur again? Why or why not?

GNP, sometimes corrected for changes in prices. If one looks at changes in GNP during the last 100 years, one would find many abrupt ups and downs in business activity. These ups and downs, depicted in Figure 17-1, represent periods of prosperity and high employment and periods of recession or depression and increased unemployment.

The Business Cycle

Ups and downs in economic activity are often associated with what is called the **business cycle.** This term is somewhat deceptive. The word *cycle* usually refers to a series of changes that are generally regular. But changes in business conditions in the United States have shown no such regularity. Nevertheless, an idealized business cycle can be visualized as shown in Figure 17-2,

In the idealized business cycle, there is a boom period, followed by a downturn. The downturn may become a **recession.** The recession leads to a recovery period, followed by a boom period of prosperity. The boom then leads to another downturn.

In recession, unemployment rises. Many workers are put out of jobs when business activity begins to decline at an alarming rate. During a recession, numerous families undergo financial hardship. Purchases that would be made in more prosperous times are put off. If a recession becomes exceptionally bad, it deepens into a **depression,** with millions of people out of work. The greatest depression in the history of the United States occurred during the 1930s.

The various phases of the business cycle are useful in describing the status of the nation's economy at any time. By itself, however, such a description does not explain why business is sometimes good and sometimes bad.

The Concept of Theory

To understand why business activity changes as it does, one needs to look at a **theory** explaining why recessions and depressions occur. A

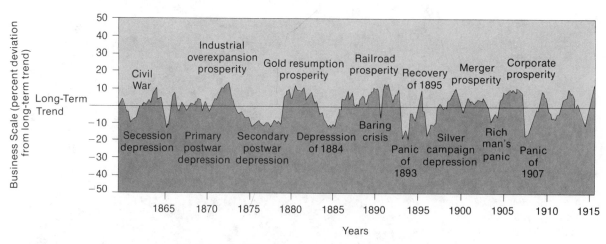

Figure 17–1. Changes in GNP over the last 100 years.

reasonable theory allows people to predict what might happen. Thus, it provides a means for determining the proper course for government policies aimed at stabilizing economic activity in the United States. Various government policies will be examined in the chapters that follow. Here it is important to realize more specifically what a theory is.

Undoubtedly you have been exposed in other courses to a number of theories about many aspects of the world. For example, if you have taken physics or biology, you have studied theories of how the universe or the human body works. You know that blood circulates in the human body. This proven scientific "fact" was at one time a theory presented by the English physician William Harvey to his colleagues. The same is true about the shape of the earth. At one time, the idea that the earth was round was just a theory. It was not until Magellan's crew circumnavigated the globe that the theory became a proven fact.

In economics, there are many theories. These are merely notions about the way the economic world works. Therefore, discussion of the business cycle is basically the presentation of ideas about the way the economy works.

Business Cycle Theories

There are many theories of why business activity goes up and down. We only have space to examine a few historically famous business cycle theories here. Later chapters will explore some additional theories that relate to the nature of unemployment.

The Sunspot Theory

Sunspots are a form of solar activity in which the sun experiences large storms on its surface. These solar storms seem to affect weather.

In the late nineteenth century, some economists believed that sunspots caused changes in business activity. Although the *sunspot*

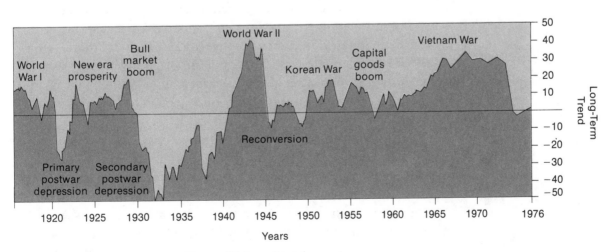

Figure 17–1 continued.

Figure 17–2. An idealized business cycle. The diagram shows that there is first a boom period at the top of the cycle, then a sliding off into recession and/or depression, and then a recovery to another boom.

theory sounds ridiculous at first, it did have a scientific base. Since sunspots affect the weather and weather affects the output of farmers, sunspots could indirectly affect the output of the entire economy. After all, agriculture was the largest sector of the economy at that time. Thus, a change in its output would mean a change in overall business conditions.

As a matter of fact, throughout most of the nineteenth century there did seem to be a direct relationship between sunspot cycles and agricultural cycles. Unfortunately, that relationship has not held in the twentieth century. It is too bad. Such a theory of business cycles could have been a most useful predicting tool, had the relationship between weather and business activity proved valid. Since scientists today can predict sunspot activity accurately, their predictions might have provided an accurate means of predicting changes in business activity.

The Innovation Theory

Many great inventions have been made in this country and elsewhere. The telephone was a great invention; the automobile was another. An invention can be defined as the creation of something new. Many inventions, however, go unnoticed because business people cannot figure out how to use them. That is, there is no *innovation.* Innovation is the adaptation of an invention to some actual production technique. Innovations may be defined as inventions that can be used and sold to the buying public. The vast bulk of inventions never become innovations.

The *innovation theory* suggests that innovations cause fluctuations in business investment, which in turn cause the ups and downs in business activities. This theory assumes that as soon as one person or firm decides to use an invention—that is, to innovate—others will attempt to hop on the bandwagon. Thus, various businesses will invest in new production processes. This will cause a rise in overall business activity as money is spent on the new production techniques. Eventually, however, investment will die down, and aggregate business activity will slow down as a consequence.

Although the innovation theory has merit in explaining some business cycles, it is weak as a predicting tool. How can people predict when innovations will be made? After the fact, certainly, people can judge which ones may have caused a particular "take-off" in economic activity. But though the theory is useful in explaining business cycles *after* they have occurred, it cannot predict when changes in business activity *will* occur.

The Psychological Theory

It is possible that people's psychological reactions to changing economic and political events cause changes in business activity. Waves of optimism may be caused, for example, by the prospects for war or peace, or by the prospects of new discoveries of natural resources. As people ride these waves of optimism up and down, so too goes the level of business activity.

However, this type of theorizing, like the innovation theory, is only useful in explaining things after they have occurred. There is little chance of using the **psychological theory** to predict when the next boom or recession will occur. Yet that is precisely what economists want to do with any theory of changes in business activity.

These theories have all fallen into disuse, mainly because they have not been able to help explain the many ups and downs in our most recent business activity. We will see that newer theories have had more success. Before doing that, let us look at one of the most pressing problems that society faces when business activity goes into a lull—excessive unemployment.

Unemployment and Employment

When people cut down on buying, businesses find that their stocks of goods for sale do not diminish as fast as in the past. Eventually, these businesses find that they cannot afford to keep all the workers they have employed when business activity was better. They also cut back on orders to suppliers, thereby reducing derived demand for labor and other factors of production. Producers are then forced to fire or lay off those workers who constitute an excessive work force.

The workers who are fired or laid off enter the ranks of the unemployed. This is where the pain of changes in business activity is first felt. The person who is unemployed must rely for survival on savings and government transfers. This is the human aspect of the business cycle—the aspect that responsible people can never forget. Many know that historically the level of unemployment in the United States has not always been socially or politically acceptable.

Historical Unemployment Rates

Figure 17-3 depicts the **rate of unemployment** in the United States over time. In the 1930s, the rate of unemployment reached almost 25 percent. That meant that out of every four people in the labor force, one was out of work. These people were actively looking for jobs but could not find them. Certainly, in comparison with unemployment rates during the Great Depression, those of the 1970s are not terrible. Nevertheless, few Americans are satisfied with an unemployment level just because it is lower than 25 percent. In fact, today most Americans favor a much stricter definition of what is the acceptable unemployment level, or the *full employment rate.*

Defining Full Employment

How does one define the magical number of employed workers that constitutes full employment—that is, the level of employment that is politically desirable and acceptable? It is not easy. Economists have no way of knowing what full employment really is. Twenty years ago, "full employment" meant that no more than 3 percent of the labor force were unemployed. In the 1960s, that number was 4 percent. By the mid-1970s, it had increased to 5 percent.

Why did the number rise? Some economists suggest that it rose because of a recognition that the labor force had become more complex. In a society that has become increasingly more technological, it is now more difficult for workers who have been laid off to find

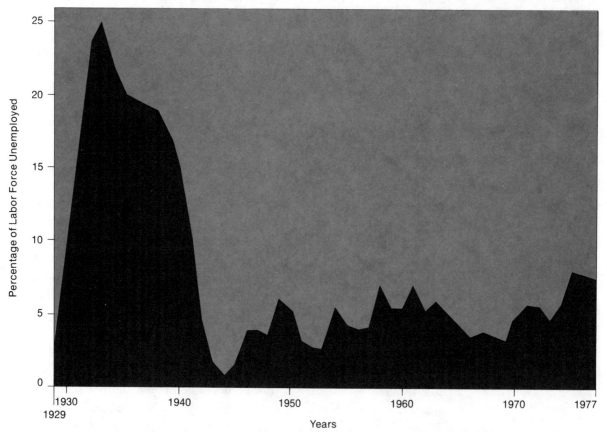

Figure 17-3. Rate of unemployment over time. Unemployment has varied in the United States from a low of 1.2 percent of the civilian labor force at one point during World War II to almost 25 percent at the depths of the Great Depression. As can be seen, the cyclical variations in unemployment are irregular. 1977 is an estimate. Source: United States Department of Labor, Bureau of Labor Statistics.

other jobs. Yet, the fact is that the level of unemployment that is called "full employment" is arbitrary and is determined politically. Nonetheless, one should be aware that when people today talk about full employment, they generally mean that no less than 95 percent of the labor force is employed and no more than 5 percent is out of work and actively seeking work.

Types of Unemployment

Government officials, particularly those who work in the U.S. Department of Labor, classify unemployment into several different types. Of course, unemployment means only one thing—not having a job. But there are a number of reasons why workers become unemployed. Economists generally look at the following types of unemployment: frictional, cyclical, structural, and seasonal.

Frictional Unemployment

Frictional unemployment is unemployment caused by friction in the system. After all, the world is not one of perfect information. When a worker is fired or laid off, it takes time to find out where the best alternative job lies. That time, or friction, is involved in a job search.

A certain amount of friction is involved in any economy. It exists whenever there is an imperfect match between job vacancies and job applicants. Many economists believe that a large percentage of unemployment is frictional unemployment. They also believe that there should be no attempt to reduce it. After all, searching for a better job is one way a worker can earn a higher income.

Cyclical Unemployment

Unemployment associated with the business cycle is called *cyclical unemployment.* When the cycle falls into a recession or depression period, unemployment rises. When the cycle enters the recovery phase, unemployment declines. Unemployment is at its lowest rate during boom periods.

Cyclical unemployment can be smoothed out to the extent that appropriate government stabilization policies even out undesired changes in economic activity. Although there have been periods of success in stabilizing the economy, there also have been failures. Thus, the elimination of cyclical unemployment in the immediate future appears unlikely.

Structural Unemployment

When the structure of the economy changes, some workers are put out of work. For example, if a new deposit of a basic mineral is found in one region of the country that can be mined at a much lower cost than deposits in another region, the workers in the declining area will suffer from *structural unemployment.*

Structural unemployment also includes technological unemployment. This is unemployment caused by machines replacing laborers —that is, unemployment resulting from *automation.*

Seasonal
Unemployment

Certain jobs require workers only during certain seasons. For example, outdoor construction work in the northern sections of the country virtually comes to a halt during the winter months. People working on such jobs suffer from *seasonal unemployment.*

Are There Other Types of Unemployment?

Discussion to this point has mentioned several categories of unemployment that economists have found useful in explaining certain elements of the overall unemployment rate. More refined definitions of different types of unemployment could certainly be cited. Issue 17 treats a type of unemployment sometimes called the "new" unemployment. It concerns unemployment caused by something most people would not think could cause unemployment. This is the unemployment associated with the current system of assisting the unemployed.

Summary

1. Business activity in the United States has never been without its ups and downs. The ups and downs in business activity make up the business cycle.

2. The idealized business cycle has four stages—boom, downturn, recession or depression, and recovery.

3. In itself the business cycle does not explain why business activity is subject to change.

4. There are many business cycle theories. Among the more important historically are the sunspot theory, the innovation theory, and the psychological theory.

5. Although most business cycle theories can explain why changes occurred in business activity, few can predict changes that might occur.

6. Unemployment occurs when business activity decreases.

7. It is difficult to define full employment. Today most people consider the full employment rate to be reached when the level of unemployment is no greater than 5 percent.

8. There are several types of unemployment. The most common are frictional, cyclical, structural, and seasonal unemployment.

Important Terms

automation
cyclical unemployment
frictional unemployment
innovation
psychological theory
seasonal unemployment
sunspot theory
unemployment rate

business cycle
depression
full employment rate
innovation theory
recession
structural unemployment
theory

Review Questions

1. What are the stages of the business cycle?

2. What is the difference between a recession and a depression?

3. In which stage of the business cycle is the level of unemployment likely to be lowest?

4. What are some theories of business cycles?

5. Why cannot these theories be used to predict business activity?

6. In general, what causes unemployment?

7. Why is it difficult to define full employment?

8. What are the four common types of unemployment?

Discussion Questions

1. Who do you think are the first people to be fired or laid off during a downturn in business activity? Why?

2. Why would the average duration of unemployment—that is, the length of time a worker is out of work—go up during a recession?

3. How serious is unemployment today? What do you think should be done about it?

4. Do you think it is possible to predict and control the level of business activity in an economy? If so, how? If not, why?

Projects

1. Obtain a copy of *Business Conditions Digest* from the school or public library. Examine some of the indicators of business activity. Which indicators do you think explain changes in business activity? That is, which ones seem to provide evidence of recession, recovery, and boom?

2. Prepare a report on various rates of unemployment for various groups of workers (age groups, occupations, racial composition, etc.). Information on unemployment statistics can be obtained from the *Monthly Labor Review*.

3. Invite a representative from the local branch of the state division (or department) of employment to speak to the class on the problems of the unemployed and the status of employment in the area. Ask the representative to talk specifically about the employment situation for young people.

Can Helping the Unemployed Cause Higher Unemployment Rates?

Definitions of New Terms

Unemployment compensation: Unemployment compensation is the payments made to workers who are unemployed and covered by unemployment insurance.

New unemployment: New unemployment is continued unemployment that results from unemployment compensation.

If a full-time worker is fired or laid off from work, he or she will probably qualify for **unemployment compensation.** The unemployed worker must file an application for benefits at the nearest state unemployment office. Under the present unemployment insurance system, the worker must serve a waiting period of one week. If the unemployed worker becomes eligible for benefits, that person will then receive weekly compensation for as long as he or she remains out of work during a specified period of time (26 to 52 weeks in most states).

The amount of compensation paid each week to an unemployed worker depends, in large part, on the wages that person earned before being fired or laid off. The goal of unemployment insurance is to provide a cushion on which people out of work can survive while they are looking for a new job. The system is designed to eliminate some of the suffering and financial hardship caused by unemployment.

Recently a number of critics have pointed out that the present system not only alleviates some suffering of the unemployed, but it also lengthens the average duration of unemployment. This, in turn, leads to a higher unemployment rate. The economics behind this criticism involves the law of demand.

The Law of Demand as Applied to Leisure

Not working is the alternative to working. A person who is not working has more leisure time. What is the cost of that leisure time? Basically, the cost is the income given up by not working. For example, suppose a person is given the choice of working five additional hours a week at $3 per hour. If that person decides not to work the five additional hours, the cost of the five hours of leisure is $15 ($3 × 5). In essence, the person "bought" five hours of leisure at a cost of $15.

Leisure, like any other good, follows the law of demand. At a higher price, less will be demanded than at a lower price. Thus, the person who decides to "buy" five hours of leisure at a cost of $15 might decide to forego those leisure hours if the wage rate became $4 per hour, because the cost for the five hours of leisure would then be $20. In other words, at higher wage rates people are willing to work more than they would at lower wage rates.

What does this have to do with unemployment compensation? Consider that for those eligible for unemployment compensation, each week without a job means a week of leisure at a cost *less* than the wages foregone. It is less because the unemployed worker receives unemployment compensation.

For example, consider a worker who was laid off from a job that paid $100 a week. If the worker does not obtain unemployment benefits, he or she loses $100 a week income for every week not worked. The leisure that is "bought" has a price of $100 per week. Now consider what happens if the worker is eligible for unemployment benefits. Those benefits make up a percentage of the lost income—maybe as much as 80 percent. Effectively, then, the cost of a week's leisure is not $100, but considerably less—say $20.

If the law of demand holds for leisure, some unemployed workers will respond to this reduced price of leisure by purchasing more. That is, some workers will remain unemployed longer, taking more time to look for a job.

Unemployment compensation provides temporary financial assistance to those who for one reason or another lose their jobs. Some critics suggest the present system creates more problems than it solves.

Can Helping the Unemployed Cause Higher Unemployment Rates?   **281**

Unemployment Compensation and the Tax System

To get an even more accurate idea of how unemployment compensation benefits the unemployed, it is important to realize that no taxes are paid on unemployment benefits. Taxes must be paid, however, on income earned. Thus, to get an accurate reflection of the actual cost of not working, one must compare the *after-tax* income that a worker was earning with the unemployment compensation to be received.

When this is done, one finds that in many cases the actual cost of leisure is small. The difference between the after-tax income a worker could make if employed and the actual unemployment benefits on which no taxes are paid is small. Studies have shown that when all taxes not paid are considered, the incentive to go back to work is greatly diminished so long as the person continues to obtain unemployment benefits.

The New Unemployment

The unemployment that results from unemployment compensation has been called the **new unemployment.** Various studies have estimated that new unemployment accounts for 1 to 3 percent in the overall employment rate. If the actual figure is 1 percent, then an overall unemployment rate of 6 percent would be reduced to 5 percent by eliminating unemployment compensation.

However, do not conclude that such studies suggest eliminating unemployment compensation. Rather, the studies recommend that the system be altered to reduce the incentive not to return to work.

One suggested alteration is to tax unemployment benefits the same as income earned. Since individuals who make low incomes do not pay high tax rates, they would be least affected by such a change in the unemployment compensation system.

Another suggestion is to change the distribution of benefits from what they are now. Today low-income families receive a small percentage of unemployment benefits. They either do not work in industries covered by unemployment insurance or have not worked long enough to qualify. Since the taxing of unemployment benefits would cost more to higher-income earners who are in higher tax brackets, they would probably use the unemployment insurance system less. The critics of the current system think such a change would be beneficial to the economy.

Summary

1. Many workers who become unemployed are eligible for unemployment compensation.

2. Those eligible for unemployment benefits must undergo a one-week waiting period.

3. Unemployment benefits are paid on a weekly basis for a specified period, as long as the person remains unemployed.

4. The goal of unemployment compensation is to provide a cushion on which people out of work can survive.

5. As the price of leisure falls, a larger quantity will be demanded.

6. Unemployment compensation has the effect of lowering the cost of leisure. Hence, it tends to lessen the incentive to return to work.

7. Several studies have suggested changes in the current unemployment compensation system. One proposal is to tax unemployment benefits.

Important Terms

new unemployment
unemployment compensation

Questions for Thought and Discussion

1. Do you believe the law of demand applies to leisure? If so, how? If not, why not?

2. Do you favor the current system of unemployment compensation? If so, why? If not, what changes do you think ought to be made?

3. What unemployment benefits are available in your state? What is the specified time limit? Who qualifies? What is the scale? Do you think the average unemployed person can survive solely on the benefits received?

18

The Decision About How to Spend Income

Preview Questions

1. What can people do with the income they make?
2. What can businesses do with the income they make?
3. How do businesses decide in what to invest?

Definitions of New Terms

Investment: Investment is the spending of income on things such as machines and plants that create new productive capacity.

Gross investment: Gross investment includes all investment expenditures, including those made to compensate for depreciation of machinery, buildings, and the like.

Net investment: Net investment includes only investment expenditures that do not compensate for depreciation.

When people are paid for working, they are faced with a decision—should they spend all they earn? Their answer determines the amount of money put directly back into the economy. If they decide to save a part of their earnings, that portion does not go directly into someone else's hands. For example, if a person puts $5 into a savings account, that $5 does not go into the economy until the bank lends it to someone to be spent.

When a business has borrowed money, saved it, or obtained it from investors, the people running the business must decide how to spend it wisely and profitably. Should the business build a new plant? Acquire more equipment? Hire more employees? Develop new products? These are just some of the things in which business firms might invest.

Individuals and large corporations alike must decide how to spend earned income. The sum of these decisions has great impact upon the economy.

Basically, what is being discussed here is the way individuals and businesses decide to use their income. When we first examined the national economy in Chapter 14, discussion centered on the measurement of GNP and its components. Here we are talking about the *disposition* of GNP, or how it is used.

According to many analyses of the way the economy works, the decision of households and businesses about how much income they want to save and invest is a major factor in determining whether there will be booms or recessions and depressions. Perhaps the best way to see this is to start with the individual business trying to decide in what to invest its money. Then, adding up the decisions of all American businesses will explain what the nation as a whole does with much of the income earned each year.

A New Definition of Investment

Before going into depth, it is important for you to understand what is meant by investment. Chapter 7 pointed out that there is a difference between the meanings of *invest* or *investment* as the terms are used in everyday language and what it means to economists.

Most people think of investment as buying stocks, real estate, or some other thing that may provide a return on their money. For economists, however, investment has another meaning. That meaning involves creating something that can help people to produce and consume in the future.

If, for example, a person buys shares of stock in a company through his or her broker, all that occurs is a *transfer* of ownership of a stock certificate. Nothing new is created. No future production is possible just because that person bought shares of stock, or a portion of ownership of a company.

However, if the person takes the same money and builds something that can produce an item for consumption, then that person has made a **investment.** The person has invested in the productive capacity of the nation. In economics, that is what investment is about.

To put it another way, in economics the terms *invest* and *investment* mean *the creation of new productive capacity*. They refer to the building of new machines, new factories, and the like.

Investing to Prevent Deterioration

Another type of investment is necessary to make sure that the machines and buildings already created do not fall apart. This type of investment makes up for the depreciation of productive capacity. The concept of depreciation was discussed in Issue 5, which dealt with the costs of running an automobile. That issue discussed the physical depreciation of a car due to wear and tear through driving. Machines and buildings also undergo wear and tear as they are used. If businesses want to prevent depreciation, they must spend income to keep machines and buildings in good repair.

The total of all investments in the economy, including those which compensate for depreciation, is called *gross national investment* or **gross investment.** If the amount of money used to take care of depreciation is subtracted from gross investment, the remainder is called *new* or **net investment.** Chapter 19 will point out how net investment at the national level has fluctuated wildly in the history of the American economy.

The Business Investment Decision

Imagine yourself as the owner of a company that is going to manufacture a new solar water heater. All of the plans to build the solar heater have been made. You know where to buy the materials. You know where to rent factory space or to lease land on which to build a factory. You have obtained "seed" money from a group of investors who want to make profits.

Now you must decide how much more money you should borrow

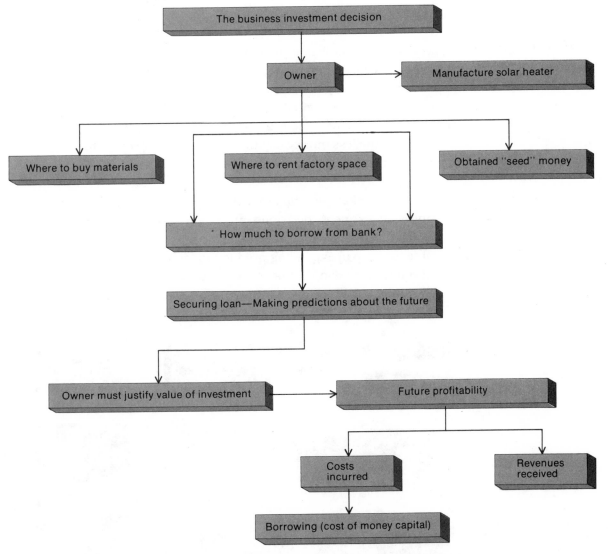

The decision-making process for investment of a business.

from a bank to develop the production facilities for manufacturing the solar heating units. Should you borrow another $50,000? Another $100,000? Another $500,000?

Making Predictions About the Future

The only way you can secure the loan is to justify to the bank the value of the investment. That is, you must try to predict the outcome of the investment to be made. The way you predict the outcome is by looking at the future profitability of the output produced by the investment.

The only way to predict profitability is to predict the costs to be incurred and the revenues to be received, assuming the product can be sold. This means that you must somehow predict future costs and future demand for solar heating units. This is not an easy task. Nevertheless, it is a job that must be done in order to determine if the investment will be profitable—that is, if the investment should be made.

The Effect of Borrowing on Investment

Of course, one factor that must be considered in investment calculations is the cost of borrowing—that is, the amount of interest to be paid on any loans to obtain money to invest. That is called the *cost of money capital*. The higher the interest rate charged for a loan, the more costly the investment becomes. Thus, the greater the cost of borrowing, the less money capital in general is borrowed to invest in additional productive capacity.

Investment Decisions in the Nation

The previous example, though simplified, is one indication of many business investment decisions made every day throughout the United States. Each day businesspersons must decide how much income to tie up in expanding production facilities so that businesses can produce more so that people can consume more in the future.

Two things determine how much businesses are willing to invest. One is the cost of money capital, or the interest rate on borrowed

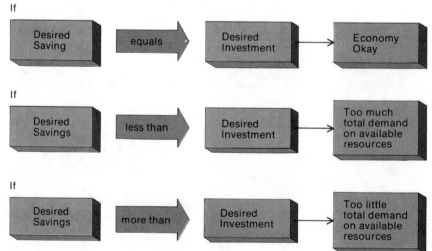

The relationship of savings and investment to the economy.

funds. The other is the expected demand for the product. Thus, whenever anything occurs that changes either of these factors, individual businesses will react accordingly. Taken altogether, these individual decisions cause changes in the amount of investment in the nation.

To put it another way, if next year appears to be promising in the eyes of the business community, businesses will predict higher demand for their product. Expecting higher demand, they will want to invest more. However, if something happens to make the cost of borrowing go up, then businesses will individually decide to invest less.

Total Investment, Saving, and the Nation's Economic Performance

By definition, if investment is money income used to create future productive capacity, then it involves taking income out of the economy that cannot be used for current consumption. In other words, a dollar put into a solar heating plant cannot be used to buy a hamburger.

Therefore, the decisions made by the business community to invest more mean that the nation as a whole must agree to consume less *at that moment in time*. People agree to do so if they think they will be better off in the future. That is, present consumption can be less when people believe they will be justly rewarded by being able to consume more later because businesses have created additional productive capacity.

Households decide to provide income to businesses for investment by deciding to save more. Thus, there is a definite relationship between the amount of saving (the nonconsumption of income in an economy) and the amount of investment made by businesses.

Everything works out fine when the amount of income households save approximately equals the amount of income businesses invest. Problems arise, however, when households want to save less—or more—than businesses want to invest.

When Households Want to Save Less Than Businesses Want to Invest

When households want to save less than businesses want to invest, then the desire of businessess to use income for future productive capacity is partially thwarted. Businesses cannot get all the investment funds they want, for consumers do not free up enough resources for them.

The tightening of investment funds occurs when there is too much demand for the available goods and services in the economy. That is, the combined demand of consumers—households and firms—is more than the supply actually available. In this situation, there is excess demand at the aggregate or national level. In such a situation, inflationary forces tend to take hold (see the exhibit on opposite page). This will be discussed in more detail in Chapter 20.

When Households Want to Save More Than Businesses Want to Invest

The opposite situation occurs when households want to save more than businesses want to invest. When that occurs, there is too little demand for available supply. In other words, the combined demand of consumers—households and firms—adds up to less than the total income or amount of resources available in the nation at the moment in time. In this situation, there is excess supply at the aggregate or national level. When this occurs, production slows down, unemployment ensues, and the economy slumps into a recession or a depression.

Summary

1. People who earn income must continually decide what portion to consume (spend) and what portion to save.

2. Businesses with income to invest must decide what to invest in and how much to invest.

3. In economics, the term *investment* refers to the creation of new productive capacity and the prevention of deterioration of current productive capacity, in addition to the common meaning of buying things that may provide a return on the money spent.

4. Investment decisions are based on the cost of obtaining money capital and on future profitability, which in turn depends on potential demand for a product.

5. Investment funds take income out of the economy so that it cannot be used for current consumption.

6. Saving provides the resources for investment.

7. When the amount of income households save approximately equals the amount of income businesses invest, things work out fine. Problems arise, however, when households want to save more or less than businesses want to invest.

Important Terms

firms
gross investment
households

investment
net investment

Review Questions

1. What do people do with the income they make?

2. What does the term *investment* mean? How does its meaning in economics differ from that used in everyday language?

3. What is the difference between gross and net investment?

4. On what are business investment decisions based?

5. What provides the resources for business investment?

6. Income taken out of the economy for investment cannot be used for what?

7. What can happen when households want to save less than businesses want to invest?

8.   What can happen when households want to save more than businesses want to invest?

Discussion Questions

1.   How do you decide how much of your available income to save?

2.   How do you think businesses decide in what to invest?

3.   Why would a rise in the interest rate cause businesses to make fewer investments?

4.   What do you think would happen to business investment if everyone thought there was going to be a depression? Why?

5.   Which situation is the less desirable—when households want to save *more* or *less* than businesses want to invest? Why?

Projects

1.   Using data collected from recent issues of *The Survey of Current Business*, prepare a report on personal saving in the United States. Does the saving rate fluctuate during the business cycle? Has saving on a per capita basis risen in recent years? What does this suggest?

2.   Invite a member of the local Chamber of Commerce to speak to the class on business investment in your area. Have the representative indicate how current investment ranks against investment five years ago. What factors account for differences? What does the rate of investment suggest about potential growth of the economy in the area?

19

Keeping the Economic Ship on an Even Keel

Preview Questions

1. Why was the Great Depression "great"?
2. What was life like during the Great Depression?
3. What caused the Great Depression?
4. How can the government act during future business downturns to prevent another Great Depression?

Definitions of New Terms

Government stabilization policies: Government stabilization policies are fiscal or monetary policies designed to control unemployment and inflation.

Monetary policy: Monetary policy is carried out by the Federal Reserve through changing the amount of money in circulation.

Fiscal policy: Fiscal policy, aimed at countering undesired ups and downs in business activity, usually involves changing the level of government spending and/or taxation.

Capital formation: Capital formation is the addition to productive capacity in the nation. Capital is formed when businesses invest in machines and equipment.

Monetarist: A monetarist is a person who believes that there is an important relationship between the amount of money in circulation and the level of economic activity.

Have you noticed in recent years that most things keep going up in price? It is hard not to notice that the United States has been suffering from inflation for quite a while. Almost everyone is touched in one way or another by the problem of constantly rising prices.

You have probably also been touched at one time or another by unemployment. More than likely someone in your family or someone you know has been out of a job. Being out of a job is a painful experience. Many Americans are unemployed at least once during their lifetime.

Certainly it would be nice if the American economy ran itself on a smooth path upward. Then no American would have to undergo the pains of inflation and/or unemployment. However, that is quite unlikely—at least given what has happened in the past in the United States and in other countries.

In order to understand why there have been periods of unemployment and inflation, one must understand what causes unemployment and inflation. An acceptable theory regarding the causes allows one to develop some rules about what government might do or should not do to even out the ups and downs in the business cycle.

When the federal government attempts to reduce unemployment and inflation, it engages in what is called ***government stabilization*** policies. There are two basic types of government stabilization policies: monetary policies and fiscal policies. ***Monetary policy*** relates to what the Federal Reserve does in controlling the money supply, the amount of dollars in circulation. ***Fiscal policy*** relates to what Congress does with respect to federal spending and taxing policies. These two concepts will become clearer later in the chapter.

First let us look more closely at a time when this country suffered dramatically because of bad economic conditions. This dark hour in American economic history has been called the Great Depression. After examining the events and conditions of the period, the chapter will present two modern business cycle theories of why the Great Depression occurred and was so long. These two theories relate directly to monetary and fiscal policies of the federal government.

The Great Depression

The decade of the 1930s was one of incredibly high unemployment rates; millions of workers could not find jobs. It was a decade of misery and despair. But before the Great Depression came the

"Roaring Twenties," a time when prices did not rise, standards of living grew at about 3 percent per year, and Americans began buying radios, refrigerators, stoves, and automobiles. Then something happened that changed the American economy for decades to come.

The Stock Market Crash

Toward the end of the 1920s, the stock market began rising rapidly. Stock prices jumped at astounding rates. Many Americans had money in the stock market and were making large profits on their money. Those who could not pay for the stocks they wanted to buy were allowed to buy on credit. That is, they only had to put up a certain percentage of the total cost. Their brokerage firm furnished the rest. Of course, they had to pay interest on the loan. But what did they care? Stock prices were rising so fast they still stood to make a significant profit.

Look at Figure 19-1. The graph plots the average stock price from 1920 to the depths of the Great Depression. By 1929 stock prices were more than one and one-half times what they had been three or four years earlier. The volume of trading was increasing every day. Something had to give. It did. By October 1929, investors became jittery. There had been continuous reports that economic activity

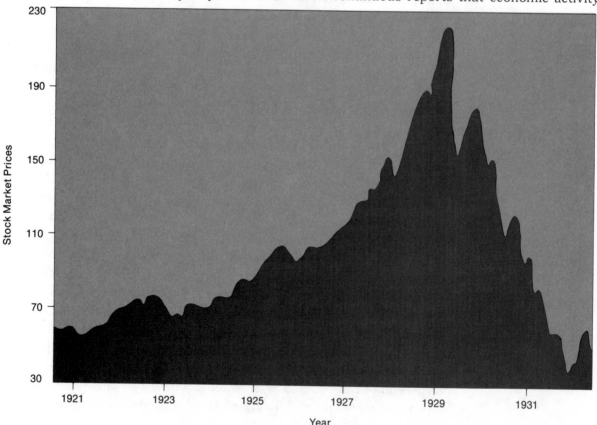

Figure 19-1. The stock market goes up and down. The "Roaring Twenties" saw common stock prices rise over 400 percent before the Crash in 1929. By 1931, prices were back to where they were in 1921. Source: *Standard Statistics Index of Prices of 421 Common Stocks*, Monthly Averages, 1926 = 100.

Panic selling during the 1929 stock market crash necessitated the use of mounted police to keep Wall Street crowds under control. What do you feel was the major reason for the crash?

was falling off. There were fears of an oncoming recession. Of course, nobody at that time conceived of the Great Depression that would follow.

On October 1, 1929, average share prices fell $5 to $10. On October 3, the same thing occurred. The next day was no better. Although the number of shares bought and sold was relatively small, prices kept declining. Toward the end of the month, when disaster seemed near, business and political leaders tried to intervene to stop the precipitous decline. Then suddenly, on October 28, 1929, there was a nationwide stampede to unload stocks. During the last hour of trading more than 3 million shares changed hands. In one day the total value of all stocks fell by $14 billion! The next day was worse. "Blue Monday" and "Black Tuesday," as they were called in later years, had arrived. Although stock prices did rise slightly during the first few months of 1930, that was the last major rally that a nation of investors was to see for many years to come. By the summer of 1932, the value of stocks had fallen by 83 percent from their September 1929 prices!

The Rest of the Economy Follows

Not long after the October stock market crash, the United States was well into a serious recession. Of course, no one suspected that it would turn into the greatest depression in economic history. At the time, noted economist Irving Fisher, a leader in the temperance movement, proclaimed in speeches to civic groups that the economic troubles of the United States were bound to be short-lived. According to Fisher, Prohibition had made the American worker more productive.

The Employment Situation.   Despite Fisher's prediction, however, the employment situation grew increasingly bleak. As Figure 19-2 shows, fully one-fourth of the entire labor force was unemployed by 1933. One out of every four adult Americans who wanted to work could not find a job. Unemployment remained high for many years. The Great Depression was not a short-term event. In fact, from 1930 through 1940, an average of 10 million Americans were unemployed in a labor force that was approximately half the size of today's.

The seriousness of the situation becomes even clearer when one realizes that the true size of the labor force at that time may have been understated—thus understating the amount of unemployment. For example, throughout the 1930s employers held to a consistent policy of "no jobs for married women." That is, married women were

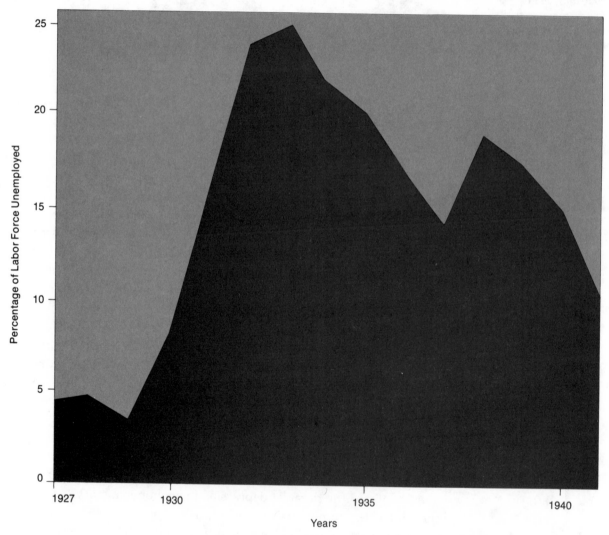

Figure 19–2. The Depression sees massive unemployment. Unemployment rose to 24.9 percent of the civilian labor force during the depths of the Great Depression in 1933. Even by the end of the decade, it was still at 14.6 percent. Source: *Economic Report of the President.*

denied jobs in favor of men. Additionally, many families moved to rural areas as squatters. Instead of looking for work in urban areas, they attempted to scrape out a bare existence in the countryside.

The unemployment rate of the 1930s is so high that it boggles the mind. Today most Americans become alarmed when unemployment climbs above 6 percent. Few young people can even conceive of a 25 percent unemployment rate. Yet that is what occurred during the depths of the Great Depression.

The Banking System.   By March 1933, the banking system of the United States virtually collapsed. Between 1929 and 1932 more than 5,000 banks—one out of every five—had failed, and their customers' deposits had vanished. Personal savings fell as income fell. By 1932 people were *dis*-saving almost $750 million, whereas they had saved over $4 billion in 1929. Not only did banks fail, but thousands of other financial institutions, such as loan companies and credit unions, failed.

Therefore, when Franklin D. Roosevelt became president, he declared a "bank holiday." That is, Roosevelt ordered all banks in the United States closed and declared a temporary halt to the collection of debts, to prevent the total collapse of the economy. Under emergency legislation, banks were permitted to reopen once they could prove they were solvent. Meanwhile, new banking safeguards were put into operation.

What Caused the Great Depression?

Why did something that could have been a heavy recession under normal circumstances turn into the greatest depression in history? The debate still continues. Although there are many theories, space permits examining only the major two.

Some notions that people had about the Great Depression have already been mentioned. One was that Americans were living beyond their means. Yet there is little evidence to support this idea. The productive capacity of the United States was not particularly strained in 1929. Others believe that the failure of the agricultural sector to prosper led to the ultimate collapse of the economy. Yet there is little evidence to support the conclusion that a small sector of a huge economy could trigger a great depression. Perhaps it could cause a recession, but nothing of the magnitude of what happened.

In the United States, the two most popular theories of what caused the Great Depression are those put forth by John Maynard Keynes and by Milton Friedman. Keynes' theory relates to the need for active fiscal policy. Friedman's theory relates to monetary policy.

The Keynesian Explanation

In 1936 *The General Theory of Employment, Interest, and Money,* by John Maynard Keynes, a respected British economist, was published. In this remarkable book, Keynes suggested that unemploy-

With the nation's unemployment rate running as high as 25% during the Great Depression, living conditions such as these began to appear in large cities.

ment might exist for a long period of time. That is, he introduced the idea that unemployment on a large scale might not be able to correct itself by natural forces within the economy. Keynes pointed out that what is necessary to keep full employment is *effective* aggregate, or total, demand.

Keynes also pointed out that one of the key driving forces in the economy is investment. To provide for investment, there has to be saving. In other words, consumers must be willing to save part of their income in order for investors to have resources for investment. But, Keynes noted, there could be times when there is not enough investment demand to use up all of the private sector's saving. When this occurs, there is unemployment, because saving is only useful when it is put back into the economy. And it is put back into the active economy only when investors use it to build houses, machines, buildings, and the like.

Proponents of Keynesian theory of income and employment point out that the public engaged in an abnormally high level of saving during the 1920s. According to Keynesian theory, such high rates of saving were dangerous. A drop in aggregate, or total, demand would result unless most of the saving was put back into the economy by investment. Unemployment would occur.

Keynesian model of the Great Depression

Consider, however, that when businesspersons keep investing, they may eventually reach a point where they have built all the plants and factories they need for some time to come. This would be much like you deciding to "invest" in making your bicycle like new again. You might buy paint and some new parts and spend a lot of time fixing it. But once you reached the point where you have made it "like new," you would stop investing.

According to one Keynesian interpretation of what happened just prior to the Great Depression, business people did reach the point where they did not want to invest much. Everything would have been okay if households had reduced their rate of saving when businesses stopped investing so much to keep in line with the lower rate of investment.

Unless something is done to increase the rate of investment or to reduce the rate of saving, total demand in the economy will fall. That reduction will result in unemployment, as workers are laid off because businesses cannot sell all of their goods. The result is a recession. Without appropriate government action, according to this theory, such a recession can lead to a depression.

Fiscal Policy.   To the proponents of Keynesian theory, the most appropriate action the government could have taken just prior to the Great Depression relates to fiscal policy. They claim that the government should have filled in the gap businesses created by not wanting to invest so much. The gap could have been filled by increasing government expenditures more rapidly. This would have been an active fiscal policy to prop up a failing economy.

Alternatively, in utilizing an active fiscal policy, the government could have reduced taxes owed by businesses and households. The reduction in taxes leaves businesses and households with more spendable income. A reduction in taxes has the same effect on the economy as direct government spending. After all, if a person obtains an increase in income, he or she probably will spend more. Therefore, everyone doing this together could prop up total demand in the economy.

Keynesian Analysis in Summary.   Basically, Keynesian theory held that the Great Depression occurred because of a collapse in the desire for new **capital formation** on the part of business. Capital formation relates to the building of new machines, new factories, and the like. In other words, during the Great Depression there was a collapse in the desire of businesses to invest. Investment fell behind saving, reducing output and thus causing large amounts of unemployment. This theory corresponds nicely to available statistics, as shown in Figure 19-3. As depicted, net investment fell dramatically in the years following the stock market crash.

However, the reduction in net investment could have been triggered by something else. According to the proponents of the second major theory of why the Great Depression occurred, it was triggered by other factors.

The Friedman Explanation

American economist Milton Friedman, while not denying that investment decisions by businesses relative to saving decisions by households are an important determinant of economic conditions, developed a theory that places considerably more emphasis on what happens to the amount of money in circulation. People who contend that there is an important relationship between the amount of money placed in circulation by the Federal Reserve and the level of economic activity are called **monetarists.** While the following sketch of Friedman's theory is simplified (perhaps even oversimplified), it points out the most obvious aspects and applies them to events during the Great Depression.

Friedman and his proponents believe that in the short run, what happens in the economy depends on the way the Federal Reserve alters the amount of money in circulation. Money, one must remember, consists of currency and checking account balances. As was pointed out in Chapter 15, the Federal Reserve System was chartered in 1913 to establish an *elastic* currency. According to Friedman and the monetarists, it did just the opposite during the Great Depression. It allowed the money supply to fall instead of rise. Why should the amount of money in circulation be so important?

The monetarist theory states that people have a certain desire for money because it facilitates transactions. That is, to live in a world without money would be quite costly indeed, for people would have to resort to barter. Therefore, people keep money in checking accounts and in cash to facilitate transactions and to keep a temporary store of purchasing power.

It seems obvious that if the number of transactions rises, the amount of money people desire would increase. In other words, there is a relationship between the level of income (and hence transactions) and the level of money desired by the public. Indeed, this relationship not only exists, but it is fairly stable, according to the monetarists.

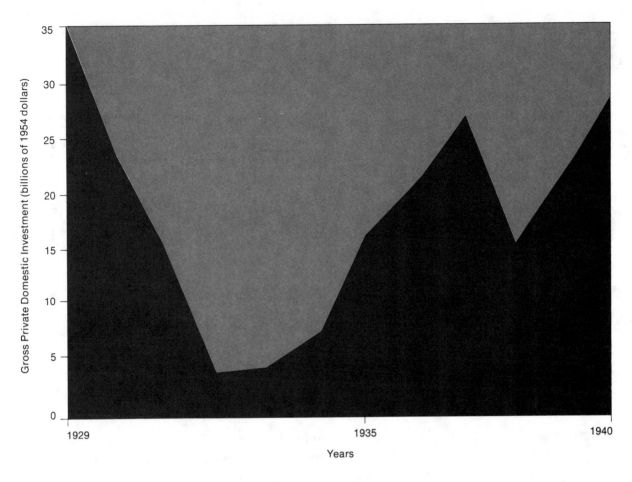

Figure 19-3. The collapse in the desire to invest. This graph shows real gross private domestic investment in constant 1954 dollars. From 1929 to 1932, it fell from $35 billion to $4 billion. Even by 1940, it had not risen to its 1929 peak. Source: Office of Business Economics.

Therefore, if the Federal Reserve increases the amount of money in circulation and transactions do not increase at the same time, some people will find that they have excess cash on hand. To get rid of the excess, these people will attempt to spend it. The only way they can get rid of their cash is by spending more money than they receive. This will lead to an increase in the amount of goods and services demanded. Hence, if there is full employment, it will lead to a rise in prices—inflation. If there is not full employment, it will lead to a rise in output.

What about the opposite situation? If the Federal Reserve decides to decrease the amount of money in circulation, then some individuals and businesses will find that they have less cash than desired. The only way they can add to their desired cash on hand is by spending *less* than they make. As they do so, total demand for goods and services in the economy will fall. Either prices or output will fall. In any case, money income will be decreased.

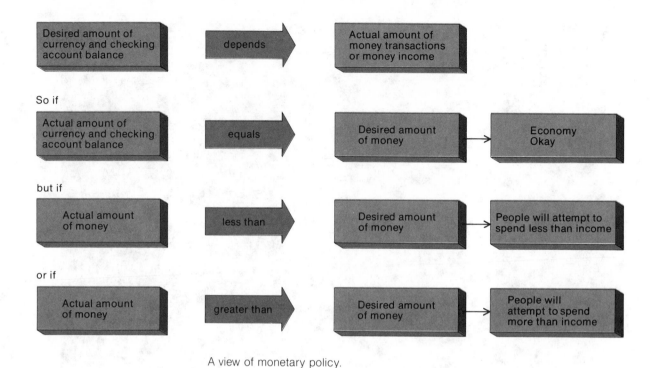

A view of monetary policy.

What Happened during the Depression?   Using this simplified version of Friedman's theory, let us look at what happened during the Great Depression. Although the Federal Reserve made many attempts to stimulate the economy, the amount of money in circulation actually decreased one-third from the start of the recession to the depths of the Great Depression. This is borne out by the data shown in Figure 19-4. The reduction of the amount of money in circulation could mean only one thing—a reduction in the total demand for goods and services and, hence, a reduction in output and employment.

The monetarists maintain that what should have been just another recession turned into the Great Depression because of the Federal Reserve's contradictory efforts during the period. As shown in Figure 19-4, the money supply decreased instead of increasing. This dealt a crippling blow to an already weak economy and hence hastened the depression.

Monetary Policy.   Monetarists point out that the Federal Reserve followed an incorrect monetary policy during the Great Depression. That is, the Federal Reserve did not allow for the orderly growth in the amount of money in circulation. The appropriate monetary policy during the Great Depression would have been to increase greatly the amount of money in circulation.

Review Chapter 15 if you do not recall how the Federal Reserve can increase the amount of money in circulation. Basically, it buys

Figure 19–4. The precipitous drop in the money supply. By 1933, the money supply had fallen by a third from its 1929 level. It again fell in 1938. Source: Board of Governors of the Federal Reserve System.

government bonds from the public; this increases the reserves of banks, which can then loan out money.

What Policies Should the Government Use?

Has anything been learned from what has happened in the past? Does the government know what to do to counter business recessions? There are no clear-cut answers to these questions.

Today the government uses both monetary and fiscal policy to counteract problems in economic activity. As previously explained, monetary policy involves changes in the money supply, and fiscal policy involves changes in the level of government spending and/or taxation. Therefore, to counter a business recession, the government might increase its spending or decrease taxes. or it might increase the money supply. To counter overexpansion, the government can decrease expenditures and increase taxes, or it can decrease the amount of money in circulation.

While it is fairly easy to understand what monetary and fiscal policy are, it is not so easy to determine when, how much, and in what combination they should be used. Nonetheless, so long as the federal government attempts to smooth out the ups and downs of business activity, Americans will continue to see it utilize monetary and fiscal policy to keep the nation's economic ship on an even keel.

Summary

1. To understand why there have been periods of unemployment and inflation, one must understand what causes these conditions.

2. Government stabilization policies are designed to control unemployment and inflation. There are two types of government stabilization policies—fiscal and monetary.

3. Fiscal policies relate to government spending and taxation. Monetary policies relate to Federal Reserve actions in controlling the amount of money in circulation.

4. The stock market crash occurred in October 1929. It was the prelude to the Great Depression.

5. The Great Depression was the most serious period of insufficient economic activity in American history.

6. During the Great Depression, unemployment rose to a high of almost 25 percent of the labor force.

7. During the early years of the Great Depression, the banking system of the United States nearly collapsed. President Franklin D. Roosevelt declared a "bank holiday" in order to restore stability to the banking system.

8. There are several theories about what caused the Great Depression. Two major theories are those put forth by British economist John Maynard Keynes and by American economist Milton Friedman.

9. Keynes argued that the major cause of the Great Depression was the lack of an active government fiscal policy.

10. Keynesian theory claims that effective aggregate demand is required to maintain full employment. To maintain effective aggregate demand, investment and savings must be kept in balance.

11. Friedman argued that the major cause of the Great Depression was the failure of the government to use a proper monetary policy.

12. Friedman and his supporters propose the notion that there is a direct relationship between aggregate demand and the amount of money in circulation. They believe that through controlling the money supply aggregate demand can be increased or decreased as the occasion warrants.

13. Today the federal government uses both fiscal and monetary policies in attempting to regulate economic activity. Still, it is difficult to know when, how much, and in what combination these policies should be used in smoothing out the ups and downs in business activity.

Important Terms

capital formation
fiscal policy
government stabilization policies

monetarist
monetary policy

Review Questions

1. To understand why there have been periods of unemployment and inflation, what must one understand?

2. In what does the federal government engage when it attempts to reduce unemployment and inflation?

3. With what are monetary policies concerned?

4. With what are fiscal policies concerned?

5. What were "Blue Monday" and "Black Tuesday"?

6. What was the Great Depression? What were some of the conditions that existed at that time?

7. What are two major theories on the causes of the Great Depression? What are the basic arguments of each?

8. How might the federal government counter a business recession?

Discussion Questions

1. The stock market crash of 1929 was a prelude to the Great Depression. What was the stock market crash? How did it come about? What was its effect on the economy? Do you think it could have been averted? If so, how? If not, why?

2. Many people have argued about the causes of the Great Depression. What do you think were the major causes? Why? Do you think it could have been averted? If so, how? If not, why?

3. There have been many notions developed regarding government action in smoothing out ups and downs in business activity. Two of the major theories are those put forth by John Maynard Keynes and Milton Friedman. Do you think one of those theories is superior to the other in combatting recession or overexpansion? If so, which and how? If not, why?

Projects

1. Prepare a report on what the Great Depression meant to the American people. Two excellent sources containing information on the social and political aspects of the depression are *The Great Depression*, edited by David Shannon, and *Since Yesterday* by Frederick Lewis Allen.

2. Canvass a group of older people who lived during the Great Depression to learn how it affected their lives and what they thought about Roosevelt's New Deal policies. Report your findings to the class.

3. With a group of students, arrange a simulated debate between proponents of Keynesian theory and monetarist theory. Obtain copies of Keynes's *The General Theory of Employment, Interest, and Money* and Friedman's *Capitalism and Freedom* from the library to use as references in preparing arguments.

Changing the Face of Economics

Perhaps the most influential economist of the twentieth century has been John Maynard Keynes. Like Adam Smith and Karl Marx, Keynes helped shape the thinking of future generations of economic scholars. In fact, one modern school of economic thought is called *Keynesian economics.*

The son of an extremely capable economist, Keynes was born in Cambridge, England, and was educated at Cambridge University. At first specializing in mathematics, he later shifted to philosophy and economics. He did not teach immediately after receiving his degree but took a civil service post in the India Office. Later he returned to Cambridge for advanced study. He then became editor of a prestigious scholarly journal and held that position for over thirty years.

Keynes was not only a brilliant academician; he was also a highly successful businessman. He involved himself in the field of investments, insurance, and publishing. It is rumored that he was able to amass a fortune lying in bed each morning for a half hour calling on the phone to buy and sell foreign currencies. He became a financial adviser to a number of business firms and chairman of the board of directors of a large insurance company.

Keynes' most influential publication is *The General Theory of Employment, Interest, and Money.* It was written during the Great Depression—when not only millions of American workers were unemployed but Europe also suffered severely from a prolonged depression. Economists of the 1930s were at a loss to explain how such a situation could continue to exist year in and year out. Where was Adam Smith's invisible hand?

During this period, Keynes became convinced that prosperity was not just around the corner. He did not believe the economy would always tend toward full employment. In fact, he pointed out that a permanent state of underemployment could exist if the total amount of desired spending in the economy were insufficient. In other words, if businesses and individuals did not want to spend enough of their income, there would be an inadequate demand for what was produced. The result would be unemployment.

As Keynes saw it, the big problem was in businesses' desire

to invest or not to invest. If the business sector did not want to sustain a high level of investment, a substitute was necessary. This substitute, according to Keynes, should be the government.

The Keynesian view of the world differs markedly from that of Adam Smith. Keynes believed the government must involve itself in attempting to smooth out the low periods in business activities. He argued that there must be increases in government spending whenever unemployment gets too high.

The importance of Keynesian economics cannot be overstated. Much of the current economic thinking in the United States is, in one form or another, based on Keynes' ideas. Keynes contended that in an economy such as this nation's, the government has to manage certain aspects of it in order to prevent severe depressions.

20

Inflation

Preview Questions

1. Do prices remain stable in the United States?
2. Which individuals are most affected by inflation?
3. What causes inflation?

Definitions of New Terms

Consumer Price Index: The Consumer Price Index (CPI) is an index of prices compiled by the Bureau of Labor Statistics of the U.S. Department of Labor. The index is based on the cost of a market basket of goods and services compared with its equivalent during a base period.

Quantity theory of money and prices: The quantity theory of money and prices is one theory that explains changes in prices and income. Basically, if the amount of goods and services in the economy and people's habits concerning how much cash they want to hold are constant, a change in the money supply will lead to an equal change in the price level.

Demand-pull theory of inflation: The demand-pull theory of inflation explains rising prices by relating them to excess demand on the part of businesses and consumers. Basically, it is a situation described as "too many dollars chasing too few goods."

Cost-push inflation: Cost-push inflation describes the view that spiraling prices are caused by the wage demands of unions or the excessive profit drive of large corporations. This type of inflation occurs when prices are rising but there is less than full employment.

Do you remember how much you paid for a candy bar when you were in junior high school? A soft drink? A hamburger? Has there been any change in the prices? Certainly there has! During your lifetime you have experienced many increases in the prices of things you have bought. You have been exposed to the worldwide phenomenon of *inflation*. You have witnessed price increases that go on year after year.

The rises in prices that you have seen in the things you buy represent the essence of a problem that has plagued nations throughout the world for generations. Consumers do not like prices to go up. Inflation is nobody's friend.

This chapter will discuss how consumers are hurt by rising prices. It also will examine why prices seem to go up all the time, not only in the United States but elsewhere. First, however, let us look briefly at the history of prices in the United States. Their irregular behavior is shown in Figure 20-1.

Who Is Hurt by Inflation?

Although by definition inflation means a sustained period of rising prices, it certainly does not always mean a period of prosperity. Even if it did, not everyone would benefit. When prices rise *unexpectedly*, people who have given credit to others are repaid in "cheaper" dollars. That is, lenders are paid back in dollars that cannot buy as much as before. When the price level goes up, any fixed obligation in dollars will cause creditors to lose and debtors to gain.

It might appear that under such circumstances it would be wise to borrow as much as one can or to buy as much as one can on credit. However, when people anticipate rising prices, the cost of borrowing (interest rates) goes up. Those who lend money demand higher interest rates as compensation. They know that rising prices mean they will be repaid in "cheaper" dollars.

Debtors who anticipate decreasing purchasing power because of inflation will pay higher interest rates. For example, a person borrowing $6,500 to buy a big car knows that the $6,500 may only buy a small or compact car at the time the loan is repaid.

To summarize, creditors who know that prices will rise a certain percent over a given time will not lend money unless they are compensated for the loss in purchasing power. Whereas they might

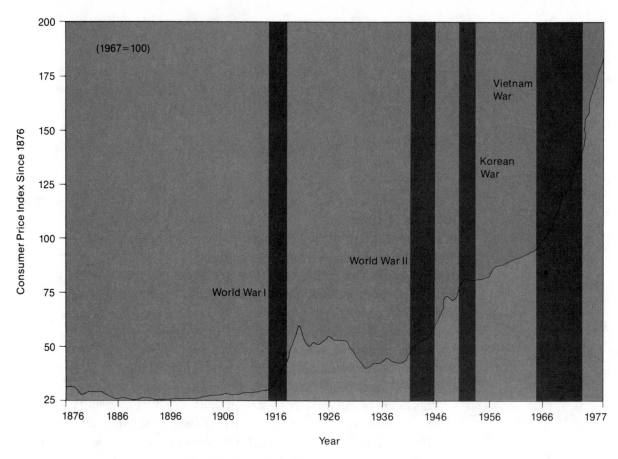

Figure 20-1. History of prices in the United States, 1876–1977. As can be seen by the graph, prices have not always been rising, even though the experience of the past few years might lead one to that conclusion. Almost every war in American history has been associated with a rise in the wholesale price index. Source: United States Department of Commerce.

charge 5 or 6 percent interest when prices are stable, they may demand 8 to 10 percent interest in times of inflation.

People Who Hold Cash

Most people hold some cash. The real value of cash is what it can buy. When prices rise, the same amount of cash no longer buys as much. If one kept on the average $10 all the time during 1977, its purchasing power would have fallen about 7 percent by the end of the year. It would have been worth only $9.30 at the end of 1977.

Inflation, then, causes people to lose purchasing power in proportion to the amount of money they generally keep on hand. The only way to avoid this loss of purchasing power is to keep no money—no currency or checking acount balance. But, as was noted in Chapter 15, life without cash can be very inconvenient.

Specific Suffering Groups

In addition to creditors and those with cash, people with fixed incomes have suffered (at least in the past) by inflation. Historically, all persons who have fixed incomes in dollars lose during unexpected inflation. Bonds and retirement payments usually pay a set amount of dollars per year. For a person who retired in 1960 with a pension of $200 per month, for example, this means that today he or she can buy less than half with that amount than when he or she retired. This problem arises when retirement payments are fixed in dollars with no cost of living scale to offset future inflation.

Rising Prices and the Individual

General information about inflation may be interesting in itself. Nevertheless, you are probably more interested in knowing how inflation affects you. You know that a rising price level is the definition of inflation. How much prices have been rising in your area is, of course, most specifically applicable to the decisions you make as a consumer.

Let us look at some of the average increases in prices of a few consumer items over the past 15 years. Table 20-1 shows the price rise of television sets, washing machines, refrigerators, and new and used cars from 1960 to 1977. It also shows the rise over the same period for the average of all prices, as represented by the *Consumer Price Index.* The Consumer Price Index (CPI) is compiled by the Bureau of Labor Statistics of the U.S. Department of Labor. The Bureau of Labor Statistics determines the CPI by pricing a market basket of goods and services every so often and computing the Index by comparing the current prices of the items to those during some base period.

Look at Table 20-1. Do you notice something strange? The price of televisions has fallen, and the price of the other items has risen at a rate less than the Consumer Price Index! What does this tell you? It indicates that the *relative* price of certain goods is lower today than it was more than 15 years ago. This is an important distinction for a wise consumer to make. As you should recall, the *absolute* price level is not as important as the *relative* price of the things one buys. To illustrate, suppose that the average of all prices rises 200 percent, but the price of a washing machine goes up only 100 percent. Although the absolute price of the washing machine is higher, its purchase is a good buy because its relative price has fallen dramatically.

Table 20-1: Price Indexes for Some Consumer Items

Year	Television Sets	Washing Machines	Refrigerators	Automobiles New	Used	CPI All Items
1960	127.1	110.7	116.8	90.6	104.5	88.7
1965	107.3	100.2	104.2	96.3	100.9	94.5
1967	100.0	100.0	100.0	100.0	100.0	100.0
1970	99.8	107.3	105.8	107.6	104.3	116.3
1977	137.1	148.0	141.0	146.0	188.0	183.0

Sources: U.S. Department of Labor, Bureau of Labor Statistics *Handbook of Labor Statistics,* 1972; *Monthly Labor Review,* February, 1977. 1977 data estimated.

But Incomes Go Up, Too!

To this point, the discussion appears academic. If everything went up in price except income, people would be in trouble. But look at Figure 20-2. It shows the average disposable income per person in the United States from 1919 to 1977. Since 1933, income has been going up at an average of 3.8 percent per year. In general, incomes not only rise each year, but they also often increase more than prices do. This means that most people are actually better off at the end of each year, even though prices have risen. They are better off because their income is rising faster than prices.

Do not be exasperated by this analysis. Many people are convinced that rising prices are hurting them. However, they should take stock of their *real* standard of living. For example, if their income has risen 8 percent and prices have increased only 6 percent in the last year, then their standard of living has gone up 2 percent in spite of the inflation. Not everyone is worse off because of inflation. Only those people who do not have income increases that match or more than match the rate of inflation are truly worse off. Historically, most people's incomes have kept up with inflation. Those who generally suffer, are, as previously noted, people on fixed incomes and the like.

Interest Rates Again

The relationship between interest rates and the rate of inflation has already been briefly discussed. However, the relationship is important enough to look at in more depth.

Every time a person borrows money, that person has to pay a price for the use of the money. Whenever inflation is anticipated, creditors

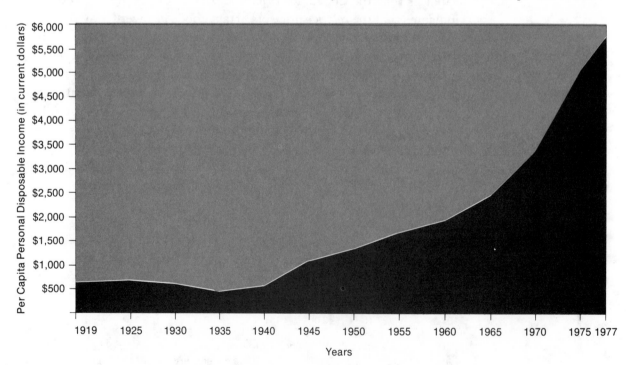

Figure 20-2. Per capita personal disposable income, in current dollars. Source: United States Department of Commerce.

want to be compensated for the cheapening of the dollars in which they will be repaid. That is, creditors tack on an inflationary premium to account for the depreciation in the dollars they will get back.

To highlight this concept, let us look at the example illustrated by Chart 20-1. A creditor lends an individual $1,000. A year later, the debtor pays the creditor back the $1,000 plus interest. If there has been no inflation, the purchasing power of the principal—$1,000—remains the same. However, if there has been 10 percent inflation, the purchasing power of the $1,000 falls over the year to $900. That is, it takes $1,000 to buy what $900 would have bought at the time the loan was made. Under these circumstances, creditors will not loan money unless, in addition to the normal interest rate, they are given an inflationary premium.

This is why people who borrow are faced with relatively high rates of interest during periods of inflation. Creditors predict future inflation on the basis of past inflation and demand an inflationary premium. Yet debtors are willing to pay inflationary premiums. They know they will pay back their debt in depreciated, "cheaper" dollars.

What does this mean for you? Does it have an important bearing on borrowing? Yes. Loans may be considerably less expensive than they seem initially. To figure out the real cost of a loan, one must subtract the anticipated rate of inflation from the interest rate. This gives the real rate of interest. That is, it gives the real cost to the borrower in terms of what he or she is giving up in purchasing power to have command over goods and services today instead of waiting. To understand this more fully, study the example presented in Chart 20-2.

The Causes of Inflation

Discussion to this point has dealt with the effects of inflation and what people can do to avoid them. Now let us turn to the pressing question of why inflation exists. Unfortunately, there is no single answer. But many theories have been developed.

Quantity Theory of Money and Prices

One of the oldest theories of inflation concerns the quantity of money in circulation—that is, "too many dollars chasing too few goods."

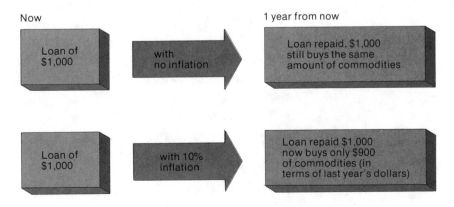

Chart 20-1. Inflation's effect on the value of borrowed money.

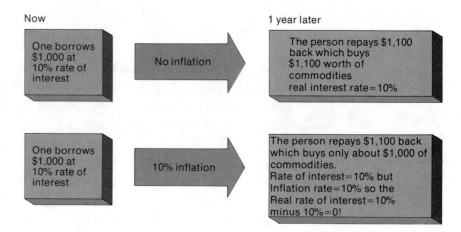

Now

| One borrows $1,000 at 10% rate of interest |
| No inflation |
| The person repays $1,100 back which buys $1,100 worth of commodities real interest rate=10% |

1 year later

| One borrows $1,000 at 10% rate of interest |
| 10% inflation |
| The person repays $1,100 back which buys only about $1,000 of commodities. Rate of interest=10% but Inflation rate=10% so the Real rate of interest=10% minus 10%=0! |

Chart 20–2. Real interest rate or cost of borrowing during inflation.

The theory is known as the ***quantity theory of money and prices.*** It states that the average level of prices varies with the quantity of money in circulation, assuming that the volume of trade and the number of times each dollar bill changes hands remain relatively stable. According to this theory, if the money supply doubled, the price level would also double. In other words, if the amount of money in circulation increased 100 percent, one might expect prices to rise approximately 100 percent.

Evidence shows that the quantity theory of money and prices works well for predicting the rate of inflation over a long period of time. For example, Spanish importation of gold and silver from the New World caused huge price increases in Spain and throughout Europe in the 1600s. The discovery of gold in the United States, Canada, and South Africa in the middle and late 1800s brought about drastic expansions in the money supply and rapidly rising prices.

However, the theory does not work as well in predicting price levels in the short run. The chief reason for this is the fact that the average number of times money changes hands varies as business activity increases or decreases.

Demand-Pull Theory of Inflation

The quantity theory of money and prices is basically a ***demand-pull theory of inflation.*** It states that there cannot be a *sustained* rise in prices unless there is too much demand for the amount of goods and services existing in the economy. Certainly there would be too much demand if too many dollars were put into circulation. Individuals, in their attempt to spend the additional dollars, would all be bidding for a limited supply of goods and services. This would cause prices to rise.

The least complex demand-pull theory indicates that inflation can only happen when there is full employment in the economy. It is known from past experiences, however, that rising prices and unemployment can occur together. Economists describe that situation as one in which ***cost-push inflation*** is at work.

The Cost-Push Theory of Inflation

The cost-push theory of inflation attempts to explain why prices rise when the economy is *not* at full employment. Cost-push inflation deals with abnormal inflation. It was this type of inflation that the United States experienced during the 1969–1970 and 1974–1975 recessions. There are essentially two explanations for cost-push inflation—union power and big business monopoly power.

Union Power. Some people believe that unions are responsible for inflation. Their reasoning is as follows: Unions often demand wage raises that are not necessarily warranted by the amount of physical output workers are producing. Since unions are so powerful, businesses usually give in to union demands for higher wages. When businesses have to pay higher wages, their costs increase. In order to maintain normal profit, the businesses must raise prices. This type of cost-push inflation often occurs when there is no excess demand, when the economy is operating at less than full capacity and full employment.

Big Business Monopoly Power. The second explanation for cost-push inflation suggests that inflation is caused by big business monopoly power. Powerful corporations are presumably able to raise their prices whenever they want to increase their profits. Each time such corporations raise prices to increase profits, the cost of living goes up. Workers demand higher wages to make up for any loss in their standard of living. This, in turn, gives corporations an excuse to raise prices again. And so goes the vicious cycle of price and wage increases.

What Has Been Learned about Inflation?

The debate is still raging about what causes inflation. In fact, there are as many theories as there are people who think they know why the cost of living has increased. Just ask anyone you know. He or she will most likely voice some variant of one of the theories presented in the chapter. Still, there is no single accepted theory that can be presented as *the* reason why prices are rising in the United States. The best that can be said is that prices are rising and will probably continue to rise in the future. So long as you anticipate rising prices, you can strive to protect yourself from their effects.

Summary

1. Prices have been rising for many years in the United States, though not at a steady rate.

2. During a period of inflation, any fixed obligation in dollars (e.g., a home mortgage) will cause creditors to lose and debtors to gain.

3. People who hold cash during a period of rising prices will suffer a loss in the purchasing power of that cash.

4. People on fixed incomes are hurt by inflation.

5. During an inflationary period, some prices will rise more slowly than others. In fact, some prices even may fall. In both cases, the relative price of such items is decreasing.

6. During all periods of inflation in American history, incomes have risen. In fact, incomes have generally increased faster than prices.

7. Interest rates rise during a period of inflation. People who lend money want to be compensated for the potential loss in purchasing power that can occur by being paid back in "cheaper" dollars.

8. There are many theories regarding the causes of inflation, including the quantity theory of money and prices, the demand-pull theory of inflation, and the cost-push theory of inflation.

9. Evidence shows that the quantity theory of money and prices works well for predicting the rate of inflation over a long period of time.

10. The demand-pull theory states that there cannot be a sustained rise in prices unless there is too much demand for the existing amount of goods and services in the economy.

11. The cost-push theory attempts to explain why prices rise when the economy is at less than full employment.

12. Some people believe that unwarranted union demands lead to inflation. Others see corporate efforts to increase profits as the catalyst.

Important Terms

Consumer Price Index	demand-pull theory
cost-push inflation	quantity theory of money and prices

Review Questions

1. Is inflation a relatively new problem? Explain.

2. What has been the general trend regarding prices in American history?

3. What has happened to prices during periods of war? Why?

4. Who is hurt by inflation? How?

5. What is the difference between absolute and relative price?

6. By whom and how is the Consumer Price Index compiled?

7. What has been the general trend regarding incomes in American history?

8. Why do interest rates rise during periods of inflation?

9. What are the differences between the demand-pull and the cost-push theories of inflation?

10. How can unions contribute to inflation?

11. How can big business contribute to inflation?

12. Do rising prices always indicate prosperity and full employment? Explain.

Discussion Questions

1. According to the text, during periods of inflation people who hold cash or live on fixed incomes suffer a loss of purchasing power. How do you think they can protect themselves?

2. People whose incomes are rising faster than prices are not hurt by inflation. Do you agree? Why or why not?

3. Which do you believe causes rising prices—excessive demand or rising costs? Why? Are there other causes of inflation? Explain.

4. What do you think can be done to control or prevent inflation?

Projects

1. Research what has happened to the Consumer Price Index since 1950. Price information can be obtained from such publications as *Survey of Current Business, Business Conditions Digest, Monthly Labor Review,* and *Federal Reserve Bulletin.* How does the current rate of inflation compare with that during the 1950s? The 1960s? To what do you attribute the differences?

2. Inflation is not a problem plaguing only the United States. It is a worldwide phenomenon. Compile a list of inflation rates in other countries. A librarian can help you find reference publications containing such information from organizations such as the United Nations and the International Monetary Fund. How do the rates of inflation in other countries compare with that of the United States? How do incomes compare? What do the differences suggest?

3. The following is a set of problems regarding inflation and purchasing power. In each case, calculate any loss in purchasing power that could have occurred during a one-year period. To make the calculations, you must use the rate of inflation that existed at the time. You also must figure any increase in the principal sum caused by interest rates.

a. John Smith put $1,000 in cash in his safety deposit box in 1970. What was the loss in purchasing power on that $1,000 in 1971?

b. In 1973, Bob and Alice Black deposited $1,000 in a joint bank account at 8 percent interest for one year. What was the real cost of borrowing the $1,000? What was the loss of purchasing power for the City National Bank?

c. In 1976 Bob and Alice Black deposited $1,000 in a joint savings account paying 5 percent interest compounded quarterly. Did they suffer a loss in purchasing power on the $1,000 in 1977? If so, how much? If not, why?

Friedman

Galbraith

Leaders in Economics

Milton Friedman is one of the nation's leading monetarists. Monetarists are people who believe the amount of money in circulation—whether a lot or a little—plays a significant part in keeping the economy on a steady keel. The underlying concept of monetarism is that people have a desire for money—currency and checking accounts. To live in a world without money would be very difficult. People would have to barter or trade for the things they want. Therefore, people desire money to avoid bartering.

In addition to being a monetarist, Friedman is a staunch advocate of a negative tax as the means of getting rid of welfare and Social Security. His plan for a "negative income tax" was put forth in his book, *Capitalism and Freedom,* published in 1962. Under Friedman's plan, everyone would be entitled to a basic minimum income. People whose yearly income fell below a certain level would receive a subsidy from federal tax funds.

Although he has never held a major government post, Milton Friedman served as Barry Goldwater's chief economic adviser during Goldwater's unsuccessful bid for the presidency in 1964. Friedman also advised Richard Nixon on economic matters during Nixon's presidential campaign in 1968. Nixon discarded Friedman's theories, however, when, as President, he instituted a wage and price freeze in 1971. In 1976, Friedman received the coveted Nobel Prize in Economics.

One of the most noted economists in the world today is John Kenneth Galbraith. Galbraith was educated at the universities of Toronto and California. After three years of teaching at Princeton University, he served as economic adviser to the National Defense Advisory Commission. In 1942 he joined the Office of Price Administration. He then served on the editorial staff of *Fortune* magazine for five years.

In 1948 Galbraith became a member of the Harvard University faculty. Although he held other posts in the interim, he remained a Harvard professor until 1975. During the Kennedy administration, he served as ambassador to India for two years.

He earned a reputation as friendly but unconventional, since he tended to ignore the State Department's general code of behavior.

Galbraith is one of the most widely read economists today. His two major books are *The Affluent Society* and *The New Industrial State.* Through his writings, his commanding position in the American liberal community, and his government experience, Galbraith has been able to exert great influence on national economic policy. For example, he helped Lyndon Johnson plan the War on Poverty. In retrospect, Galbraith considered there were two major problems with that program. He believes considerable more government assistance should have been given to educational programs and the training of teachers, and he now thinks the budget planned for the program was too low.

Can Wage and Price Controls Stop Inflation?

Definitions of New Terms

Black market: A black market is an illegal market in which goods are bought and sold at prices higher than the legal prices.

Repressed inflation: Repressed inflation exists when rising prices are held in check by wage and price controls.

Rationing: Rationing is a means of allocating scarce resources by some government formula or system.

As discussed in Chapter 20, rising prices seem to be almost as inevitable as death and taxes. Therefore, the question is: Can something be done about inflation?

Politicians and citizens alike are convinced that something can be done. Periodically the cry for controls on prices and wages rings forth. In fact, at some time in your lifetime you will more than likely see the government establish, at least on a temporary basis, wage and price controls in an effort to stem inflation. To determine whether such controls work, let us examine some previous experiences.

Old Forms of Price Controls

Nearly 2000 years before the birth of Christ, the ruler of Babylonia decreed that anyone caught violating the empire's wage and price freeze would be drowned. History reports that Babylonia endured more than 1,000 years of such price fixing. In spite of such drastic measures, prices in Babylonia rose.

In A.D. 300, the Roman Emperor Diocletian fixed maximum prices on grain, eggs, beef, and clothing. He also set wage ceilings for teachers, lawyers, physicians, tailors, and bricklayers. Anyone who violated such price fixing was subject to the death penalty. But, according to a Roman named Lactantius, writing A.D. 314:

There was . . . much bloodshed upon very slight and trifling accounts; and the people brought provisions no more to market since they could not get a reasonable price for them; and this increased the dearth so much that after many had died by it, the law itself was laid aside.

What Happened During World War II

Wars are often associated with pressures on prices because of the great expenditures for war-related activities. World War II was no exception. Since government officials anticipated high rates of inflation, controls were put into effect almost immediately.

The Price Control Act of 1942 established the Office of Price Administration (OPA). By mid-1943, fully 95 percent of the nation's foodstuffs were rationed, and maximum prices on most commodities, as well as rent ceilings, had been established. The Anti-Inflation Act of 1942 created the Office of Economic Stabilization (OES). Its purpose was to limit wages and salaries and to curb prices and rents that were not subject to the regulations set by the OPA.

At the height of price controls these two offices, along with the Office of War Mobilization (OWM), created in 1943, were aided by some 400,000 paid and volunteer "price watchers" scattered throughout the country. As a result of this enormous nationwide effort, wholesale prices rose only 14 percent from November 1941 to August 1945. Many observers feel that price controls did work during World War II.

The United States was not the only country to believe that the war necessitated drastic measures. Nazi Germany also controlled prices. So-called economic crimes, such as selling products on the **black market** (above the maximum legal price) were punished harshly. When the Allies occupied Germany after the war, they did not end rationing immediately. Although punishment was lessened, the Allies believed that without a rationing scheme, pandemonium would have broken out in an already chaotic situation.

For three years, strict price controls remained in effect. Yet something very strange occurred. Available money in circulation increased 400 percent, while output fell 50 percent. Barter inevitably developed as the German mark became useless for obtaining goods and services because of widespread shortages. American cigarettes became the unofficial currency.

Repressed Inflation During World War II

During World War II, there existed what is known as **repressed inflation.** That is, within the economy there were factors that could result in inflation, but inflation did not actually show up in price statistics because of price controls.

Some economists claim that during World War II workers and businesses had a significant amount of extra cash to spend. They wanted to spend this cash. Hence, there was a situation of excessive demand. On the other hand, the amount of resources (commodities) was limited since so much was going into war production. Normally, excessive demand for goods or services causes prices to rise. But prices were not allowed to rise because of price controls.

In addition, **rationing** was put into effect. Under government rationing, consumers were given ration coupons. These gave people the right to buy a certain quantity of gasoline, meat, and other items. In principle, it was illegal to obtain more gasoline, meat, and the like than was allowed by rationing.

Black Markets

With rationing in effect, a black market sprang up. A black market is any illegal market in which goods and services are sold at higher than controlled or legal prices.

There were also numerous other ways that individuals could circumvent rationing and price controls to get goods and services they wanted. Special favors could be done for the supplier of a rationed good or service. Special arrangements could be made for under-the-counter payments. Ration coupons could be traded or bought from people willing to forego consumption of an item or service.

It is not clear how much of this actually occurred during the war. Many accounts indicate that illegal and semilegal wheeling and dealing were quite rampant. Price controls were lifted after the end of hostilities in 1945. Then prices rose dramatically, as can be seen in Figure I–20–1.

The dramatic price rise lends further support to the contention that repressed inflation existed during World War II. When price controls ended, prices rose sharply. This indicates that prices would have steadily risen in the absence of controls. Note, too, that it took a large amount of human effort to police controls effectively during the war—that is, during a period of active patriotism. Although inflation was checked, it remained unclear whether a similar price control endeavor could work during peacetime, and without a large body of price watchers.

Price Controls During the 1970s

Under President Richard M. Nixon, price and wage stabilization programs, known as Phases I–IV, were put into effect, starting in 1971. Phase I was a 90-day freeze on all wages and prices commencing August 15, 1971. Phase II, initiated in November 1971, reduced the number of controls. It lasted until the end of December, 1972. Phase III, announced in January 1973, set acceptable increases in wages at 5.5 percent and in corporate profits at 1.5 percent. Under Phase III, most price-control categories were shifted to voluntary restraints. This triggered re-

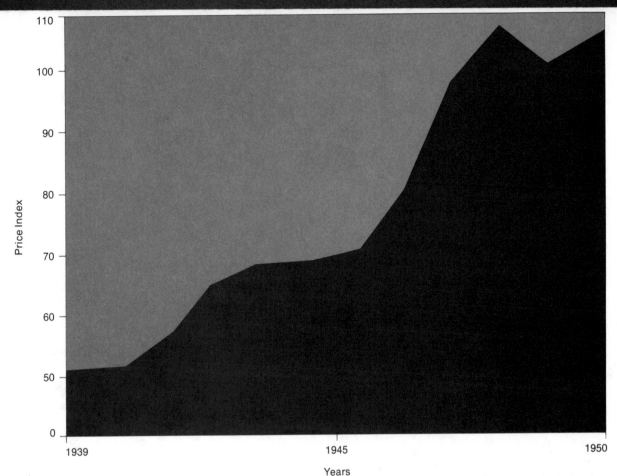

Figure I–20–1. Stemming inflation during the war effort. This index of wholesale prices for all commodities shows that during World War II prices held relatively steady. After termination of hostilities, however, prices jumped drastically. Source: Bureau of Labor Statistics.

newed inflation. Phase IV was instituted in August 1973. The price freeze on all items except beef, gasoline, and diesel oil ceased. Phase IV gradually petered out when all price restraints were removed in April 1974.

If one looks back at prices during 1971–1974, he or she will find that prices were rising more rapidly than they had previous previous to the imposition of controls. Of course, this does not mean that Nixon's price stabilization program caused the rise.

What it does mean is that, if the underlying forces of inflation are not repressed, inflation will continue no matter what the government tries to do. During Phases I–IV, federal monetary and fiscal policies were, on the average, quite expansionary. That is, there were large amounts of government spending and a significant increase in the money supply. For much of the time, it was a situation of "too many dollars chasing too few goods." Of

© 1976 NYT SPECIAL FEATURES

course, this demand-pull theory of inflation cannot explain all that transpired during the period.

People who lived while Nixon's price stabilization program was in effect can attest to the ineffectiveness of its wage and price controls. People find a way to circumvent controls when it is in their own best interest. Just from a practical standpoint, can you imagine how difficult it would be for any government official to control every single price in the economy? There are literally hundreds of thousands of items and millions of prices. How could one ever hope to control even a significant portion? Whatever may be the appropriate method of stemming inflation, wage and price controls have their drawbacks.

Summary

1. Systems of wage and price controls date to ancient times.

2. During World War II, rationing and wage and price controls were strongly in effect throughout the American economy.

3. The chief effect of wage and price controls during World War II was to repress inflation.

4. Some people find ways to circumvent wage and price controls and rationing when these are in effect.

5. Wage and price controls and rationing give rise to black market operation.

6. During the 1970s, the Nixon administration sought to check inflation through a series of wage and price controls. Nevertheless, the nation experienced an extremely high rate of inflation.

Important Terms

black market
rationing

repressed inflation

Questions for Thought and Discussion

1. Do you favor or oppose wage and price controls as a means to check inflation? Why?

2. How might people circumvent wage and price controls and/or a system of rationing? Why do you think some people do it? How can such circumvention be prevented?

3. How does repressed inflation differ from inflation in general?

4. Do black markets exist when wage and price controls are not in effect? Why or why not? What recommendations would you make for controlling black market operations?

UNIT SEVEN

DUTY FREE

The International Scene

21

Trading with Other Nations

Preview Questions

1. Does the United States buy from and sell to other countries?

2. How do Americans benefit from trading with the rest of the world?

3. Can Americans buy goods from other countries with dollars?

4. How do Americans engage in the financial transactions necessary for foreign trade?

Definitions of New Terms

Imports: Imports are goods and services purchased from other countries.

Exports: Exports are goods and services sold to other countries.

Free trade: Free trade is trade without restrictions.

Import quota: An import quota is a limit placed on the quantity of a certain good that is allowed to enter a country.

Importer: An importer is a person who specializes in buying goods from abroad for resale.

Foreign exchange market: The foreign exchange market is the place in which the currencies of different countries are bought and sold.

Floating exchange rate system: A floating exchange rate system is a system of international money dealings in which there are no restrictions on the value of any currency. Supply and demand determine the price of each currency.

Fixed exchange rate system: A fixed exchange rate system is a system in which governments fix the value of one currency in terms of another.

Balance of payments: The balance of payments is the accounting of the value of everything sold abroad compared with the value of everything bought from abroad. When the value of everything sold is less than the value of everything bought, there is a balance of payments deficit.

Depreciation: Depreciation occurs when the value of a currency falls in the foreign exchange market under a floating exchange rate.

Devaluation: Devaluation occurs when a nation's central bank lowers the value of that nation's currency in a fixed foreign exchange rate system.

What would happen if suddenly the United States could no longer buy goods from other countries? Before you answer, be aware that the value of what the United States buys from foreign countries accounts for less than 10 percent of GNP. This implies that if world trade stopped, the United States would not be too different a place in which to live. However, there would be many differences without *imports,* goods bought from other countries for domestic consumption.

For example, tea and coffee drinkers would have to switch to other beverages. There would be no chocolate, bananas, or pepper. Consider also that nearly 90 percent of the radios, 50 percent of black-and-white television sets, and 96 percent of the motorcycles sold in the United States are imported. Many raw materials—one of the key factors of production—come from foreign sources. More than 90 percent of the bauxite, from which aluminum is made, is of foreign origin. All tin, cobalt, and chromium, and most of the platinum, nickel, and asbestos are imported. In fact, Americans buy literally tens of thousands of products that come from foreign countries.

Even though imports account for only 10 percent of the nation's total economic activity, there would be a tremendous disruption of the American way of life if foreign trade suddenly ceased. If American businesses were not allowed to sell to other countries, there would also be a tremendous disruption in the agricultural and manufacturing sectors of the economy.

Selling to the Rest of the World

Imports tell only half the story. Foreign countries do not sell their goods for money alone. The United States has to *exchange* (give up) some of its goods, too. The goods sold to foreign countries are called *exports.*

Great numbers of workers are employed in the nation's export industries. For example, one-fifth of the cotton, one-fourth of the grains, and one-fourth of the tobacco produced in the United States are shipped abroad. One-third of the sulfur and one-fifth of the coal mined in the country are sold to foreign nations. More than 12 percent of the nation's auto production, 25 percent of its textile and metal-working machinery, and 30 percent of its construction and mining machinery go overseas. Between 3 and 4 million jobs are

While imports account for only a small percentage of the total GNP, many imported products have become central to American lifestyles.

involved in the export end of production within the United States.

If world trade were to end, these jobs would cease to exist. However, those 3 to 4 million people would not be *permanently* out of work. New industries would spring up to provide *substitutes* for the *imported* goods Americans could no longer buy. Workers who lost their jobs in *export* industries would, in time, find jobs in newly created industries. Nevertheless, the nation would be worse off. World trade is important to a society's material well-being.

The Benefits from World Trade

Why do people exchange money for goods and services? Usually because the value they place on a good or service is at least as great as the value they place on the amount of money they give up. In other words, they voluntarily engage in economic exchange with others because it makes them better off. If it did not, they would not make the exchange.

Voluntary exchanges have to make both parties feel that they are better off or the exchange would not take place. How do people benefit from exchanging with others? Each gets what he or she wants. In the process, everyone is better off.

Just imagine what would happen if exchange were prohibited. All people would have to become self-sufficient. They would have to grow their own food, make their own clothes, and furnish their own recreation. Life would be hard and most likely dull.

Exchange is essential to specialization. Specialization usually leads to individuals doing what they can do best in society, while it leads to the exchange of the fruits of people's labor so that everyone is better off. Whenever you question whether trade or exchange among individuals is beneficial, think about how you would live if you could not exchange with someone else.

Trade Among States

Many of the things produced in the United States are not necessarily produced within the state in which one lives. For example, New Yorkers buy oranges. Oranges are not grown in New York, however. They come mainly from California and Florida. People who live in Montana know that the books they read were most likely not printed in that state.

Within the United States, lots of trade goes on among the states. As consumers, all Americans find such trade beneficial. Americans have within their reach a huge variety of products that would not be available if trade were prohibited among the 50 states. In fact, the Founding Fathers were well aware of the benefits of trading among the states. In drafting the Constitution, therefore, they prohibited any taxes on interstate trade. Article I, Section 9, Paragraph 5 reads:

No tax or duty shall be laid on articles exported from any state.

Article I, Section 9, Paragraph 6 reads:

No preference shall be given by any regulation of commerce or revenue to the ports of one state over those of another; nor shall vessels bound to, or from, one state, be obliged to enter, clear, or pay duties in another.

And Article I, Section 10, Paragraph 2 reads:

No state shall, without the consent of the Congress, lay any imposts, or duties on imports or exports, except what may be absolutely necessary for executing its inspection laws; and the net produce of all duties and imports, laid by any state on imports or exports, shall be for the use of the Treasury of the United States; and all such laws shall be subject to the revision and control of the Congress.

Again, if you doubt that Americans benefit from trade among the several states, ask yourself what life would be like if the state in which you reside were prohibited from buying goods from other states. Suppose you lived in Delaware. How much fresh fruit might be obtainable? Or suppose you lived in Oregon. How many new automobiles would be produced?

Unrestricted trade among the states is something all Americans accept as part of the nation's economic activity. No American would suggest that trade be stopped within the nation's borders. It would be difficult, if not impossible, to make an argument showing that any American is worse off because *free trade* (trade without restrictions) is permitted.

Free trade allows both American and foreign businesses to grow. Write a list of foreign products you have recently used or purchased.

Free trade allows individuals to specialize in whatever they can do to make the highest profits. People find that out by doing whatever yields them the greatest income and satisfaction for the use of their time. The same is true for states. These principles can also be applied to trade among nations.

World Trade

The reason the United States engages in foreign trade is because Americans benefit. Trade is usually voluntary. Voluntary exchange between two parties has to benefit both. Otherwise, exchange does not take place.

The reasoning behind this argument often goes unnoticed by some politicians. They complain about foreigners "underselling" American businesses by offering relatively cheap goods for sale in the United States. Nevertheless, when free trade exists among nations, each nation can specialize in whatever it can get the highest reward for doing. It can exchange with other nations those goods it specializes in producing for the goods that other nations specialize in producing.

Since the beginning of human society, there has been trade among nations. Since trade usually involves acts of voluntary exchange, it must be assumed that nations generally benefit from trade.

Advantageous Trade Will Always Exist

As entities, nations have different collective tastes and different collective resource bases. Therefore, one might expect that potential gains will always exist from trading among nations. Furthermore, the more trade there is, the more specialization there can be. (Figure 21-1 shows the growth in world trade since 1958.) In most instances, specialization leads to increased output. Since well-being can be measured by output levels, increased output leads to increased well-being, or satisfaction.

Self-sufficiency on the part of individuals undeniably means that they forego the opportunities to consume more than being dependent would offer. Likewise, self-sufficiency on the part of a nation lowers its consumption possibilities. Therefore, self-sufficiency lowers the income level of a nation's inhabitants.

Costs of Trade

Trade has costs, however. For example, if in the United States one state has an advantage in producing agricultural crops, other states may not be able to survive as centers of agricultural production. Farm workers in those states will suffer decreases in their incomes. Eventually they may be forced to find other work.

As tastes, supplies of natural resources, and prices change throughout the world, countries might find their trading advantage in some exports slipping. When this happens, it means severe hardships for some people.

An example of a changing advantage in world trade is the

production of steel. In recent years, Japan has become increasingly competitive in steel products in the world market. As Japan has become more competitive, United States steelmakers have been hurt. American steel companies—including the stockholders and employees—are feeling the pinch of Japan's ability to produce steel products at low prices.

Arguments Against Free Trade

The numerous arguments against free trade have merit. However, many of these arguments are incomplete. They point out the costs of trade without considering the benefits. Nor do they consider possible alternatives for reducing costs while reaping benefits.

Protect Infant Industries. Many nations believe that if a particular industry is allowed to develop domestically, it can eventually become efficient enough to compete in the world market. In light of this reasoning, they favor placing some restrictions on imports. Restrictions give domestic producers time to develop their own techniques. Eventually, they may be able to compete without any restrictions on imports. The idea of protecting infant industries

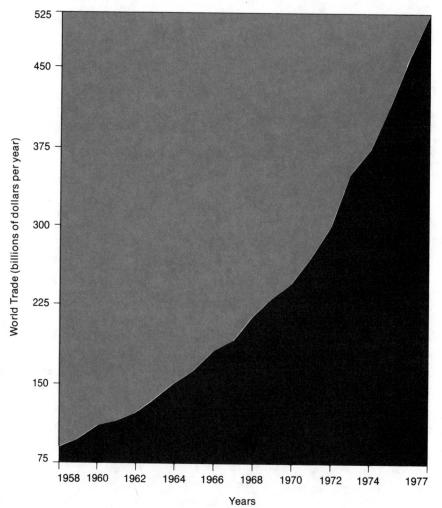

Figure 21–1. World trade per year. World trade has grown rapidly over the last decade or so. In 1974, it had reached the $300 billion mark. Source: United States Department of Commerce.

against foreign competition has some merit. The United States has used **protective tariffs** (taxes on imports) to protect a number of American industries in their infancy.

Such policies can be abused, however. Even after an infant industry has matured, protective import restrictions are often not removed. The people who benefit from this situation are obviously the stockholders (owners of the companies) and perhaps the employees in the industry that is being protected from world competition. The people who lose out are consumers, who must pay a higher price than the going world price for the product in question.

Provide for National Security.

It has been argued that the United States should not rely on foreign sources for many products. Those that claim this point out that in times of war the United States might not have those sources on which to rely. Thus, it should strive to build up its own industry.

A classic example of this involves oil exploration. For reasons of national defense, President Dwight D. Eisenhower instituted during the 1950s an oil **import quota** system. At first voluntary but then mandatory, the system restricted the amount of foreign oil that could be imported into the United States. Eisenhower's idea was to force American oil companies to undertake more exploration of American oil. In time of war, the United States would then have a ready and available supply of oil for tanks, ships, and planes.

Keep the National Economy Stable.

Many people argue that foreign trade should be restricted because it introduces an element of instability into the American economic system. They point out that the foreign trade activity goes up and down. Its ups and downs add to the ups and downs in the domestic employment rate.

If this argument is followed to its logical conclusion, however, trade among the states should be restricted as well. After all, changes in the volume of trade among certain states can cause unemployment in some states. Although displacements are sorted out over time, workers suffer during the adjustment period.

Nonetheless, the desire of certain countries to allow themselves to become specialized in one crop through extensive free trade cannot be played down. When a country does that, its economy is at the mercy of any severe price changes affecting that crop. For example, if Brazil's economy relied only on exporting coffee to the rest of the world, the nation would be in serious difficulty should the price of coffee on the world market drop. Furthermore, when a country specializes completely, it becomes much more dependent on other nations. In times of emergency, this may pose a problem. Traditional trade routes might be disrupted, thus depriving the dependent country of critical materials.

How We Make Foreign Exchanges

The United States uses dollars as its money. But France uses francs, Britain pounds, and Japan yen. In fact, almost every country in the world has its own unique currency system. Therefore, how can one purchase a Japanese-made 10-speed bicycle for dollars? To see how, let us trace an imaginary transaction.

Buying a Japanese Bicycle

Let us simplify discussion by assuming that you live in a town in which there are no Japanese bicycles. Nevertheless, you have heard about one you would like to buy. Although the local bicycle shop has British-made, French-made, and American-made bikes, the dealer does not carry Japanese products. You give the dealer the exact description and model number of the Japanese-made bicycle you want to buy.

The dealer then calls an *importer,* a person who specializes in buying goods from abroad. The importer looks at a catalog of Japanese products to obtain the order number. The importer then informs the bicycle dealer that the order will be placed and estimates the length of time it will take to get the bicycle from Japan.

Chart 21–1. Examples of foreign currency.

The order is then placed with the Japanese manufacturer. The Japanese firm, however, does not want to receive dollars in payment for the bicycle. The firm must pay its workers in Japanese currency. After all, its workers want to be able to spend their wages for the goods and services they want to buy in Japan. Therefore, the Japanese manufacturer quotes the American importer a price for the bicycle in yen. The importer then goes to the foreign exchange market to purchase yen.

The Foreign Exchange Market

Basically, the foreign exchange market is like most other markets. Instead of buying and selling goods and services, however, the *foreign exchange market* buys and sells currencies.

Let us assume for the moment that there are only two currencies in the world, U.S. dollars and Japanese yen. When the American importer goes to the foreign exchange market, he or she finds a quotation for Japanese yen. For example, on April 5, 1977, the quotation was 273 yen for $1.00. Suppose the bicycle cost 21,840 yen. That translates to $80. The importer purchases $80 worth of Japanese yen and mails it as payment for the bicycle.

The bicycle is then shipped to the importer. The importer in turn sells it to the dealer for $80 plus a normal markup. The dealer then sells it to you for cost plus a normal profit.

The bicycle purchase is an example of the way foreign goods are purchased. Generally most foreign goods are bought in the same way domestic goods are purchased. There is one additional step, however: U.S. dollars must be exchanged for the currency of the product's origin. This is done in the foreign exchange market.

What Determines the Price of Foreign Exchange?

Why was the Japanese yen selling for less than 4/10 of a penny on April 5, 1977? Like anything else, it sells for a price that equates supply with demand. The price of yen is determined by the forces of supply and demand. The only difference is that demand for yen is a derived demand, derived from the demand for Japanese products by foreigners.

If you were to go to Japan, you would find that when Japanese importers want to buy American products, they go to the foreign exchange market to purchase dollars with their yen. What determines the price of dollars in that foreign exchange market? The demand for dollars by Japanese who want to buy American products and the supply of dollars from Americans who want to buy Japanese products.

The type of foreign exchange market just described is called a *free* or *floating exchange rate* market. In it the forces of supply and demand are allowed to make the prices of various currencies what they are. This type of market, in a modified form, has been in use since the early 1970s. How long it will remain the general system of foreign exchange is another question. Many international bankers want a *fixed exchange rate* system.

Fixed Exchange Rates

Fixed exchange rates exist when the price of foreign currency remains *fixed* by government edict. The only way to fix price is by intervening in the market. Recall the discussion about price supports for agricultural products in Issue 9. The only way agricultural price supports were maintained for a long period was by the federal government essentially purchasing surpluses of agricultural products.

The same analysis can be used to understand a fixed exchange rate system. If, for example, there is a surplus of dollars on the foreign exchange market at a fixed exchange rate, somebody has to buy them. That somebody is either this nation's central bank—the Federal Reserve—or the central bank of another country. The same is true if there is a surplus of French francs, German marks, British pounds, etc. Somebody has to buy them up in order to maintain the fixed exchange rate.

For many years, there was a system of fixed exchange rates. And for many years the world had continuous "crises" in international dealings. Just as it is very difficult to fix the price of any product, it is very difficult to fix the price of foreign exchange permanently. Today's world is dynamic; it does not lend itself to rigidities. When a system of fixed exchange rates existed, the United States lost tremendous quantities of gold trying to maintain the price of the dollar.

Losing Our Gold

From the 1950s until the 1970s, the value of everything Americans bought from abroad was more than the value of what the rest of the world bought from the United States, expressed at the fixed exchange rate. This created a problem. In trade between nations, other countries ended up with more than they spent on U.S. goods. In other words, the United States had a *balance of payments* deficit, as it is called. The United States spent more than it sold at the fixed exchange rate.

Look at Figure 21-2. It shows the balance of payments deficits that the United States had experienced for many years. Under the existing international monetary and trade rules, foreign countries holding surplus dollars could demand that the United States exchange gold for their surplus dollars. At that time gold had a fixed price in the world market. That price was $35 an ounce.

Due to trade deficits, U.S. holdings in gold dwindled from $20 billion to $10 billion in 15 years. Figure 21-3 shows the losses on a year-by-year basis. Finally, after much pressure and heated debate, in 1971 the world bankers agreed to put gold on a floating exchange rate system.

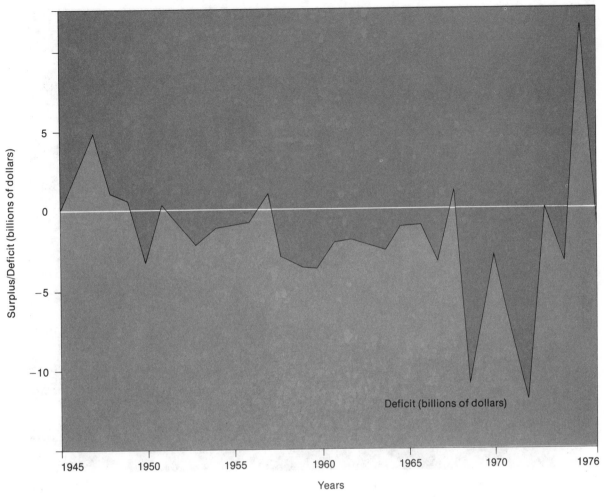

Figure 21–2. United States balance of payment deficits. In the 1950s, the United States fell into an almost perpetual balance of payments deficit. That is, the value of our out-payments has continually exceeded the value of our in-payments. Source: Council of Economic Advisors.

Balance of payments takes account of all economic dealings between nations. Thus, it includes borrowing and lending. However, if discussion is limited to the commodities that are bought and sold, one talks of the *balance of trade* as opposed to the balance of payments between nations.

What Happens When the Price of the Dollar Falls?

When the price of the dollar falls on the foreign exchange market under a floating exchange rate, the dollar has depreciated. That is, the fall in the foreign exchange value of a currency is one of *depreciation.* In a fixed exchange rate system, the only way the price of the dollar can fall is by an official action. That is, a *devaluation,* which is a fall in the foreign exchange value of a currency, is mandated by the government.

In either case, if the price of the dollar falls, it means that foreigners can purchase dollars with less of their own currency. When that happens, it means that the price of American goods to foreigners also falls. Let us look at a simple example.

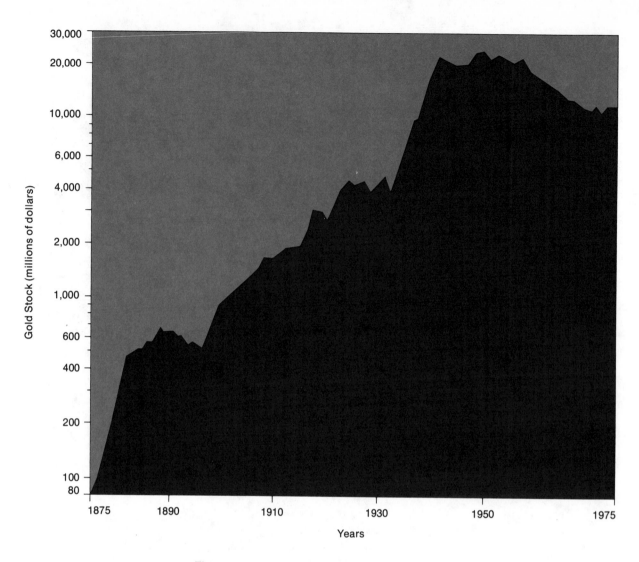

Figure 21–3. Dwindling United States gold stock. By the middle of World War II, we had amassed more than $20 billion worth of gold at the official price of $35 an ounce. By 1970, we had a little more than $10 billion worth of gold. Our chronic balance-of-payments deficit was responsible for this drain. Source: Federal Reserve Bulletin.

Suppose a pair of jeans costs $10 in the United States. If the exchange rate is 5 French francs for $1, a French citizen would have to pay 50 francs for those jeans. What if the price of a dollar falls? What if a dollar can be purchased for only 4 francs? Then to buy that same pair of jeans, the French citizen has to pay only 40 francs.

Basically, the depreciation or devaluation of a country's currency improves its competitive position with respect to other countries. That is, it makes its goods relatively cheaper expressed in other countries' currencies. That same depreciation or devaluation makes other countries' goods more expensive.

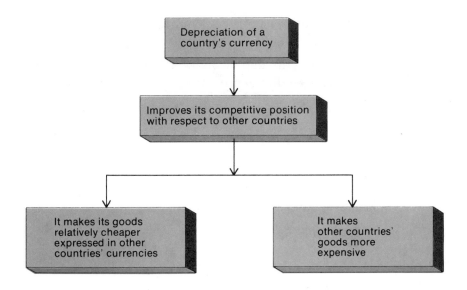

Depreciation, or devaluation, of a
country's currency, and its effects.

Summary
1. Foreign trade accounts for less than 10 percent of GNP. Yet there would be a significant difference in everyday living should foreign trade cease.

2. Products bought from foreign countries are imports. Products sold to foreign countries are exports.

3. Trade is beneficial for those parties who voluntarily engage in it.

4. In principle, there is no economic difference between trading among individuals, states, or nations.

5. Because trade allows for increased specialization, the economic well-being of a nation can be increased if free trade is allowed.

6. There are numerous arguments against free trade. The arguments include the need to protect infant industries, the need to provide for national security, the need to keep the national economy stable, and the desire to avoid dependence on other nations.

7. To engage in foreign trade, buyers must obtain other nations' currencies. This is done in the foreign exchange market.

8. There are two types of international financial systems—a floating exchange rate system and a fixed exchange rate system.

9. In the floating exchange rate system, supply and demand determine the value (price) of each nation's currency in international money dealings. In a fixed exchange rate system, governments fix the value of one currency in terms of another.

10. In international money dealings, the value of currency can fall either through depreciation or devaluation.

11. When the price of a currency falls, foreigners can purchase the goods of that nation more cheaply.

12. Basically, the depreciation or devaluation of a country's currency improves that country's competitive position with respect to other countries.

Important Terms

balance of payments	foreign exchange market
depreciation	free trade
devaluation	import
export	import quota
fixed exchange rate	importer
floating exchange rate	

Review Questions

1. Foreign trade accounts for what percent of GNP?

2. What is the difference between imports and exports?

3. Why is trade beneficial?

4. In drafting the Constitution, what prohibitions did the Founding Fathers make regarding trade among the states?

5. What are the arguments in favor of free trade?

6. What are the arguments against free trade?

7. What must buyers obtain to engage in foreign trade? Why? How do they obtain it?

8. What is the difference between a floating exchange rate and a fixed exchange rate?

9. What is the difference between depreciation and devaluation of a currency?

10. What happens when a nation's currency depreciates or is devaluated?

Discussion Questions

1. Do you think your life would change if all world trade were to stop? If so, how? If not, why?

2. Why do you think the Founding Fathers favored free trade among the states? What problems might have arisen if states had been allowed to tax imports?

3. Do you favor *free* or *restricted* trade on a world basis? Why?

4. What do you think are the advantages and the disadvantages of a floating exchange rate system? A fixed exchange rate system? Which of the two systems do you favor? Why?

5. Are there disadvantages in international trade for a country whose currency has depreciated or has been devaluated? If so, what? If not, why?

Projects

1. Throughout most of American history, the United States maintained a protective tariff policy. Using an American history text as

reference, prepare a report on American tariff policy in the nineteenth or twentieth century.

2.   Various tariff acts have given rise to much heated debate. With a group of students, prepare and present a simulation of a Congressional debate on one of the following tariff acts: Tariff of 1828 (popularly known as the "Tariff of Abominations"), the McKinley Tariff of 1890, the Underwood Tariff of 1913, or the Hawley-Smoot Tariff of 1930.

3.   Using a copy of *The Wall Street Journal,* list the current exchange rates for French francs, British pounds, German marks, Japanese yen, etc. Compare the current exchange rates with the rates that existed a year ago. Which currencies have depreciated? Which have increased in value? Can money be made by investing in foreign currencies? Explain.

Should Cheap Foreign Competition Be Stopped?

Definition of New Term

Tariffs: Tariffs are taxes on imports.

Imagine that your parents work for a shoe manufacturing firm in the northeastern region of the United States. How would they feel if they were given notice of a layoff? The notice given indicates that the shoe plant is being closed because the firm can no longer compete against foreign competition.

Naturally, you would be upset. Your parents might be angry. Suddenly they would have to go on unemployment, draw on their savings, and look for alternative employment opportunities. They would have to do these things because workers in foreign countries were able to produce shoes that could be imported into the United States at prices lower than those for shoes made by the firm for which your parents worked.

Now put yourself in the place of the owners of the firm that could not meet foreign competition. They would suffer losses in wealth and income. They too might feel cheated and indignant that foreigners were allowed to undersell American firms in the United States.

If you look at the history of trade in the United States, you will find that the hypothetical shoe manufacturing case is not unrealistic. It represents a situation that has been repeated many times. For example, American manufacturers of black-and-white television sets have been undercut by Japanese firms. During the early 1970s, American automobile manufacturers lost many sales to foreign competitors, especially to Japanese and German car makers. Many auto workers in Detroit were laid off because of the problem. Thus, free trade obviously does not benefit everybody.

Who Is Hurt by Free Trade?

Whenever another nation obtains a trading advantage in the production of a good or service that competes directly with a good or service produced in this nation, certain individuals in the American economy suffer. Who are those individuals?

Basically, they are the workers and the owners of firms in the affected industry.

Most of the negative effects of free trade are known as *sectoral* effects because they affect certain sectors of the economy rather than the whole economy. There will always be sectoral effects. Trade advantages continually change in the world economy.

You should realize that trade conditions constantly change within the United States, too. For example, what might happen if suddenly a previously unknown supply of natural gas were discovered in Arizona? Let us suppose that so much natural gas was discovered that energy from the wells in that region could be sold at 1/100 of the current price of energy produced elsewhere in the United States. Under such circumstances, Arizona could become a major manufacturing center because it would have low-priced energy. Its competitive advantage would shift to manufacturing. Other regions in the United States would suffer. Manufacturers in the Northeast might have to move to Arizona or lose their businesses. Workers in manufacturing industries in the Northeast might find themselves out of jobs.

There is not much difference between the Arizona example and what does, in fact, happen in world trade. Trading advantages of nations change all the time. Discoveries of raw materials and new production techniques lead some nations to become comparatively better off in the production of goods. In

"TAKE IT OFF! TAKE IT ALL OFF!!"

Should Cheap Foreign Competition Be Stopped? **345**

Import tariffs are designed to protect American business and labor from foreign competition which can produce the same products more inexpensively because of lower labor rates.

recent years, other nations have gained some advantages in industries in which the United States once held a most dominant position. For example, the United States dominated the production of high-technology equipment for many years. Today Japan, Germany, and other countries have a competitive advantage in producing some high-technology products. Declines in these markets mean that American manufacturers may have to shift to producing items in which they will not be faced with a competitive disadvantage.

Protecting American Industries

Because unrestricted trade can have sectoral effects—that is, can cause people to be unemployed and businesses to lose income—concerted efforts have been made in the history of the United States to restrict free trade. One of the main ways by which free trade has been restricted and specific American industries protected is by taxing imports from abroad. Taxes applied to imports from other nations are known as **tariffs.**

U.S. Tariffs

The first U.S. tariff was passed in 1798. It had an average tax rate of 8.5 percent. This meant that on any import item that was not excluded (a *free list item*), the American importer would have to pay a tax of 8.5 percent to the federal government. For example, if an importer obtained $1 million of taxable imports from other countries, that importer would have to pay the U.S. Treasury $85,000 in tariffs.

During the early decades of the nineteenth century, the average tariff rate grew steadily higher. It reached a peak in 1828 and then declined to conservatively low rates until after the Civil War. During the post-Civil War period, the tariff rate rose again. Just before 1900, it reached a high with the enactment of the Dingley Tariff. Although the tariff then declined sharply, it rose once more during the 1920s. In 1930, it peaked with the enactment of the Hawley-Smoot Tariff. Since then, tariff rates have fallen steadily. Today they are at their lowest levels since 1920. Figure I–21–1 shows the average rate of tariffs since they were first enacted in 1798.

Who Benefits from Tariffs?

It is interesting to analyze who benefits from a tariff. Obviously, American consumers do not benefit from tariffs on imports. Tariffs mean that consumers have to pay higher prices for imported products. Who, then, gains?

The people who gain directly from a tariff are the owners of businesses of protected industries. With tariffs on imports, they do not have to fight so much competition. A tariff raises the price

Should Cheap Foreign Competition Be Stopped?　**347**

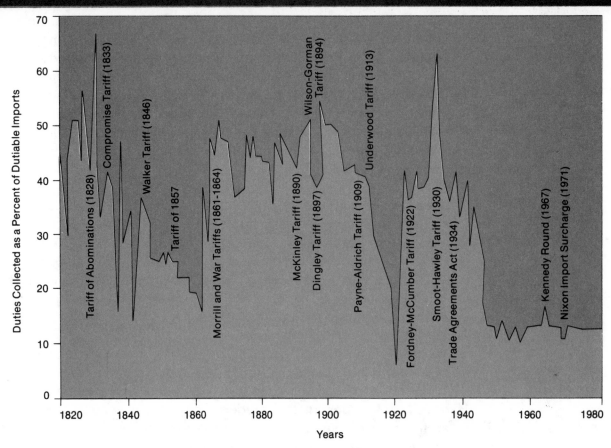

Figure I–21–1. Tariff rates in the United States since 1820. Tariff rates in the United States have bounced like a football, and, indeed, in Congress, tariffs do represent a political football. Import-competing industries prefer high tariffs. In the twentieth century, the highest tariff we have had was the Smoot-Hawley Tariff of 1930, which was almost as high as the Tariff of Abominations in 1828. Source: United States Department of Commerce.

of goods from abroad but not the price of goods produced in the United States. Hence, industries competing with imported goods do not have as much competition. Of course, this is the main reason why tariffs are enacted. In addition, workers in the protected industries find that their jobs are less in jeopardy. Nevertheless, tariffs do not benefit the nation as a whole, only specific protected groups.

Distortions
What is clear is that a tariff in most cases causes an economic distortion. After all, to obtain the highest economic value from scarce resources, one must use those resources in a manner that provides the highest comparative advantage. If other countries can produce goods at a lower price than the United States, Americans have to adjust in order to maximize economic welfare—even though certain industries may be hurt in the short run.

On the other hand, American businesses may have to concentrate on producing those goods in which other nations do not have a comparative advantage. By doing this, the United States can export the latter and import the former. That is what free trade is about. That is why some economists are opposed to setting up tariff walls around nations.

Summary

1. Whenever free trade is allowed, certain sectors of the economy will suffer because of foreign competition.

2. Since 1798, the United States has imposed tariffs to protect American industries against foreign competition.

3. Tariff rates have varied. Today rates are at the lowest levels since 1920.

4. In general, consumers do not benefit from tariffs placed on imports.

5. Those who benefit most from tariffs are the owners of firms and workers in industries that compete with low-cost foreign products.

6. Tariffs introduce distortions in worldwide relative prices.

Important Terms

free list item   tariff

Questions for Thought and Discussion

1. Who can be hurt by free trade?
2. What are the sectoral effects of free trade?
3. Who benefits from a tariff? Who is hurt by a tariff? How?
4. Do you favor a high tariff policy or a low tariff policy? Why?

22

Economic Growth in Developing Nations

Preview Questions

1. Why do some nations grow faster economically than others?
2. Why are humans so important in a nation's economic development?
3. Do nations need lots of natural resources in order to develop?

Definitions of New Terms

Subsidization: Subsidization is the provision of financial help to firms or persons to allow them to stay in business. Often done by a government agency, it is to aid an industry that is not making a profit.

Service sector: The service sector is the part of the business community that provides services, such as cleaning, auto repair, medical care, and so on.

It is probably impossible for you to imagine what it would be like to grow up in a country with an economic standard of living drastically lower than that of the United States. However, try to picture what life would be like in rural India. There most people live three to a room. Most houses have no running water, no electricity, and are probably constructed of mud. As primitive as these accommodations appear, many people in India must make do with even less. Present trends indicate that for some time the housing shortage in India will continue to increase at a rate of over 2 million units per year.

Even the poor in the United States have many times more than what most people have in nearly every less-developed country in the world today. Look at Table 22-1. It shows the per person income in some selected countries. Can you imagine getting by on $120 a year? It sounds impossible. Yet much of the world does get by on just that amount.

Of course, the $120 figure is not an accurate representation of the standard of living in many countries. Nevertheless, it gives some idea of how much richer the United States is than less-developed nations. This nation, with only 6 percent of the world's population, consumes between 30 and 40 percent of the world's resources.

Although many Americans go to bed hungry, many more *non*-Americans do. The less-developed nations today are facing many age-old problems. Some of these problems seem even greater today, partially because of available information.

Table 22–1: Per Person Income in Selected Countries (1975)

Switzerland	$8,754
Sweden	8,450
Denmark	7,106
United States	7,099
Norway	6,944
Canada	6,935
West Germany	6,842
Australia	6,168
France	6,386
Japan	4,425
Kenya	185
Sudan	120

Source: U.S. Department of State

Poverty exists in one form or another in all nations. In what ways do you feel your definition of poverty would differ from that of the woman pictured here?

The Problems of the Information Explosion

Today the less-developed countries are no longer content with their economic situation. Information about how citizens in rich countries live is now known in remote villages of the most backward nations. Many know about the comforts of modern living. Hence, the relative poverty of the world's masses is not as accepted as before. The downtrodden know that a better life exists elsewhere. That is the life they are striving for.

What do they want? They want the "good" things—better health, food, and housing. These people do not exactly seek what Americans call the "good life." Still, they are demanding that their governments do something about their poverty.

The governments of less-developed countries, in turn, have sought the help of economists to develop policies that might increase the rate of economic growth for their nations. The policies economists suggest are often determined by what economists believe have caused the rich nations to get rich. Unfortunately, there is no generally accepted theory to explain why nations such as the United States became so much richer than other countries. Nevertheless, economists have developed some theories of why nations grow at different rates.

Theories of Why Nations Grow

Geographical Theories

One of the most simplistic theories of growth concerns geographical location. This might be called the *north-south theory of economic development*. It suggests that nations in colder climates will be more developed than nations in warmer climates. This theory seems to be supported by some evidence. In the United States, for example, the North has a higher per capita income than the South. Northern Italy is more developed than southern Italy. The same is true for France. On the other hand, this is not the case in England, Sweden, Norway, or Australia.

Moreover, if this theory were sound, it ought to apply to the past. It does not. Most ancient civilizations were in hot regions of the world. Recall the great river civilizations of Egypt and Babylonia and the Mayan civilization of Central America. Even Greece and Rome had milder climates than those of the industrial powers of the nineteenth and twentieth centuries.

As a variation of the north-south theory, some economists have hypothesized that geographical distribution of natural resources is important. They suggest that development is often tied to location of mineral deposits, good soil, useful rainfall, etc. While this may have some validity—particularly in the past, when trade was not so widespread—Japan, Denmark, and Israel show how nations without numerous natural resources can do well economically.

A Racial Theory

Even more simplistic, and certainly less defensible, is the racial theory of development. According to this theory, economic well-being is a matter of race—some races are more productive than others.

This assumption, however, is not borne out by history. No one race has historically proved to be more productive than others. One need only look at the success of the Japanese in raising their standard of living and compare it with the success of Anglo-Saxons. A look at the history of the Chinese, Egyptian, Greek, African, and Indian cultures further strengthens the argument that there is little evidence for race as the determining factor in economic development. In other words, race is not a useful device for explaining why or predicting where relative prosperity will occur in the world economy.

Modern Theories

As might be expected, more sophisticated theories of development are voiced by today's economists. One of the most widely discussed theories concerns the need for balanced growth.

Industry and Agriculture Together.

One characteristic of most developed countries is a high degree of industrialization. In general, countries with relatively high standards of living are more industrialized than countries with low standards of living. Some economists have taken this to mean that industrialization can be equated with economic development. The policy that should be followed is then obvious. Less-developed countries in which a large percentage of total resources are devoted to agriculture should attempt to obtain a more balanced growth. They should industrialize.

While at first glance the theory appears acceptable, it can lead to some absurd results. For example, some underdeveloped countries have built steel factories and automobile plants. Yet the people are actually worse off because of this attempt at industrialization. Why? These countries do not have an advantage in producing steel or automobiles. They can engage in such industrial activities only by heavy *subsidization* and by massive restrictions on competitive imports from other countries. In India, steel mills produce steel at two to three times the resource cost that would be required if the steel were imported from the United States or Japan. Therefore, it seems that India is worse off, not better off, because of this attempt at industrialization. Although owning steel mills may raise national prestige, the citizens get less economic value out of their resources than they would otherwise.

The circumstances just described occur throughout much of the less-developed world. Import restrictions such as quotas and tariffs abound, preventing the purchase of cheaper foreign substitutes for industrial products that the country produces in a subsidized environment.

Sometimes the subsidization is not obvious. Nevertheless, it usually exists in one form or another. In general, when an industry must be subsidized to exist, the subsidy leads to a misallocation of resources and to lower economic welfare for the country as a whole. Obviously, the owners of firms and the workers with skills specific to that industry are better off. But consumers end up paying a higher *total* cost for domestically made goods. In addition, the total output of the nation remains less than it could be were resources allocated correctly.

A Theory of Stages of Development.

If one looks at the development of modern nations, one will find they go through three stages. First is the agricultural stage, when most of the population is involved in that endeavor. Second is the manufacturing stage, when much of the population becomes involved in the industrialized sector of the economy. Finally, there is a shift toward the **service sectors.** This is exactly what is happening in the United States. The service sectors of the economy are growing by leaps and bounds, whereas the manufacturing sector is falling in its percentage of total employment.

Nevertheless, it is important to understand the need for early specialization in what one does *relatively* best. If free trade is allowed among nations, a nation is best off if it produces what is has a relative advantage at producing and imports the rest. This means that many underdeveloped countries should continue to specialize in agricultural production. However, they should diversify rather than concentrate on production of one crop. If the world price of a crop falls, a one-crop economy can suffer.

Problems with Agriculture. Continued specialization in agriculture by less-developed countries does face a problem. Many industrialized countries have continually subsidized their own agricultural sectors in order to eliminate in part the relative advantage that less-developed countries have in agricultural pursuits. If people lived in a world without subsidization, they might see much less food being produced in the highly industrialized nations and much more being produced in the less-developed nations of the world. Under such circumstances, the less-developed nations would trade food for manufactured goods and the industrialized nations manufactured goods for food. Accepting this reasoning, one can argue that one of the "bad" aspects of U.S. economic policy, from the viewpoint of Third World nations, has been the continued subsidization of the American farmer.

Nonetheless, even within the current situation, a policy of balanced growth—of increased industrialization—may be difficult to accomplish in the less-developed countries of the world. Industrialization is generally more beneficial if it comes about at its own pace. When economic conditions are such that businesspersons freely decide to build factories instead of increasing farm output, then industrialization will probably add to the prosperity of a nation.

Humans Are a Resource

Large amounts of natural resources are not by themselves sufficient to guarantee economic growth. Many Latin American countries, for example, are quite rich in natural resources. However, they have not always used those resources to maximize economic growth.

In order for natural resources to have an effect on economic growth, humans must be included. It is humans who devise the methods by which other resources can be converted into usable forms. The immigrants who came to the New World to escape the strict life-styles in the countries of Europe were the people who would devise new methods to utilize the natural resources of America.

Education has improved the lot of both Americans and the United States. This has been done by formal and informal schooling and training. Many workers have increased their value by going to college, others have obtained on-the-job training. Figure 22-1 shows that the number of years of education completed has been increasing since before the turn of the century.

With this in mind, many economists have suggested that one road to economic well-being for less-developed nations may lie in increased expenditures on education. However, education provides no guarantee. For example, many young people in less-developed nations study political science and foreign diplomacy in high schools and colleges while using government resources. Some people feel these nations would probably be better off training engineers, technicians, and food specialists, instead of diplomats. As always, care must be taken when a government decides to adopt a program designed to expand a certain sector of an economy—be it industry or education.

Capital Requirements

Some observers believe that economic development would require less-developed countries to have more capital—machines, factories, raw materials, and the like. Indeed, highly developed countries do have much more available capital per person. The United States, as well as other developed nations, has given massive amounts of capital to those countries seeking economic development. In fact, this nation has given away more than $25 billion to other countries.

The lack of capital, however, is not the only reason for under-development. After all, since World War II, immense sums have

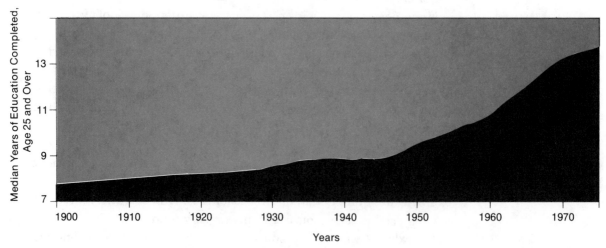

Figure 22–1. Median years of education completed. In the United States, the median years of education completed by the adult population has risen from under 8 years at the turn of the century to over 12 years by the 1970s. Source: United States Department of Commerce, Bureau of the Census, *Long-Term Economic Growth*, p. 43.

been made available to developing nations. To some extent, these funds have been well applied and have produced sound results. In other cases, foreign aid has been applied to economically unsound purposes, or to good projects that have been poorly planned and executed.

To spend large amounts of money capital efficiently and to use large amounts of physical capital effectively require organization, experience, and a high level of skill. Taking this into account, it appears that large injections of capital into developing nations cannot guarantee good results.

Productivity

The importance of the productivity of individuals within respective societies cannot be overemphasized. Countries such as the United States, Germany, and Sweden, which have high output per work hour, have tremendous advantages over nations with lower rates of productivity. The things that determine productivity—schooling, management techniques, attitude, capital investment, ingenuity, and so on—are critical. When a nation, an industry, or a company lacks or begins to slide in regard to such determinants, bad times are on the way.

Productivity appears to be suffering dramatically in some developed countries. Many observers have suggested that this is a problem Great Britain is experiencing. In fact, one astute observer has contended that Britain might eventually turn into a goat pasture if reductions in productivity continue. Just the opposite seems to be true in such countries as Japan and Germany. The United States, on the other hand, has had both ups and downs in national productivity in recent years.

Many Americans know that productivity has to get started in less-developed countries. But it cannot come out of the blue. The United States has attempted through various means to help these nations help themselves.

What About the Future of Less-Developed Countries?

Although a number of less-developed countries have moved toward increased economic well-being, many are still languishing. Observers contend that one reason less-developed countries have remained that way is that they have not been able to stop high rates of population growth. If these nations are to improve economically, they must find ways to solve their population problems.

Summary

1. Per capita income varies greatly among the nations of the world.

2. The United States is the richest of all nations. With only 6 percent of the world's population, it consumes between 30 and 40 percent of the world's resources.

3. There are many theories to explain why some nations grow faster than others. One of the most simplistic concerns geographical factors—location and resource distribution.

4. Although it has been put forth as a theory, race is not a determining factor in economic development.

5. Some economists support the ideas of establishing a balance between the growth of industry and agriculture and allowing for stages of development to take their normal course.

6. Subsidization can lead to misallocation of resources and to lower economic welfare for society as a whole.

7. In order for natural resources to have an effect on economic growth, humans must devise methods by which such resources can be converted into usable forms.

8. If properly directed, increased expenditures in education might be one road to economic well-being for less-developed nations.

9. Large injections of capital into less-developed nations will not necessarily guarantee sound economic development.

10. Productivity is an important determinant of economic well-being.

11. Some observers believe that many less-developed nations will not begin to increase their economic well-being until they find ways to solve their population problems.

Important Terms

balanced growth
per capita income
industrialization

productivity
less-developed countries
subsidization

Review Questions

1. Why can it be said that the United States is the richest nation in the world?

2. Why do some of the age-old problems that less-developed nations are facing seem even greater today?

3. What do the people of less-developed countries want?

4. What is the north-south theory of economic development?

5. Is race a useful factor for explaining why or predicting where relative prosperity will occur?

6. What is a major characteristic of most developed countries?

7. How can subsidization hurt economic development?

8. Why are humans perhaps the most important resource?

9. Is the lack of capital the chief reason for underdevelopment? Why or why not?

10. Why is productivity important to economic well-being?

Discussion Questions

1. Do you think individuals living in very poor countries know what it is like to live in a rich country such as the United States? If so, how? If not, why not?

2. How important do you think geographical location and the distribution of natural resources are in determining the economic well-being of nations? What other factors do you consider to be important? Why?

3. Countries with relatively high standards of living are more industrialized than countries with low standards of living. Does this mean that less-developed countries should industrialize? Why or why not?

4. How do you think less-developed nations might best improve their economic well-being?

Projects

1. Prepare a report on a less-developed nation that has large quantities of natural resources, explaining why it is less developed. Countries that might be researched include India, Brazil, the Congo, Nigeria, Venezuela, and Indonesia.

2. Prepare a report on a highly developed nation that has a small natural resource base, explaining why it is developed. Countries that might be researched include Great Britain, Japan, Switzerland, the Netherlands, and Denmark.

3. Research American foreign aid to Third World nations from 1960 to the present. Information on foreign aid can be obtained by writing to the U.S. Department of State, 2201 C Street NW, Washington, DC 20520 or to the Agency for International Development, 320 Twenty-First Street NW, Washington, DC 20523. The librarian at the school or public library may also be able to help you find appropriate sources. Do you think this nation's foreign aid policies have been helpful in promoting development among Third World nations? Why or why not?

Biography: Thomas Robert Malthus (1766–1834)

The Malthusian Trap

Thomas Robert Malthus believed that the world was destined to face a food crisis unless people began resorting to birth control. Malthus himself was an ordained minister and economist who graduated in the late eighteenth century from Cambridge University, where he studied population statistics and agricultural production.

Malthus anonymously published *An Essay on the Principle of Population, as It Affects the Future Improvement of Society* in 1798. The essay basically sums up Malthus' observations made while traveling in other countries. In it he claimed that food supplies increase arithmetically from generation to generation, whereas population, through natural growth, increases geometrically. Malthus' conclusion—that eventually there would be insufficient food to feed the population unless the birth rate is reduced drastically in situations in which population growth exceeds economic growth—is commonly known as the *Malthusian trap.*

Malthus' essay was a direct attack on the English Poor Laws, which provided relief to poor people. Malthus thought that direct relief to the poor would only make things worse. Gifts of goods and clothing, especially to large families, would tend to encourage laxness and still larger families.

After becoming a history professor, Malthus published a revision of his essay under his own name in 1803. Although he modified his original arguments, he still claimed that population had a tendency to outrun the supply of food. He thought that only wars, famine, and pestilence served to check population growth.

It is not surprising Malthus' theory was criticized severely by clergymen, politicians, and journalists. However, a few economists, including his friend David Ricardo, based their own theories on his ideas.

Malthus' theory has some validity. It accurately reflected the history of population growth and food production *before* the Industrial Revolution. Perhaps it is even applicable to many underdeveloped nations in Asia, Africa, and Latin America today.

The Industrial Revolution had a major effect on Malthus' thinking. That time in England was very hard. Machine industry

360 The International Scene

was rapidly displacing craftsmen, and many could not find jobs. Many people believed England was overpopulated.

In this century, some nations have definitely suffered from overpopulation and food shortages. Nevertheless, the Malthusian theory of overpopulation has had little meaning for the United States and Western Europe. First, improved farming techniques and soil conservation practices in these areas have greatly increased the supply of food. Second, the population of these areas has not grown at the enormous rate predicted by Malthus, in spite of the fact that people live longer. However, as the world grows "smaller," problems that affect non-Western nations inevitably also affect the West.

23

Alternative Economic Systems

Preview Questions

1. What are the origins of socialism?
2. What is Marxian economics?
3. What are some features of the Soviet economy today?
4. What are some features of the Chinese economy today?

Definitions of New Terms

Socialism: Socialism is an economic system in which the government owns the major factors of production.

Surplus value: Surplus value is the term Marx applied to the difference between the market value of a product and the cost of materials and wages paid to workers. To put it another way, it is the profit realized by the capitalist.

Dictatorship of the proletariat: The dictatorship of the proletariat (the workers) is the first stage of communist society. Under it the state controls the economy to prepare society for the communist ideal.

Communism: Communism is an economic system in which the "people" own the major factors of production, and the relationships of production and distribution are "from each according to his ability, to each according to his need."

Imperialism: Imperialism is, according to Lenin, the final stage of capitalism. When it is reached, the economy is completely dominated by monopolies.

Bolsheviks: The Bolsheviks were the communists in Russia who overthrew the provisional government and established a communist state.

Mixed economy: A mixed economy is one in which elements of socialism and capitalism are mixed together.

Those of you who read this book live in the United States. Some of you have already decided what job you would like to have after completing your education, although your decision may change in time. Others may not make a decision until they have been in college awhile. No one dictates what you must do with your most valuable productive resource—yourself. You decide what to do on the basis of available opportunities, advice from your parents, friends, and teachers, and your abilities and talents. You do not usually have to ask government officials about what you should do. One reason is that you live in a private enterprise, or capitalist, system.

The American Capitalist Economy

The American economy is a capitalist economy in which individuals usually can pursue their own productive activities without interference from a central authority. Actually, the American economic system is a mixed economy. Although it contains many elements of capitalism, government officials do make some decisions about what is to be done in the economic sphere.

Capitalism is not the only economic system in the world today. There are others. Comparisons among the various economic systems can be made by comparing the degree to which economic decision making is politically centralized or decentralized.

The Degree of Decentralization

Chart 23-1 shows the degree of decentralization in various economic systems throughout the world. At the extreme right-hand side of the

Scale of Decentralization

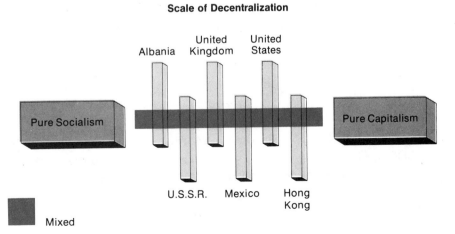

Chart 23-1. Degree of decentralization in different economic systems throughout the world. On the extreme right, we find pure capitalism which no country follows. The extreme left is pure socialism, which again no country follows. Between these extremes are all the world economies, with just a few shown here as representative.

chart is shown the system called *capitalism*. It is a system in which the government has practically no control over economic decision making. At the extreme left-hand side of the chart is shown the system called **socialism**. Socialism is an economic system in which the uses of the major factors of production—machines, land, and labor—are decided on by central political bodies.

Socialism is the leading alternative economic system to capitalism. Before turning to a discussion of some of the major socialist systems in the world today, let us briefly examine the origins of socialism.

The Origin of Socialism and Marxian Economics

Socialist ideas have existed for a long time. However, it was not until the middle of the nineteenth century and the writings of Karl Marx that socialism took root as an economic system. Marx, more than any other individual in the history of economic thought, is responsible for the foundations of socialism as it is known today.

In almost every socialist system, the government owns all major productive resources, such as land and machines. Individuals generally own their own consumer goods. They are not allowed to own the means of production as are individuals in a capitalist system.

As practiced today, socialism is generally consistent with the principles outlined in Marx's writings. Marx believed that the owners of capital (land, machines, and the like)—the capitalists—exploited the owners of labor services (the workers).

Exploitation of Labor

Marx contended that in a capitalist system, the capitalists took advantage of workers. The way they took advantage of workers was by keeping for themselves what Marx called the **surplus value** of production. Marx defined surplus value as the difference between the cost of labor and the total value of the product.

According to Marx, workers in a capitalist system work part of each day without payment. They create for the capitalist a surplus value, which is a source of wealth and profit for the capitalist. Marx believed that the true, or total, value of any good was directly related to the total amount of labor used in making it. This means if a worker works all day to make $100 worth of shoes but is paid only $50, the difference after deducting the cost of materials is surplus value. In the capitalist system, the capitalist gets the surplus value, even though he or she has not contributed to the production of the product. In other words, Marx believed that the capitalist gained from the labor of workers, and he saw this as exploitation.

Economic Crises and Business Cycles

According to Marx, capitalists strive continuously to get richer. The only way they can do this is by producing more. Eventually the market becomes saturated, and all the things that capitalists produce cannot be sold. Then the only way capitalists can increase their profits is by introducing more sophisticated means of production—

new equipment and techniques. Eventually all sources for increased profits run out. Recession and depression develop. In fact, Marx foresaw a continuous series of recessions and depressions in all capitalist economies. These, however, are different from those discussed in Chapter 17.

According to Marx, economic cycles would get worse and worse, eventually exploding in the collapse of capitalism. He predicted that industrial power would become increasingly concentrated in fewer monopolistic firms. Wealth would also become increasingly concentrated in the hands of a few capitalists. Eventually, workers would unite and revolt. The capitalist system would be overthrown by a more rational system. That is, socialism would prevail. In Marx's words, the world would see:

The revolt of the working class, a class always increasing in numbers and discipline, united, organized by the very mechanism of the process of capitalist production itself. [1]

The Fall of Capitalism

Marx predicted that capitalism would fall. Its fall was to lead to the rise of a socialist world ruled by a ***dictatorship of the proletariat*** (the workers). Eventually the socialist world would give way to the communist ideal. Then, under communism, the state—the government— would wither away.

Communism would theoretically differ from socialism in that the relationships of production and distribution are "from each according to his ability, to each according to his need." The ideal communist world that Marx predicted would eventually emerge is unrealistic. It has never happened, and most likely it never will.

Lenin—A Disciple of Marx

One of the great followers of Marxist thought was Vladimir Ilyich Ulyanov, popularly known as Lenin. He led the Russian Revolution of 1917, which disposed of the provisional government that had replaced tsarist rule in Russia. Under Lenin, the first communist state in the world was created.

Lenin spent much time in analyzing what has been called ***imperialism,*** the final stage of capitalism. According to Lenin, economies in the imperialist stage of capitalism are completely dominated by monopolies. As capitalist countries become more monopolized, their governments strive to gain access to protected markets. The attempt to partition the world into various international monopolies results in ugly competitive wars between nations. National conflicts inevitably result. This struggle for economic dominance thus hastens the eventual demise of the capitalist world.

---

[1]Karl Marx, *Das Kapital*, Vol. 1, page 763, (Moscow: Foreign Language Publishing House, 1961).

Lenin, the founder of the first communist state, firmly believed that capitalism would eventually fail.

When Lenin and the **Bolsheviks** (the communists) succeeded in establishing a revolutionary government in Russia, not all capitalist institutions were immediately eliminated. In fact, during the civil war that erupted and lasted until 1921, Lenin was forced to modify some Marxist principles. By 1921, however, the communists were in total control. Lenin then introduced his New Economic Policy in an attempt to industrialize the Soviet Union.

After Lenin died in 1924, Joseph Stalin came to power. In 1928, Stalin introduced the First Five-Year Plan. It outlined the goals of the economy and set a pattern for the future. The First Five-Year Plan emphasized rapid industrialization under state direction and a high rate of economic growth. In addition, it stressed the modernization of agriculture through *collectivization*, the establishment of state farms.

The Soviet Economy Today

Today the Soviet economy follows many of the concepts laid out by Marx, Lenin, and Stalin. The economy of the Soviet Union is socialist, although in each socialist country some capitalist features exist. Today the state—the central government—owns almost all factors of production in the Soviet Union. Workers are paid government-set wages. They do have some freedom in what they spend their lives doing. Nevertheless, Soviet citizens do not have the same range of choices as Americans in their movement around the country to seek better employment.

Until recently, physical quotas were set for factory output. This caused many problems. Factories would produce to meet their physical quotas, but often the products were of poor quality. The typical Soviet factory is now evaluated according to a concept of

Traditionally, the Soviet government has owned and controlled all means of production. Some elements of the capitalist system have recently been adopted in an effort to improve both the quantity and the quality of manufacturing.

profitability. Profitability, however, is not yet measured in the same way it is in the United States.

Within the factory itself, managers obtain special benefits that workers do not have. In addition to such benefits as housing priorities and allowances, travel expenses, and perhaps the right to own a car, managers are paid a higher salary. Just as in the United States, workers are paid according to a scale of importance. The difference is that the government, rather than the marketplace, determines the scale.

In terms of resource allocation, there are regional economic councils and planners who decide what industries should do. However, the decision as to how many economic resources should be used in producing consumer goods as opposed to producing other goods is made by the government's central planners.

Since the 1920s, there has been a concerted effort to devote as much production as possible to the production of capital goods—that is, goods used in the production of other goods. This has meant that Soviet citizens have not been able to buy as many consumer goods as they might like. Nevertheless, in the future they can have more than they might otherwise have because of the decision, until recently, to concentrate on the production of capital goods.

Mao Tse-Tung led China to its present collectivist economic system.

Until recently in the Soviet Union, little market information was used to determine which consumer goods should be produced. This, of course, resulted in a lot of things being in short supply and many products being produced that were never bought. Today, however, central planners realize that production should be slowed down when consumer goods are not bought and should be increased rapidly when goods are bought.

Soviet planners are even starting to engage in marketing surveys to see what consumers want. People from the central planning office go out with questionnaires and interview consumers as to their needs and desires. This is a common practice in the United States, too, to find out where industry should be started, which products should be produced, and so forth.

Communist China

One of the economic systems that is most different from that of the United States is the Chinese communist economic system. Since the late Mao Tse-tung, Chairman of the Chinese Communist party, took power in 1949, China has become a model of collectivist economic planning and operation.

Maoist Economics

The main features of the Chinese economy include public ownership of all industries, agricultural communes, and massive central planning. The state makes all decisions regarding investment versus consumption, how labor is to be supplied to various sectors of the economy, and the prices of goods and services.

In the Chinese economy, there is always full employment. Although workers have complete freedom to change jobs in theory,

Full employment is one advantage of the Chinese economic system. However, workers do not have the same degree of mobility within the nation as we do in the United States.

police regulations and quota systems prevent complete job mobility. For example, university students are generally assigned their future positions while in school.

The Planning Operation

After coming to power, the Chinese communists set out to restore a country that had been devastated by years of internal and external strife. They devised plans to set China on the road to economic well-being. The First Five-Year Plan was instituted in 1952. It stressed investment in heavy industry, retention of small handicraft industries, and land reform. As early as 1946, in those areas "liberated" during the struggle to overthrow Chiang Kai-shek's nationalist government, the Chinese communists confiscated the holdings of wealthy landowners and gave them to poor peasants. Under the First Five-Year Plan, farms were collectively organized into communes.

In 1958, the Second Five-Year Plan was put into effect. Known as the "Great Leap Forward," the plan stressed rapid economic growth. The central leadership—the policymakers—wished to increase output by more than 25 percent per year. Heavy industry was to be developed even more rapidly than under the previous plan. More labor was to be used to reduce underemployment of the labor force. Instead of directing all heavy industrial operations under a central plan, however, there was some decentralization. Local managers were given more control over what their plants bought and sold and what production methods were to be used.

From its beginning, the Great Leap Forward ran into problems that resulted in tragic consequences. The program was too ambitious. Many goods were produced that were not needed or wanted in the economy. Many large-scale projects were poorly planned and managed. The results were often a fiasco. For example, steel was produced by unskilled workers under unsafe and primitive conditions using poor production techniques. Much of the steel produced was so poor in quality that it could not be used.

In agriculture, shortages in production quotas developed. Not only did severe weather conditions result in poor harvests, but many workers were transferred from farm communes to the city to provide the labor for the great industrial expansion program. The consequence was too little production of food, leading to minor famine.

Finally, a New Economic Policy was instituted. Under it, the Chinese communist leadership showed recognition that agriculture had to be built up before industrialization could be achieved. Thus, agriculture became the foundation of the economy.

Milder Forms of Socialism

There are milder forms of socialism than the communist style practiced by the Soviet Union and Communist China. Great Britain has a type of socialism that vacillates between increased government ownership of the means of production and increased private ownership. For example, British steel mills have been nationalized and denationalized several times. When the Labor Party came into power after World War II, it did an effective job of nationalizing the railroad, coal, and electric power industries. Today, however, there is considerable debate within the Labor Party about the advisability of increasing socialist economic institutions.

The same kinds of debates are taking place in other countries that have experimented with socialist practices. These countries include Norway, Sweden, Denmark, Australia, and New Zealand. In recent years, the more socialist countries have tended to adopt elements of capitalism, while the more capitalist countries have tended to adopt elements of socialism. The result is what is known as a *mixed economy*—neither socialist nor capitalist, but a mixture of the two.

Summary

1.   Today the United States has a mixed economy. Nevertheless, its economic system is basically capitalistic and highly decentralized.

2.   The major alternative economic system to capitalism today is socialism. The most socialistic economies are those of communist countries such as the Soviet Union and Communist China.

3.   Under socialism, the state—the central government—owns the major factors of production, and most economic decisions are made by central planners.

4.   Although socialist ideas have existed for many centuries, it was not until the writings of Karl Marx in the middle of the nineteenth century that socialism took root.

5.   Marx contended that capitalism is a system of exploitation. The capitalists—the owners of capital—take advantage of labor by taking for themselves the surplus value created by workers.

6.   Marx believed that the exploitation of workers by capitalists is the basis for a class struggle. He thought that as capitalists strove to become richer, they would adopt measures that ultimately would result in depressions that would explode into revolution and the overthrow of the capitalist system.

7.   Marx predicted that capitalism would fall because of a growing class struggle between capitalists and workers (the proletariat). Capitalism is supposed to give way to socialism, which will eventually give way to the communist ideal.

8.   One of the major disciples of Marx's ideas was Lenin. He was the leader of the Bolsheviks, who overthrew the provisional government in Russia in 1917 and established the world's first communist state.

9.   Lenin expanded some of Marx's ideas. Once in power, he sought to industrialize the Soviet Union. Because of internal strife and the devastating effects of civil war, Lenin introduced his New Economic Policy in 1921. This permitted some capitalist features to exist within the Soviet economy.

10.   After Lenin's death in 1924, Joseph Stalin came to power. He introduced the First Five-Year Plan in 1928. It outlined the aims of the economy and set the pattern for the future. In fact, it established a model that has generally been followed by all communist countries since that time.

11.   Today the Soviet economy is socialist. Economic priorities are established by central planners. Although producers are still subject to physical quotas, production is evaluated according to a concept of profitability.

12.   Like workers in the United States, Soviet workers are paid wages in accordance with a scale of job importance. The difference is that the government, rather than the marketplace, determines the scale.

13.   The Chinese economy is even more centralized than the Soviet economy. Its main features are public ownership of all industries, economic decision making by central authority, and agricultural communes.

14.   The spiritual, economic, and political leader of Communist China from its birth in 1949 until his death in 1976 was Mao Tse-tung.

15.   The Chinese economy has full employment. Today China is no longer faced with the terrible problem of famine that had existed for centuries.

16.   One of the major disasters in Chinese economic planning was

the Second Five-Year Plan. Known as the "Great Leap Forward," it was much too ambitious in its emphasis on massive industrialization.

17. As a consequence of the failure of the "Great Leap Forward," Chinese leadership came to recognize that agriculture had to be built up before industrialization could be achieved. Agriculture thus became the foundation of the economy.

18. There are milder forms of socialism than that practiced by communist nations. Systems such as that of Great Britain vacillate between increased government ownership of the means of production and private ownership.

19. Today many of the economies of the world are mixed economies. That is, they are a mixture of socialism and capitalism.

Important Terms

Bolsheviks
communism
socialism
Five-Year Plan
"Great Leap Forward"

imperialism
mixed economy
dictatorship of the proletariat
surplus value

Review Questions

1. What is the American economic system?

2. What is the major alternative economic system to capitalism today?

3. What is the difference between the two systems?

4. Who was Karl Marx?

5. What did Marx predict about capitalism? What was his reasoning?

6. What did Marx mean by surplus value?

7. Who was Lenin?

8. How did Lenin expand Marx's ideas?

9. Who was Joseph Stalin?

10. What is a five-year plan?

11. What are the chief features of the Soviet economy?

12. How does the determination of wages in the Soviet Union differ from that in the United States?

13. Who was Mao Tse-tung?

14. How does the Chinese economy differ from the Soviet economy?

15. What was the Great Leap Forward? Why did it fail? What was the result of its failure?

16. What are some milder forms of socialism than that practiced by communist nations? How do these economies differ from communist economies?

Discussion Questions

1. Karl Marx described the communist ideal as a society in which the state has withered away and the economy is organized on the principle "from each according to his ability, to each according to his need." What do you think Marx meant by this? Do you think such a society is possible? Why or why not?

2. Marx believed that the overthrow of capitalism by a revolt of the proletariat (the workers) would first occur in advanced industrial societies. However, communist revolutions have taken place in less-developed agricultural countries. How do you explain Marx's miscalculation? In developing his theories, what premises did Marx make that now appear inaccurate? What factors did he not consider?

3. How would you compare capitalist and communist economies? What are the advantages and disadvantages of each?

Projects

1. Prepare a report comparing either the Soviet economy or the Chinese economy with that of the United States. Data on the Soviet and Chinese economies can be obtained from *Allocation of Resources in the Soviet Union and China, Soviet Economic Prospects for the Seventies,* and *China: A Reassessment of the Economy,* which are U.S. Government Printing Office publications. Data on the American economy can be obtained from *Statistical Abstract of the United States* or *The President's Economic Report,* which are annual publications of the U.S. Government Printing Office.

2. Based on Marxism and modeled somewhat after the Soviet and Chinese economies, Cuba's economy is currently the only communist economy in the Western Hemisphere. Established as a communist state by Fidel Castro in 1960, Cuba serves as an interesting case study. Research Cuban communism and report your findings to the class. Information on Cuban communism can be obtained from *Communist Economies* by Helburn, *et al,* (Reading, Mass: Addison-Wesley, 1977).

3. With a group of students, prepare and hold a panel discussion contrasting the theories of Adam Smith with those of Karl Marx.

4. With a group of students, hold a debate on the following proposition: *Resolved,* that communism is doomed to failure since it is based on numerous fallacies.

The Theory of Class Struggle

The *Communist Manifesto* was published in 1848. In it Karl Marx called on the workers of the world to unite in revolt against the capitalist ruling class. Marx contended that all history was represented by the control of one class of people over another class and that the rulers (the owners of property) exploited the laborers.

Marx believed that class conflict would continue until the capitalist system was destroyed. He thought only by overthrowing capitalism and establishing a communist society in which everyone would be equal could class struggles finally be eliminated.

Marx's theories are important because they guide the thinking of leaders in communist countries. Although his theories have been modified by others, they serve as the philosophical foundation for communist society.

Marx was born and educated in Germany. He attended the universities of Bonn and Berlin, and he received a Ph.D. in philosophy from the University of Vienna at age 23. While at the university, Marx became very interested in the ideas of philosopher Georg W. F. Hegel. Hegel's ideas were to have a profound influence on Marx's thinking—particularly the idea that history constantly changes. Marx based his idea of historical materialism—that the condition of the economy affects the course of people and their ideas—on Hegelian principles.

During the 1840s Marx met Friedrich Engels, who was to become a lifelong friend and colleague. As coauthor of the *Communist Manifesto,* Engels worked very closely with Marx. In fact, it is often difficult to know to whom ideas belonged, as each had a hand in almost everything the other wrote.

Marx moved to London in 1849. There he spent most of the remainder of his life, much of it in poverty. While in England, Marx spent long hours daily at the library of the British Museum gathering information for his monumental work, *Das Kapital (Capital).*

In *Das Kapital* (of which Volumes II and III were completed by Engels following Marx's death in 1883), Marx concluded that no changes could save a system that could create such terrible problems for society. He predicted the eventual overthrow of the capitalist system and its replacement by the dictatorship of the proletariat. He looked forward to a stateless society where workers would direct and govern themselves and divide the products of their labor according to their needs.

It is important to remember that *Das Kapital* was Marx's review of capitalism as it existed in the nineteenth century. The book appeared at a time when many problems were being caused by rapid industrialization. Crowded slums, poor working conditions, and the abuse of women and children who were forced to labor long hours in factories and mines were visible to all.

Although not widely known in his own time, today Marx is known the world over. Because his economic theories have had such a profound effect on the modern world, Marx ranks as one of the most significant figures of history.

UNIT EIGHT

Politics and the Future

24

The Politics of Economics and the Economics of Politics

Preview Questions

1. What social values enter into economic policymaking?
2. How is policymaking carried out at the federal level?
3. What does scarcity have to do with politics?

This book has made a number of references to the American system of private enterprise. Chapter 23 contrasted the capitalist system with several socialist systems. However, a closer view of what goes on in the United States shows that the American economy does not follow the model guidelines of a *pure* capitalist system. Politics is much involved in the national economic system. In fact, economic policymaking is probably one of the most important functions of government today. If all the economic decisions made by government instead of by individuals and businesses were listed, the list would be long indeed. Because economic policymaking is so important, it is worthwhile to spend some time describing how it is done.

Economic policymaking takes place in the context of the nation's entire political process. That process is an attempt to bring together the desires, wants, and needs of all Americans to achieve maximum welfare for the nation as a whole. Of course, *maximum* welfare may never be obtained. Nevertheless, people try to get as close to it as possible.

In a pure capitalist system, individuals in their quest for their own welfare theoretically cause the total welfare to be as great as possible. But Americans do not live in that kind of society. Rather, many decisions are taken out of the hands of individuals and put into the hands of elected or appointed representatives. As politicians, these people must attempt to satisfy much of the electorate to stay in office. Thus they attempt to satisfy the social values of their constituents in the policies that are considered by government.

What Are Social Values?

What are the social values in the United States? According to most observers, one major social value is equal opportunity.

Equal Opportunity

Equal opportunity is one of the key elements in a successful democracy. Obviously, economics has much to do with equal opportunity. It is *economic* opportunity to which most people refer when discussing equal opportunity. Whether a person is born into a working-class family or a wealthy family should make no difference in that person's ability to rise to the top in whatever endeavor he or she engages.

In recent years, the federal government has taken increasingly stronger steps toward ensuring equal opportunity for everyone regardless of race, creed, or sex. A government dedicated to improving opportunity for its citizenry is a government that attempts to eliminate discrimination in educational opportunity, in vocational development, etc.

Economic Policymaking at the Federal Level

The most important elected government official in the United States is, of course, the president. Part of the president's job is to influence economic policymaking at the congressional level. Congress basically holds the power to translate desired social policies into laws.

Economic lawmaking, as well as any other type of lawmaking, is indeed a complex process. Figure 24-1 presents a schematic diagram showing how the executive branch influences Congress. You can see that it takes months—sometimes years—for an idea coming from the president or the executive branch to become law.

Lawmaking itself is an extremely complicated process, as can be seen in Figure 24-2. With such a complicated process, one might wonder how laws actually come into being. But they do. Although

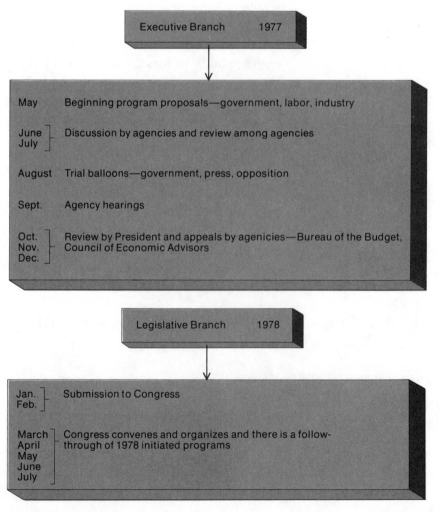

Figure 24-1. How the Executive Branch influences Congress.

thousands of bills are enacted into law, most proposals do *not* become laws. They are introduced but never get through committees.

The intermingling of economics with politics once caused Karl Marx to say that economics is the mirror image of politics.

The Politics of Scarcity

If one could go backward from today to any moment of the past, he or she would find some striking resemblances in the political problems facing each generation in every society. Once we leave the area of economic policymaking in response to social values, we find that much political action has been involved in giving something to one part of society, and hence, by necessity, taking something away from another segment. The taking away is "by necessity" because of the age-old problem of scarcity. At any moment in any society, the amount of resources available is fixed. Whether it be today, 100 years ago, or even 1,000 years ago, someone must pay for anything that is provided. Therefore, politicians—whether in a democratic or a totalitarian society—are deeply involved in economic problems, whether they like it or not, and whether they admit it or not.

Politics Past and Present

If this were a book on American political history, the emphasis would be different. Many of the historical facts examined would also be different. Nevertheless, a basic similarity would still hold.

To prove the point, glance at a short political history of the United States. You will find that it presents a number of topics that are similar to those discussed in this book. Although there would certainly be more discussion of such topics as political elections, much of the book would examine things having to do with economic welfare. Even though 100 years ago the United States was a lot poorer than it is today, it appears that the nation was just as materialistic. Then, as today, citizens were concerned with what a politician would do if elected to improve their lot in life.

Many people are aware of the fundamental political problem of

Politics and economics are closely related. The government has always been in a position to make economic decisions which affect each and everyone of our lives. Read today's newspaper. How many articles can you find which illustrate this point?

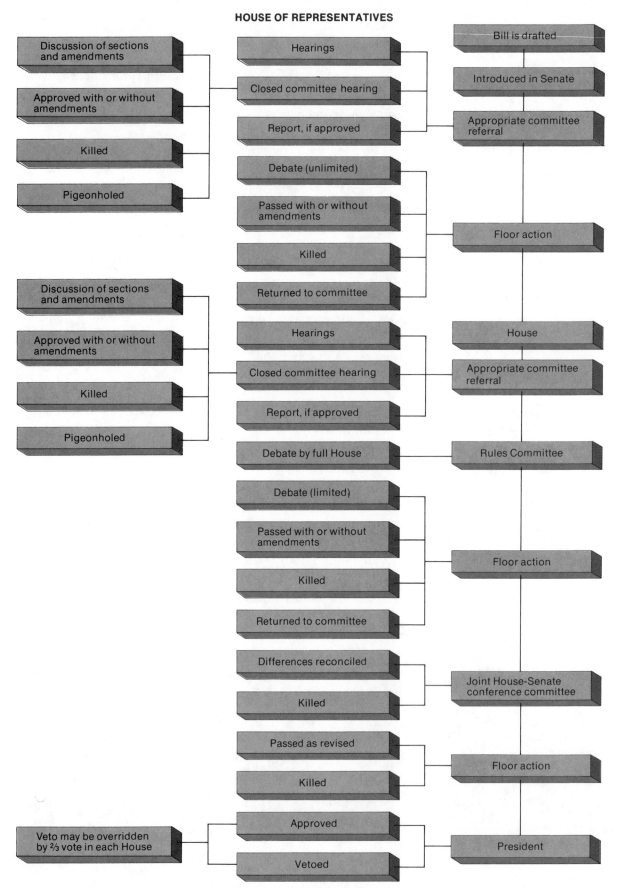

HOUSE OF REPRESENTATIVES

Bill is drafted

Introduced in Senate

Appropriate committee referral

Hearings

Closed committee hearing

Report, if approved

Discussion of sections and amendments

Approved with or without amendments

Killed

Pigeonholed

Debate (unlimited)

Passed with or without amendments

Killed

Returned to committee

Floor action

House

Appropriate committee referral

Hearings

Closed committee hearing

Report, if approved

Discussion of sections and amendments

Approved with or without amendments

Killed

Pigeonholed

Debate by full House

Rules Committee

Debate (limited)

Passed with or without amendments

Killed

Returned to committee

Floor action

Differences reconciled

Killed

Joint House-Senate conference committee

Passed as revised

Killed

Floor action

Approved

Vetoed

President

Veto may be overridden by ⅔ vote in each House

Figure 24–2. How a bill becomes a law in the House of Representatives.

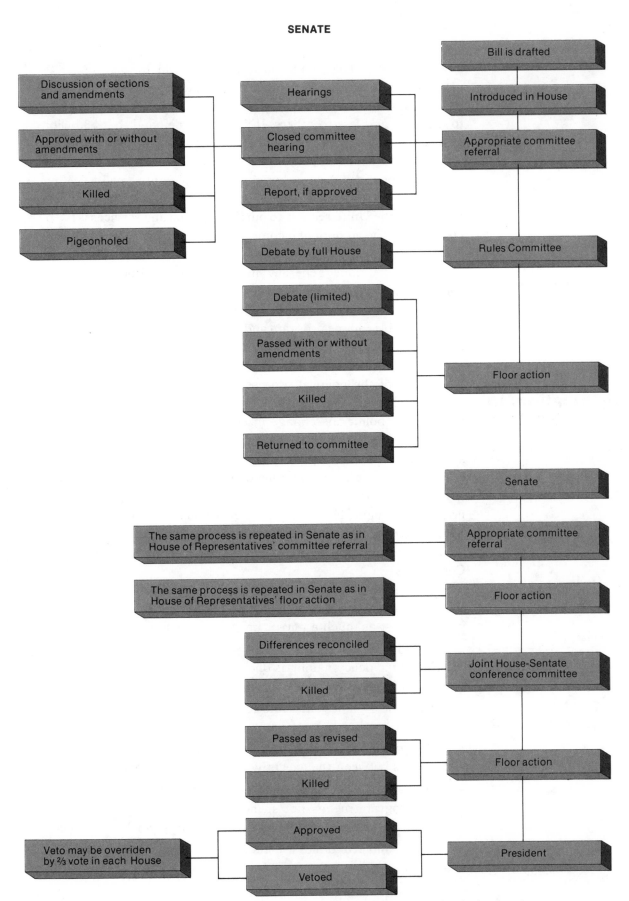

Figure 24–2 continued. How a bill becomes a law in the Senate.

how the fruits of economic production should be distributed to various members of society. When politicians argue for increased medical care for the aged, they are, in fact, asking that more be given to the aged and less to others. If politicians demand that $3 billion more be spent on pollution control, they are stating that $3 billion should not be spent on some other activity.

Not all political desires can be translated into reality. Why? Because of scarcity. At any given time, the total amount of income available in the United States to purchase goods and services is fixed. Necessarily, the amount of income that the government has to spend is even smaller. Hence, any political problem about what should or should not be done generally involves the creation, expansion, contraction, or removal of a government program. Whatever action is taken can be translated directly into an increase in the amount of funds available for one program and a reduction in funds available for other programs that benefit groups of people.

An Oversimplification, to Be Sure

Discussion of the political process in this chapter has been oversimplified. Nevertheless, a cursory glance at various government actions that politicians engage in every day reveals the economic nature of politics. Just as strikingly, an examination of economic activities often indicates that politics is lurking in the background. For example, the economic phenomenon of large grain surpluses during the 1950s can be explained by government support of grain prices at too high a level. Why the government would support grain prices at that level, even though surpluses resulted, involves the political question of why the farm bloc has had so much power in Congress.

Such intertwining of economics and politics leads to the conclusion that economics is a mirror image of politics. On the other hand, politics is just as much a mirror image of economics.

Summary

1. Economic policymaking is one of the most important processes that go on in government today.

2. Many social values enter into economic policymaking. One of the most important is equal opportunity.

3. Economic policymaking at the federal level involves complicated interactions between the executive branch and Congress.

4. Since at times government revenues are limited, spending funds for one program means not spending on another. Moreover, the more government spends, the less the private sector has to spend.

5. Politics and economics are intertwined. That is, each is a mirror image of the other.

Important Terms
economic policymaking   politics   equal opportunity
equal opportunity

Review Questions

1. What is one of the most important functions of government today?

2. What is one of the key elements in a successful democracy?

3. To what do most people refer when discussing equal opportunity?

4. Why is lawmaking a complex process?

5. Why cannot all political desires be translated into reality?

6. What does scarcity have to do with political decision making?

Discussion Questions

1. The chapter noted that one of the major social values in American society is equal opportunity. What other values do you think that Americans commonly hold as important?

2. Is there a conflict between individual freedom and the desire of government to do things for individuals? If so, how? If not, why not?

3. The chapter has suggested that politics and economics are so intertwined that each is a mirror image of the other. Do you agree with this idea? Why or why not?

Projects

1. Write to your representative in Congress, asking for information on major bills currently being considered by Congress. How many of those bills are related to economic questions? Who would benefit by passage of each bill? What are the costs?

2. Research any major proposal currently before Congress. Does the bill involve increased federal spending? From what source will the revenues be drawn? What impact might the bill have on the economy as a whole? Why?

What Does the Future Hold?

Definitions of New Terms

Futurologist: A futurologist is someone who predicts what will happen in the future.

Planned society: A planned society is one in which government, with the help of business and citizens, attempts to formulate economic plans with specific goals to be accomplished within a given time period.

Can you imagine a world without electricity, gasoline, and the comforts to which you have become accustomed? Can you imagine a world in which pollution has become so widespread that people no longer have clean air to breathe or fresh water to drink? Can you imagine a world in which the population has become so large that there is standing room only? Even if you cannot imagine such horrendous conditions, there are those who contend that the future may be that grim. According to these critics, the only salvation is individual restraint in the use of resources on a level never before experienced in the United States.

The political processes involved in economic decision making were outlined in Chapter 24. Many observers, however, suggest that the role of politics in economic decision making must become even greater. It must take over what to date has been taken care of by individuals acting on their own in the marketplace. Before examining the need for such massive governmental economic planning, let us first look at the future of scarcity.

Scarcity in the Future

As you know, economics is the study of the exchange of scarce resources. Will economics change in the future because resources have become scarcer? Perhaps. Yet you know people can never have everything they want. Nature does not provide people with everything. That was true 1,000 years ago and 100 years ago, and it will be true 100 years from now. Nevertheless, many economic observers contend that the world's primary resources—coal, iron ore, oil, and the like—are becoming scarcer today than they were in the past. They believe that people

© Chronicle Publishing Co. 1977

"Tell me again how it was back in 1977 before we ran out of everything"

have been greedy in their use of those resources. Let us look at minerals, for example.

Mineral Shortages

When there was an energy crisis in 1973–1974, modern Malthusians predicted the end of the world as people knew it. Why? Because people were exhausting the resources necessary to generate energy. One of the main resources used in energy production is petroleum. During the energy crisis, observers pointed out that at current rates of consumption, known oil reserves might last only 30 to 50 years. Eventually, the world would run out of oil. Although their analysis may have seemed correct, they forget to take into account the fact that the quantity of oil and oil products demanded is basically a function of how much those products cost.

If the price of oil were to rise (and indeed it did), the quantity of oil and oil products demanded would fall. Moreover, as the price of oil rose, the relative profitability of exploring and extracting more oil would increase (and it did). In fact, in less than a year after the energy crisis, oil companies began to report surplus reserves on hand rather than shortages. Why? Because many had started exploring for new oil sources, on a scale not previously anticipated. Predicted profits were now very high, given the higher price level of oil.

This analysis can be applied to most other natural resources. As economists D. B. Brooks and P. W. Andrews once stated, "The literal notion of running out of mineral supplies is ridiculous."[1] It seems that the quantities of minerals even in the upper kilometer of the earth's crust approach the infinite in size. A single cubic kilometer of crustal rock contains 2 billion tons of bauxite, 1 billion tons of iron, 800,000 tons of zinc, and 200,000 tons of copper. Much the same commentary could be made about seawater.

Why are these minerals not being used today? The reason is simple. At current world prices, it is not economical to mine them. But as they become relatively scarcer, their price will rise. Businesses will then find it profitable to engage in more expensive production techniques to provide these minerals to demanders.

The notion of reserves for any resource—oil or anything else—greatly understates the availability of these resources. Reserves are figured on the basis of today's prices and today's technology. However, tomorrow's technology will be different.

Future Needs and Future Supplies

Those who predict that people will not have what they "need" in the future make arithmetic computations. Let us take electricity, for example.

Generally, scientists predict the future needs of the nation. How do they do it? They base their predictions on the past rates of use and growth. For example, if the demand for electrical energy has been growing at 10 percent per year, they predict that same growth rate into the future and arrive at a figure for total kilowatt-hours demanded. Then they look at current and anticipated increases in supplies of electricity, and come up with a number as to what will be supplied. Inevitably, the difference is negative. That is, supplies will be less than demands. This is generally labeled an *electrical energy deficit*.

The analysis, however, ignores a crucial determinant of both quantity supplied and quantity demanded—the relative price of

---

[1] D. B. Brooks and P. W. Andrews, *Science*, Vol. 185: No. 4145, (July 5, 1974), p. 13.

the product. At a higher relative price, people will find ways to conserve electricity. Moreover, at a higher relative price, suppliers will find ways to get more electricity from the earth's given amount of resources.

This supply and demand analysis, in which price plays an important role, is often ignored or even scoffed at by **futurologists,** those who predict what will happen in the future. This basic disagreement with economists regarding analysis brought futurologists to the conclusion that unless nations stop their current rates of economic growth, humankind will be heading for worldwide suicide.

Does Growth Mean Suicide?

A few years ago, a number of studies were published showing that, unless living habits changed drastically, humankind faced potential extinction. These studies claimed that pollution would overwhelm people, resources would dry up, and food would become unavailable. Figure I–24–1 presents a typical example of a computerized chart drawn for these studies.

Look at the graph closely. According to the lines plotted, food supplies will prove inadequate, even with ample natural resources, pollution controls, and a decrease in population growth. But who drew the curves? And how did they do it? In a

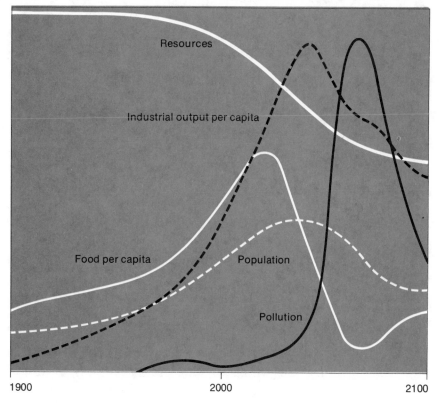

Figure I–24–1. The limits of growth. Taken from the popular book, *Limits to Growth,* this chart takes a look into the twenty-first century. The prediction is humankind will run out of food, even though the world may have ample natural resources, sufficient pollution controls, and better birth control. Source: Potomac Associates.

Technological advances alone will not solve the problem of limited resources. Peoples' values and attitudes must also change. Can you think of a related instance where your own attitudes have changed?

study called *Limits to Growth,* scientists at Massachusetts Institute of Technology (MIT) set up many mathematical equations using information on what determines industrial output, food production, pollution, population, and the relationships among those factors. A computer was then used to calculate and project the behavior of each trend as it related to the other trends.

The computer forecast drastic consequences for the world if current trends in each variable continued. Before A.D. 2100, the world would reach a point at which the population could no longer be supported by existing resources. This grim finding apparently holds even if important advances are made in birth control, food production, natural resource output, and pollution control.

The MIT equations show ever-increasing growth for everything except food production. Even breakthroughs in technology will not prevent the final collapse of the world. For example, take the computer run that actually underlies the curves shown in Figure I–24–1. To get the curves shown, the MIT scientists assumed that recycling technology would reduce the input of raw materials per unit of output to 25 percent of the amount currently used. They also assumed that birth control would eliminate all unwanted children. Additionally, pollution would be 75 percent below its present level.

What happens? Resources are sufficient. But the growth of industry is so great that higher output soon offsets the 75 percent decline in pollution. That is, even with less pollution per unit of output, the tremendous increases in output result in an overwhelming absolute amount of unwanted waste. Additionally, even when all unwanted pregnancies are eliminated, population will get out of hand. This, in turn, will lead to a food crisis. Moreover, increases in agricultural technology will apparently have little effect. There will still be overuse of land that leads to erosion, causing food production to drop. This is what the computer predicted.

The authors of *Limits to Growth* point out that even if there are tremendous scientific breakthroughs, these breakthroughs must be matched by equally dramatic changes in the world's social institutions. Otherwise the breakthroughs—be they birth control devices or high grain yields—will not be distributed effectively to those in need of them. Needed changes will not appear.

Limits to the *Limits of Growth*

Limits to Growth presents humankind with a frightening perspective of what might occur in the future. However, it seems only fair that the deficiencies of the study should be mentioned. There have been enough doomsday foreseers in the past to warrant some suspicion. After all, Malthus predicted disaster more than 150 years ago, and it has yet to happen.

Relative Prices.   In developing their predictions, the authors of *Limits to Growth* gave no consideration to the effect of price change on the quantity of resources demanded. By now you know, however, that when specific resources become scarce, their price rises. People are then motivated to find substitutes for or to do without the more expensive goods and services. That is something many ecologists forget. Nevertheless, it is an unchanging economic fact.

If a good becomes scarcer (with a stable demand curve), one expects a rise in price. The quantity sold then falls. If timber should become scarcer, for example, its price would rise, and substitutes would be found. The same holds true for steel, coal, and copper. The history of an economy is in part a history of the ways changing relative prices reflect relative scarcity.

Production and innovation respond to such changes in relative prices. If the price of steel should go up because iron ore becomes scarcer and more expensive, more attempts will be made to find steel substitutes. Perhaps there will be an increase in the use of plastics. In any event, such is the way of the economic world.

Consider also that economic growth does not necessarily

have to involve wasting resources or generating tremendous amounts of pollution. For example, increased use of computers may involve no pollution relative to the dramatic increases in economic growth made possible by increased computer capacity. Additionally, increased pollution control might cause producers to learn to recycle unwanted by-products. If pollution abatement involves higher costs, consumers will be confronted with higher prices. They, in turn, will alter their consumption accordingly. Then products and services that do not involve pollution in their production and, therefore, do not involve increases in relative price will experience increased demand. In this way, pollution will be reduced, not increased, as growth continues, provided the "necessary" amount of restriction is placed on those who might otherwise generate pollution.

Growth Rates.   Another suspicious characteristic of *Limits to Growth* is its assumption that problems are growing at an ever-increasing rate and the ability to solve those problems is growing at a constant rate. This is exactly the same kind of reasoning that led Malthus to predict a potential food crisis for the world's growing population. According to Malthus' theory, population was growing exponentially, or geometrically, and the food supply was growing only arithmetically. Somehow that has not been the case. Perhaps it will not be the case in the future either.

There Are Problems

Do not conclude from what has been said to this point that there are no problems in the United States or in the world. Indeed, there are many. Issue 1 pointed out the ecological disasters that must be avoided. Continuing environmental destruction is not something that can be brushed aside because it will supposedly solve itself. One way to improve the ecological mess invading the United States is to make polluters pay for the pollution they bestow on Americans. Another way is to establish or reestablish property rights in certain resources so they will not be ruined for eternity.

To be sure, the *way* this nation is growing may not be appropriate. There may be certain sectors in the economy that should grow faster than others. But does this mean that the American economic system must be drastically altered? That is what a growing number of economists contend. They want no less than a planned society.

The Planned Society

What is a **planned society**? Basically, it is a society in which government, with the help of business and citizens, attempts to formulate economic plans with specific goals to be achieved by the end of the given time period. For example, a five-year plan might state that the agriculture sector of the economy will have grown by 25 percent in terms of output at the end of five years.

The plan, of course, should only be formulated by a consensus of opinion. Individuals from all phases of government, business, and consumer groups should strive to reach consensus on what type of plan is best for the nation as a whole. However, it may be difficult to reach consensus in terms of economics. Most people have different ideas of what is best for the nation. The only thing they know is what is best for themselves and perhaps for the people closest to them. It would be most difficult to draw up a plan that would satisfy everyone.

What, then, will determine the final economic plan? Obviously, it will be determined by the effectiveness of various pressure groups. In a way, this goes on today. Pressure groups influence much legislation that affects various sectors of the economy. Tariff legislation is one example. A particular industry sends lobbyists to Washington, DC, to persuade members of Congress to support tariff provisions protecting that industry.

Once any national economic plan is drafted, it must be implemented. This can be done in various ways. Taxes and subsidies can be used either to discourage or to encourage various sectors in the economy. Government control can be established over particular sectors. Or the government might actually take over some of the operations in a sector. That is, it may own particular businesses. Currently the federal government owns the Tennessee Valley Authority, which provides electricity to a large area of the South. Government ownership of basic means of production and basic services desired by Americans could be multiplied throughout the land.

The debate over the issue of increased government planning continues. Those in favor of more planning fear that the economy is too complex and resources are "too" scarce to leave the workings of the economy to individuals. Those opposed to more planning worry about loss of economic freedoms and increased inefficiency due to incorrect plans. Much of the economics in this book can help you to analyze both sides of this important social issue.

Summary

1. Today many economic observers contend that the world's primary resources are becoming scarcer. They predict a grim future if humankind does not place some limits on growth.

2. In making their predictions, most of these critics fail to take into account the fact that the quantity of any resource demanded is basically a function of how much it costs.

3. Some economists believe that the idea that the world will run out of mineral resources is absurd. They note that the earth's crust contains an almost infinite amount of essential elements.

4. Those who predict doom make arithmetic computations. Inevitably their calculations show that supplies will be less than demands. However, they ignore a crucial determinant—relative price.

5. In recent years, a number of studies have been published on the prospects of continued economic growth.

6. One of the major studies, *Limits to Growth,* predicts that the

world will run out of food in the twenty-first century even though it may have ample natural resources, sufficient pollution controls, and better birth control. According to the MIT study's findings, even breakthroughs in technology will not prevent the final collapse of the world.

7. In making their predictions, the MIT scientists gave no consideration to the effect of price change on the quantity of resources demanded. They did not consider the economic fact that as something becomes scarcer, it tends to increase in price. As it increases in price, demand falls. People seek substitutes.

8. Economic growth does not necessarily have to involve wasting resources or generating tremendous amounts of pollution.

9. There are many problems today. Many economists thus favor increased government planning. Others are against more planning. They worry about loss of economic freedoms and increased inefficiency due to incorrect plans.

10. Since no economic plan would satisfy everybody, any economic plan will be determined by the effectiveness of various pressure groups.

Important Terms

futurologist   planned society
limits to growth

Questions for Thought and Discussion

1. What do many economic observers predict about the future? On what basis do they make such predictions? What economic fact do they tend to ignore?

2. What happens when a resource becomes scarcer? What effect does this have on reserves?

3. Do you think there are limits to economic growth? If so, what? If not, why not?

4. Today many people argue for increased government planning. Why? Other people are opposed to the idea of a planned society. Why? What do you think about this issue?

APPENDIX

Economics as a Career

The importance of economists continually grows as our need to understand the economic system increases and our efforts to keep this system healthy intensify. As this book has shown, the American economic system can be immensely complicated and often very confusing. Imagine the continual frustration of business leaders and government officials trying to make proper decisions when they do not understand our economy and how it works. If corporation executives make a wrong decision, they will probably see profits decline, their company loses money, and they might even lose their jobs. If our government officials enact the wrong policy, our tax dollars will be squandered and valuable public resources will be wasted. Preventing these costly mistakes and helping business and government leaders allocate their resources in the wisest and most efficient manner is the economist's job. It is an extremely important job because unprofitable businesses or wasteful public policies hurt every citizen. As long as we desire a healthy and vigorous economy, there will be a growing need for men and women who understand our economic system.

Careers in Economics

Never has the prestige and prominence of the economic profession been greater than it is in our society today. In the not too distant past, economists were rarely seen and seldom heard by the general public. Today, as more and more people have realized the necessity of sound and learned economic opinions, economists have become more visible throughout our society. In newspapers and on television, economists are often quoted and interviewed. Their opinions are valued and their advice is heeded. With the enormous attention given to economic matters, such figures as the Chairman of the Federal Reserve Board have almost become household names. Equally noticed and respected is the President's Council of Economic Advisors. In this book, you have read about many of the country's leading economists and have seen how important and influential they are in our society today. But these well-known figures are only the most visible representatives of a thriving profession whose members work in all facets of our society.

Private industry provides many well-paying jobs and offers exciting careers for professional economists. All large corporations and many smaller companies hire economists. Many of the nation's largest corporations, such as General Motors, United States Steel, or Exxon, maintain full-time research divisions staffed by highly trained economists. When working for a corporation, the economist's responsibilities are often varied but always important. Crucial to any business, no matter its size, is accurate information about market trends, consumer behavior, and the general condition of the economy. You will recall from chapters 8, 9, and 10 how important to companies are issues like marketing, pricing, and industrial organization. Equally important are such issues as wages, labor, and production, which we discussed in chapters 11, 12, and 13. In most companies, all of these problems we have covered are the primary concerns of economists. If there is a problem in one of these areas, an economist is usually consulted or called in to resolve the issue. Perhaps even more important, economists are called upon to forecast the condition of the economy in future years. With such predictions, businesses can continue making profits even though markets, prices, or other factors may have changed. Let's take, for example, a bicycle company that wants to expand its production. Before making such an important decision, the company's executives must know if the demand for bicycles will continue to grow in future years. They must also know if the economy will keep expanding, providing full employment and high wages. If the economy should slump and people could no longer afford bicycles, the company's expansion plans would be foolish and probably disastrous. The bicycle company's executives could not make these decisions without the expert advice of professional economists.

Besides the many opportunities available in private industry, there are many equally important jobs for professional economists in government service. Outside the private sector of our economy, the Federal government is the largest employer of economists. As we discussed in Chapter 16, the Federal government plays a central and constantly expanding role in our nation's economic life. Throughout the Federal government, therefore, our leaders depend upon the experience and expertise of economists to help them enact wise and efficient policies. This is especially true in the Executive Branch, where economists work in all major cabinet departments and many federal agencies. All the issues we discussed in Chapters 17 through 20, such as inflation, public spending, measuring economic activity, and stabilizing the economy, are challenging problems that these economists face every day. In the Department of Agriculture, for example, economists study the demand for agricultural commodities so that they may develop policies that benefit the American farmer. In the Office of Budget and Management, economists help devise a federal budget that will, depending on the immediate need, either stabilize or stimulate our economy. At the international level, many economists work in the State Department analyzing some of the same problems that you read about in Chapter 21. Since our government has such a large and important role in the economy, the opportunities for economists in the Federal government are plentiful.

State and local governments also need economists. Though their number is not as great, many economists have similar duties in state and local governments as do their counterparts in the Federal government. Economists have crucial roles in solving some of the most important and controversial problems that confront communities across the nation. Welfare and tax policy, the financing of education, public health, and urban planning are some of the more significant problems which economists are actively trying to solve.

Teaching is another career open to economists. Since we must understand our economic system, our need for competent people to teach economics in our schools and colleges continues to grow. Most secondary schools now offer courses in economics. In addition, economics is one of the most popular courses taught in colleges and universities. Not only are there many economics majors, but most college students realize the necessity of understanding our country's economic system. Many students, therefore, attend economics courses for personal as well as professional reasons. College and university professors will always be needed, though the competition for these prestigious positions is extremely keen.

Planning a Career in Economics

The first step in an economist's career is to go to college and choose economics as one's major field of study. Most colleges and universities offer similar, though not identical, programs for the economics major. In most schools, students take a series of introductory courses that cover the principles of economics, much like the one you are now taking. Following this introduction, students must take several courses in microeconomics and macroeconomics. Along with these courses, most students usually take a few courses in statistics.

These statistics courses are essential, because more advanced economic theories are often founded on sophisticated mathematical methods and research. Economics majors conclude their study with several specialized courses on one aspect of economics, such as monetary theory. All students, of course, must take a variety of non-economics courses that satisfy the general requirements for the Bachelor's degree. These non-economic courses are very important, for they enhance the economist's understanding of how non-economic variables affect the economic system.

A typical economics program might look like this:

ECONOMICS PROGRAM

Introduction to Economics

Statistical Method and Interpretation

Economic Analysis

Microeconomic Theory

Macroeconomic Theory

Industrial Organization

Public Finance

Monetary Theory

Money and Banking

Survey of Labor Economics

American Economic History

Introduction to Econometrics

International Economics

After graduating from college with a Bachelor of Science degree in economics, the aspiring economist must make an important decision: whether to find a job immediately or continue working toward a higher academic degree. Many students choose the first alternative and are able to find excellent jobs as junior economists in corporations or government agencies. For example, one might be employed by the Environmental Protection Agency to help a senior economist analyze the economic impact of a clean water standard on a community. Some students plan to continue their education, but feel that a short stint in business or government will contribute to their knowledge of economics as well as earn them a salary.

For those students who do not seek jobs immediately, the next level in their education is the Master's degree. This degree usually takes one or two years to complete, depending on the school and the specific program. Most Master's degree programs require students to take numerous courses on specific economic topics and pass a series of comprehensive exams that rigorously test the student in several fields of economics. Also, some colleges require students to write a long research paper, called a thesis, before the degree is granted. After completing this program, most economists with Master's degrees can obtain higher paying jobs with greater responsibilities than those with Bachelor's degrees.

After the Master's degree, a limited number of highly qualified students may choose to pursue the Ph.D., a Doctorate in Economics. At a minimum, this advanced degree requires three years of study after the student earns a Bachelor's. However, most Ph.D. programs involve many more years of study. All Ph.D. students are required to take several more years of courses, pass difficult comprehensive examinations, and write an original, book-length research project called a dissertation. People with the Ph.D. are trained to handle the most complicated economic problems facing our society. As a consequence, men and women holding this degree are respected highly and their opinion is highly valued. With this training, the economists can obtain high-paying and important jobs in teaching, private industry, or government.

Our society will always need professional economists. If you choose a career in the economics profession, you will find it both rewarding and challenging. Regardless of your decision, however, learning about economics is an ongoing process of personal growth and education. And if you continue to study our economic system, you will find that the knowledge you gain will help you in your daily life. As we discussed in our second unit, you are constantly faced with tough personal economic decisions. You don't have to be a professional economist to realize how important are these decisions that you make. Informed citizens not only help themselves, but they benefit our society as a whole. Through wise personal economic decisions and intelligent political action, you will help our economy to continue growing and working for the benefit of everybody. Furthermore, you will show that the doomsayers were wrong, as through your actions our future will be bright and prosperous. We hope that the understanding and knowledge you have gained through your first economics course will prove invaluable and will continue to serve you in the years ahead.

Selected Bibliography

General Economics Texts

Heilbroner, Robert L., *The Making of Economic Society* (Englewood Cliffs, N.J.: Prentice-Hall Book Company, latest edition) (also available in paperback).

McConnell, Campbell R., *Economics: Principles, Problems, and Policies* (New York: McGraw-Hill Book Company, latest edition).

Miller, Roger LeRoy, *Economics Today* (San Francisco: Canfield Press, latest edition) (also available in two separate paperbacks and an abbreviated hardback brief edition).

Samuelson, Paul A., *Economics* (New York: McGraw-Hill Book Company, latest edition).

Reference Volumes

Board of Governors of the Federal Reserve System, *Federal Reserve Bulletin* (published monthly).

Economic Report of the President (Washington, D.C.: U.S. Government Printing Office, published each January or February).

U.S. Bureau of the Census, *Statistical Abstract of the United States* (Washington, D.C.: U.S. Government Printing Office, published annually).

U.S. Department of Commerce, *Business Conditions Digest* (published monthly).

U.S. Department of Commerce, *Survey of Current Business* (published monthly).

U.S. Department of Labor, *Monthly Labor Review* (published monthly).

Periodicals and Newspapers

Barron's, weekly magazine reporting on current industry trends.

Business Week, a weekly magazine related mainly to items affecting businesses.

Challenge, published every two months, containing articles by leading economists on various economic problems.

Forbes, a business magazine, particularly related to investment news.

Fortune, a monthly magazine on economic and business events.

Newsweek, contains sections on the economy.

The New York Times, contains complete financial section.

Time, contains business news and financial information.

U.S. News & World Report, contains information on business and finance.

Wall Street Journal, the nation's daily business newspaper.

Readings for Unit 1

Deacon, Robert, "The Environment: A Challenge for Public Policy," in Phillips, Llad and Votey, Harold L., Jr., *Economic Analysis of Pressing Social Problems,* 2d. Ed. (Chicago: Rand McNally College Publishing Company, 1977).

Maher, John E., *What Is Economics?* (New York: John Wiley & Sons, 1969).

North, Douglass C. and Miller, Roger LeRoy, *The Economics of Public Issues* (New York: Harper & Row, Publishers, Inc., latest edition). Contains several chapters on ecology and the environment and gives many areas where economic analysis applies in our society.

Readings for Unit 2

Bailard, Thomas E., *et al, Personal Money Management* (Chicago: Science Research Associates, Inc., latest edition).

Engel, Louis, *How to Buy Stocks* (Usually available free from Merrill Lynch, Inc., a large stockbrokerage firm) or latest edition (New York: Bantam Books, Inc.).

"Life Insurance: What You'd Better Know Before You Buy," *Changing Times,* March 1977.

Miller, Roger LeRoy, *Economic Issues for Consumers* (St. Paul: West Publishing Company, latest edition).

North, Douglass C. and Miller, Roger LeRoy, *The Economics of Public Issues* (New York: Harper & Row, Publishers, Inc., latest edition). See chapter on the automobile.

Troelstrup, Arch W., *The Consumer in American Society: Personal and Family Finance* (New York: McGraw-Hill Book Company, latest edition).

U.S. Department of Agriculture, *Family Economics Review* (published monthly).

Readings for Unit 3

Adams, Walter, Editor, *The Structure of American Industry*, 4th. Ed. (New York: The Macmillan Company, 1971). See Chapter 11 on monopoly.

Friedman, Milton, *Capitalism and Freedom* (Chicago: University of Chicago Press, 1962).

Galbraith, John Kenneth, *Economics and the Public Purpose* (Boston: Houghton-Mifflin Company, 1973).

Galbraith, John Kenneth, *The New Industrial State* (New York: New American Library, 1967).

Green, Mark J., Editor, *The Monopoly Makers* (New York: Grossman, 1973).

Hayek, F. A., "The Meaning of Competition," in *Individualism and Economic Order* (Chicago: University of Chicago Press, 1948).

Henderson, Hubert, *Supply and Demand* (Chicago: The University of Chicago Press, 1958).

Heyne, Paul T., *The Economic Way of Thinking*, 2d. Ed., (Chicago: Science Research Associates, Inc., 1976).

Mansfield, Edwin, Editor, *Monopoly Power in Economic Performance* (New York: W.W. Norton & Company, 1968).

Mundell, Robert A., *Man and Economics* (New York: McGraw-Hill Book Company, 1968).

North, Douglass C. and Miller, Roger LeRoy, *The Economics of Public Issues* (New York: Harper & Row, Publishers, Inc., latest edition). See chapter on agriculture.

Simon, Julian, *Issues in the Economics of Advertising* (Urbana: University of Illinois Press, 1970).

Swerdling, Daniel, "The Food Monopolies," *The Progressive*, January 1975.

Trivoli, G. W., "Has the Consumer Really Lost His Sovereignty?" *Akron Business and Economic Review*, Winter 1970.

Weiss, Leonard W., *Economics in American Industry* (New York: John Wiley & Sons, Inc., 1967).

Readings for Unit 4

Cohen, Sanford, *Labor in the United States* (Columbus, Ohio: Charles E. Merrill Publishing Company, latest edition).

Freeman, Richard B., *Labor Economics* (Englewood Cliffs, N.J.: Prentice-Hall, Inc., 1972).

Gilman, C. P., *Women and Economics* (Boston: Maynard & Company, 1898).

Harrington, Michael, *The Other America* (Baltimore: Penguin Books, 1962).

Kennedy, Thomas, "Freedom to Strike Is in the Public Interest," *Harvard Business Review*, July 1970.

Kennedy, William, "Working and Dissatisfaction: Is Money Enough?" in Llad, Phillip and Votey, Harold L., Jr., Editors, *Economic Analysis of Pressing Social Problems*, 2d. Ed. (Chicago: Rand McNally College Publishing Company, 1977).

Kreps, Juanita M., *Sex in the Marketplace: American Women at Work* (Baltimore: Johns Hopkins Press, 1971).

Mayer, Lawrence A., "We Can't Take Food for Granted Anymore," *Fortune*, February 1974.

Miller, Roger LeRoy, *The Economics of Energy: What Went Wrong and How We Can Fix It* (New York: William Morrow & Company, 1974).

North, Douglass C. and Miller, Roger LeRoy, *The Economics of Public Issues* (New York: Harper & Row, Publishers, Inc., latest edition). See chapters on poverty, welfare, income, and professional sports.

Rees, Albert, *Economics of Trade Unions* (Chicago: University of Chicago Press, 1962).

Tuckman, Howard P., *The Economics of the Rich* (New York: Random House, Inc., 1973).

Readings for Unit 5

Board of Governors of the Federal Reserve System, *The Federal Reserve System: Purposes and Function* (Washington, D.C.: U.S. Government Printing Office, latest edition).

Bernstein, Peter L., *A Primer on Money, Banking, and Gold* (New York: Random House, Inc., 1965).

Economic Report of the President (Washington, D.C.: U.S. Government Printing Office, published each January or February).

Heilbroner, Robert L. and Bernstein, Peter L., *Primer on Government Spending* (New York: Random House, Inc., 1971).

Klein, John J., *Money and the Economy* (New York: Harcourt Brace Jovanovich, Inc., latest edition).

Pechman, J. A. and Okner, B. A., *Who Bears the Tax Burden?* (Washington, D.C.: The Brookings Institution, 1974).

Pechman, Joseph A., *Federal Tax Policy,* 3d. Ed. (Washington, D.C.: The Brookings Institution).

The Brookings Institution, *Setting National Priorities* (Washington, D.C.: latest edition).

United Nations Statistical Office, *Basic Principles of the System of Balances of the National Economy* (New York: United Nations, 1971).

U.S. Department of Commerce, *The Economic Council of the United States: Retrospect and Prospect* (Washington, D.C.: U.S. Government Printing Office, 1971).

Readings for Unit 6

Chandler, Lester V., *America's Great Depression, 1929–41* (New York: Harper & Row, Publishers, Inc., 1972).

Dillard, Dudley, *The Economics of John Maynard Keynes* (Englewood Cliffs, N.J.: Prentice-Hall Book Company, 1948).

Galbraith, John Kenneth, *Money: Whence It Came, Where It Went* (Boston: Houghton Mifflin Company, 1975).

Gordon, Robert A., *Economic Instability and Growth: The American Record* (New York: Harper & Row, Publishers, Inc., 1974).

Lekachman, Robert, *Inflation: The Permanent Problem of Boom or Bust* (New York: Vintage Books, 1973).

Miller, Roger LeRoy, *The Economics of Macro Issues,* 2d. Ed. (San Francisco: Canfield Press, 1978). See part on inflation, including wage and price controls.

Mitchell, Broadus, *The Depression Decade* (New York: Reinhart, 1947).

Soule, George, *Prosperity Decade,* 1917–29 (New York: Harper Torchbook, 1947).

Terkel, Studes, *Hard Times* (New York: Avon Book Div., 1971).

Readings for Unit 7

Bastiat, Frederic, "Petition of the Candlemakers," in *Economic Sophisms* (New York: G. P. Putnam's Sons, 1922).

Bornstein, Morris and Fusfeld, Daniel R., Editors, *The Soviet Economy,* 4th Ed., (Homewood, Ill.: Richard D. Irwin, Inc., 1974).

Brunner, John, *Stand on Zanzibar* (New York: Ballantine Books, 1968). A novel about population problems.

Ehrlich, Paul and Ehrlich, Anne, *Population, Resources, Environment,* 2d. Ed. (San Francisco: W. H. Freeman, 1972).

Engels, Friedrich, "Socialism: Utopian and Scientific," in the *Marx-Engels Reader,* edited by R. C. Tucker (New York: W.W. Norton & Company, 1972).

Harrington, Michael, *Toward a Democratic Left* (New York: The Macmillan Company, 1968).

Hirschman, A. O., *The Strategy of Economic Development* (New Haven, Conn.: Yale University Press, 1958).

Howe, Irving, *Essential Works of Socialism* (New York: Bantam Books, Inc., 1971).

Malthus, Thomas R., *First Essay on Population* (London: Rural Economic Society reprint, 1926).

Myrdal, Gunnar, *Asian Drama: An Inquiry Into the Poverty of Nations* (London: Allen Lane, Penguin, 1968).

Pen, Jan, *A Primer on International Trade* (New York: Random House, Inc., 1967).

Schumpeter, Joseph A., *Capitalism, Socialism, and Democracy,* 3rd. Ed. (New York: Harper & Row, Publishers, Inc., 1950).

Smith, Adam, "Restraints on Foreign Imports," in *The Wealth of Nations,* Vol. I (New York: Random House, Inc., 1937).

Stevens, Robert W., *A Primer on the Dollar in the World Economy* (New York: Random House, Inc., 1972).

Readings for Unit 8

Cole, H. S. D., *et al*, Editors, *Models of Doom* (New York: Universe Books, Inc., 1973).

Downs, Anthony, *An Economic Theory of Democracy* (New York: Harper & Row, Publishers, Inc., 1958).

Haveman, Robert H., *The Economics of the Public Sector* (New York: John Wiley & Sons, 1970).

Meadows, Donnella H., *et al, The Limits to Growth* (New York: Universe Books, Inc., 1972).

Mesarovic, Mihajlo and Pestel, Edward, *Mankind at the Turning Point* (New York: E. P. Dutton & Company, Inc., 1974).

Scott, Andrew M., *Competition in American Politics—An Economic Model* (New York: Holt, Rinehart & Winston, Inc., 1970).

Tullock, Gordon, *Private Wants, Public Means* (New York: Basic Books, 1970).

INDEX

Photo Credits